CLASSICS IN PSYCHOLOGY

CLASSICS IN PSYCHOLOGY

A NOTE ABOUT THE EDITOR

MARTIN L. REYMERT was born in Holmstrand, Norway, in 1883. He studied at the University of Oslo but emigrated to the United States in 1916 and received a doctorate at Clark University the following year. After a brief return to teach at the University of Oslo, Reymert moved permanently to the United States in 1925. At first he was the head of the Department of Psychology at Wittenberg College, where the symposium on which the present volume is based was held. In 1930 Reymert was appointed Director of the Mooseheart Laboratory of Child Research, an organization which tested and aided children with psychological disturbances. At Mooseheart, Reymert held a second symposium on feelings and emotions, which was published in 1951. In an active scholarly career, Reymert edited several periodicals and conducted research on motor learning, language, the psychology of emotions, educational psychology, and child psychology. He died in 1953.

FEELINGS AND EMOTIONS
THE WITTENBERG SYMPOSIUM

Edited by

MARTIN L. REYMERT

ARNO PRESS
A New York Times Company
New York ★ 1973

Reprint Edition 1973 by Arno Press Inc.

Reprinted from a copy in
The University of Illinois Library

Classics in Psychology
ISBN for complete set: 0-405-05130-1
See last pages of this volume for titles.

Manufactured in the United States of America

————◆————

Library of Congress Cataloging in Publication Data

Wittenberg ███████ on Feelings and Emotions,
  Wittenberg College, 1927.
  Feelings ███████████

  (Classics in psychology)
  Reprint of the 1928 ed. published by Clark
University Press, Worcester, Mass., in series The
International university series in psychology.
  Includes bibliographies.
  1. Emotions—Congresses. I. Reymert, Martin
Luther, 1883-1953, ed. II. Title. III. Series.
[DNLM: W3 IN918 1927F. XNLM: [BF511 I61F 1927F]]
BF531.W57 1927b   152.4   73-2986
ISBN 0-405-05158-1

FEELINGS AND EMOTIONS
THE WITTENBERG SYMPOSIUM

LONDON: HUMPHREY MILFORD
OXFORD UNIVERSITY PRESS

THE INTERNATIONAL UNIVERSITY SERIES IN PSYCHOLOGY

FEELINGS AND EMOTIONS
THE WITTENBERG SYMPOSIUM

by

Alfred Adler
F. Aveling
Vladimir M. Bekhterev
Madison Bentley
G. S. Brett
Karl Bühler
Walter B. Cannon
Harvey A. Carr
Ed. Claparede
Knight Dunlap
Robert H. Gault
D. Werner Gruehn
L. B. Hoisington
D. T. Howard
Erich Jaensch
Pierre Janet
Joseph Jastrow

Carl Jörgensen
David Katz
F. Kiesow
F. Krueger
Herbert S. Langfeld
William McDougall
Henri Pieron
W. B. Pillsbury
Morton Prince
Carl E. Seashore
Charles E. Spearman
Wilhelm Stern
George M. Stratton
John S. Terry
Margaret F. Washburn
Albert P. Weiss
Robert S. Woodworth

Edited by
Martin L. Reymert

WORCESTER, MASSACHUSETTS
CLARK UNIVERSITY PRESS
1928

PREFACE

This book contains the papers and proceedings of the Wittenberg Symposium on Feelings and Emotions, held at Wittenberg College, Springfield, Ohio, October 19–23, 1927, on the occasion of the inauguration of the new Psychological Laboratory.

Plans for a mobilization of international scholastic talent in the interest of clarifying the psychology of feelings and emotions were first formed in May, 1927. Preliminary conferences and correspondence with several American psychologists revealed an encouraging attitude, but also made clear the seemingly insurmountable difficulties inherent in the project. The untimely death of Dr. Edward Bradford Titchener, who had kindly consented to act as Honorary Chairman of the meeting, created an added difficulty. A most happy solution to this new problem came about through the courteous attitude of Dr. James McKeen Cattell, who upon urgent request graciously consented to assume the Honorary Chairmanship.

Inquiries addressed to scholars both in this country and abroad brought prompt and heartening responses. It was clear that the choice of topic for the conference was meeting with general approval. Additional indication of this was evidenced by word from one of our contributors to the effect that the Division of Psychology and Anthropology of the National Research Council, Washington, D. C., had appointed a Committee on Feelings and Emotions. Correspondence with the chairman of this committee, Dr. Margaret F. Washburn, brought further encouragement.

Representative American and European scholars particularly qualified to contribute to the special theme of the conference were invited to participate. In due time, the program was complete.

Invitations were sent to members of the American Psychological Association, the American Philosophical Society, the American Psychiatric Association, and other scientific bodies presumably interested. The meeting opened Wednesday, October 19, 1927, with an audience numbering several hundred. Those in attendance included official representatives from the foremost universities and colleges, the United States Bureau of Education, and from scientific and educational societies such as the National Research Council, the American Sociological Society, and many others.

In the necessary absence of Dr. Cattell from the opening session, the meeting was formally opened with the following remarks by the editor:

"*Ladies and Gentlemen:* As convener of the Wittenberg Symposium on Feelings and Emotions I take the liberty to call this first meeting to order and have the honor to introduce to you, the President of Wittenberg College, Dr. Rees Edgar Tulloss. President Tulloss received his Harvard doctorate in the field of psychology and is deeply interested in the problems before us. From the start, he has whole-heartedly sponsored this project, and has spared no effort to make it successful."

A brief address of welcome was then given by President Tulloss, followed by the opening address of the chairman, both of which are printed elsewhere in this volume.

Upon the program appeared the names of fifteen European scientists, who had prepared papers especially for the occasion. These contributors represented the following countries: England, Germany, Italy, France, Denmark, Austria, Switzerland, Russia, and Estonia. Papers were presented by twenty Americans. The papers of the European contributors and of the two or three Americans who were unable to be present at the time appointed were read by members of the Wittenberg psychological staff.

The formal inauguration of the new Psychological Laboratory took place on Friday afternoon, October 21st, in the presence of a representative audience. The inaugural address delivered by Dr. Cattell is printed in the Appendix. On this occasion the Honorary Chairman referred, in sympathetic and appreciative words, to Dr. E. B. Titchener, and gave expression to the great loss sustained by science in the untimely death of this distinguished scholar. By unanimous agreement, telegrams of sympathy were sent to Mrs. Sophie Kellogg Titchener, and to President Farrand of Cornell University. Their responses by wire, together with well-wishes for the meeting, were later read to the conference.

This same day was marked by a general academic program in connection with the formal dedication of the new Chemistry-Psychology Building at Wittenberg. In this exercise the psychologists and their friends were joined by the delegates to the National Conference on Chemistry, which was being held during the same week under the direction of the Wittenberg Chemistry Department. The dedication ceremonies, conducted by President Tulloss, included an impressive academic procession and a dedicatory address by Dr. Edgar Fahs Smith, former Provost of the University of Pennsylvania and an early teacher of science at Wittenberg. The program reached its climax in the conferring of honorary degrees upon a number of distinguished scientists in both fields. Degrees were conferred upon the following contributors to the Symposium on Feelings and Emotions:

James McKeen Cattell, L.H.D.
Walter Bradford Cannon, LL.D.
Margaret Floy Washburn, Sc.D.
Joseph Jastrow, LL.D.
William McDougall, Litt.D.
Karl Bühler, Austria, LL.D.
Charles Spearman, England, LL.D.
Felix Krueger, Germany, Sc.D.
Wilhelm Stern, Germany, LL.D.
Henri Piéron, France, LL.D.
Pierre Janet, France, LL.D.
Federico Kiesow, Italy, LL.D.
Edouard Claparède, Switzerland, LL.D.
Alfred Adler, Austria, LL.D.
Vladimir M. Bekhterev, U. S. S. R., LL.D.

At a joint banquet of the Psychology and Chemistry Departments in the evening, Dr. Edwin E. Slosson and Dr. Joseph Jastrow delivered the addresses which are printed in the Appendix.

As the program was carried out, ample time was given for the discussion of each paper. As will be seen from this publication, the participants in this notable gathering voiced their opinions freely. Great interest in the Symposium was manifested. The press throughout the country carried daily accounts of the sessions. Many important publications sent special representatives to report the proceedings.

The editor is, of course, indebted to so many for the success of this first International Symposium on Feelings and Emotions that it is hardly possible for him to record here his gratitude to all. The Symposium would have been impossible without the understanding support and cooperation so heartily given by the president of the college, Dr. Rees Edgar Tulloss. To Dean C. G. Shatzer, chairman of the general committee on arrangements, great credit should be given for the way in which he foresaw and cared for the problems connected with the arrangements for the gathering. The Board of Trustees of Wittenberg gave their unreserved moral and financial support. The entire faculty were interested and cooperative. The members of the Department of Psychology should be especially commended, including: Dr. H. G. Bishop, Dr. P. L. Mellenbruch, Dr. Margaret Kinkaid Bishop, Dr. C. H. Schneider, Miss Ruth Immell, and Mr. H. J. Arnold. Mention should also be made of the efficient help of the department assistants: Dorothy D. Markley, Donald B. Lindsley, and William Schwarzbek.

In the early planning and preparation for the Symposium, the editor is deeply indebted to Dr. E. B. Titchener, Dr. James McKeen Cattell, and Dr. Edwin G. Boring, who gave freely of their time both in personal conferences and through correspondence.

Prompt responses and helpful suggestions also came from contributors, whose interest made the Symposium and this book possible. It should likewise be mentioned that some, being unable to accept our invitation on account of pressing academic duties or for other reasons, sent their sincere regrets and best wishes for the success of the meeting. Among these were: John Dewey, Edward L. Thorndike, and H. L. Hollingworth, *Columbia;* Raymond Dodge and Robert M. Yerkes, *Yale;* Howard C. Warren, *Princeton;* Victor Kuhr, *University of Copenhagen;* A. Grotenfelt, *University of Helsingfors;* B. Hammer, *University of Upsala;* A. Herlin, *University of Lund;* T. Parr, *University of Bergen;* G. Heymans, *University of Groningen;* and K. Koffka, *University of Giessen.* Comments from several of these scholars as well as from our contributors were to the effect that the conference would mark a most needed step in contemporary psychology.

Sincere thanks are also extended to the translators of the foreign papers, most of which reached the editor in the original languages; namely, German, French, and Russian. The translations were undertaken by members of the psychological staffs of Wittenberg College and Cornell University, at which latter institution Dr. L. B. Hoisington very kindly and efficiently carried out the promises of Dr. Titchener in this regard. The editor, however, will have to accept the final responsibility for all translations. He asks the contributors and readers to be lenient in their judgment of an exceedingly difficult task. In some cases, the final translation has been approved by the author.

The scientific sessions of the Symposium were brought to a close Saturday, October 21, 1927, when the honorary chairman, Dr. James McKeen Cattell, according to extracts from the stenographic report of the proceedings, was kind enough to give voice to the following words of thanks: "I think no formal arrangement has been made for a vote of thanks, but we ought not to go without most cordially stating our obligation and appreciation. I doubt whether there has ever been held a meeting of psychologists in which were presented so many papers of such high average merit. What I wish to do now is to present to Dr. Reymert and to the president and authorities of this university our most sincere thanks."

In closing these introductory notes, which are in the nature of a brief historic record of the first International Symposium on Feelings and Emotions, I venture to express the hope, referred to also in my opening address as chairman, that other gatherings of a similar character may in due time follow.

This book, to the appearance of which Dr. Carl Murchison of the Clark University Press has given so much personal attention, is now sent forth in the hope that it will be of value to scholars as representing a view of the general status of the field of Feelings and Emotions in 1927, and that it will so stimulate research and discussion that if, in five or ten years from now, scholars again assemble to consider the problems of this field, we may then be able to point to material advances.

MARTIN L. REYMERT

WITTENBERG COLLEGE
SPRINGFIELD, OHIO
December, 1927

TABLE OF CONTENTS

APPENDIX

LIST OF ILLUSTRATIONS

ALFRED ADLER

F. AVELING

VLADIMIR M. BEKHTEREV

MADISON BENTLEY

3

G. S. BRETT   KARL BÜHLER

WALTER B. CANNON   HARVEY A. CARR

4

Ed. Claparède

Knight Dunlap

Robert H. Gault

L. B. Hoisington

D. T. HOWARD   ERICH JAENSCH

PIERRE JANET   JOSEPH JASTROW

6

CARL JÖRGENSEN

DAVID KATZ

F. KIESOW

F. KRUEGER

HERBERT S. LANGFELD

WILLIAM McDOUGALL

HENRI PIÉRON

W. B. PILLSBURY

MORTON PRINCE

CARL E. SEASHORE

CHARLES E. SPEARMAN

WILHELM STERN

9

GEORGE M. STRATTON

JOHN S. TERRY

MARGARET F. WASHBURN

ALBERT P. WEISS

ROBERT S. WOODWORTH

J. McKeen Cattell   Martin L. Reymert

Edward B. Titchener   Rees Edgar Tulloss

12

CHEMISTRY-PSYCHOLOGY BUILDING, WITTENBERG COLLEGE

PART I

General Problems in the Psychology of Feeling and Emotion

IS "EMOTION" MORE THAN A CHAPTER HEADING?

MADISON BENTLEY
Cornell University

Those who meet to contend against their fellow psychologists are scarcely in a position to deny the existence of the emotions. Whatever the temper of their psychological creeds, the temper of their assertions, denials, and retorts bears testimony to our eyes and ears that emotions—or things similar to them, however denominated—exist and are observable in our midst.

The question before us is primarily a question of scientific feasibility. Is it profitable—we may first ask ourselves—to psychologize a class of phenomena which we shall agree to call the emotions? And then, if profitable, we shall have to seek a feasible manner of regarding the class for purposes of concrete study and delineation.

Long before the emotional life achieved an independent recognition (while contended against by German rationalists, French sensationalists, English empiricists, and other advocates of the more renowned intellect), the passive affections of the soul—*les passions de l'âme*, in the Cartesian phrase—had caught the attention of certain expositors of the nature of man. These "passions" included the perceptions, the emotions, and much besides. The affective and emotional aspects of experience were, however, long subordinated to the faculties of reason and will. But the nineteenth century, with its romanticisms, its naturalisms, and its humanisms, seems easily to have turned the reflective attention of men toward the feelings. Along with Spencer's didactic evolution of human reason appears Bain to insist that the emotions be given a place coordinate with the intellect and with the will. In France the physician-psychologists found the feelings to play a major part in the aberrations of mind, and in Germany and America the affective phenomena came generally into prominence among psychologists. Charles Darwin and G. H. Schneider brought in the instincts and the emotions as adaptive devices of service in survival, and Wundt drew an elaborate doctrine of emotion and voluntary action out of the integration of his simple feelings. And finally, by their experimental attack upon the circulation, the muscles, and the viscera, the physiologists contributed their share in adding the details of bodily resonance to the emotive stirs which thrill and afflict the human organism.

The common result has been to add a large and important chapter to our textbooks and other general treatises. Has anyone ventured, within the last half-century, to compose a comprehensive work without according to the *emotions* one of the most prominent places in the book? I don't recall an important exception. What have been the contents of these chapters? Usually a section upon classification; a section devoted to James-Lange (usually the longest); a section on "expression"; sometimes a little description and often practical reflections upon the uses and the inconveniences of emotive disturbance. I recall that when I read and returned the manuscript for Titchener's emotive chapter in his *Text-Book* I exclaimed (not having essayed the terrible task myself!): "But why bury James-Lange again with such elaborate rites!" The author's retort was: "What *would* you put in? You've got *somehow* to fill up the chapter!" I fear that many other authors have had as good an occasion for frankness and that few have had the courage to leave out what had already been said too many times. But who would dare to speak authoritatively upon the emotions without showing his audience that he was *au courant* with his subject by discussing and criticizing these alien twins! You may have noticed that they were by no means neglected by the hard-headed committee of researchers into emotion which met last year in strategic counsel upon our common enemy. Why do men continue to whet their knives upon the broken fragments of this hard stone of exaggeration? Is it because psychology has so few respectable theories that it fears to let one escape or die? The virtue of the theory seems to lie in drawing attention to the widespread seizure of the organism whose *Gemüth* is moved. But language, both vulgar and literary, had many times picturesquely referred to the straightened chest, the yearning bowels, the palpitating heart, and the rigid muscles. Besides, the physiologists were bound, without inspiration from the theory, independently to describe the organic details as soon as appropriate methods could be devised. I doubt whether the psychology of the emotions would not have ripened faster without the huge academic discussion through decades as to whether the emotion had any substance not contributed by viscus, blood-vessel, and unstriped muscle. Energy otherwise expended might, for example, have enlightened a certain graduate student who wished to begin a doctoral research on emotion because, as he explained, he had discovered that elusive object in his stomach and intestines, and wished an appropriate apparatus that he might demonstrate his discovery to the psychological world.

As to whether the instincts supply, or are likely to supply, the key to the emotions, opinions (even inspired opinions) are bound to differ. The concept of instincts we chiefly owe to biology; and biology's knowledge of the matter comes mainly from field-stories, casual observation, and speculation. One of the inveterate tendencies of the biologist has been, when pressed by difficulties in the organism, to refer to past generations as an alleged cause. The creature does so-and-so because it was so born. As certain plausible facts are set forth, it is difficult to check the speculation, which creates convenient instincts to account for observed emotions. An added danger is that for actual emotive descriptions is likely to be substituted the mere stock label of fear, anger, jealousy, or rage, and for actual instincts are substituted alleged powers which match these labels. The concept of instinct has, as it seems to me, never been really naturalized within psychology; and it is, as I venture to think, the loose adoption of it from a speculative biology which is in large measure responsible for the destructive critical attacks which have lately been made upon it.

You may be inclined, in your reaction, to go with extremists of an opposite camp who allege that the human infant is so nearly neutral in its functions that its "conditioning" creator can make of it what he will. But until the boast has been confirmed by, say, a dozen children of various extractions, reared by and answering to a prescription and a plan of design published at the birth of these neutral individuals, I shall be skeptical about the alleged powers of the creative behaviorist.

As regards classification and description, I doubt whether anyone can boast. Leaving purely logical schemata aside, the titles to our emotions generally refer (1) to the situation or context in which the organism is placed (the terrifying object, the taunting aggressor, the rival in love, the uncertain and worrying turn of events), and (2) to the bodily indicators of the way in which the individual "takes" the situation (trembling, striking, cowering, blanching, reddening, and what not). Instead of the emotive experience itself, the first kind of reference gives its setting and the second its indication or symptom. What we call "expression" of emotion is, in large measure, the "social indicator" which advertises how the organism is affected. These indicators have high social value since they grant the observer important information about the precise way in which the sufferer is moved. Under human sophistication we all learn to modify them, by way of repression, exaggeration, and emphasis, for our own social purposes. Cannon was inclined to doubt whether visceral changes were sufficiently diverse to characterize the emotions. But some of the states and conditions which Cannon induced were scarcely authenticated as "emotions" (save by an arbitrary definition); and, moreover, he was confined to a small number of indicators. The very fact that we recognize in our fellows the shades and varieties of emotion (even injecting them anthropomorphically into other animals) argues for a wide variety in these bodily indicators, even when taken in their grosser forms. Of course, bodily variety might be present and still not be constitutive of a like emotional variety. And I should always look for the latter in the emotive experience itself. But then others are more interested in the secretion of adrenin or thyroxin, or in vascular turgidity, or in electrical conductivity of the skin; and their interest in emotions may well be as authentic as mine.

This remark leads me to comment upon the last of the big sections which I find in the chapter devoted to the emotions. The history of "expressive methods," as they are called, is extremely interesting; but you know this history as well as I. Interesting, I should say, but melancholy. Enchanted by the principle of "parallelism," men have diligently sought, as they earlier sought the philosopher's stone, to discover some fundamental indicator among our bodily functions which should run in simple parallel to the "mind" or "consciousness." Fechner sought to express a general function and relation in a quantitative way in the Weber-Fechner Law. The Wundtian School sought the function in feeling, on the one hand, and in changes in muscular contraction, circulation, and breathing, on the other. To the behaviorists, all movement is expression in the form of "response," and response runs parallel to the initial way in which the organism is stimulated or moved by outside agents.

But we are concerned at the moment with the *emotional* expressions. You remember the technical devices by which they were harnessed: sphygmograph, sphygmomanometer, pneumograph, laryngograph, planchette, ergograph, and plethysmograph. There was initial success, the hint of a simple parallelism, then a doubt, then a repetition, then the discovery of instrumental errors, negative cases, and new complexities, and then a recasting of the method. The most integrative and persistent attempt appeared in the Wundtian tables and graphs of bodily symptoms in circulation, secretion, respiration, and muscular tension which regularly accompany the course of the typical emotions. As the emotion was conceived to be the unified resultant of many simple feelings, integrated into typical courses under centralizing processes of the brain, it was natural that the typical course should have had definable and decipherable symptoms among the bodily processes mentioned. This was the logic of the emotive expressions. The logic was beautiful and the experimental program of verification brilliant. Many think that the attempt failed; that the delicate instruments fail to detect either a parallelism or a differential bodily outcome and expression of the emotions. And we may well doubt whether, under the vast complexities of organic function, so simple a parallelism is to be looked for. Too many organic events influence in too many ways blood-pressure and pulse and smooth muscle for the emotion of anger or fear or jealousy to have its undisputed way with these great bodily systems and so with the organism at large.

In the nineties the project revived when galvanometric deflections were observed with certain emotional states and the absurd hybrid name of the "psychogalvanic reflex" suggested new hope in a universal indicator of the emotions. Faith in the galvanometer is still to be found; but at least we are beginning to understand that deflections sometimes occur without emotions, and emotions sometimes without deflections. Moreover, it is common to find the most meticulous care exercised with the electrical measurements and controls and the most appalling looseness with the descriptive side of the emotion which the changes in bodily resistance are supposed to register. As a physiological aid the method holds out promises; but as a plain and unequivocal indicator of emotion it does not impress us. And the case for the glands seems at the moment to be in about the same state; though the frank recognition by all who really know something about the vast complexity of the subject is here a good augury.

Well, emotion is at least a topic! It is something to talk about and to disagree upon. To me its essential characteristic is a progressive activity of the organism when faced by a predicament. As a psychological function it is related to the various forms of action. It has beginning, course, and ending. It is to be described in terms of its inception, its successive stages, and its outcome. It comprehends, in a peculiar way, the internal regulation of the body by chemical and neural means. Whatever concerns emotion by way of experience and by way of bodily process is proper material for its description. Its varieties, its history, its pathology, and its subsequent effects upon the organism are all thrilling matters for investigation. But to another psychologist, emotion means glandular products and visceral incidents; to a third, the action of the autonomic nervous system; to still another, a type of external bodily activity or deportment; or again a pleasant or unpleasant reaction upon events or a "mental state." Once more, emotion may be defined as a quality of excitement which accompanies the operation of an instinct, or a kind of drive under which the organism whips itself into action, or a certain kind of response to a certain kind of stimulus. All these conceptions and understandings of emotions, and more, do we find current among psychologists. And yet we speak of emotion as if it were the common intellectual and professional property of all of us. At this moment the flag of emotion floats above us announcing to a mildly interested world that we are convened to discuss and possibly to solve its problems. And there *are*, doubtless, problems of emotion; as there are problems of reducing poverty and of preventing war. But is emotion here more than a label, or a general topic of discourse, or a banner? It certainly represents a subject of human concern. For example, few human concerns in current academic and medical matters now rival men's interest in the power and the therapy of the emotions. The lay-world has been given to understand that its passions, perplexities, tortures, and lusts stand among the chief agencies of personal and social order and disorder; that a man may be made or marred by worrying about his limitations, his father's debts, or his mother's lovers; that childish tantrums and adolescent longings may scar him for life. He is also encouraged to believe that these same thrilling emotions may be interestingly discussed in the clinic and set right by the new doctors. Naturally he is all for the emotions. But are the emotions a center for coordinated psychological research? That is to say, is there *a* scientific problem of emotion? This query suggests, as I suppose, one of our main objects in coming together in this hospitable place by the courtesy of this generous college. At the least, the interests of all of us are bound to be made more catholic, more tolerant, and more enlightened, and the discriminations of all of us made sharper for our own problems and for the problems of our neighbors.

As a logical matter, our present status is fairly clear. It seems to me that our problems have prospered best when the emotions have been considered as one phase of the general affective life and when the feelings were properly coordinated with all the other aspects of experience and of the psychological organism. While the mere analysis into affective qualities has never carried us far in the understanding of emotion, it seems to me that reasonable accounts of the feelings have. Just now I have been reading a manuscript of this temper, a judicious and enlightened book upon the affective life of man which will soon (as I hope) come to

publication.   It gives a psychological setting for the emotions
which would include in a coherent way most, if not all, of the
current problems of which we have been hearing.   But most men
care less for a general understanding than for the exploitation of a
private interest or a particular problem.   And perhaps this individuality of interest is well for research.   It may lead us ultimately to
a common topic and to common coherent knowledge.

But whether emotion is today more than the heading of a
chapter, I am still doubtful.   Whether the term stands—in the
regard of most of us—for a psychological entity upon which we are
all researching, I do not know.   Whether it is the common subject
of our varied investigations, I am not sure enough to be dogmatic.
But that is precisely one of the desirable issues which we may
confidently expect from this international symposium of psychologists.

CHAPTER 2

THE PLACE OF EMOTION IN
MODERN PSYCHOLOGY

JOSEPH JASTROW
University of Wisconsin

I am accepting the uninspiring rôle of an unofficial guide to the realm of emotion, and shall be content if my offices prove of service. At most I may aspire to arrange in one reel the several shifts of scenes and plots of the story of the emotions in the motion picture of modern psychology. True to the function of guides, I shall be pointing out what is familiar, but commonly omitted from statement because assumed. A certain measure of completeness is desirable, while yet limiting the survey to what has become significant in the status of the affective life in the present-day empire of the mind.

I

The first setting may be assigned to emotion as motive. The common root of several energetic words, *m-o-t*, indicates that that whereby we live, wherein we have our being, leads to our moving in that we are moved to response. Motive, emotion, and motion are of one psychological as well as philological family.

Yet there is rivalry within the family circle, not, as the Freudians would have it, a family romance, in which the romantic appears to be more frantic than fond (and to the more normally minded, more fiction than fact), but a family faction as well as affection, a friendly contention for the supremacy of the "why." Those who answer the "why" with a motive—it may be revenge, it may be sympathy, it may be deviltry—are emotionalists; those who answer it with a reason—it may be to obtain advantage, to save trouble, to avoid disaster—are the emotionalists once removed, whom we call rationalists. They stress the means-to-end relation in its plan and mechanism, its logical device, and do not choose to uncover any deeper motivation-level for the choice of behavior or its defense. Motives and reasons present two sides for the same shield; it is not easy to say which is gold and which silver, as so often either is gilt or glitter, or even brass or dross. The aptness at supplying good reasons for poor motives is an ancient one, and was not left for Freud to discover; even Aesop was late in the field. The discovery that grapes are sour when out of reach is made by many humans whose I. Q. does not entitle them to be called foxy. The tendency to rationalize is encouraged by the need of defending or disguising motivation—again an evidence of rivalry or conflict between feeling and thinking. In tracing the service of reason in defense of emotion, we come upon the more vital urge or drive that stimulates both.

II

Next in the overture arises a question: Why this belated regard for what is now so cordially recognized as a clue to the entire psychic nature? Why was emotion so long the Cinderella of the psychic household? The answer requires a historical reference. It was not so at the outset. To the ancient Greek mind the "*psyche*" was an integrated activity, of which the "*phrene*" was the problem-working partner. Had not the term been bastardized some time before the needed advent of its birth, *phrenology* would have been the name of the "mental philosophy" concerned with the logical equipment.

Yet that fateful tendency to assign value, which makes not cowards but moralists of us all—all but the most abandoned or the most tolerant seeking to moralize the rest—is responsible for the greater dignity assigned to the soarings and explorings of the intellect in contrast to the homely beckonings and reckonings of the feelings. Yet no Greek or Roman philosopher, however equally under the sway of moralizing bents, could anticipate that the marriage ties of *Psyche* and *Phrene*, which he respected, would under Christian influence lead to the distrust of all but a prescribed range of feelings, and to a castigation of the flesh as the seat of the passions. But this recognition of the closer moralization-value of the emotions is itself a distrustful avowal of a truth that led modern psychology to the rescue of Cinderella. We are virtuous or vicious more by how we feel than by what we know.

One hesitates whether to go back to Plato or to Adam for the further intrusion or confusion of the tree of knowledge, and the fabled loss of a Paradise in which ignorance secured bliss. The doctrine that no one would knowingly or willingly do wrong suggests to the irreverent Freudian disciple that Adam and Plato alike should have been psychoanalyzed. Idealism, intellectualism, rationalism, were all set going in that active ferment of the mind that through the ages made Plato and Aristotle household words, and made the *Story of Philosophy* a twentieth-century best seller

among the many cherishing the volume as a sign of intellectualism
rather than as a guide to their perplexities by which the majority
of these philosophers-by-purchase were untroubled, having no
vitiating contact with the tree of knowledge, but much with the
range of feelings, including the pride of intellect. Man will not
easily give up the hope that he is a rational animal by definition
if not by fact. Behaving like human, all too human, beings does
not imply any striking measure of rationality, if we accept a happy
mean between Nietzsche and Dorsey.

Dessoir in his *History of Psychology* offers a convenient distinction
to indicate the two streams which, when they converged, made
the current of modern psychology: the one psychology proper, as
the accredited ruler of the affairs of the thinking mind, and the
other *psychosophy*, which gathers the reflected wisdom growing
out of experience and behavior. The psychosophic attitude was
congenial to the Roman mind, like the American given to practical
affairs, to engineering of aqueducts and highways and boom-towns.
To take things philosophically is a Roman expression; the Stoic and
Epicurean were emotionalized practical rather than scholarly
attitudes toward life. A continuous stream of doctrine reflecting
both interests is that relating to character, from the delineations
of Theophrastus, their revival in Renaissance Europe, and the
sturdy survival of the "humors" or temperaments from Galen
down—all engaged with the psychic life in the concrete and
emotionalized reality. The practical stress of modern living has
played its part in focusing upon the actual realistic motivation
that keeps us going. The feelings are so real that their claim
to attention was congenial to our modern interests.

Of like antiquity is the recognition of the abnormal. For medical
psychology, though a modern term, is an ancient body of knowledge, emerging from the observation of disturbed emotional
states—of excitement and anger, like mania, of fear and depression,
like melancholia. Yet in this field also the false accents of rationalism and moralism appear. Until recently the insane were regarded as those unable to reason straight—a distinction which if
democratically applied would require more asylums than apartment
houses—or again, were supposed not to know the difference between
right and wrong, on which many asylum-residents have more
emphatic views and defend them better than many who read the
daily papers and do as they are advised. Elation and depression
as fluctuations of mood and as characteristic of temperament form
early data of emotional psychology.

When psychology became an established discipline, yet long
attached to the apron-strings of mother philosophy, the very

addiction to psychologizing was an invitation to intellectualizing. Professor Stratton has stated it simply and well.

"In the older days the philosopher took his own mind as the type and standard by which all minds were to be interpreted; the psychologist applied universally whatever stood in the forefront of his own consciousness. The intellectual interest, so powerful in the observer, made him see little but intellectual interests and devices wherever his eye might rest   Today in the effort to correct his prepossession we have come to a careful study of rudimentary minds, where there is risk that our judgment be distorted in an opposite way, man being now conceived as made in the image not of pure reason but of the beast. But in this way we are attaining to a knowledge, never before had, of the driving forces of inheritance, of the impulses, of the passions of the human mind. When new corrections are made in the light of these, then our intelligence is seen not as a thing apart, moved solely by laws of consistency and evidence, but swept this way and that by deep currents of longing and anger and fear."

III

We may now approach at closer range. The emotions could hardly come to their own before a very considerable convergence of modern interests had prepared the way for the consummation. A set of sign-posts may indicate the route. These are:

a) the *evolutionary* doctrine in general and the signal service of Darwin's study of emotional expression as a link between man and beast;

b) its application to *primitive man* and the widening of the psychological horizon by a comparison of culture stages, as notable as the expansion of the geographical horizon by travel and acquaintance with the variety of customs and their emotional support;

c) the *genetic* unfoldment of the *child*, so different from the adult in many ways, but emotionally most instructive and authentic;

d) the *differential* psychology of *sex, race, type, temperament, age, and organic disposition;*

e) the *abnormal* emotions, particularly the upsets of psychoneuroses and the dominant part which disturbed and distorted emotion plays in mental disorder;

f) convergent as well as divergent streams among these by way of the specialized study of the *criminal, defective,* and *delinquent* classes, all examples of the emotional-social *maladjustment;*

g) the *social* embodiments and agencies of the crowd-mind, and the sway of socialized motives that must be understood and controlled if men are to be governed, including also the *institutional* products that themselves arise out of the emotional needs of men—the church as well as the school, the courts as well as the forum;

h) the specific contributions of the *Freudian psychology* centralizing upon the primitive *urges*, the drives, the libido, the *élan vital*, the horme, the what-not that men live by and for;

i) the advance in *experimental* knowledge making it possible to include the study of emotion by laboratory methods, and to define its *organic basis;*

j) the specialized study of the lower and the higher reaches *of the affective life* (including the fine arts) and the *theory* of the interrelation and integration of all the world of affect in its own domain from instinct to sentiment, and by this route returning to the philosophical orbit, but with the enrichment of a biological, genetic, comparative, psychopathic, social approach;

k) finally, the applicational side of this cumulative insight for which the term *emotional hygiene* is itself a summary. To live wholesomely and happily requires affective health. We must feel rightly to act rightly. Morale is largely emotional.

IV

My further course is to comment upon the significance of these contributions and their place in the picture.

a) The evolutionary renaissance was a general one. Yet the demonstration was easier that animals behave like human beings because they feel as human beings feel than that they behave so because they think as human beings think. In so many ways animals put what mind they have upon different ranges of activity, though with much in common with the human scene, as in the emotionalized pursuit of food and sex. But these typical appetites are highly though differently emotionalized, as well as organized; and the struggle for existence, so largely a struggle for meals and mates, was indelibly written in the bodily gesture of desire and attack, and most intricately in the palimpsest of the face. Here are to be read the original pre-human records of fear and anger, as well as the courtship gestures and the maternal attentions—far earlier and more convincing records than the selected laboratory registrations that have only the advantage of measurability. We eat and pout, we chew and gnash with the same outfit, greet friend and meat with the same smile, reject distasteful food and disgusting conduct and even express disdain with the same pooh-pooh; we thus show that we and our animal friends or enemies have been through the same school of Mother Nature, though in a more advanced class. Where the dog snarls, we sneer, but both

have the same muscle to uncover the "canine," our single vestige
of a pointed tooth. It is in uncovering this amazing record of
the emotional past preserved in the smile and laugh, the cries
and tears acquired without learning, that Darwin may be said
to occupy the first place in the Hall of Fame of modern emotional
psychology.

   b)   Among the group of early Darwinians there were, in addition
to the zoölogists and the geologists, for whom the long aeons for
the play of variation and natural selection seemed a "special
creation," a group of anthropologists to whose pioneering ventures we owe the inclusion of primitive man as a psychological
inquiry. One may mention Spencer and Tylor as distinctive.
A survey of the fauna and flora of human races and institutions
brought forward the close dependence of custom, belief, and invention upon modes of feeling and satisfaction of affective needs.
The mores, rites, and ceremonies gave up their dead secrets as
modes of relief or expression of fears and angers and hopes and
sympathies. Primitive man was much more *homo sentiens* than
homo sapiens or *volens;* and, if he acted or believed strangely to
our so differently centered systems, we can still meet and understand our primitive forbears on the. common basis of the desires
and rewards, the dreads and avoidances of so much that remains
our common fate. Despite other days and other ways, we maintain the same hopes and fears, establish similar prides and shames
to regulate our conduct. The extended anthropological record
proclaims the emotional as well as the anatomical brotherhood
of man, despite the difference of behavior magnified to our sophisticated vision. The recent proof—from Boas to Lévy-Bruhl,
to Radin—that primitive mentality approaches, far more nearly
than we supposed, our own mind-processes, through a common
service of curiosity and orderly satisfaction of intellectual cravings,
is another brilliant example of a correction through the consideration of the emotional ingredient of knowledge.

   c)   Emotions have profited as much from the rich contributions
of the genetic approach in its modern restatement as have the
knowledge-functions. Parallel with the intelligence tests as
marking the stages of growth are the emotional tests, that have
more recently and imperfectly come to their own. The will-tem-
perament and personality schedules and the indications of traits
through types of response suggest the promising line of advance.
Equally significant is the emotional (instinctive) dominance in
the early infantile stages as set forth by Gesell, in whose program
the affective genesis finds a proper emphasis. Here, too, belong
the evidences of original emotional responses by Watson—a part

of the solid core of the behavioristic contribution, which remains valid despite the extravagant and so sadly misleading superstructure that has been based upon it. Here more than elsewhere is the inadequacy apparent of what a hurried guide may mention. Sufficient to say that the genetic concept has been enriched perhaps more than any other by the recognition of the emotional support and direction of growth. The story of feeling parallels the story of thinking as part of the story of psychic growth more intimately, more indispensably, than in any other chapter of the Story of Mind.

I must not leave it without indicating sentence-wise what would require a chapter-scale of presentation. The psychic growth of childhood is dominantly an affective development. Childhood is even more characteristically an emotional condition than a stage along the route to intellectual grasp and motor control. The stream of childhood behavior is set by the emotional course. Affect is more authentic, plays a larger and more directive rôle in the ensemble of childhood than later. It is because the emotions in the child are so strong, so sweeping, so devastating if unwisely hampered, that childhood is a problem as well as a clue to the intricacies of later adjustment. The concept that must be given a far wider recognition than it has yet received is that of *emotional age*. The stages and levels of growth, so rapidly shifting in the earlier periods, are distinctively affective, native reflexes of organic insistence, primitive craving and avoidances, expanding to tastes, desires, longings, and their antipathies. Viewed from its later issue, there arises the concept of *infantilism*, the relative failure to outgrow with the maturity of years the bondage of the early emotionalism. Genetic psychology alone would require the intensive study of emotion which this survey outlines.

d) Continuing the theme, we may with similar emphasis and similar inevitable foreshortening, set forth that the study of individual differences equally requires the centralization of the emotions in the total picture. Each of the rubrics of differential psychology carries an emotional story, sex above all. To be masculine or feminine implies a distinctive and pervasive emotional composite. I cannot stop to do more than characterize as elaborately foolish and futile the attempts to make out that boys and girls are substantially alike in their "psyche" because they do equally poorly in algebra or in supplying missing words in sentences. Of course coeducation shows that the mediocrity or, if you like, the super-mediocrity of college students follows no lines of sex, and that I have only a fifty-fifty chance in correcting examination papers to guess whether the inadequacy is that of a

John or a Jane. But to allow this trivial fact to offset the overwhelming contrast of the rest of John's and Jane's natures, merely
because in other unenlightened days their similarities were overlooked and a false view of their meaning shaped the whole system
of lives for men and lives for women, is to throw out not only the
child with the bath but the whole human family and its record.
For the relatively unemotionalized sections of behavior, sex may
have slight meaning as affecting performance. But one of the
major contributions of affective psychology is to show how exceptional is the behavior with the but slight or remote affective
determination; and no less, that what is decreed by nature carries
farthest in reach and authenticity at whatever level of expression.
The problem of social adjustment is to shape living conditions to
the needs of men and of women, not to ignore nor yet to thwart
them. We shall lead more rational lives as we use our rationality
to recognize and not to disguise or distort the psychology of sex.
To this much-desired conviction the psychology of the emotions
contributes notably.

Less can be and need be said of race. The affective traits of
race are real, however difficult to formulate and however overlapping. In the social aspect they again come to the front, as
Porteus has interestingly set forth. The study of racial prejudice
is one of the most illuminating demonstrations of the realities of
the affective life. How far animosities can be regulated by cultivation of tolerance through rationality, is an uncertain but vital
issue. Through the recognition of the emotional factor in race
contacts, as well as in race proficiencies, the future of racial psychology is more secure, as well as more imperative.

The psychologies of differences, whether of sex, of race, of age,
or of type, have a common or an overlapping orbit. I am convinced that in every psychology of the future, the chapter devoted
to psychological types will be an increasingly important one.
Between the individual and the species stands the type. The
plan of personality is neither a standardized repetition of a uniform unit nor a haphazard medley or mosaic; there runs through
its designs a limited set of groupings or configurations (again
with subvarieties) which compose the type. Consideration for
type is the logical and humane principle for treatment and specialization. Type likewise starts from the affective clue or drive, of
emotional push and pull; it is temperamental. The study of
type, whether introvert and extravert or some more refined division, is bound to follow the lead of affect, again justifying the
focus upon the psychology of the emotional distinctions.

Growth includes decline. The genetic and the individual converge. Such a survey as that of Hollingworth is most useful to establish the correct vicissitudes and regulations in terms of age periods. It brings adolescence and senescence into one picture. Life proceeds in a cycle; the ages of man have their dominant affective aspects, their compensations, and handicaps. An affective psychology of the cycle of life has as marked a regulative as an informative value.

e) In terms of influence, the abnormalities of emotion have presumably contributed more directly to the "emotional" renaissance which this occasion celebrates than has any other phase of interest. Its early and continuous play in shaping the doctrines of temperament, its later invitation to consider the poles of elation and depression, have been noted. The most casual visit to the wards of what we by tradition call mental disorders offers convincing and distressing proof that we are traversing the halls of aberrant emotion. An established principle of abnormal psychology is that the fundamental psychic relations and mechanisms, the dispositions and conditions of behavior, are the same in sane and insane; the derangement indicates only that the psychic clock is no longer keeping correct time, may be permanently disabled for such normal function, while yet it keeps going as a timepiece of some sort. Because in normality it is so vitally and intricately an emotional going concern, its false movements are largely emotional ungearings, as MacCurdy's thesis elaborately indicates.

In the newer insight the psychoneuroses have yielded a rich psychology; they are representative of the common meeting-ground of the psychologist and the psychiatrist. If we specify only the hysterical and the neurasthenic complexes, the lessons are sufficiently clear and comprehensive. Sanity broadens to emotional balance and a mental hygiene of their control; mental stability becomes emotionally poised and maintained. Hysteria must be outgrown and checked if the stability of human relations is to endure. The incapacities of neurasthenia must be reduced and the waste and menace of fatigue be broadcasted. We become aware through the psychoneuroses—those of the war-shock adding to the tale—of the delicacy of the psychic balance, the perils of the strains that modern strenuosity places upon the more sensitive. Thus reconstructed sanity acquires an affective rather than an intellectual implication. Reasonableness becomes an issue, not a condition of emotional integrity. The coming of age of abnormal psychology, the establishment of the clinical attitude toward behavior, the close alliance in intent and technique of psychology and psychiatry—all converge upon and have been, in part, prompted by the significance of the affective life. The same conclusion appears in further extension and detail in the Freudian approach.

f) With emotional maladjustment thus brought into the psychic scene, the practical stress of its social consequences naturally intensified the interests in its manifestations. Poverty and crime, weakness and sin abound; the salvaging of humanity is a persistent need. Humanized psychology becomes a necessity, not an academic ideal. How the newer insight has affected our concern and treatment of the defective, delinquent, and criminal classes and our understanding of the offender, is familiar. Through the reconstruction of emotional psychology, what has been too exclusively regarded as a moral failure appears as part of the liability of aberrant emotions and faulty instinctive responses. Much of the problem falls in the sphere of adolescent and youthful stress, where emotion runs high and readily becomes unruly, where the spark of impulse, when in contact with the tinder of neurotic constitution, readily produces the psychic conflagrations which become social menaces. Juvenile and adolescent stresses are real. To many dispositions, emotional maturity and stability become a difficult achievement, requiring all the aid of sympathy and understanding that we can command for their wise direction, and in more serious incapacities become an almost hopeless consummation. The guiding hand of psychology replaces or supports the stern arm of the law.

g) How intimately the affective life is a socialized venture has become clear through much the same shift of view and emphasis. The great majority of the psychic responses, the affective ones dominantly, move in a social milieu; we react to others far more intimately and more formatively than to situations of things and processes of the mechanical order. The socialized emotions express at the same time a field of reference and a reconstruction. Social conflict and mutual aid are alike emotionally supported. Social psychology is so recent a discipline that it has grown up under the same set of influences as have crowned our emotional Cinderella.

In addition, collective emotion, herd-traits, mental contagion, class conformity, social conflict, racial and communal prides and shames, rewards or disgraces are seen to derive from the extensions of the emotionality of the individual in the only setting in which it can reach complete expression. The development as well as control of the crowd-mind, the guidance of public feelings and sentiments buttress the structure of collective emotion. More specifically must institutions be considered and developed in terms of emotional values.

h) In emotional psychology Freud requires either a page or a volume. The single-page, the front-page reference would be to the commanding fact that here first appeared the motive psychology in its own right as a star performer, assigned the leading part in the play. Freudian psychology is deep psychology; exploring below the surface, it comes upon the hidden and suppressed motives and mechanisms, exposes a subconscious activity, discloses the sources of conflict within the competing motives and the imposed struggle between the individual and the encircling collective forces of restraint—the family, society, moral censorship, custom, law. All this striving is essentially emotional, as being alone sufficiently organic, natural, instinctive, driving. Libido is emotionalized psychic energy. That Freud came upon it in the rôle of sex and forthwith sexualized all striving is but one version, one configuration of libido in the natural, in the raw. Hence the need of sublimation of emotional refinement, of affective development through civilized outlets for primitive, romantic, or cultural urges; hence later the inclusion of the power or mastery motives and the total personality, the ambitions, disappointments, and rewards in the drama of life. Each measures himself against the rest, emerges or struggles with an inferiority complex, a superiority delusion, a compensation device, a rationalization system, or a normal "know thyself" adjustment. We Freudianize ourselves clumsily or expertly, deliberately or deceptively.

The coincidence of the Freudian era and of the emotional renaissance is not accidental. The twenty-year period of resistance —itself a Freudian symptom—was doubtless in the main the result of a medical prejudice and suspicion of irregular practice, but in a secondary way also a scepticism towards emotional disturbance as so causative an agent in the production of neuroses, and in the details of making and dreaming experience. After Freud performed the matrimonial ceremonies uniting motive and emotion, it has been hazardous for a psychologist to put them asunder, while his ardent disciples regard such attempt as sacrilege. Freud is a notable name in the emotional renaissance.

i) The experimental psychology of the emotion can hardly be summarized. Most distinctive is the demonstration of its organic bases in the complex glandular mechanisms—a chapter unknown when Wundt ventured to call his pioneer textbook *Physiological Psychology*. Yet there is today hardly a beginner's text that does not present the relation of thyroid deficiency to apathy and inertia, of thyroid overaction to undue excitability, of the adrenals to strenuosity, of endocrine balance as a condition of normal functioning of the emotional life. Sex finds its place in a glandular psychology. Through Cannon's monumental demonstrations, emotion becomes an emergency-meeting device, mobilizing the organism for fight typically and for other vital emotional situations as well by virtue of the same integrated mechanisms. Rage, fear, hunger, and sympathy no less overlap in their glandular registration. More than one writer has been struck with the analogy of the doctrine of "humors" to the secretions. A fanciful guess with a stroke of luck and a large dose of baseless notions has been replaced by laboratory findings undreamed of in the philosophy that, when revived in no less sporadic relation to scientific evidence, gave us the phrases, still current, of good humor and bad humor.

This fascinating story of the glands is quite as dramatic in its further relation to the organic background of the affective life. The mediumship of the autonomic nervous system has revealed itself as bringing glands and the central direction of the new brain, to whose extraordinary development man owes his behavior as a human being, into one genetic integration. The life of feeling and emotion is aeons older than that of thought, of cerebral redirection and control. We are far older emotionally than intellectually and can never deny, never outgrow our evolutionary birthright, whatever its handicaps. In the duality of the nervous system is written the organic preamble to the chapters on feeling and thinking.[1]

j) Here again, a summary becomes an enumeration. I select for mention the theories of emotion, for which the James-Lange contribution represents the modern starting-point, and the several attempts to define pleasure and displeasure in subsequent development. Next, the close relations between instinct and emotion, suggested by Shand, made current by McDougall, widely influential in social psychology, critically present in Allport. There is the large chapter on the sentiments and the intricate relations which they assume under intellectual reflection and institutional support. The most elaborate work is that of Shand. The specialized treatment of the great trunk-line emotions is the next step. A brilliant example is Stratton's treatise on *Anger* with its further specialization in the field of religion. It was part of Stanley Hall's ambition to bring together his several contributions to these phases of emotional psychology, and his name belongs among

[1] As experimental findings do not lend themselves to summary the handbook of Smith may be referred to, and the many studies of the emotional components of character and personality not yet collected. The chapter in Roback's *Psychology of Character* is an available summary. Studies in aesthetics and in social products of emotional trends have also, in part, proceeded experimentally.

the foremost of its pioneers. But to the making of lists there is no end, except the limitation of time and space.

k) The regulative side of the emotional life I have referred to in my prologue. From the nursery school, which owes its being to the recognition of affective control as the basis of the first steps in right growth, to the university, which harps upon the training of character but flounders in attempting to find a place for it in its crowded and too commonly aimless curriculum, the theme of the emotional life is asserting its claims. Emotional hygiene, genetic and social, has come to stay.

V

My epilogue determines itself: how to harmonize the life of feeling and of thinking in one living symphony. Ours must be a "life of reason," a phrase expanded to a series of volumes by one who has lived it significantly—Santayana; he has felt as sensitively as he has thought nobly. For the most of us, the program must be reduced to humble dimensions, to simpler terms. Edman has used the caption "Career of Reason" in surveying for college students the several contributory disciplines to the reflective and institutional occupations of mankind.

In this humanized version of psychology we must recognize that we cannot trust our feelings uncritically, however much we must feel as well as think our way to the solution of our problems, to the attainment of the attitudes that represent what we have made of our lives. We must definitely recognize the emotional impediments of thought. Superstition, prejudice, dogmas form a human record vast and dismal, a permanent warning of the dangers attending the life of reason. From moods to philosophies the affects rule. The arts of ruling men organize or exploit their sympathies and sentiments. Leaders are experts in gauging the composite tempers of their following; their insight is a tact far more emotional than rational in its technique. Thus the renaissance of emotional psychology derives its largest warrant from its practical value in understanding and directing human motives as the mainsprings of action. The adjustment of feeling and thinking in that cause remains the great desideratum.

For its establishment our survey provides a few hints and guides. The neurological approach leaves a deposit of advice. The neurotic must be understood and avoided; a sound organic basis is indispensable to the sane life of reason. The neuroses indicate the untoward liabilities. If we are hysterical, we shall live and love and think not wisely, but too well, too intensively, too narrowly, with too heavy an affective load, with a too much prejudiced and fitful vitality. If we are neurasthenic, we shall feel and think too timidly, with too much repression, too much troubled anxiety, too ready discouragement, too shrinking a venture, too sensitive a responsiveness to the give and take of an imperfect world. If we are paranoiac, we shall be burdened with suspicion and distortions, see the world too much in the image of our own deviations, be prone to fanaticism and the erratic. The avoidance of the neurotic is the first condition of the affective stability.

In further illustration, note that the neurotic liabilities, the recognition of which grows out of emotionalized psychology, throw the weight upon hereditary factors, despite the recognized influence of wise direction in mitigating and avoiding neurotic catastrophe. But disposition is fundamental and offers aid or resistance to discipline. As long as psychology was so largely concerned with the intellectual processes, learning was paramount and much of it acquired, redirected, artificial. With the emphasis directed to the emotional basis of the psyche, the hereditary rather than the environmental appears in the determining rôle. Traits are deeper than habits; the laws of psychic heredity must be read first in the emotional, temperamental make-up, and the conclusions transferred to the logical traits as of a derivative order.

Constructively we shall seek the normal by a rightful satisfaction of the dominant urges, not by way of crippling, denunciation, denial, or escape, but by whole-hearted employment and enjoyment of the stages of growth. The slow, yet natural expansion of motives must be accepted; for such is the law of emotional age. The disciplines of early life assume a corrected perspective under the recognition of the validity of natural urges, free expression, and levels of emancipation and growth. The emotions have themselves been rationalized by giving them an accredited place in the life of reason.

The older intellectualism has receded to its proper place in the psyche. Motive psychology has replaced it, yet has incorporated the most valued of its findings, including its laboratory and clinical technique. In the recognition of mechanisms the advance of knowledge is congenial in both fields. Perceptive and apperceptive mechanisms as aids to logical and objective control are of one order; emotional mechanisms for guiding instinctive satisfactions and their derivative issues up to the complications of character and personality are of another order for self and socialized assertion and control. But as we go far in a life of reason we require the logical techniques for the combined direction of the psychic, the integrated rational life. Motives lead to goals and ideals, by way of principles and formulated experience; insight belongs to both—a humanized scientific habit of mind. It is in view of these converging and supplementing contributions that we are warranted in speaking of an emotional renaissance and in commemorating it so worthily, as by the program of the present occasion.

BIBLIOGRAPHY

BOAS, F. The mind of primitive man. New York: Macmillan, 1911.

CANNON, W. B. Bodily changes in pain, hunger, fear, and rage. New York: Appleton, 1915.

DARWIN, C. R. The expression of emotion in man and animals. New York: Appleton, 1873–1913.

DESSOIR, M. Outlines of the history of psychology. New York: Macmillan, 1912.

DORSEY, G. A. Why we behave like human beings. New York: Harper, 1925.

EDMAN, I. Human traits and their social significance. Boston: Houghton Mifflin, 1920.

FREUD, S. A general introduction to psychoanalysis. New York: Boni & Liveright, 1920.

GESELL, A. Mental growth of the pre-school child. New York: Macmillan, 1925.

HOLLINGWORTH, H. L. Mental growth and decline. New York: Appleton, 1927.

JAMES, W., AND LANGE, C. G. The emotions. Baltimore: Williams & Wilkins, 1922.

LÉVY-BRUHL, L. How natives think. London: Allen & Unwin, 1926.

———. Primitive mentality. London: Allen & Unwin, 1923.

MACCURDY, J. T. The psychology of emotion, morbid and normal. New York: Harcourt, Brace, 1925.

MCDOUGALL, W. Introduction to social psychology. Boston: Luce, 1918.

PORTEUS, S. D. Race and temperament. Boston: Badger, 1926.

RADIN, P. Primitive man as philosopher. New York: Appleton, 1927.

ROBACK, A. A. The psychology of character. New York: Harcourt, Brace, 1927.

SANTAYANA, G. The life of reason; or, the phases of human progress. (5 Vols.) New York: Scribner, 1905–1918.

SHAND, A. F. The foundations of character, being a study of the tendencies of the emotions and sentiments. London: Macmillan, 1914.

SMITH, W. W. The measurement of emotion. New York: Harcourt, Brace, 1922.

STRATTON, G. M. Anger: its religious and moral significance. New York: Macmillan, 1923.

TYLOR, E. B. Researches into the early history of mankind and the development of civilization. London, 1865; Boston: Estes & Lauriat, 1878.

———. Primitive culture. London: Murray, 1870–1903.

WATSON, J. B. Psychology from the standpoint of a behaviorist. Philadelphia: Lippincott, 1924.

WUNDT, W. Principles of physiological psychology. New York: Macmillan, 1922.

There has been no general survey of the "Psychology of the Emotions" since that of Ribot (1889), but many and varied special contributions.

CHAPTER 3

A NEW METHOD FOR INVESTIGATING THE SPRINGS OF ACTION

Charles E. Spearman
University of London

I. Present Lack of Scientific Progress

Few topics of inquiry could be more fascinating than that of the fundamental human impulses, desires, and emotions. The behavior of every one of us at every moment is not only always caused by such urges in ourselves, but also for the most part aims at being effective by activating those of other persons. As much may be said of all public legislation, and even of all social customs and institutions.

With small surprise, then, we find a pre-eminent place ceded to this topic already in the writings of Plato. Familiar enough is his beautiful simile wherein the organization of the mind is likened to that of a charioteer driving two horses, the one noble and the other base. The former steed represents the higher tendencies, such as courage to face danger; the baser animal stands for the sensory appetites; whilst the charioteer symbolizes the controlling "Logos" or "Reason." And upon such a ground—the constitution of the individual person—it is that he builds up the constitution even of the model state itself.

Hardly less well known is the kindred line of argument adopted many centuries later by Hobbes. For again the make-up of the state is derived from the inclinations of the individual citizen. But since this motivation of the individual is now conceived in a totally different manner—that is, as essentially directed towards his own happiness and preservation—so too the whole state and statecraft are now entirely remodelled.

Great, however, as has always been the interest displayed in this paramount branch of psychology from the earliest times, there are grounds for doubting whether it has made any corresponding amount of scientific progress.

Take, for example, the most fundamental and elementary step towards submitting the natural inclinations to exact investigation; namely, the making out of a list of them. Such lists have been drawn up, indeed, abundantly enough; but they have varied most disconcertingly from one author to another; and, what is worse, they seem to remain as discrepant nowadays as in the most ancient times. Thus, nothing could be more unlike than, on the one hand, the "original tendencies" of Thorndike, and, on the other hand, the "instincts" of W. McDougall. Have we at any rate the consolation of knowing that, although controversy has not abated, yet it has been continually passing on to new and more modern phases? Even this comfort is vouchsafed to us only in meager degree. For instance, any attempt to trace back the parentage from which McDougall's doctrine of emotion has sprung would not rightly, I think, go to such immediate predecessors of his as Ward, Bain, James, or Wundt, but rather would jump right back to Malebranche. In fact, that which in current literature has been universally accepted and yet is characteristically modern comprises little more than a thoroughgoing adoption of the biological standpoint. To the preservation of self as advocated by Hobbes has now been added the preservation of the offspring and the herd; whilst the conscious motivation towards these ends has been replaced by a system of blind drives subserving them. For the rest, the most notable general modern characteristic would appear to be a decisive—indeed, contemptuous—rejection of what in the older doctrines plays such a dominant part as the "will"; by this, it used to be said, all the natural impulses and acquired desires are alike brought under supreme control.

II. Scope of Results Needed

Since, then, the situation seems to warrant some misgivings and scrutiny, let us begin by inquiring what extent of information has really been elicited by psychology ancient and modern, and how far it goes towards covering the whole scope prescribed by science.

To begin with, there are the already mentioned lists of natural inclinations, as also of emotions, sentiments, and so forth. The supply of these, however it may err on the side of discrepancies, leaves at any rate nothing to be desired in respect of elaborate detail. But still such lists are primarily and in themselves nothing more than classifications.

And herewith is at once furnished a key to some part at least of the discrepancies. For one and the same material may with equal truth be classified in any number of different ways. The question really at issue between them may be—and usually is—not as to which is the more correct, but only as to which is scientifically the more fruitful. And to answer this may require many years, or even centuries.

In addition to all such analysis, but necessarily in intimate connection with it, has been supplied a great amount of further analysis. For this latter alone can furnish the characteristics upon which the former is grounded. In analysis, accordingly, it is that the acumen of psychologists has always been most conspicuously manifested. What unbiased reader, for example, can fail to admire the beautiful analysis of the emotions by Malebranche? Or who does not wonder to find even him over-topped by McDougall?

But for the purposes of science we need something more even than all this. We require, not only analysis and classification to gratify the understanding, but furthermore laws of causation and sequence to confer the power of prediction. Exact investigation is wanted, both of the manner in which the inclinations and emotions are influenced by circumstances and also of the way and degree that they themselves influence conduct.

Now the work hitherto done in these causal directions, however admirable in quality, would seem to have been lamentably defective in quantity. Indeed, most often the required causation and sequence, instead of being definitely evidenced, have only been surreptitiously and illegitimately inferred from what was really no more than a classification. This has been done by the old, old fallacy of confounding names with things; what in truth were only classes of mental events were taken to be unitary mental entities. Consider, for example, the immense share in school life that has been allotted to games which involve teamwork, the reason offered being that thereby the children's inclination to teamwork in general will be developed and they will become correspondingly better citizens. Typical of this view has been the popular myth that Wellington declared the Battle of Waterloo to have been gained on the playgrounds of Eton. But in vain one may look for efforts to support this view with serious evidence. And as for the evidence that may be picked up casually, even this is far from favorable. In the World War, for instance, did those nations who had been most devoted to team-games really display any the more cordial teamwork between, say, regimental officers and staff officers? Rumor says otherwise. For all we know at present, development of the one kind of teamwork will no more bring with it that of the other kind than, say, the watering of one rose tree will serve as a watering of its neighbor.

Turning to quite a different type of causal problem, suppose that we have analyzed any complex emotion, as exactly as may be, into its constituents. How far will the effects of the whole emotion be the same as, or even resemble, the sum of the effects of these constituents occurring separately? Into such matters there seems never to have been any investigation. Or, to take yet another type of problem in causality, psychologists have from the earliest ages attributed the utmost importance in forming a child's character to the kind of literature with which he is supplied. Nevertheless, so far as I know, none of them have ever tried really to ascertain the nature and amount of such influence by way of reliable experiment.

Alongside of and supplementary to this universe of problems in causation and sequence is the further universe of the problems of coexistence. In the make-up of the individual, what qualities tend to go with what? If there have been investigations of this, at least one may run through the gamut of current psychological textbooks without finding any trace of them.

III. New Aids to Research

Confronted with all these grave difficulties and deficiencies in the sphere of inclination and emotion, I venture to suggest that some assistance may be derived from the "noegenetic" doctrine, which has been found of service in so many other domains of psychology.

To begin with, the three noegenetic laws of quality can at least help the science of purposive action by showing in what manner any ends, or means to these ends, can possibly be brought into the mind of the purposer at all. Suppose a person to encounter some novel situation. How can he so much as think of any appropriate behavior, on the adoption of which he has to decide? The solution to this paramount problem has been shown, especially by Laycock, to center upon the noegenetic laws of eduction and reproduction.

Further assistance in the causal problems may be supplied by the noegenetic doctrine through the quantitative laws which it has evolved. For these, originally shown to govern the whole field of cognition, have since proved themselves to be also applicable in at any rate large measure to the sphere of inclination and emotion. Consider, for example, how the "law of retentivity" has been corroborated by the "motivation tracks" of Boyd Barrett. As for the "law of energy," this finds confirmation ubiquitously: in experimental work, as that of Ach and Aveling; in pathological observations, as those of Déjerine and Gauckler; or again, in the most familiar mental therapeutics, as when some morbid desire is suppressed by exciting a healthy one. Even the "law of fatigue" would seem to have far more extensive bearings here than is commonly suspected; it may perhaps supply the real key to so strange and momentous a phenomenon as that of "abreaction."

But still more in need of aid than all these problems of causation and sequence, it seems to me, are those of the coexistence of qualities in the individual make-up. Nor can it ever suffice merely to calculate numerous correlational coefficients. Science demands also that the results obtained in this way should be systematically interpreted in relation to one another. The most significant feature about correlations, as a rule, is not so much their absolute as their relative values, together with the theorems deducible from these. The well-known cognitive theory of "Two Factors" is only one instance out of very many possibilities in this direction.

Furthermore, even the most elaborate systematization will be quite inadequate if put aside into a watertight compartment labelled "individual differences." It ought, rather, to be thoroughly incorporated with psychology as a whole. The present unnatural divorce between the two—on the one hand the novel method of correlations, and on the other hand the ancient and still dominant method of analysis and classification—cannot but doom both alike to sterility. In order to illustrate how they can be combined, let us briefly consider an actual case.

IV. The Case of Egoism

Throughout the literature of the natural inclinations, no tendency has been so copiously, so emphatically, and, it would seem, so justly urged as that of exalting one's self. Such terms as self-assertion, self-regard, self-esteem, egoism, *amour-propre*, and so forth have filled the most eloquent pages—mostly in censure, but sometimes in praise—from the earliest times down to this day.

Now, for the most part, this inclination has been assumed to constitute one single entity in the constitution of an individual. But is this justifiable? In an investigation conducted by Dr. Webb in my laboratory an attempt was made to put this and many similar assumptions on trial. Six different versions of self-exaltation were formulated, so as to ascertain how far these are correlated together. Only in so far as the correlations approach unity will the prevalent assumption be corroborated.

These six versions—their titles together with some explanations of what these titles were taken to express—are given below:

1. "*Desire to excel at performances (whether of work, play, or otherwise) in which the person has his chief interests.*" (a) Desire to do well for the sake of excelling *another*, not so much for the

work's sake. (b) The keenness with which he followed his favorite work. (c) Desire to beat all rivals. (d) The "plus" characters were patently anxious to do better than their fellows; they believed in their own powers and made no secret of it. (e) The wish to distinguish one's self, not ostentatiously, but in order to give one self-satisfaction.

2. "*Desire to impose his own will on other people* (*as opposed to tolerance*)." (a) Desire to be a leader. (b) Want their own way and sulk when they do not get it. (c) Degree to which he desires to override the opinions of others, and press forward his own. (d) Desire to have his own way. (e) Dogmatic and inclined to be intolerant of the views of others. (f) No wish to hear both sides. (g) Blindly believing that his ideas are the only correct ones. (h) An autocratic attitude towards his fellows.

3. "*Eagerness for admiration.*" (a) Acting or speaking, not naturally, but to gain the applause of his fellow-men. (b) Playing to the gallery. (c) Desire to be appreciated and tendency to talk of their own "prowess." (d) Long speeches to win approval. (e) "Conceit." (f) Extent to which a subject would go in order to display his talents, and thereby gain the applause of others. (g) Enjoys being in the "limelight." (h) Will set aside principles for the sake of admiration.

4. "*Belief in his own powers.*" (a) Self-confident. (b) Absence of diffidence with regard to the work. (c) Boastful. (d) Plenty of self-confidence. (e) Believes himself equal to any task. (f) Spoke of superiority to others.

5. "*Esteem of himself as a whole.*" (a) Feeling of satisfaction with himself as a member of society from the point of view of general ability to "cut a figure." (b) Decidedly the reverse of modest and self-depreciatory. (c) Boastful of capability to overcome practically all difficulties. (d) The general estimate or summing up of himself by himself. (e) This includes belief in one's own powers and a considerable satisfaction with everything belonging to or connected with one; at the same time this feeling caused the owners to regard others in a pitying manner. (f) Thinking one's self above criticism. (g) Subject's good opinion of himself, especially of his personal actions.

6. "*Offensive manifestation of this self-esteem* (*superciliousness*)." (a) 5 carried to excess. (b) This follows from the last, 5, in a way, though a man might think very highly of himself without offensive manifestation. (c) 5 pushed to excess. (d) Overdoing 5. (e) Looking down upon others. (f) The "plus" characters did not disguise the low esteem in which they held such opinions as did not fit in with their own ideas. (g) Looked at times upon everyone

else with contempt. (*h*) Subject's overbearing manner, due to too much self-confidence, and too great opinion of himself. (*i*) A person possessing this quality in a high degree always carries an air of superiority and seizes every opportunity for giving vent to his high opinion of himself. (*j*) Always talking of themselves—always imposing their esteem of themselves on other people unwilling to hear it.

To begin with, an interesting comparison is afforded between the titles (as given in quotation marks at the beginning of each version of self-quality) and the explanations (as indicated by the letters of the alphabet). In general, the titles represent the results of a priori analysis on the part of the experimenter. Whereas the explanations show what the estimators, on trying to interpret the titles, actually observed in the subjects. We may note incidentally that the different estimators often interpreted in diverse manners.

Passing on to the correlations between these six self-qualities, they are as given in Table 1.

TABLE 1

Raw Correlations

	1	2	3	4	5	6
1. Desire to excel		+.36	+.28	+.47	+.36	+.26
2. Desire to impose will	+.36		+.71	+.59	+.66	+.62
3. Eagerness for admiration	+.28	+.71		+.57	+.61	+.71
4. Belief in own powers	+.47	+.59	+.57		+.69	+.54
5. Esteem of self	+.36	+.66	+.61	+.69		+.73
6. Offensive manifestations	+.26	+.62	+.71	+.54	+.73	

As there were 194 subjects, the largest probable error is under .05.

TABLE 2

Correlations Corrected for Attenuation

	1	2	3	4	5	6
1. Desire to excel		+.48	+.39	+.65	+.51	+.37
2. Desire to impose will	+.48		+.94	+.78	+.90	+.88
3. Eagerness for admiration	+.39	+.94		+.78	+.86	+1.00
4. Belief in own powers	+.65	+.78	+.78		+.97	+.77
5. Esteem of self	+.51	+.90	+.86	+.97		+1.00
6. Offensive manifestations	+.37	+.88	+1.00	+.77	+1.00	

Accordingly, we see that in many cases the assumed functional unity does receive some degree of corroboration. For despite the diversity in interpretation, several of the correlations are very high indeed. Notably is this the case between eagerness for admiration, esteem of self, and offensive manifestations. But, on the other hand, there also occur several correlations which are remarkably low; in particular, the desire to excel has no high correlation with any of the others. On the whole, it seems impossible to concede that all the self-qualities are reducible to one and the same functional unity.

There remains still, however, the question as to whether or not they contain, at any rate, some common element. Here, our first impression is favorable, seeing that all the correlations are positive. But really this fact takes us only a little way. To establish the unitariness of function we require further that all the "tetrad differences"[1] should vanish (within the limits indicated by their probable errors).

And this is very far from being so. Out of the 30 different tetrad differences (of the raw correlations), no less than 22 are more than five times larger than the probable error; several are about eight times as large.

But, on the other hand, 20 out of the 22 turn out to involve one and the same correlation; that between desire to excel and belief in one's own powers. And both the remaining involve the correlation between desire to impose will and eagerness for admiration. When these two correlations are left out of account, all excessive tetrad differences disappear. On the whole, then the most plausible interpretation of the table seems to be that all six self-qualities do possess a factor in common, besides each having a factor specific to itself; whilst additionally there is a large group factor common to 1 and 4, with a smaller one common to 2 and 3.

The next great point at issue is as to which of the six qualities depend on the general self-factor in highest degree. We find that five out of the six are very nearly the same in this respect, the moment of the general as compared with the specific factor being in each case about 2:1. But the remaining or sixth quality stands out in remarkable contrast to all the rest, the ratio this time being only about 2:5.[2]

Besides these correlations of the six self-qualities with one another, however, there have also to be examined their correlations with the further qualities—over fifty of them—which were included in the investigation. Out of this great mass of information we will

[1] C. Spearman, *The Abilities of Man* (New York: Macmillan, 1927), p. 73.
[2] *Ibid.*, pp. 74–5.

for the present pick only a very small part; namely, the group of qualities, again six in number, which may be regarded as ethically "good." These and their correlations with the self-qualities are given in Table 3.

TABLE 3.

	Kindness on impulse	Kindness on principle	Corporate spirit	Trustworthiness	Conscientiousness	Interest in religion
	1.	2.	3.	4.	5.	6.
1. Desire to excel	+.07	+.30	+.49	+.49	+.50	+.24
2. Desire to impose will	−.08	−.60	+.08	−.64	−.72	−.72
3. Eagerness for admiration	+.04	−.57	−.17	−.72	−.69	−.50
4. Belief in own powers	−.21	−.22	−.03	−.40	−.50	−.31
5. Esteem of self	−.16	−.33	−.04	−.54	−.57	−.42
6. Offensive manifestations	−.47	−.79	−.04	−.83	−.78	−.47

This time the results are very striking indeed. The desire to excel does not merely differ in degree from all the other self-qualities; it is absolutely opposed to them all. For it shows throughout significantly positive correlation with the good qualities; whereas the other five have overwhelmingly negative ones.

Such results, no doubt, cannot be accepted without much further investigation and corroboration, seeing that research of this kind is beset with very great difficulties. But should the corroboration be eventually forthcoming, then there would seem to ensue corollaries of immense magnitude. The fact that the desire to excel correlates in low degree with all the other self-qualities, but in high degree with all the good qualities, appears to supply a foundation pillar for education and even for legislation.

V. "W" AND "DECISION"

The space at our disposal admits of only one more extract from Webb's research to illustrate the method of investigation here recommended. It is a theorem which was already obtained by himself, and indeed was very rightly taken by him to be his most important discovery. Expressed in his own words, it is that—in addition to the intellective "g"—

"A second factor of wide generality exists; this factor is prominent on the 'character' side of mental activity." It may be taken as "consistency of action resulting from deliberate volition or will."[3]

This second general factor he calls "w".

Verily a strange upshot! On investigating character with what seems to be far greater thoroughness than ever before (or afterwards), and on employing the new incomparably more powerful technique than available previously, what ensues? That ancient entity, which almost all modern authorities are now pluming themselves as having abandoned as an effete supersitition! Over and above all the impulses, inclinations, instincts, etc., struggling with one another there re-emerges an all-controlling "will." A will, too, as Webb shows, the strength of which has high correlations with all the representative "good" qualities.

Furthermore, this result of Webb some dozen years ago has just recently been followed and illuminated by a no less momentous discovery to stand beside it. It is that of Aveling,[4] according to which a volitional "decision," far from being nothing more than the victory of one struggling conation over another, does not in itself contain any conation at all! It proves to be an act *sui generis*, neither cognitive nor conative. With this result of the most perfect experimental conditions as yet realized, we seem to have returned to something curiously like the original "Logos" of Plato.

Be this as it may, Aveling's "decision" together with Webb's "w" would appear to restore to us at last some solid foundation for the ethical distinction between right and wrong. A distinction which, perhaps fortunately, the usual modern writers on character have not seen that they have eliminated.

[3] *British Journal of Psychology, Monograph Supplement*, 1915.
[4] See recent numbers of the *British Journal of Psychology*.

CHAPTER 4

EMOTION, CONATION, AND WILL

F. AVELING
University of London

It is an opportune time for a symposium on the psychology of feeling and emotion. These aspects of mental process have not been investigated so thoroughly as those of cognition, but already sufficient experimental work has been done in their regard to warrant the bringing together of psychologists to discuss them. What is wanted is more exact and agreed definition of the terms we are currently employing, and sympathetic criticism of such researches as have so far been carried out.

In contributing to this symposium my attempt shall be to analyze briefly the qualitative and quantitative changes in concrete conscious experience which give rise to the notions of feelings and emotions; to examine, in particular, the temporal properties of conscious process by reference to which I believe we may be helped in our distinctions; and to define some at least of our terms in the light of certain experimental evidence which I shall advance. The paper thus falls under two heads: Introspection, showing the phenomena to be related; Experiment, in which we shall hope to find indications of their relation. A final paragraph will deal with Nomenclature.

I. INTROSPECTION

In attempting to determine what a "feeling" or an "emotion" is, we must clearly begin with the concrete experience of an affective or an emotional state of consciousness. There is no difficulty in deciding that we are experiencing such states, though there may be a difficulty in saying why they are affective or emotional. Simple introspection, however, is enough to enable us to differentiate qualitatively one feeling state or one emotional state from another, as well as to analyze a number of irreducible phenomena which enter into the constitution of the latter. "Feeling," though this term is ambiguous, I shall restrict in the present paper to the "pleasure-unpleasure" couple, which I take to be a modality of self-awareness. My reason for this is that pleasure and unpleasure seem to be irreducible to any other conscious experience; whereas all other "feelings" can be reduced either to cognitive or to conative processes. We experience these affective states when *we* are pleased or unpleased; and (though, in accordance with popular usage in speaking of objects as pleasant or unpleasant, some psychologists would group such "feelings" with sensations) it seems to be introspectively clear that they are subjective states of mind rather than objective presentations.

Similarly, we experience anger, fear, and the like, when *we* are "emotionally" affected. To make these statements is to bring the Self which experiences (without prejudice as to any explanation as to its nature) into the very forefront of the science of psychology. I believe this to be a necessary position to take up, but, as I have argued the point elsewhere and supported the argument with experimental data, it need not be labored here.[1]

Accordingly, like the feeling states, the emotional states are prominently subjective; and we are able to distinguish a very considerable number of them introspectively—the large number of terms in ordinary language expressive of emotions and shades of emotion being proof of the fact. All psychologists will agree that many different emotions are actually experienced; but they are certainly not all in accord as to what an emotion is, by what it is conditioned, or what, in turn, it effects. The causal relations of emotion are, of course, a matter for experimental investigation. We can judge only by results, in the presence or absence or variation in amount of which causal sequences can be ascertained. But the fact of the occurrence of emotion and its descriptive analysis are open to introspection, and to introspection alone.

In such an analysis of any normally aroused and moderately intense emotional state, over and above cognized (and significant) objects or situations, feelings, and impulses or conations, we find coenaesthetic and kinaesthetic elements. Doubtless these are all abstractions from the concrete state in question, none of which can be taken to occur in its own right or to be capable of existence alone; but the problem is to discover which of these elements constitutes the state an emotional one, or gives it its emotional character. The fact that we are also able to report quantitatively as to the intensity of emotion or feeling helps us here. We currently describe these experiences by the use of quantitatively comparative adjectives, and adverbs. It is quantitative variation which makes it possible for us to form notions of feelings and emotions at all, and to say what element in the total state makes it emotional, since observable variations in some of its aspects ap-

---

[1] F. Aveling, "The Standpoint of Psychology," *British Journal of Psychology*, (Gen. Sect.), XVI (1925), 159–170.

parently occur in the absence of variations in others. There are times in which the emotional aspect is found to have thrust all others out of focal consciousness, just as there are times when the cognitively objective or conative aspect is predominant in it. These are commonplaces, but they form the raw material out of which psychology is built up.

Much confusion in the present use of the term "emotion" is due to the failure to distinguish two absolutely different characters of experience. Emotion is sometimes looked upon as a pathic, sometimes as a dynamic state, but quite as often as a combination of both. The confusion is ancient. The "desire" of Aristotle can be analyzed into two factors. The "passion" of the Schoolmen was something suffered, but equally expressed an active aspect of mind. The two aspects have almost invariably been confused, even in recent psychology, not excluding psychoanalysis. It is probably this fact which has led a representative psychologist to say that the term "emotion" should not be used at all; or, if used, only in a very general sense, since we cannot make it precise or give it a definite meaning.[2]

It is clearly necessary to distinguish within an orectic process whatever can be distinguished in introspection; the dynamic impulse (namely, appetition or aversion) and the massive and pathic aspect which enters into every emotion popularly and properly so called. Abstract this from the impulse, from the feelings and from the objectively cognitive items which accompany (or precede) it, and there is no emotion left. To this it may be objected that, since the massive and pathic element is clearly in the main coenaesthetic, and since this forms a part of all conscious states, all consciousness must be emotional. I am not concerned to deny it, but merely to assert that in what are commonly called emotions the markedly "stirred-up" character of consciousness is essential. As in the case of feeling, with a neutral point between pleasure and unpleasure, so in the case of emotion the habitual coenaesthesio-kinaesthetic tone may be neutral.

This is a version of the James-Lange doctrine—taught, in substance, long before the time of James and Lange. It lays stress on the usually vague (but sometimes partially quite determinate) sensational aspect of the emotional state as the characteristic of emotion. Bodily changes (principally visceral, glandular, and analogous ones) are mentally experienced as a massive sensational complex, and it is in proportion to the massiveness rather than to the clearness of this complex that the emotion is said to be

[2] D. Wechsler, "What Constitutes an Emotion?," *Psychological Review*, XXXII (1925), 235–240.

greater or less. Here, again, any connection between the bodily and the mental phenomena is not a matter for introspection but for experiment. The massive and sensational character of emotional experience, however, is an immediate fact of consciousness, and in its absence emotion is not commonly said to be experienced. Bearing in mind the fact that it is an abstraction, there would seem therefore to be no very grave objection to calling this the emotion.

In the emotional state, however, apart from the qualitative and quantitative changes due to the inrush of vague somatic sensation, there is also variation in the conative impulses as well as in feeling. In my opinion the former is of the greatest importance. I have been led, both by introspection and experiment, to the view that what is experienced as massive and unclear sensation complex is invariably consequent upon conative impulse. Almost literally, in the picturesque language of William James, "we feel sorry because we cry, angry because we strike, afraid because we tremble," and so on; or at least we experience these emotions because of a previously aroused conation which constitutes the "set" of the conscious organism towards action. Stated in purely psychological terms, the order of events would seem to be: first, cognition of a significant stimulus; second, conative "set" towards it; and, last, the "stirred-up" characteristic of emotion proper. Feeling may also enter into the total state of consciousness at any phase of its development from the initial cognition to the full-blooded emotion.

All these abstract phenomena can be discriminated introspectively, provided care be taken to arrange suitable conditions in which one or the other is emphasized, and the experiments repeated a sufficient number of times to allow of adequate characterization of the phenomenon in question. This is a *sine qua non* of all serious introspective work, since what in reality is introspected is (cognized) experience, and not all that enters into a single given experience can ever be taken to be cognized adequately—a fact due to the law of the limitation of mental energy.[3] We are directly aware only of an infinitesimal part of our external sensory experience at any given moment. Our span of consciousness is likewise limited for any aspect of experience whatever. Very many observations, accordingly, may be necessary to disentangle the phenomena of the simplest mental process.

[3] C. Spearman, *The Abilities of Man* (London: Macmillan, 1927), p. 98 ff.

II. Experiment

We have now to ask what evidence there is of any causal order between the phenomena we have been able to distinguish introspectively, and of what functions each may subserve. This is a matter for experimental investigation, so planned as to vary the introspectible phenomena in a relatively independent way, and to observe the objective results. I propose to offer the evidence of two or three researches as a contribution towards a partial solution of this many-sided problem.

It need hardly be argued that conation and emotion are conditioned by experience of a cognitive character. I use "experience" here in order to cover all possible (even pathological) cases, since it may be admitted that conscious feeling, and even emotion, may be a consequent of cognitions of which we are neither intensely nor determinately aware.[4] And this may happen in two ways: either by reason of a natural set (e. g., instinct), or because of a set intentionally adopted.

It will be convenient, especially in connection with the latter, to consider first the relation between will-acts (decisions, resolutions, etc.) and the conations involved in their performance. It has been shown that the determination to perform a task (acceptance of an "instruction") sets up a determining tendency in virtue of which the task in question is carried out. Ach's rhyming experiments[5] (even though they may not have provided a method of measuring the strength of the will) and Michotte's researches on choice[6] are, among others, demonstrations of this relation. Work in our own laboratory, embracing a very considerable number of mental processes, not only corroborated these demonstrations, but allowed us also to obtain graphic records which suggest that the will-act itself is not conative (in the sense of a striving), whereas the carrying-out of the decision most frequently is. From the outset in these researches, together with other instruments for recording bodily changes taking place during the reaction period, we made use of the galvanometer, subjects regularly being placed in circuit with it in all the experiments. Almost at the beginning it was noticed by some of the subjects that it came to be designated as "alertness," as roughly equal to, or greater or less than, a previous experience of a similar nature. And it was found that the galvanometric deflections

---

[4] C. Spearman, *The Nature of Intelligence and the Principles of Cognition* (London: Macmillan, 1923), p. 164 ff.

[5] N. Ach, *Ueber den Willensakt und das Temperament: eine experimentelle Untersuchung* (Leipzig: Quelle & Meyer, 1910).

[6] A. Michotte, *Étude expérimentale sur le choix volontaire* (Louvain, 1910).

correlated in a significant manner with the estimates. At the time "alertness" was identified with "consciousness of action" (Michotte) or "act" (Ach); but the distinction was not then clearly drawn between will-acts on the one hand and conations on the other.[7]

In a later research definitely planned to investigate the nature of the deflections occurring in connection with will-act and conation respectively it was found that they were usually greater with the latter, and often did not occur at all with the former. A brief report of this work was communicated to the VIIIth International Congress of Psychology at Groningen.[8] The main conclusion which is relevant to the present paper, however, was that will-acts (resolutions, etc., to perform difficult mental or bodily tasks) are both introspectively and objectively different from the conations involved in the actual performance of the tasks. The conations are clearly strivings and effortful; the will-acts as such appear to be neither. While we must doubtless allow that conations may issue from non-voluntary dispositions (as instincts) also, it is clear that causal sequences obtain between true volitions and conations, from which, accordingly, they should be distinguished.

An objection to the foregoing argument lies in the commonly asserted emotional character of the psychogalvanic reaction itself. This objection seems to be due to the confusion between the pathic and dynamic aspects of consciousness noted above; and in meeting it we shall find, I believe, evidence of a real causal sequence between conation and emotion. In all the researches conducted by us, we not only photographed the galvanometric deflections, but also measured reaction-times and recorded full introspections. The last named covered the period between the giving of the stimulus and the end of the performance of whatever task was in hand—choosing one of several alternatives; reacting by rhyming, reversing, etc., to a syllable which has been learned in association with another; attempting "to have and to hold" one of several alternating visual after-images; trying to get the meaning of an imperfectly learned nonsense word; mentally working out mathematical and logical problems; and the like.

On comparison of the times of occurrence of the deflections with the times of the reactions, it is clear that whatever bodily changes are indicated by the former almost invariably take place *after* the whole introspective period is over. The somatic resonance

[7] The distinction is drawn in: F. Aveling, "The Psychology of Conation and Volition," *British Journal of Psychology*, XVI (1926), 339–353.
[8] *Proceedings of the VIIIth International Congress of Psychology*, p. 227.

can, therefore, neither be the antecedent nor the concomitant of the experiences related in the introspections. It can be only the consequent. And similarly with any mental concomitant or consequent it may itself have. These are effects and not causes of the conation to perform or the performance of the task.

Hardly ever were emotional experiences reported in the very large number of introspections recorded. Sometimes feeling was noted, but mostly only cognitive and conative phenomena—especially in the difficult mathematical, after-image, and meaning tasks. Accordingly, since, as has been said, the size of the deflections varies with the estimated amount of a conative phenomenon, it can only be taken as indicative of this; and, since the somatic resonance is regularly subsequent to the conation, conation is the cause of emotion.

An alternative account of emotion would make it due not to conation but to a *choc* or general excitation of a large number of cranial and sympathetic nerve centers not habitually affected by the stimulus causing it. Variations of physiological activity (heart, respiration, secretion, etc.) and variations of impulse (to run, to strike, etc.) would be two parallel expressions of the emotional stage.[9] Not to emphasize the fact that this is a conational explanation, making emotion the mental counterpart of a neural rather than of a glandular-vascular-muscular activity does not seem to be satisfactory for the following reason. In the greater emotions, at any rate, definite organic sensations often stand out from the vague coenaesthesio-kinaesthetic mass, and these, together with that mass, certainly seem to form part—indeed the prominent part—of the emotion itself. Moreover, certain secretions, toxins, and organic diseases produce, or concur in the production of, emotional states. It would be impossible to say that this action is not by way of the nerves, and that the *choc* is not the cause of the emotion. But this has to be shown rather than stated.

My contention above is that variation of impulse and of physiological activity are not synchronous, but related as cause and effect. A consideration, however, arising from our own researches might seem to lend color to the opposing view. One observer in our work on will-acts and conations designated the initial phase of what we have termed alertness as a "shock," and describes it as a "passive endurance of enjoyment rather than active striving or willing."[10] This seems to be the "something has

[9] D. Wechsler, *loc. cit.*

[10] R. J. Bartlett, "Does the Psychogalvanic Phenomenon Indicate Emotion?," *British Journal of Psychology*, XVIII (1927), 30–50.

happened to me but I do not know what" state of mind which had been noted in another (yet unpublished) research made in our laboratory. The experience in question is one in which various peripheral stimuli were presented to the subject under conditions in which he was unable to say to what sensorial sphere they belonged; and the term "primary pathic state" was used to characterize it. This is a state of cognitive order, but clearly antecedent to determine cognition.[11] It is feeling in the sense of inadequate apprehension.[12] And it might be confused with emotion, not in the sense in which I have used this term, but in that in which some psychologists have postulated an "interest" as a limiting case of emotion in their treatment of instinct.[13] For, though it seems to display both aspects, it is a subjective state rather than an objective content. It is unclear, more in the sense of being indeterminate than necessarily lacking in intensity. And it is identified with the initial phase of conation.

The truth would seem to be that conation is an introspectible mental process which has a temporal development, but a far more speedy one than the physiological adaptation of the organism to the situation; that it has usually come to full expression before anything like emotion, in its common meaning, is experienced; but that, nevertheless, the emotional (or interest) aspect of consciousness so quickly superimposes itself upon the cognitional and conational that it is not, except in carefully arranged experimental conditions, easy to discriminate between them. Conation thus would initiate emotion as even unclear cognition initiates conation, each developing phase tending to overlap and intermingle with the preceding one.

There remain many questions to be asked, among which two (concerning the reciprocal bearing of emotion on conation, and of feeling on cognition) have had some beginnings of investigation.

It is generally considered that emotion reinforces conation; and this would well fit in with the view put forward in this paper. Certainly more can be accomplished under emotional stress than in its absence. This, again, is a commonplace; but, so far as I am aware, it has not been the subject of detailed investigation and measurement.

On the other hand, experiments which we have been carrying out indicate that feeling (pleasure-unpleasure) has upon cognition an effect similar to that of conation. Conscious pleasure and unpleasure provoked by auditory, gustatory, olfactory, etc., stimuli

[11] C. Spearman, *The Nature of Intelligence and the Principles of Cognition* (London: Macmillan, 1923), p. 48 ff.
[12] R. J. Bartlett, *loc. cit.*
[13] J. Drever, *Instinct in Man* (Cambridge, 1921), p. 130 ff.

have an enhansive effect upon the perception of visual stimuli. A greater number of letters tachistoscopically shown can be perceived, and in their true order, under the influence of feeling than otherwise. The research in which these experiments figure is not yet published, but it shows that with feeling (when the subject adopts a passive or receptive attitude) the percentage of letters reproduced is of the order of those reproduced, without feeling, in an attentive attitude. Feeling considerably enhances the results of reproduction.

A final mention may be made of a research on the influence of conation upon the duration of visual after-images (perception). Having secured disparate and alternating after-images for each eye, it was found possible "to have and to hold" one or the other to some extent at will by trying (conation). Within the range of the experiment, this indicated that cognition is the effect of conation [14]

III. NOMENCLATURE

The foregoing brief notes, which touch only upon some of the problems of feeling and emotion, permit us to make several psychological distinctions between introspectible aspects of a mental process, and to define terms which may be used to denote them.

A volition, as an act of the Self by which we resolve, decide, etc., to do anything, is in essence effortless, and is to be distinguished from a conation, of which it may be the cause.

A feeling is the experience of pleasure or unpleasure enjoyed by the Self.

A conation is an experienced act, mental or bodily, of doing (striving or effort).

An emotion is the massive and generally wholly unclear experience of coenaesthesio-kinaesthetic sensation.

These terms, thus defined, are clearly not employed in the ambiguous meanings of current psychologies, but it is suggested that, so defined, they would make for precision in thought. Admittedly, they signify no more than abstract phenomena of concrete experiences. But, short of discarding them altogether and substituting an entirely new terminology, only some such drastic limitation of their meaning can bring agreement among psychologists, who often dispute, not about facts and events, but words.

[14] Messer, Thesis for Degree of M. Sc. (University of London Library).

CHAPTER 5

THE ESSENCE OF FEELING

OUTLINE OF A SYSTEMATIC THEORY

F. Krueger
University of Leipzig

Whatever pleases one, whatever interests him, whatever depresses him, whatever excites him, whatever he perceives as the comic; even more, how easily and how continuously he is moved internally in these ways—this is the particular characteristic of his "being," his character, and his individuality. Such has prescientific thought unanimously been since ancient times. Feelings embrace or penetrate all other mental events in some way. The "emotional" testifies in a unique way to the structure of the "inner," the mental life. Apparently it is generally typical of life itself.

I. The Psychological Status of the Problem

Since science with its analysis and schematic abstraction shatters the naïve belief in the seriousness of "matters of the heart," the most fervent and the deepest experiences have, consequently, fought from the beginning against their investigation (*Beobachtung*) by science. The results in mechanically constructing and in quantitatively determining "objective" reality are generalized into a materialistic metaphysics in which everything which may not be subjected to the procedure of reduction is said to be unreal. Physics, chemistry, and mathematics, with proven right, seize the phenomena of life, seize even the structures of life. These unmistakable advances create a prejudice that scientific problems may be exhausted with settling these questions and using these methods; that whatever phenomena of life might be understood physically and chemically would, if they might not be at the same time mentally (*erlebnismässig*) qualified or closed within themselves, lose all psychological relations; that if they should be "accompanied" here and there by mental data it would then be superfluous to observe those mental phenomena as such within the science.

Out of epistemological and empirical necessity a special science of mental reality and its particular laws developed, nevertheless, especially among those nations which were creative in natural sciences. But even from those psychologists who are opposed to materialism (Stout, Lipps), we have heard recently that "feelings are secondary phenomena"; they have no particular "psycho-motor" force; they are "something parasitical." Such paradoxical statements, as a rule, are co-determined by certain depravities of later civilization. Enthusiasms, aesthetic and snobbish over-refinements, also moralizing tendencies can, in fact, generate emotions which are, so to speak, mere "luxuries" in the household of mind; or they are even "ungenuine," merely imaginative feelings consciously created to deceive. With mental attitudes like these—they are sufficiently important—science must occupy itself without judgments of evaluation. In so far as the conceptions just mentioned are valid, in general, for all mental events, they are regularly deduced from certain theories or from one-sided "principles" of generalization.

The whole qualitative variety of mental phenomena is, sensual-istically, reduced to "sensations," besides these, perhaps, to their "images" or to psychological residues, or to Herbartian statics or mechanics of block-like "imaginations." Other psychologists construct mental events according to the reflex movements of a beheaded frog by a scheme of stimulus-response, to which the "movements" of mood do not in the least correspond. Finally, since the days of the Greeks, psychological thinking has always been inclined to correct reality anew, according to the model of rationalization, and to confuse its empirical regularity with logical ideals. Schopenhauer and, in a more exact way, Wundt have struggled indefatigably against this confusion.

It is instructive that those thinkers who render most decided homage to psychological intellectualism, e. g., the French meta-physicians of the seventeenth century, take most pains to arrange "affections" in their systems. They are, as a whole, in a contra-dictory fashion reduced to influences of the body, which ought not to happen, or they are interpreted as pathological disturbances.

We learn from history as a whole that since the victory of Chris-tianity, the real emotionality—including the ethically or artisti-cally informed emotionality—is placed more and more in the center of the struggle of opinions and of psychological doctrine. When the Germans at the end of the eighteenth century fully overcame the enlightenment, storm and stress had prepared the way for the classicists in art as well as in thinking by means of its conviction of the originality, productivity, and all-determining power of the emotions. Kant, Tetens, Goethe's friend, K. Ph. Moritz, recognized in the faculty of feeling a particular, genetically early, and fundamental class of mental functions. Since that time psychology, especially in the German countries, has mainly followed that direction of ideas. At least the problem remains a psychologically fundamental one. Whoever intends to penetrate into and explain mental realities, whoever would describe fully any one of their phenomena and would understand that they are necessary, is compelled to understand feelings and emotions as one whole. (Cf. 14 in the bibliography, p. 17 ff.)

The results obtained up to the present time as a scientific solution of this problem are out of proportion to the admittedly central significance of the problem. Even the most exact observers today not infrequently describe the psychophysical development of animals, young children, and primitive peoples as if primitive experience were poor in emotions, or at least not mainly determined by them (12). In general, mental, emotional phenomena are mentioned as something qualitatively particular, but keen-minded specialists always seek anew to lose them again by speculation. One "reduces" them to "relations" of "imaginations" (Herbartians), to indwelling constant "tones" of sensational elements (Wundt at the beginning), or to organic sensations (W. James), while others, especially German theoreticians, considered these weighty facts once more as unimportant "concomitant phenomena." Recently C. Stumpf has made a special class of sensations related to tickle, itch, pain, the basis of all emotions (20). Besides explaining teleologically, one uses all kinds of objective expediencies; on the other hand, somewhat the same psychologists set up the old hypothesis in many new forms. At all events the finest, most spiritual emotions are caused by *intellectual* processes which are admixed with some known and more "elementary" data. Thus the border line fluctuates, and the qualitative relationship of the higher to the lower emotions remains incomprehensible.

One would expect that we should be clear at least about what well-circumscribed phenomena have to be interpreted in a theory of emotion. As a matter of fact, however, scarcely two books agree on how to draw a line between the emotional in, or with, our experience and the non-emotional, even in a rough way. What have the facts called emotions, phenomenologically and immediately compared, in common with one another? A related question about the *classes* of feeling is still answered in the most contradictory way. For example, Th. Lipps, for good reasons in our opinion, decided, until future researches are made, in favor of an unlimited manifoldness of emotion. More than fifty years have passed since Wundt created his theory of the three elementary classes or principal directions of qualitative differences in this field. Until this very hour, however, professional psychologists maintain that feeling, in the scientific sense of the word, is identical with *pleasantness* and *unpleasantness*. Some critical spirits submit to this algedonical restriction, not only because Wundt surely confused his well-founded descriptive division with unclear and incorrect theories (13, 14), but, more clearly stated, mainly for the reason that they were afraid of losing every basis for an unequivocal answer to the fundamental question, "What is 'the emotional'?"

II. DIFFICULTIES OF CONTENT AND METHOD

Whatever a sensation of green or the taste experience of bitter may be, the mental datum of the tone *a*, or the memory-image of such a partial experience (*Teilbefundes*)—those questions, like all psychological ones, are not ultimately definable. They may be only exhibited, not defined. For the normal man, however, conditions of great exactness may be created in which he finds and recognizes definite experiences of seeing, of tasting, or of hearing. And we can as well look at every such field as a total, as we can divide it, with general validity at least, into main directions of general similarity and into "modal" differentiation without gaps. There are highest and lowest tones. Every sensory experience can be classified according to intensity by the determination of absolute and relative limens.

On the other hand, does not the world of emotions elude every effort to classify or even limit them? In our language we call the most different and the most heterogeneous things "feelings": data of the sense of touch and all sensitivity of the internal organs; complex, especially diffuse, or weak sense experiences of every kind; vague images; unclear ideas; even the "subjective" in aesthetic enjoyment and in artistic creation, and many other things—almost every reality, in as far as it cannot be exhausted in intellectual "objective" relations. Whatever is difficult to name, whatever cannot be fully conceived in any other way, one is inclined to call by that name. Is there something of quality or function in common which positively needs the name "emotional" and exalts it to the significance of an identical concept?

Whatever has been differentiated scientifically until now as "feelings in the narrower sense"—pleasantness, tension, excitement, etc.—everything of this kind can pass over *steadily* from one into another and even change into its qualitative *opposite*.

Such a phenomenon seems to dissolve easily into indifference, but variations of the conscious attitudes in general are unnoticeable. Moreover, sense experience or thought experience, whichever you choose, can "develop" out of it without a break, and conversely. Of all forms and colors of our experience the emotional are the most fleeting, labile, or, as the name implies, motile. Many of them are of a directly intangible fragility. All movements (*Regungen*) of feeling, as they are experienced, have originally and in common the peculiarity that the experiencing person must *attend* to them to some degree. But when he changes the direction or the intensity of this attending, moreover when he thinks about it, they unavoidably change themselves. That may be formulated in a more precise and at the same time more general manner— *ceteris paribus*, an emotional complex loses in the intensity and plasticity (*Ausgeprägtheit*) of its emotional character to the degree that it becomes analyzed, so that its parts become relatively separated or that the partial moments in it come out clearly as such. This law can be reduced still further in an explanatory manner as we shall see. Those facts of which we spoke here, at first propaedeutically, must be observed in continuity by psychology.

Two touch impressions, brightnesses, optical shapes, or two experienced verbal meanings can be observed one beside the other and be directly compared. Concerning emotional life, however, we have theoretically good reasons to claim that two *feelings* are never experienced at exactly the same time. The experimental principle meets with difficulty with them in that they are influenced by *every* variation in the condition of simultaneous experiences with which their particular ability to be blunted is connected. Quantitative units like the just noticeable differences are extremely problematic in our field. The concept of "adequate stimuli" is here scarcely compatible with the actual complications, some of which we have called, not unsuitably, the "universality of the excitant of emotion."

The founder of scientific methods in psychology, Wilhelm Wundt, toward the end of his life assigned the more central mental functions almost exclusively to "folk psychology," i. e., to ethnological and historical comparisons. Thus he gained fruitful insight into the genesis of language, and into the social conditions of primitive civilization (14). But the continuity with his remaining doctrines of general or individual psychology is unsatisfactory. He took this social-genetic course from a certain despair about the utility of the methods of experiment and measurement introduced by himself and, last but not least, from the realization that they are, in fact, unsuited to the investigation of emotional life. In the matter of feelings Wundt had amplified the experimental quantitative method up to the nineties. Following the example of physiological registration but without a real contact with the other methods of psychology, he conceived the important idea of the "expressive methods" (23, II, p. 278 ff.). He knew very well that with them he took only the first steps in a way full of promise but to a high degree "indirect." Only haltingly and occasionally did he recognize, for example, the measurement of *Sprechmelodie* as an expressive method. He restricted himself mainly to the symptomatic correlation of certain variations of breathing and circulation of the blood with the three fundamental qualities of his theory of feeling. With these experiments and with his theory of affections, Wundt methodically approached the theories of Lange and James but in a more exact way. He did not contradict the principle when one said to him that at every moment the *total* mental state is mirrored in the *whole* attitude and in *every* movement of the organism; in this "expression," above all else in the expression of feelings, every organ of the body (including the glands) participates in ever changing arrangements which ought to be observed systematically.

To restrict itself to "objective" methods in the physical sense, much less to limit its view materialistically, is in general remote from European science since Kant, Herder, and Hegel. Wundt was fortified against it in detail by his axiom that all true psychology rests more or less directly upon "introspection." This is epistemologically an indispensable truth. To be sure, Wundt as an experimenter interpreted it so one-sidedly and limited it so narrowly that other necessary ways of comparison, for example, in animal and child psychology, were therefore denied him.

Positivism, as it is known, used the criticism against all psychology that the process of observation, if it be directed upon the particular experience of the observer, always changes these experiences themselves. This is true in the highest degree, as we saw, for the psychology of feelings. Skeptical conclusions may be drawn only with precaution. It is the task of science, however, to recognize difficulties and then overcome them step by step by suitable methods.

III. EMOTION AND PSYCHICAL TOTALITY (*Gefühl und Psychische Ganzheit*)

Psychology has been educated to scientific exactness by the natural sciences, its earlier matured sister disciplines. But in the middle of the nineteenth century it took as an example not biology but physics and chemistry. It incorporated into the psychological events of life not only the methods of experiment and measurement but also problems, fundamental concepts, and the mechanistic scientific ideal of these sciences of inanimate and non-genetic reality.

A. *The Totality of Inner Experience* (Erlebens)

Wundt claimed even to the end that it is the principal task of psychology to analyze the concrete complex "contents of consciousness," which are always manifold, into a limited number of atomistic "elements" out of which those contents (*Tatbestände*) are "composed." He maintained that such "mental elements" were, besides "simple" sensations (i. e., not analyzable and not changeable by experience), "elements of feeling": pleasantness, unpleasntness, tension, relaxation, excitement, calm. He felt obliged, however, to extend these analytically in several directions by the introduction of special processes which established *cohesions;* namely, assimilation, apperception, and, superior to them all, creative synthesis (16, 14). Tension and relaxation were believed to be mainly dependent upon apperceptive conditions. In the general theory of feelings he worked with a special principle of "unity of disposition of feeling" (*Gemütslage*), and he placed them in the foreground, in a significant way, more and more as time passed (23, II, p. 325, cf. p. 316 ff., 363 ff.; III, p. 99 ff.). But in contradiction to these supplements, the original atomism of sense experiences and their constant "affective tones" led to confusion everywhere. He related his symptomatic results of expression immediately to the proportionate participation of those elements of feeling. The affective impression of the major chord, for instance, was believed to be composed of the isolated effects of feeling of the partial tones and intervals contained in the chord. He even taught with great emphasis, concerning affections, that each one of them could be analyzed, without remainder, into sensations and into many "partial feelings" of pleasantness and unpleasantness, of excitement, etc.

This summarizing, atomizing mode of observation has been in the meantime essentially completed, and to a high degree overthrown by mere exact description and comparison of real data, as well as more critical concepts. The Austrian school of psychologists made clear for instance that a chord, a melody, a rhythmic sequence possesses, as far as they are immediately experienced, particular qualities as *wholes*, which are independent of all actual analysis, and that those qualities of shape (*Gestalt-qualitäten*) cannot be reduced to qualities of existing parts of experience. Furthermore, it follows from this insight that similarity of complexes of experiences is not based exclusively and in many cases not at all on similar or identical parts, as experience very often shows (15, p. 82). However, the corresponding synthetical-total conception of feelings has not satisfactorily succeeded as yet. When H. Cornelius transferred the concept of *Gestaltqualität* (quality of shape) to them unequivocally (1, p. 74 ff., 362 ff.), almost nobody considered this a far-reaching hypothesis. Von Ehrenfels himself opposed us violently, in private in 1897 and publicly since that time, and until today scarcely one professional psychologist, except my pupils and colleagues, has considered it seriously to say nothing of discussing it fundamentally. In the psychological congress at Würzburg in 1906, C. Stumpf gave a survey of the possible fundamental conceptions of feeling and added his sensualistic construction of *Gefühlsempfindungen* to them. When I explained this shaped-qualitative (*gestaltqualitativ*) or better still complex-qualitative conception, it seemed to be new to all those present, and Stumpf declared it incomprehensible. (20, p. 211 ff.; Stumpf has moderated this here.)

For thirty years I tried continuously to refine the new theory of the essence of emotions and feelings and of mental totality in general. I applied it to the experience of evaluation (*Werterleben*) and found it confirmed in extensive experiments upon chords, consonance and dissonance, *Sprechmelodie* (6, p. 30 ff.; 7, p. 617, cf. 344 f., 364 f., 373 ff., 592 ff.; 9, p. 239 ff.; 11, I, p. 375 ff.; 11, V, p. 401; 10). Here I placed the more inclusive concept of "complex quality" above the original quality of shape by an experimental as well as theoretical basis, (11, II, p. 221 ff., cf. H. Volkelt, 21, who, by the way, in 1914 did not dare to accept the consequences of the theory of feeling; see esp. p. 79 ff., cf. 15, p. 104, note 2). I early, and with increasing variety, connected those two concepts with the still more inclusive one of mental totality (*Ganzheit*) (15), especially the totality of inner experience (*Erlebens*). This expansion and differentiation is necessary, mainly for two reasons: first, because of the fact that immediately given and comparable qualities of experienced *totalities* are realized, even above all other ways, in sharply limited, heterogeneous, and diffused, yes, absolutely unorganized data (e. g., in the lower senses, in the consciousness of place or time, in primitive thinking)—and are indeed realized much more frequently and genetically earlier in the narrower sense of correlated "parts" actually excluding one another than in the sense of "shapes" (15a, p. 7 f., 11 ff.;

15, p. 71 f., 82); second, because we need a special concept for the existence (*Gegebensein*) and conception of specific forms of organization (*Gliederungen*), e. g., of geometrical, musical, logical ones, and this is the concept of shape (15, esp. p. 96 ff. Please read this summary together with all the following). All these concepts have proved themselves fruitful, even indispensable in the various fields of experience since that time—not only in Leipzig. They have been determined in increasing exactness by quantitative experiments. (Cf. *Neue Psychologische Studien*, München, since 1926; especially I, *Komplexqualitäten, Gestalten und Gefühle*, and IV, *Gestalt und Sinn*, now in press.) But the majority of the exact psychologists continue either not to consider them, or to confuse them with one another and with things not belonging to them.

The problem of *shape* has, however, forced general attention recently. It has many industrious workers in different countries. The danger exists already that the name Gestalt will be used as a magical lamp for any psychological darkness, and especially that the misuse of such an important concept will prevent the completeness of *analysis* both of phenomena and of conditions. Nevertheless, the assured results of Gestalt psychology will sometimes be favorable, even if only indirectly, to the theory of feelings and of mental totality in general.

It is necessary, to this end, that all attempts at *explanation* be put aside at first as premature, both the physical analogies, as Köhler has ingeniously presented them, and Wertheimer's *Querfunktionen* of the brain. Whatever we would explain scientifically, we must above everything else know exactly as it is. We must take the task of a pure and complete *description* of the phenomena very seriously. Then we recognize, among other things, that the homogeneous, sharply limited, and objectively organized "perceptions" of the higher senses, which are prevalent in experimental observation today on account of tradition of method, are, at best, very specialized, genetically late results of an abstracting attention; not infrequently they are the artificial products of the laboratory far removed from life. This is true to a particular degree in the scientific attitude (*Einstellung*) of the conventional observation of "animal intelligence" toward the static, and at the same time spatial "contact" (*Zueinander*) of purely optical parts of a sensational complex and toward its purposeful, intellectual application (15, p. 96 ff.). Although experimental *Gestaltpsychologie* and also *Denkpsychologie* tried to describe mental events which have hitherto been isolated, their concepts directly hide the character of totality of true experience and close the main entrance to the world of feelings. In reality, the experience of a normal individual (and also all social experience) consists in its main bulk of indistinctly bounded, diffused, slightly or not at all organized complexes in whose genesis all organs and functional systems take part. It is significant and not at all obvious that, at least in adult human beings and higher animals, the total state of their experience often unfolds into a multitude of relatively closed part-complexes. But even in the highest stages of development, this is not always the case, e. g., in states of the highest, permanent excitement, great fatigue, most complete self-subservience. Even where we observe experience in relief, its organization, as a rule, does not correspond at all and may never correspond exactly to the limitations of objects created by intellect, or to objective "situations," or even to the physically and physiologically mediated or constructed "stimulus"—relations ("*Reiz*"-*beziehungen*). Never are the differentiable parts or sides of real experience as isolated from one another as the parts of physical substance, i. e., its molecules or its atoms. All things which we can differentiate there, by comparison, always grip into one another and around one another in the greatest elaboration. And every time it is, without exception, imbedded within a *total-whole*, by which it is penetrated and more or less completely enclosed (15, p. 36 ff., p. 117 ff.). **Feelings are the qualities of experiences of this total-whole.** (*Erlebnisqualitäten des Gesamtganzen*).

In so far as part-complexes are more or less sharply excluded (*sich ausgliedern*), they have their specific qualities, i. e., *complex qualities* of the most different kinds, notwithstanding whether they are organized or in how far they are themselves organized (*gegliedert*) or shaped (*gestaltet*). They also possess specific similarities. One chief task of a descriptive psychology consists specifically in a systematic comparison of these two kinds of total-qualities. It happens that phenomenologically the qualities of the part-complex (e. g., a clang, tint, or "dull" and "hot-humid") are allied to the feelings, more allied by all means than the qualities of the unanalyzable parts of experience (e. g., the tone *a*, sharply limited pressure or temperature sensations), which are stamped in the same way. The complex qualities are of the nature of feeling (*gefühlsartig*); the more the corresponding complex includes of the existing total-whole, the more indistinctly it lifts itself out from the "background" of the remaining simultaneous experience and the less penetratingly it is organized in itself, under equivalent circumstances. The natural, the most frequent, and genetically earliest kind of experiences like the following are determined by complex qualities, therefore emotionally (*gefühls-mässig*): the experiences of an optical-motor situation, the perceiving of a sequence of sounds or noises, the consciousness of a change in our bodily state, our seeking, finding, or willing, our being disposed or being directed toward something—stated briefly, all are mental reactions. Recognizing, remembering, knowing, and concluding also—every kind of "thinking" naturally uses related total-complex forms.

In the same direction, to mention the first description of real facts, there pressed in from various sides the results of the psychology of thought (*Denkpsychologie*), which was founded in the beginning of the twentieth century at Würzburg. Külpe and his pupils dared to investigate experimentally what educated adults find in themselves whenever they understand and correlate verbal meaning or meaningful sentences, form judgments, or arrange concepts logically. The result was that sometimes exclusively "imageless" data were found that such "conscious attitudes" or states of awareness (*Bewusstheiten*) difficult to name have an important share in them, that sometimes there is very "definite knowing" of the *direction of thought*, of *gaps* in the continuity, which the experiencing person often tries passionately to close or feels painfully obliged to close. All classifications and qualitative schemes usually attempted failed with respect to *those including heterogeneous complexes*, which here came into play regularly. The flight into the totally "unconscious," which some older psychologists tried, is impossible, because those "states of awareness" or "tendencies" frequently possessed a sharply cut contour and, with suitable experimental technique, were clearly recognized in their specific qualities (*Eigenqualität*). The crude data of such experiments, published in a completeness meriting our thanks, contain very much which nobody has as yet evaluated psychologically, especially concerning simultaneous *feelings* of the most diversified quality and manner in which they come to an end, as well as concerning feeling-*like* (*gefühlsartige*) forms of experience, dispositions, and attitudes of the observer. But the school was prevented by a fundamental prejudice from observing facts like these sufficiently, to say nothing of building a theoretical bridge across to the life of feelings. Külpe himself more decidedly than any other psychologist had determined that scientifically only *pleasantness* and *unpleasantness* could be called *feeling;* all others were not emotional. And all his successors agreed with him in this (cf. 13).

One could object to what has been said because the terms are arbitrary. I answer that the terminology here used agrees better than the one reigning in experimental psychology hitherto with the terminology of civilized nations and the practical observers of men, which terminology is itself psychologically instructive. It can be carried through without contradiction for all facts which demand the fundamental concept of totality, for those·recognized as emotional, and, at the same time, for many others which were recently found to belong to them; they are above all closely related phenomenologically. The total-whole of experience always has a specific, immediately observable quality which changes in a particular, continuous way. Such qualities of the total-whole are the different kinds of pleasantness and unpleasantness, excitement, tension, relaxation, and many other manifold tintings, shadings and forms of flight of total experience, cannot be limited by number and, until some future time, cannot be completely classified.

These total-qualities, phenomenologically, all have something in common: that is what I call *bewusstseinerfüllende Breite* (13), a spread which fills consciousness completely. Seen from another angle, it is, as Lotze saw it, their inability to be indifferent (*Nichtgleichgültigkeit*) or, positively expressed, their "warmth" or their "weight." Whatever can otherwise be distinguished in or within our experiences qualitatively approximates the qualities mentioned (feeling-like) to such extent that it fills out even the total zone of experience (*Erlebens*) and, on the other hand, does not leave the experiencing person in indifference.

This is mostly true for the specific qualities mentioned, which are attached to the largest part-complexes and which, at the same time, by weight of experience, overbalance both the qualities and the relations of those part-complexes decisively encompassing them with "withinness" (*Innigkeit*). (Compare for this concept G. Ipsen: 2, p. 247 f., 263 ff.; 3, 336 ff, 447 ff.) This again fits the fact that everything actually given is always imbedded in simultaneous feelings, most deeply in the most pronounced ones and those of weighty intensity.

Does not the clearness of the fundamental conceptions suffer, however, under this kind of observation? Is not the opposition between the emotional and the non-emotional eliminated? From our point of view, in a science of living processes and especially in its descriptive introduction, less depends upon excluding opposite views than upon approximation to reality, upon completeness, and upon combining everything which essentially belongs together. It is certainly a fact that feelings (e. g., of excitement without an object, of excitement resembling fury, or of purely moody excitement) always pass over into qualities of more circumscribed and, primarily, of less organized *part*-complexes, e. g., into the consciousness of that about which I become excited, of that for which I hope, of that which I seek or of which I am afraid; and, conversely, it is a fact that the one set of events is, moreover, qualitatively related to the other. The conception of the feeling-*like* is necessary in order to designate those phenomenological similarities and transformations. As far as it is possible, without violating the facts, our theory, which, it seems to me, is more unequivocal than those propounded up to the present time, primarily determines more descriptively what *feelings* in the particular sense of the word *are*, as they are differentiated from all other kinds of experience, even from the most circumscribed and most complicated ones, but in connection with them, **feelings are the complex qualities of the experienced total-whole, of the experienced totality.**

B. *Functional Interconnections*

Only when we put the total as well as the partial *totality* into the center of observation is it possible to exceed the description of compared phenomena and "functionally" to understand living experience as necessary in the sense of full analysis of *conditions*. A fundamental conception of the essence of feelings must prove its correctness by being theoretically applied to the unitary explanation of definite facts.

Three things follow necessarily from what has been said before which permit of unprejudiced and careful observation:

1.   The universality,
2.   The qualitative richness (*Qualitätenreichtum*),
3.   The variability and lability of feelings.

1. *The Universality of Feelings.* Whether the events that can be met with now and then in my own inner life are so accentuated or otherwise, are sharply organized or diffused, significantly combined or are immediately quite without division, the experience-whole always has its own particular quality as such. Of course, this coloring may be more or (in the case of approximation to indifference) less expressed and dominating.

Nearly everybody admits this fact now for *part*-complexes. That they unquestionably possess *total*-qualities would scarcely be seriously disputed now. This has been exactly investigated with part-wholes which are organized in themselves, especially with sensory shapes. The consciousness of an "organizedness" or "shapedness" is itself always totally formed and conditioned. But if a complex is experienced as unorganized, chaotic, unarranged, even as something completely diffused, the cause is exactly the same. A part-complex must in every case be totally qualified in order to be set off from the remaining states of experience as something particular, something more or less closed. What then is the phenomenological fact if we meet no kind of organization or accentuation or no plurality at all in an experience-whole? That this happens is obvious even in a dogmatic, most objectively prejudiced inspection. Nobody doubts there are in the total experience steps of organizedness, steps of simultaneous as well as of successive plurality. Should the infinitesimal limiting case never appear here? We have found examples of it already. Very likely the duration and the relative frequency of such unorganized states decrease, in general, with the rising civilization of the individual and of peoples. The conditions, however, under which they happen certainly become more and more manifold.

Here is the place to emphasize a social-genetic relation: the density of the population and of traffic, the growth of large cities and whatever belongs to them always create new opportunities to experience that which is common by fits and starts in unorganized masses. The larger their numbers, the more unorganized are the mental events, *ceteris paribus*. Demagogues change the original magic of the world into a rhetoric of many forms. Technicians of mass suggestion develop from holy ceremonies, from faithful devotion and enthusiasm. Furthermore, we think of the use and misuse of many intoxicants or of the growth of crude tensions and excitements in places of sport, in the movies, etc. On the other hand, those forms of enthusiasm which seize one totally for some time and those which persist are increasingly refined, music, for example. These are only a few main directions of the phenomenological as well as of the functional relationship. Do all those mental events lack a specific experience-quality? The demagogues, the producers of the films, also the artists, the prophets, see reality more clearly than the algedonically restricted theorists. They know that the strongest emotions of the most different, often sharply defined qualities originate under such circumstances from necessity, and that they do not harmonize sometimes with any form of experience which is *not* emotional; they repress all critics; they watch comparison, judgment, and meditation; they oppose every clear, analytical behavior. Inner states and functions of this kind are unanimously called emotional (*gefühlsmässig*).

Seen genetically, many of them bear the character of the primitive. We observe such behavior much more regularly among primitive people, young children, animals, crude and depraved adults than in the educated. On the other hand, the forms of organization which grow out of true culture and penetrate even the most personal experiences are even more regularly accompanied and penetrated by them. Consider the devotion of the religious mind, or how artistic forms, especially those thoroughly shaped ones, seize one totally and tax fully all one's mental powers. Those, of course, are emotions of particular and much more manifold quality. In the laboratory, however, the one as well as the other kind of complete strongly emotional experience cannot easily be observed. But by suitable methods we are able to create some of the genetic relations in an abbreviated form and observe their regularity. The "actual genesis" (*Aktualgenese*), as we say in Leipzig, (cf. 19, sect. 5) shows everywhere that isolated sensations, perceptions, relations, also memories, clear ideas, decided volitions—in brief all experience-organization (*Erlebnisgliederung*)—split off only after some time from the diffuse tendencies of emotion, and, secondly, that they always remain functionally dominated by them. In any case they always remain more or less imbedded within the emotion, which, as it were, fills in the "gaps" in the total experience as it exists and forms the common "background" for all outstanding experience. Feeling is the maternal source of all kinds of experience and their richest fostering soil. Whenever something happens mentally to a living being, we always observe or with good reason we discover an *emotional* mood. If anything at all changes in an experience, then the emotion always changes, either alone or together with other simultaneous experiences determining it. To the degree that we, as psychologists, try to explain anything, we never are allowed to neglect those facts nor their specific qualities and effects. This is, briefly, what "universality" of emotions should mean.

The ideal of the older psychologists to relate changes of experience as completely as possible to unequivocally definite varieties of physical stimuli arose out of discreet (*Zusammenhangslos*) observation and "analysis" of sensations which demanded an object (*objektgebundene "Analyse"*). Behaviorism has recently exalted this ideal almost to the status of the sole principle of psychological investigation. In reality, it can never seriously be applied in the total field of pyschophysical events and especially to emotions and feeling-like experiences. The totality of experience is fundamentally opposed to it, and totality is especially marked in experiences of the kind under discussion. No constellation of stimuli can ever predict that it will positively initiate feelings at all, to say nothing of releasing this or that definite feeling. On the contrary, every intentional change of psychophysical experience can be an initiating (*komplementär*) condition of every kind and intensity of emotions, by means of a suitable constitution of the experience-totality. On the other hand, a really existing emotion must color everything that one experiences at the same time. These threefold consequences necessarily follow from the principle of emotional universality. If one does not observe it, then every exact investigation of psychological conditions falls into confusion. Functional psychology pre-eminently needs this principle as a guide at every stop.

Speaking from the standpoint of general psychology, even now certain pervading regularities are recognizable where the accompanying genetic investigation is still in its swaddling clothes. Whatever we have emphasized hitherto as constant processes and brought into a system is empirically the more impressive; the more intensive the observed feelings are, the longer they last and the more completely they fill consciousness, the more exclusively they dominate the total experience with significant specific quality. Advances and notable transitions, etc., result if any change in the course of experience suddenly enters, if we devote ourselves "totally" to any object, or if we are "totally" absorbed in it. Under certain circumstances, the high intensity of a certain inner vent, and even of a sensation, works in this direction. Our method of comparing *part*-complexes with feelings under the point of view of totality is thoroughly useful for an exact understanding of those relations. The total-qualities here as well as there are exactly similar to one another, and they functionally determine everything else. Feeling corresponds to the remaining *total* content of experience just as the specific attributes of every *part*-whole correspond to that which may be differentiable within it or in it.

2. *The Qualitative Richness of Feelings* (Qualitätenreichtum). We expect, according to the rules of combination, that there are many more complex qualities than qualities of the final, unanalyzable parts of experience. In the field of hearing, we have an especially good ability in perceiving homogeneous pluralities as such and as manifold.

At this point, on the other hand, the immediate, phenomenological dissection, even of simultaneous experiences, is highly developed; and the functional analysis of conditions has progressed far in relation to both. One may investigate, for instance, what a definite number of (let us say vibration frequency and amplitude) six distinctly different, physical, tonal stimuli will arouse as single-tone sensations (under otherwise equal circumstances there can be only thirty-six different ones), and then compare with that the richness of mental qualities which result specifically from the cooperation of those thirty-six single sensations taken in pairs, in threes, etc., simultaneously or successively; i. e., what can be experienced in clang-tint and harmony, in melodies and rhythm. With a plurality of tones very many things are given simultaneously or in temporal relations: roughness, beats, noises, even heterogeneous, non-sensuous (*unsinnliche*) experiences. Every further combination of this kind increases potentially the manifoldness of the concrete experience-shades. It is necessarily greatest for the momentary, *total* experience-whole. The comparative observational results agree with this. A tone perception, a cutaneous pain, an optical-shape experience, a thought, or a judgment can essentially remain "the same" whether I have or do not have, besides it, this or that kind of other sensation, memory, etc. On the contrary, the feeling found simultaneously never stands as much "besides" another experience as those partial events which can run along beside one another. The emotions are demonstrably influenced by every variation in the total content of experience as well as its total qualitative, intensive, temporal, etc., constellation. Here "smallest" causes have the most manifold and in every psychological sense the "greatest" effects.

This explains:

3. *The Variability and Lability of the Feelings.* A chord of two notes can become something very different if a third tone sounds at the same time; if this one stands in a "disturbing" relation, or stands in a relation "not suitable" to one or both of the fundamental tones, then the feeling which belongs to them changes color extremely, even reciprocally. Or a recognition changes much more penetratingly if certain sensations, perceptions, memories, which are related to it, spring up or change; all the more does a shape of higher intellect or of volition with its manifold similarities, states of being directed (*Gerichtetheiten*), and experienceable relations change. Feeling is, however, always immediately related to everything which is found simultaneously with it or in experience neighboring upon it. Think of synaethesias, of surprising intuitions and rushes of thought, or think of the plays of imagination; they all collectively are mediated by their relations to emotion (*Gefühlsbeziehungen*).

Liminal methods have been exactly applied to experience-complexes only for a few years. One of the most certain results is that we possess an extremely fine *just noticeable difference* for them *as wholes.* Children and animals possess it for complexes suitable to them, complexes always heterogeneous and widely inclusive (*viel umfassend*), therefore proportionately all the more *feeling-like.* If one compares the distribution or the mean limen for the "most" simple, i. e., the most isolated sensations with the corresponding measurements for closed shapes, which among many others contain the same sensations as one member, the limens are there very much higher. (In all fields investigated until now, cf. *Neue Psychologische Studien,* I and II. Newer results which belong here, e. g., for motor-kinaesthetic differences, will soon be published in IV.) One can state as a law that the *variation of total-complexes is more certainly observed and more exactly perceived than the variations of their parts,* and this is the case the more complete, the more organized, and at the same time the more closed those complexes are; besides this, of course, it depends whether the compared "parts" mean much or little for the whole. For conceivable reasons, especially from methodical difficulties, the just noticeable difference for emotions has not yet been exactly investigated. But the agreement with the facts found up to the present permit carrying it on theoretically in just the same direction that our conception of the essence of the feelings demands. Facts which are manifoldly proved fit in very well. Primitive consciousness reacts by sensitivity (*Feinfühligkeit*) even more sharply and in a more differentiated way than in all its part-functions. It has been observed a thousand times in laboratories, although mostly as a by-product, that the smallest variations in any part of the field of experience come into consciousness "emotionally" long before one can say "where" something changed and what really happened earliest.

The three main directions by which we functionally determine an object, when we try to understand penetrating features of the life of emotion, converge most exactly one upon another. The variability of feelings, their lability, and the capacity they have to get blunted rapidly (*rasche Abstumpfbarkeit*) by an especially great variety of constellations of conditions in contrast with the adaptation of sensations—all this can be regarded as the dynamic counterpart of their more static richness in qualities. Both again are necessarily combined, together with the universality of feeling, with the fact that they alone are never absent from the state of experience as it is found (*Erlebnisbefunde*), that every noticeable change of events appears in an emotional way more than in any other and that those emotional fluctuations are subjected to the most manifold conditions. They seem demonstrably to accompany the most heterogeneous variations of experience, and the most different experiences seem to be carried by them.

4. *Analysis versus Totality of Experience.* From all this we understand better a regularity which had to be mentioned above

on account of its methodological importance—that contradictory character of mental functions which occupied psychological thinking for a long time, most strikingly in the popular form of a polar conflict between "head" and "heart." In fact, the feeling of absolute devotion is diminished to a high degree by intellectual activity, and conversely. It loses in plasticity and strength, nay, what is more, it evaporates into experience of indifference if the experiencing person, by abstraction, emphasizes definite currents in the given experience, turning away from all else, if he judges, or if he makes clear distinctions and binds things together from one point of view, or if he, by his concepts, makes the flowing events stand still and cuts them into bits. Analogous effects occur as "attention" focuses sharply upon something there, outside or purely within, as soon as memory, expectation, or volition are directed upon something definite, etc. If we summarize these experiences among themselves and with what has been said before, we may formulate these facts in the following general law: *Every dissection, every analysis of the experience-totality is destructive to the whole as such, acts against its particular form of phenomena and forms of existence, is functionally in discord with it.* Otherwise, and perhaps more audaciously expressed: the more a mental *part*-function becomes dominating, just that much more does the functional totality of the mind become rickety; its unity, at least, is endangered.

A great wealth of facts, both concrete and pathological, confirm this rule and unite undividedly under its concepts. Again our method of comparing *part*-complexes with the *total*-whole of experience, and both with its organizations, justifies itself, a method which in turn goes back to our fundamental conception of the essence of emotions. The opposition between total experiences and attention to their parts has been observed more closely in the field of acoustics in my experiments on *Zweiklänge und Konsonanz.* If one were to try here to describe *emotional* impressions comparatively, it would have to be done in the beginning of every experiment, because the rise of partial phenomena and their aftereffects in consciousness would otherwise make the feeling unclear, weaken it, and even destroy it. The results were the same in the total impression of part-complexes such as "consonant," "harmonious," "discordant," "chord of the 4th and 6th," etc., (cf. 7, p. 539 ff., 618; 9, p. 242 f.; see also 12, 13, 15). Since that time numerous experimenters, mostly independent of one another, have hit upon the same regularities with very different material (cf. *Neue Psychologische Studien,* I and IV).

5. *The Dominance of the Whole.* We have already pointed out several times, for instance, in connection with the universality, qualitative richness, and inconstancy of the emotions, that changes in any part of the experience-totality appear most frequently in a dyeing another color of the total-quality, especially of the feeling. In this way, the smallest changes in mental events and the finest stratification of their profiles in terms of complex quality, are potent *for experience,* even those part-contents whose mental place, "particular quality, and relations" are otherwise not recognizable at all. (Cf. 9, p. 44 f. and 11, I, 324 f.; concerning *"An-gleichung* [Assimilation] *und resultative Nachwirkungen früheren Erlebens.")* The emotional life offers the most tangible and the most manifold proofs of this, as is to be expected. Who has not experienced that a "mood" which dominated him totally arose or changed in a moment, even to its qualitative opposite, when something happened in the background, when something was out of its place or was gone, something that, considered in itself alone, seemed to be extremely unimportant, even seemed to be without relation to the remaining content of experience? Very often one discovers only uncertainly and after a long search what it really was, or one never understands why such a mood intruded or was "destroyed."

Cases of such a kind belong to the field of *reciprocal* action between the experience-total and its parts or members. Total-qualities and isolated qualities have the tendency to influence one another, assimilating one another into a resultant (*"resultativ" angleichend*). As the coloring of a part-whole and especially that of the momentary total-whole of the feeling beams upon everything that belongs to it, as it penetrates everything to a greater or less degree which can be differentiated within the whole, so the quality of the whole, on the other hand, is dependent always upon the attributes, the relations, and the total constellation of the parts, in case there exists any organization of the experience at all. With a certain measure of exactness we penetrate those complicated coalitions of relations at the present time only in clearly limited partial complexes, especially in organized pluralities in the sphere of audition and vision. We can show that it is essential for the total impression of dissonance, that at least one chord out of tune is contained in the given tonal plurality, if it also, as usual, is perceived for itself, not separately, and shares its roughness, its bifurcation—in short, if it shares its qualitative character with the clang-whole of the moment, and, as a rule, if it spreads itself out over this part-complex in a feeling-like manner far into the total-whole of the experience (11, V, p. 368 ff.). This is not the place to add single facts to this important problem, which is still too little worked out from our point of view. The newer experimental investigation has shown many kinds of insight, even some quantitatively determined, into the reciprocity between wholes and their parts. In certain cases we recognize rather exactly what part-determinations are noticed genetically first, what ones are noticed at all, and what ones operate most strongly afterwards upon memory. One can say, in summary, that functional overweight regularly comes to those part-determinations which have greater significance for quality and erection of the experience-totality, in short, to those related to totality (*ganzheitsbezogenen*) in the highest degree. To these belong contours, in the visual as well as in the symbolic sense, of that which closes a complex and limits it; rhythm in the broader sense of the word; shape character (*Gestaltcharakter*); the form of organization (*Gliederungsform*) in itself; (cf. *Neue Psychologische Studien*, I and IV; and Sander, 19). These and features or aspects of our experience related to them take a significant position in the total experience in relief. If they possess decided character of inclusion (*Gliedcharakter*), as well as a regular, known, or beautiful shape in the field of vision, then such separate qualities appear and work as *dominating* part-contents within the whole at that moment. If they have, as in the case of rhythm, a characteristic change between some kind of "accentuated" and unaccentuated members, then the accentuated ones are, by nature, more important for the total impression and are more sensitive to every change. If, by way of exception, a relatively unaccentuated, peripheral part or moment, apparently dislodged from the structure of the whole, becomes impressive for us, strikes us, then this usually fleeting constellation passes over very soon into the normal one previously indicated.

More exact analysis shows, too, that from the beginning intimate relations existed between the problematical component and the *part*-whole to which it belongs, especially between these two and the *total*-whole. These are not infrequently conspicuous at first in an especially feeling-like complex quality of inescapableness, confusedness, unattunedness (*Nichzusammenstimmenden*), annoyingness (*Störenden*), states of the given (*Gegebenheiten*), which go regularly hand in hand with an experienceable *urge*, with a more or less definitely directed striving to close the "contour," to reconstruct regularity or order, to "supply" missing details from which most of the illusions of sense and memory arise; in short, to experience the whole as a closed unity of the highest possible degree of stability.

These are the observations which I called *Dominanz des Ganzen* (dominance of the whole) and later summarized in the concept

Drang nach Ganzheit (striving for totality). (Cf. 15, p. 22 ff., 27 ff., 55, 72, 80 ff.) After our comparative orientation concerning part-complexes, their more or less feeling-likeness, and on the other hand concerning the type of phenomena of the total-whole and its function, we understand now much more exactly that feelings, as we said before, are naturally *attended* to. It is their nature always to dominate. Even the most distant, the most excluded parts of an experience-constellation always remain interwoven into the simultaneous feeling, alloyed with it and embraced by it, according to the behavior of the totality (*Ganzheit*).

In this manner even the most dismembered inner events are directed in their qualities as well as in their functions. The emotion always strives powerfully to penetrate everything which goes on in us with its color, to quench resistance or to recast it, and to carry through its own total rhythm by overlapping.

Actually it always fills consciousness totally only that it may quickly and perpetually pass over into other feelings. The emotional gives the main direction to all mental behavior. Whatever has been regarded otherwise until now, as strengthened "attention," as forms of domination of the psychophysical life, such as intensity of sensations, as relative weight of the palpable, of the spatially spread out or the long continuing, of the sudden and sensational, as the power of the customary, of exercise, and of repetition, as the compelling effect of the closed "shape" and of form of organization, all these may be arranged as corollaries of our principle of the *dominance of the whole* and can be conceived in a more unitary manner through it.

C. *Durable Forms* (Dauerformen)—*The Psychophysical Structure*

Of all mental functions the emotional obviously has the greatest weight for life in general. Since the emotions are themselves products of the *total* psychophysical state and *totality* of function, it so happens reciprocally that totality maintains a well-rounded, filled-up life, without breaking apart or wearing away, and always generates itself anew, principally through feelings. Furthermore, in the endless whirlpool of manifold influences, ultimately of the total universe, these little beings, which we know as living things, can remain alive at least a few hours or decades; this means, then, that they maintain themselves for a certain time as structures (*Gefüge*) of a psychophysical kind formed for some time (*psychophysischen Dauergeformtheit*). (Cf. 15, p. 53 ff., p. 9 f.; 15a, p. 16 ff.)

Regarded from this angle, we see in a new light that man and probably animals, especially the young, always strive for "experiences" (*Erlebnisse*), playing, hazarding, even intoxicating themselves for experiences which are emotionally combined and motivated, which are wherever possible wholly filled out by strong feelings. The sick cling to these warming waves even in the enjoyment of their pains. The immature seek by pathos or sentimentality to quiet their longing for a full being alive (*Lebendigsein*); those of broken nature wear themselves out for it by assuming the sentiment of another, and at the same time by all kinds of self-criticism. "All joys," says Friedrich Nietzsche, "long for eternity." So far as this quotation is true, it is valid for every quality of inner total-fullness (*Ganzerfülltheit*), although in no way at the same degree everywhere. But, as we saw, the emotional, on the other hand, is labile to the highest degree, even fragile. This is true especially of those emotions which, determined moment by moment contrary to structural determination (cf. 6, p. 30 ff.; 15, p. 57; 15a, p. 15), have roots no deeper than in an accidental constellation of the psychophysical reality only for a moment; they never remain long as they were; they blunt swiftly; they reverse or dissolve without control. A continuous sequence of mere moods, to say nothing of strong effervescence of the emotions, is a thing for which man does not seem to be constructed.

Now it is an established fact of our lives, which has been considered only a little hitherto in research and theory, that different kinds of emotions can become blunted to *different degrees*. If one considers the amusing effect of verbal witticisms, or of a crudely comical situation, and, in contrast with that, if one considers a truly humorous occurrence, one finds that the latter presupposes a set spirit and especially a formed emotionality (*Gemüt*), that it is combined harmoniously with other phenomenologically similar and functionally related mental efforts in a *perpetual* attitude of the mind, which is maintained even in storms.

In the same way all mere thrills can be distinguished, and especially the most boisterous can be distinguished as momentary ones from spiritual emotions of a healthy kind, e. g., from perpetual, strongly established thrills of friendship, of art, or creative work. Still within a field of experience conditioned by culture as, for instance, art, there are broad tensions. The decorations of a festival may be very effective, but one cannot use them a second time. A street-song is rather pleasant sometimes when we hear it the first time, or a catchy tune from an operetta seems to be pretty the first time, but after even a few repetitions it becomes uninteresting to one who is musical or it becomes torture. On the other hand, a fugue of Bach always seizes one anew just as a painting by Rembrandt or an engraving of the "Kleine Passion" does; one discovers new beauties in it every time. Even the untrained can hear an original folk song, a minuet of Haydn, or a melody of Mozart many times, even again and again, with undiminished enjoyment.

To conceive such facts psychologically one must become free from the dogmatic phenomenalism which in the nineteenth century, according to the false example of physics, narrowed scientific psychology (cf. 15a, p. 17; 15, p. 100). One must have the courage to view stable, penetrating duration-forms of the mental, and to go back, at least hypothetically, to the dispositional set (*Angelegenheit*) of experience, finally to its structural coherence (*Strukturzusammenhang*), i. e., to the working totality of the mind and the organism. For this purpose we need in every case *genetic* and also cultural-genetic comparisons and analyses (15, p. 120 f.). For instance, the appertaining ability of emotions to be blunted does not differ to the same degree at all steps of the development. Primitive people and children, up to about the eighth year, can devotedly repeat innumerable times one and the same harmless joke which bores us to death.

The problems presented here can be reached to a certain degree even by measurement and experiment. Sander, starting with the basic ideas of the Leipzig laboratory, successfully investigated the *Aktualgenese* (actual genesis) of limited shape-formations. Besides establishing results for the *genetic primary* and for the penetrating, phenomenological, and functional *dominance of the feelings*, he gained instructive new views, even of the structural condition of those processes. In that he regularly cut back the effect of the outside stimulus by temporal abbreviation, diminished brightness, diminution of size, etc., he showed, by steps, that the dispositional sets became preponderating; in this manner, certain mental part-structures and their persistent cohesion became clearly recognized (cf. 19, and IV, *Neue Psychologische Studien*).

These data must be completely coordinated with numerous other experimental results. It is no accident that exact psychology recently investigated the problem of set (*Einstellung*) from different angles. Thus, in a way rich in consequences, it broke down the ban of the atomistic conception of ideas and theories of images (*Vorstellungen*), which for centuries retarded scientific knowledge in the field of "memory," of so-called "association," of "attention," and which, checked elsewhere, led the theory of feelings into confusion, and immediately tied up the investigation of the "imagination." (It is wholly dominated by feelings; cf. 15, p. 31 f.; 15a, p. 12.)

What combines systematically, or at least what ought fundamentally to combine those new significant problems and methods, is the idea of mental *totality;* on the one hand, totality of inner experience (*des Erlebens*), above all, of the emotions; secondly, totality of the universal coherence of function; and thirdly, totality of their structural foundations, foundations of the mental and finally of the psychophysical structure (15a, p. 16 f.).   With strenuously refined methods, we dare not fall back again into that way of thinking which was a stranger to totality and therefore to genetic development.   The part-coherences of mental events, necessarily isolated when investigated in the laboratory, are in reality always imbedded in more embracing unities of experience; they are always embraced and conditionally dominated most effectively by the *whole totality* which we recognized as the *emotional.*   The mental *part*-structures which are now tangible here and there, must, correspondingly, be theoretically incorporated within the structural whole of the psychophysical organisms in their genetic regularity and ultimately within the structure of culture.

This very far-reaching requirement means, to be sure, among other things, that we psychologists must by no means be satisfied with the juxtaposition of infinite dispositions, shape-phenomena, or artificially (e. g., by training) produced and arbitrarily variated forms of "structural" reaction, as one says equivocally (cf. 15, p. 96, 99 ff.).   The "urge to form shapes" (*Gestaltungsdrang*), which can easily be observed in visual figures (*Darbietungen*) and also in tests of intelligence, to mention only this one fact critically, is certainly considerable in the right connection.   Often this is to a great extent nothing but a kind of self-defence of the observers, however, who try continually to get rid of the boredom imposed upon them.   Shapes which are in conformity with the structural conditions of the inner experience and with its genetic necessities look absolutely unlike.   They are always penetrated and mainly determined by feelings.   They are subjected to more inclusive principles of the blood-warm, whole totality, and the same is valid concerning those artificial products, if we observe them completely. Much more regularly than would be expected according to present-day theories, highly differentiated men are inclined, to a high degree, to behave in an unorganized way, purely emotionally, even to give in totally to a state of drunkenness of the mind, although scarcely in the laboratory.   Of course they do not long remain in it.   Living perpetual shapeness (*Geformtheit*) forbids it.   The morning-after headache follows every intoxication the more developed the organism is, and the more civilized his environment.

It is also important that the habit, particularly of purposefully creating ecstasies, makes one unfit for life. It soon damages the organization itself, the mind as well as the body. On the contrary, high art, or wisdom, especially deep, sound religion are fruitful or grow strong in that they at the same time lend enduring *warmth*. Their true experiences with all the intimacies (*Innigkeit*) of the corresponding emotions filling us to the full, are, to the highest degree, structurally conditioned, built according to structure, and they therefore promote structural growth.

Manifold and strongly organized inner experience which, at the same time, is powerfully infused with feeling is indeed demanded, biologically, in forms prescribed according to the state of development. Even the finest, most spiritual form of human existence is corporally typified as far as it does not sever itself from the cycle of life.

From a totality more than from an individual we see all living beings, from the beginning of their existence, endowed with a great number of inherited adjustments of their behavior to regularities in the environment. These innate constancies of the psychophysical course (*Ablaufs*) interweave with manifold, acquired, dispositions for a longer or shorter time; they interweave with individual dispositions, just as in ourselves, as human beings, they interweave with historically developed dispositions (e. g., rites, customs, institutions, etc.). All those dispositional facts are of the kind that I call part-structure; their structural unity, the psychophysical total-structure of the experiencing person is meant if one speaks of the constitution or personality or character, as the standpoint of observation may be. None of the determinations of the direction of the events is absolutely unchangeable or fixed; otherwise it would be torn out of the developing structure of life. They are in thorough reciprocity with one another and with the structural whole. They are plastic, even the bones and the teeth, the instincts and acquired traits (*Dressurerfolge*), and even the reflexes. They are changed by the shaping, restoring, and combining powers of the total organism equally as well by the powers of the individual as by the powers of the larger social one. In diseases, bodily or mental crises, in revolutions, they can fall to pieces or fully demolish themselves.

What threatens the duration-form of life most is the irreconcilable conflict of structural dispositions with one another. We experience it, like all structurally conditioned psychophysical events, in experiences of palpable "depth" (13, p. 6; 15a, p. 15; 15, p. 53 ff.). To them belong all feelings of valuation in contrast with momentary excitements; all emotional awareness of significance but also thoughts "deeply" conditioned and full of coherence in contrast to unstable intuitions, or imitated, merely copied judgments; and also voluntary decisions from the consciousness of duty, and final responsibility. Such forms of behavior are realized when the experiencing person always feels unequivocally, and often very strongly unequivocally, and under the proper conditions clearly knows, at the same time, that the whole (*ums Ganze*), even the substance of existence in the ever ascending stages of life is concerned. The depth of the emotions descends into another level than the total remaining richness of colors and the richness of shapes of the inner experiences. It is essentially different, especially from the mere intensity and momentary force of the emotions. So far as these facts are not determined by values and systems of evaluation, are not rooted in the structure of the personality, so far as they remain without continuous connections with the central conditions which determine their course (*zentralen Gerichteheiten*) and with duration-form we recognize it immediately in the flatness of the experience, and conversely. The depth dimension of mental events corresponds sympathetically to the functional unity of life, better symbolically, in phenomena of great consequence. In it is reflected the formation of the structures (*gefügehaftes Wesen*) which combines all expressions of life from within and thus reflects the stage of development of the structures and the necessity for their growth as well as for their decline (15a, p. 19 ff., 24 ff.; 15, pp. 53, 57, 75, 83, 110 ff.; cf. *Zur Entwicklungspsychologie des Rechts*, München, 1926).

Deep inner experience is essentially conditioned by the bipolarity of feelings. All growing-deeper, all shape-getting of the individual as well as of society comes inescapably by way of hard opposition. It requires struggle and sacrifice, deprivation and unceasing suffering. From the most serious conflict of duties and primarily from hard wrestling for eternal "salvation" it happens the heart does not "return whole." There is a remainder, then, unquenchable perhaps in a whole life and yet the one possessing it will not overcome it; and if it could be, they would continue on, be blessed in the continuous growth of such suffering.

The limited shape-formation, as we create it, methodically change it, and measure it in our psychological laboratories, has its theoretical value. Although they lie relatively at the surface, these phenomena and these connections in their rich complexity give much to think about to one who reflects. Out of the parts of the living, if one observes them correctly, the whole always shines. The wonderful closure, impressiveness, and indentation even of those small bits of experience with their tensions against one another and against unshaped events, all those part-phenomena whose regularities we now begin to suspect, must become incorporated genetically into the structural necessity of the total course of life. To the mental manifestations of this necessity and to their duration-forms science has a particular entrance, the psychological one. Here we may be allowed to look from the inside because we have full inner experiences ourselves, where we who have the inner experiences observe and describe them, carefully compare, analyze, and combine them anew. Whatever has been conscientiously observed in this way can finally be brought under concepts in so far as they have been cleanly determined. Life itself seems to demand more vividly at the present than in ancient times that some of its bearers in diverse lands observe mental experiences scientifically. We must ponder them as total men, clear of vision, but humble before its mysteries.

BIBLIOGRAPHY

1. CORNELIUS, H. Psychologie als Erfahrungs-wissenschaft. Leipzig: Teubner, 1897.

2. IPSEN, G. Ueber Gestaltauffassung. Erörterung des Sanderschen Parallelogramms. *Neue Psychologische Studien*, I (1926), 167–278.

3. ————. Zur Theorie des Erkennens. Untersuchungen über Gestalt und Sinn sinnloser Wörter. *Neue Psychologische Studien*, I (1926), 279–471.

4. KLEMM, O. Sinnestäuschungen. Psychologie und experimentelle Pädagogik in Einzeldarstellungen. Leipzig, 1919.

5. ————. Wahrnehmungsanalyse. Aus "Handbuch der biologischen Arbeitsmethoden," hrsg. v. Abderhalden. Berlin, Wien: Urban & Schwarzenberg, 1922.

6. KRUEGER, F. Der Begriff des absolut Wertvollen als Grundbegriff der Moralphilosophie. Leipzig: Teubner, 1898.

7. ————. Beobachtungen über Zweiklänge. *Philosophische Studien*, XVI (1900), 307–379; 568–663.

8. ————. Zur Theorie der Combinationstöne. *Philosophische Studien*, XVII (1901), 186–310.

9. ————. Differenztöne und Konsonanz. *Archiv für die gesamte Psychologie*, I (1903) 205–275.

10. ————. Beziehungen der experimentellen Phonetik zur Psychologie. *Bericht über den 2. Kongress für experimentelle Psychologie in Würzburg, 1906.* Pp. 65.

11. ————. Die Theorie der Konsonanz. Eine psychologische Auseinandersetzung, vornehmlich mit C. Stumpf und Th. Lipps. *Psychologische Studien*, I (1906), 305–387; II (1907), 205–255; IV (1908), 201–282; V (1910), 294–411.

12. ————. Ueber Entwicklungspsychologie. Leipzig, 1915.

13. ————. Die Tiefendimension und die Gegensätzlichkeit des Gefühlslebens. Festschrift zu Joh. Volkelts 70. Geburtstag. München, 1918.

14. ————. Wilhelm Wundt als deutscher Denker. *Beiträge zur Philosophie des deutschen Idealismus*, II (1922), 1.

15. ————. Ueber psychische Ganzheit. *Neue Psychologische Studien,* I (1926), 1. (Auch separat erschienen.)

16. SANDER, F. Wundts Prinzip der schöpferischen Synthese. *Beiträge zur Philosophie des deutschen Idealismus,* II (1922), 55–58.

17. ————. Ueber räumliche Rhythmik. I. Mitteilung: Experimentelle Untersuchungen über rhythmusartige Reihen und Gruppenbildungen bei simultanen Gesichtseindrücken. *Neue Psychologische Studien,* I (1926), 123–158.

18. ————. Optische Täuschungen und Psychologie. *Neue Psychologische Studien,* I (1926), 159–166.

19. ————. Ueber Gestaltqualitäten. Sonderdruck des *Vortrags 8. internationalen Psychologenkongress in Groningen, 1926.*

20. STUMPF, C. Ueber Gefühlsempfindungen. Vortrag. *II. Kongress für experimentelle Psychologie in Würzburg, 1906.* Leipzig: 1907. Pp. 209–273. Abgedruckt in *Zeitschrift für Psychologie,* XLIV (1907), 1–49.

21. VOLKELT, H. Ueber die Vorstellungen der Tiere. Arbeiten zur Entwicklungspsychologie, I. Leipzig: Engelmann, 1914.

22. ————. Fortschritte der experimentellen Kinderpsychologie. Jena: Fischer, 1926.

23. WUNDT, W. Grundzüge der physiologischen Psychologie. 3 Bde. 6. Aufl. Leipzig: Engelmann, 1908–1911.

24. ————. Grundriss der Psychologie. 15. Aufl. Leipzig: Engelmann, 1922.

DISCUSSION

DR. REYMERT: You may think we have given undue time to this particular paper. There are two reasons for this: one, that we have a pupil of the author here, Dr. Carl Schneider, so that the paper can actually be discussed, and the other, that the system of Wundt's successor in the Leipzig laboratory should call for particular attention in an American psychological audience.

DR. GEISSLER (*Randolph-Macon College*): I do not quite understand the relation between the intensity of feelings or emotions and the total consciousness. I should like a restatement.

DR. SCHNEIDER (*Wittenberg College*): Feelings in this theory mean that they are a quality of a total experience. Now, of course, that does not mean that the more total the experience is, the more intensive the feeling is. This would be the easier answer but it is not so simple. The intensity of the feelings does not depend absolutely on the richness of the total experience. At least we cannot observe this experimentally. But we may say that the richness of the inner experience is mirrored in the depth of the feelings. Depth and intensity are different. In the Krueger system there is great difference between a deep joy and a flat joy in their qualitative aspect. Depth is a qualitative term and can be seen better the more closely we arrive at a totality of the experience. But, on the other hand, there is really no difference in intensity alone without a difference of quality. Difference of intensity alone is an abstraction which measures difference of quality. Therefore we cannot speak of pure intensity of feeling; we can speak only of a kind of measured differences of emotional quality, and from this standpoint we also can say we measure indirectly the different intensities by measuring the different states of more or less total experience—but indirectly, of course, not directly.

DR. GEISSLER: I was wondering what that had to do with the possibility of comparing feelings in their relative strengths with each other. We can compare geometric forms with each other: "I like that best"; "that one has the lowest feeling for me"; "that one has the highest feeling." Now, can we make comparisons, put these feelings into pairs, and compare them? I don't quite understand the relations.

Dr. Schneider: Of course we can do it methodically, but the results show that there is always a difference of quality, too. No two emotions are always so alike that they may be differentiated by intensity alone. They are always differentiated by the qualitative state as well. It is, therefore, not surprising that the Leipzig *Ganzheit* psychology has created and is creating a new technical vocabulary.

Dr. Reymert: I wonder if this would be of any help in clearing up the question which Dr. Geissler has raised. I think this is a fundamental one. May I ask this question? Would it be somewhat comparable to saturation and brightness as we use these terms in speaking, for instance, of one particular color? These two attributes of a color-tone might be regarded as the intensity and the color-depth of that hue. Of course intensity and saturation are abstractions—or singled-out aspects of the total—i. e., the hue under observation. Changes in either one aspect—or in the total experience—are, of course, interdependent. Changes in brightness are naturally experiential of a qualitative nature. The total—the hue under immediate observation—may, like feeling, be changed in infinite dimensions, or experiential qualities. The naming of these infinite totals in vision is not farther advanced than Krueger's emotional qualities.

Dr. Schneider: Every change in the emotion or feeling from the one aspect means at the same time a change in the other, too. Using your terminology any change in "brightness" means also a change in intensity, saturation, etc. Not only one "attribute" is changed, but the total. Therefore it is not so easy to compare two emotions. It is impossible to measure emotions quantitatively only.

Dr. Reymert: Would you say then that, so far as it goes, my reference to color experiences helps to clarify the situation?

Dr. Schneider: Yes, with the mentioned restrictions.

Dr. Reymert: Of course no strict parallels may be drawn.

Dr. Pyle (*Kansas State Teachers College, Pittsburgh, Kansas*): If the measuring of the various intensities are abstractions, could you say that you would never get a knowledge of what the law is?

Dr. Schneider: No, I should say this. Although we cannot measure the emotions qualitatively, we can see in indirect quantitative measurements laws concerning the quality. You remember what Krueger said on the least perceivable difference. We can measure indirectly the expressions of these total states and these expressions as we find them. In measuring the least perceivable difference we find in it regularities of the qualitative experience.

Dr. Pyle: But the measuring again would seem to be analytical and therefore aside from the whole.

Dr. Schneider: Only as a methodical necessity which lends to a fuller description of the whole by various, mainly genetic methods.

Dr. Erickson (*East Orange, New Jersey*): It was a little difficult for me to follow certain points in Professor Krueger's paper, though I think it was made perfectly clear. One point, however, I should like to have covered again—whether we may think of Professor Krueger as tending toward the functionalistic concept more than, say, toward the structuralistic? Is my question clear?

Dr. Reymert: Very clear.

Dr. Schneider: By all means more towards the functionalistic concept, but he is no functionalist in the classical sense. Of course emotions have a functional character, but they have only a functional character so far as all total experiences have a functional character—not in the sense of elementary functions. As they are always simultaneous and successive they are similar to functional experiences of a total state. And thus, of course, his theory is neither structuralistic nor functionalistic. These qualities which we finally experience in every state of life, these are qualities which are imbedded in experience as a closed total experience.

DR. MABEL FLORENCE MARTIN (*State Psychological Clinic, New Jersey*): But if we are to dispose with elements and analysis, in what terms can totalities be described?

DR. SCHNEIDER: We have to have in many respects a new terminology in psychology. Of course many things can be described in the terminology which we now have. But our present psychological terminology is too much under the influence of physiological and chemical vocabularies. You will find in Krueger's terminology many new words which simply had to be created for naming totalities.

DR. MARTIN: I am not sure that that quite answers my question. Suppose that you can create new terms of description, are not these in themselves elements, or are not they at least products of analysis?

DR. SCHNEIDER: No, that is just what we deny. They are not products of analysis, but they are descriptive symbols of experienced phenomena. Even the application of the language of the mathematical formula in psychology means always only organization, as it were, part-shapes (*Gliederungsformen*), and is absolutely dependent on the whole which is given with the part.

DR. DICKINSON (*University of Maine*): Would I be right in understanding from the presentation of the paper that we have a continuum of qualitative changes which in any given time would be the aspect of emphasis at that particular time in relation to the total? I am trying to formulate the question in my own mind: I mean would I be right in understanding that there is a continuum of qualitative change, and that the parts in relation to the part-whole at any particular time would be the emphasis of the aspect at any particular time?

DR. SCHNEIDER: Yes, there is just the main essence of the theory. Of course, there is a continuous change and we divide this into parts as compared to the total. The task of psychology is to observe laws of this change. As for those questions of organization of shape—we organize diffuse, chaotic total experience into arranged, organized experience, and we divide this first total into parts; but always so that the parts have relation to the total. These are the problems of this kind of psychology. They are not elementary problems. The relation between parts and whole is the most interesting phenomenon.

DR. REYMERT: Having to close this interesting discussion, I feel that Dr. Krueger's paper when published will give all of us much food for thought and fruitful discussion.

CHAPTER 6

THE FEELING-TONE OF SENSATION

F. KIESOW

Royal University of Turin

The phenomenon of consciousness, with which we shall deal in the following pages, belongs to those psychic processes which are generally comprised under the concept of the life of feeling. What is common to all the experiences included in this concept is that they are not referred to objects of the outer world, of which one's own body is regarded as a part, but remain, as it were, in consciousness, forming a necessary basis for the development of the processes of the will and the empirical ego. We cannot here treat of the development of the latter, nor of the connection in which the feelings stand to the will-processes.

Since investigation of the domain of feeling is among the most difficult tasks of psychology, it is not surprising if, in spite of the manifold work on the subject carried out both in the past and the present, not only is the problem as a whole still unsolved, but even respecting certain fundamental questions, no agreement has yet been compassed by the various investigators. One of these fundamental questions relates to the nature of the phenomenon which we call the *feeling-tone of sensation*.

What has rendered the psychological investigation of feeling difficult for a long time is the fact that it was carried out under the influence of metaphysical premises, as well as ethical valuations and epistemological considerations. We cannot here deal with all the perturbations which the problem of feeling has consequently been subjected to, but I cannot refrain from mentioning that these influences are responsible for our speaking even at the present day of "higher" and "lower" senses and of "higher" and "lower" feelings, and for our assigning the feeling-tone of a sensation to the lower feelings. Such valuations are useless to psychology as an empirical science. Psychology demands that we should, as far as possible, separate into their ultimate component parts the complexes of consciousness which emerge from the ceaseless flow of psychic events as relatively independent forms, in order to comprehend the cause of their internal structure and their modes of origin, and, at the same time, the building-up and ulterior development of psychic life. What further value is to be ascribed to the results of psychic analysis, psychology, as an empirical science, is not called upon to decide. It is the task of metaphysics, of ethics, and of epistemology to turn to account the results of psychological investigations. Psychology may not set to work in the opposite way, but in saying this I certainly do not mean that it can fully dispense with philosophy.

On this premise let us endeavor to avoid expressions like those mentioned above and make use instead of terms which are psychologically free from objection. Just as we designate as *sensations* the ultimate constituents of which objectifiable complexes of consciousness are composed according to the principle of psychic synthesis, so we call those which form the basis of the unobjectifiable feeling-complexes *elementary feelings*. No other than a purely psychological valuation lies at the bottom of this concept. In this sense the feeling-tone of a sensation is an *elementary feeling*.

Instead of elementary feelings we frequently hear the expression "simple feelings" used. Since, however, it is a question of really fixing a designation for the last, not ulteriorly divisible contents of feeling, the expression "elementary feeling" is, in my opinion, preferable to that of "simple feeling," and for this reason, that the term "simple feeling" may lead to misunderstanding: those feelings which accompany complex objectifiable contents of consciousness, that is, representations, and which are certainly not final elements of feeling, give, owing to their unitary character, the impression of simple feelings and are generally called so. We are unable to reduce a composite feeling of such a kind into its components by pure subjective effort, and must, in order to recognize these, have recourse to special experimental aids. In this respect there is an essential difference between representation-complexes and feeling-complexes. To put it briefly, every elementary feeling may be conceived as a simple feeling, but not every feeling, appearing as a simple feeling, is an elementary feeling.

It is clear from all this that by the feeling-tone of sensation is to be understood that purely subjective something which accompanies the sensation, and which is yet essentially different from it, and which is called agreeable, disagreeable, etc. Of course we may also speak of the feeling-tone of a representation. We shall not, however, here discuss this part of the domain of feeling. In the feeling-tone accompanying a sensation in its greatest possible isolation, we have the elementary feeling in its purest form and therein lies, I think, the fundamental importance of this psychic phenomenon for the comprehension of the whole life of feeling.

In what I have said, I have already expressed a personal conviction, which is not shared by all the psychologists of today. On the contrary, it is vigorously opposed by very distinguished representatives of our science. The latter conceive of the feeling-tone of sensation in a sensualistic way, thus reverting to older conceptions. At the same time it must be pointed out that the opinions, even within the sensualistic school, deviate considerably from one another. As we can see now from this general survey, the opinions about the actual nature of the elementary experience here under discussion are so widely different that the struggle raging on this point between the various authors will not end, I think, until either the one or the other view has fought its way through to general recognition. A conciliation of views may be regarded as impossible.

As for the origin of the expression "tone of feeling," it is sufficient here to point out that the Herbartian school used it in the form "tone of sensation." The fundamental idea of the Herbartian school, long dominant in psychology, is, we may say, a thing of the past. We know now that the feelings cannot be explained by Herbart's mechanism of representations. This must be said in spite of full recognition of the various introspections concerning feeling which are to be found both in Herbart's own works and in those of adherents of his theory, such as W. F. Volkmann, Náhlovski, and others. The term "tone of feeling" has also met with some hostility. If, however, we emphasize the fact that by this term nothing more is meant than the universally recognized elementary experience which accompanies sensation, then the designation "tone of feeling" (considering the difficulty of finding, in all languages, adequate terms for given psychic experiences) may surely be accepted as the one best answering the purpose and not likely to lead to misunderstanding.

The term "sensory feeling" (*sinnliches Gefühl*) seems to me more open to criticism. My opinion is that we should avoid this expression. Not only does it imply a valuation, inasmuch as the so-called "sensory" feelings are not infrequently placed in opposition to the "intellectual" feelings, as experiences of a lower nature, which psychologically is inadmissible, but such a designation may give rise to the erroneous notion that a "sensory" feeling is essentially different from an "intellectual" feeling. This is not the case, as a comparison of the two processes shows. The feeling of pleasure which I experience during a simple intellectual process is not essentially different from that which I experience, for instance, when looking at a saturated color in a dark room. Further, the attribute "sensory" favors, to an extraordinary degree, a sensualistic interpretation of the phenomenon in question, which I, for my part, must reject.

As our time is limited, we must pass over the older opinions on the feeling-tone which are to be found in the literature of the subject. We must be content to take into account those chief directions which, at the present time, struggle for supremacy. These, in my opinion, are connected principally with the names of Carl Stumpf, Theodor Ziehen, and Wilhelm Wundt. We shall, therefore, consider the theories of these three authors with particular care, thereby touching on the opinions of other investigators in so far as they relate to the problem before us.

Carl Stumpf expressed his opinion on the feeling-tone of sensation first in 1906, at the Second Congress of the Association of Experimental Psychologists at Würzburg, and published his lecture in the following year in Volume XLIV of the *Zeitschrift für Psychologie* (pp. 1–49) in amplified form under the title, "Ueber Gefühlsempfindungen." A further treatment of the same subject was published by Stumpf in 1916 under the title, "Apologie der Gefühlsempfindungen" in Volume LXXV of the same journal (pp. 1–38).

Stumpf's conception is, in the most rigid sense, sensualistic. This is indeed indicated by the title of his above-mentioned paper. Sensations of feeling (*Gefühlsempfindungen*) are, according to Stumpf, all so-called sensory feelings, that is to say, all tones of feeling accompanying sensations. Stumpf thus rejects both the opinion that in these processes we have to do with a particular category of psychic experiences and the view of earlier authors, who regarded feeling as a function of sensation, and maintains that all sensory feelings represent a "particular class of sensations of sense" (*Sinnesempfindungen*). Nevertheless Stumpf is for a rigorous differentiation between sensations of feeling on the one hand and aesthetic feelings and the emotions on the other. The two latter groups of experience are designated by him as "states of a particular kind" (*Zustände eigner Art*) which, according to him, are not "disintegrable into sensations of sense."

As for the term "sensation of feeling" itself, it is to be found also in Brentano, to whose school Stumpf originally belonged. We find it, however, still earlier, in the works of older authors. Ernst Heinrich Weber, for example, has the term "sensation of common feeling" (*Gemeingefühlsempfindung*), which likewise is to be understood in a sensualistic sense, and with which he designates all those psychic processes which, according to him, are not included in the five senses derived from the Aristotelian doctrine of mind. This, in Weber, is explainable, because the physiology of his time took no special interest in the subjective experiences accompanying sensations and representations, in spite of the notice taken thereof by Ackens and, more particularly, by Kant; and further, because physiology, owing to the fact that the German language of every-day life makes no essential difference between feeling and sensation had given the name "sense of feeling" to the "fifth" sense. This influence is still traceable in Weber, although he himself speaks, instead of the "sense of feeling," of the "sense of touch," which term has been metamorphosed in our time, as we know, into the concept of the "skin-sense" with its manifold subordinate senses.

I have directed your attention to these facts because in Stumpf's views their influence is, I think, to a certain extent, recognizable. Otherwise, the juxtaposition of the concepts "feeling" and "sensation," with which the psychology of today designates totally different contents of consciousness, is difficult to understand.

Stumpf, too, has the concept of the sense of feeling. For the most part, however, he speaks of the "sensory" feelings which are, for him, precisely, sensations of feeling. Stumpf enumerates among the sensory feelings—"sensory pains," the "feeling of bodily well-being" (with the "pleasure components of titillation, the feeling aroused by itch, and the sexual feelings") and, finally, the tones of feeling which are linked to the sensations of temperature, smell, and taste, as well as to the several tones and colors.

The views held by von Frey and his followers on the subject of the cutaneous sensation of pain have, as I imagine, contributed essentially to the propounding of Stumpf's theory of sensations of feeling. Stumpf adheres to these views. On the other hand, however, since he classifies pain as a "sensation of feeling" of a disagreeable character, he is obliged to look upon the two factors —the actual pain quality and the concomitant unpleasantness— as a unitary single experience. Through von Frey's researches, Stumpf says: "The sense of feeling has, so to speak, been success-fully isolated, like a culture of absolute purity." Stumpf rejects, therefore, Thunberg's opinion, which ascribes to pain sensations a specific tone of feeling, and arrives at the really paradoxical conclusion that pain possesses no tone of feeling. "It possesses only *one* quality, and it is this which is expressed by the designation 'pain.'" According to Stumpf, this holds good for the delayed pain sensation noticeable in pathological cases, as well as for the secondary pain sensation first observed by Goldscheider and Gad. Pain sensation has, according to Stumpf, whenever and wherever it appears, only the one quality, namely, that it is painful. This means, in other words, that it is an unpleasant sensation in itself.

The second chief quality in the sense of feeling is, according to Stumpf, generally speaking, agreeableness. Stumpf leaves the question open whether, just as, according to von Frey, there are particular pain nerves, there may be particular pleasure nerves also. He writes: "Perhaps there are such for the pleasure sensations excited at the periphery, while for those arising in the inside of the body—for the sensation of satiety, of rest, of general well-being—only definite central processes are perhaps called into action, as concomitant effects of the modified circulation of blood in the brain." "Pleasure sensations" as opposed to pain sensations must, according to Stumpf, be characterized likewise by one quality only. This means, from his point of view, that they have no tone of feeling. Among such sensations, pleasant in themselves, Stumpf includes voluptuous sensation.

In the cases mentioned up to this point, we have been dealing with sensations of a high degree of intensity. But what about sensations of a low or intermediate intensity? Besides pleasant and unpleasant sensations of a high degree of intensity, such as pain and voluptuousness, smells, tastes, colors, tones, etc., as generally observed in our laboratories, there are sensations of intermediate or low degree of intensity. And yet they may be all more or less characterized by a tone of feeling. According to Stumpf's premises this would mean that they are not characterized, like pain sensations and the really pleasant sensations, by one quality only, but are accompanied by a second sensation, that is, by a sensation of feeling. This raises the question: How does this sensation of feeling arise, which Stumpf likewise defines as a "sensation of sense"? Since it can scarcely be due to the agency of a special nerve-apparatus with definite peripheral end-organs, Stumpf regards it as highly probable that it be owing to centrally aroused concomitant sensations. According to Stumpf this opinion is borne out by the fact that the specific sensation and the concomitant sensation can neither be separated from one another nor modified independently of one another and that, further, wherever they are artificially separated, this can only be effected through a change in central conditions. Concerning the last point, he calls attention to his own auditory observations and to my experiments of isolation, systematically followed up in the domain of sensations of taste and their concomitant tones of feeling.

Summarizing, we may say that Stumpf differentiates, finally, two classes of feeling-sensations: one which he holds to be characterized by the fact that the qualities belonging to it, such as pain, voluptuousness, etc., are absolute pleasant or unpleasant sensations, that is, require no accompanying tone of feeling and come into existence through peripheral stimulation or through central processes of excitation; and a second to which belong feeling-sensations conditioned exclusively by central concomitant excitation, whose pleasant or unpleasant character is, according to him, to be regarded merely as a supplement to any one specific sensation (colors, tones, tastes, odors).

Stumpf's theory of feeling-sensations has repeatedly been subjected to criticism. Passing over the resultant polemics, I intend merely to state briefly what prevents me personally from agreeing with this distinguished scientist.

In the first place, the assertion is incorrect that pain possesses no concomitant tone of feeling but is, in the absolute, an unpleasant sensation. In high degrees of intensity both factors are certainly so bound up with one another that isolation is difficult, if not impossible. But pain does not always appear at once in the highest degree of intensity, but may increase gradually from a slight degree onwards through a series of stages, until it reaches a point where it is unbearable. In all the intermediate and weaker degrees, the feeling-tone of displeasure is, I think, clearly distinguishable from the actual pain quality. There are, besides, different pain sensations with varying feeling-tone. Conversely, I am able to produce on the skin pain sensations free, or almost free, from feeling. Moreover, the question as to the existence of pleasure-toned pain sensations must be more amply investigated.

Stumpf's assumption that tickle and itch sensations, as also voluptuousness, are, in the absolute, pleasure sensations is erroneous. So far as voluptuousness is concerned, it is a very complicated process which will not be here analyzed. As for tickle and itch sensations, I cannot personally sense these two experiences, in agreement with Stumpf, as pleasure; rather do I experience them as fraught with unpleasantness, indeed, given continuance, they may become a torture. The tickle sensation, conditioned by the touch apparatus, is, besides, no simple process, while the itch sensation must really be looked upon as a low-degreed pain sensation accompanied by a distinct tone of feeling. True, pleasantly toned sensations may be produced by simply stroking certain regions of the skin, for example, the skin of the back, but these are neither tickle nor itch sensations but touch sensations accompanied by an elementary pleasure feeling.

There is, again, great difficulty in the way of accepting Stumpf's second class of sensations of feeling. If there are not elementary feelings, but, as Stumpf maintains, real sensations, they ought then to obey the fundamental psychophysical law to which all real sensations are subjected. I know of no single sensation which ever changes its quality during increasing stimulation. During the gradual increase of stimulus every real sensation attains at last a degree of intensity, the so-called acme of stimulation, beyond which no additional intensity is perceived. In tones of feeling I observe the opposite phenomenon. Beyond a certain point of stimulus-increase the quality of feeling generally changes to its opposite, and, in certain cases, a stage of indifference may even be observed. This justifies, at any rate, the conclusion, that the "sensations of feeling" may not, as Stumpf proposes, be considered as equal to other sensations.

This applies likewise to the process of concomitant central excitation to which Stumpf ascribes the suscitation of the different tones of feeling. I do not understand how, in this way, *new* qualities of sensation can be called forth. When, commonly, we speak of centrally aroused concomitant sensations, we mean, beyond a doubt, sensations aroused in a reflex way, which were suscitated in the first instance through the agency of a particular nerve-apparatus with special peripheral terminations. Here, however, we are called upon to accept as a fact that a completely new quality of sensation is produced exclusively through concomitant central excitation. This opinion seems to me to conflict so with all other known psychophysical processes that it fails to carry conviction.

There still remains the further question whether tones of feeling, as such, are localizable. Only if this were the case might we, I think, speak of them as sensations. The numerous observations relating to this question which I myself have carried out force me to assume a negative attitude. Stumpf himself admits that the feeling-tone may, to a certain extent, be isolated experimentally from the sensation which it accompanies. When I perform experiments of this kind with colors, for instance, I observe that the various tones of feeling induced by the colors are not projected externally.

These are my chief objections to Stumpf's theories. They lead me to conclude that his views on the sensations of feeling are not well founded.

The views of Theodor Ziehen are likewise sensualistic. He holds that tones of feeling are not essentially different from the sensations which they accompany. Taking them all together Ziehen looks upon them as constituting a "sixth sense." He has also designated the tone of feeling as a property of sensation. As regards this opinion in particular, Oswald Külpe combatted it as far back as 1893. Stumpf likewise expressed his complete agreement with Külpe. We find the same negative attitude in Edward

Titchener (*Lehrbuch der Psychologie*, 2nd ed., p. 194). And indeed the tone of feeling can under no condition be a property of sensation, whether we take the expression in its stricter or wider sense. No dialectic argumentation, such as Ziehen attempts in Volume II of his *Grundlagen der Psychologie* in 1916, can help us over this difficulty. The theory, in my opinion, is even in contradiction with Ziehen's own conception of the nature of the feeling-tone. A sensation, as Ziehen, at bottom, must take the feeling-tone to be, can never be a property of another sensation, nor a characteristic (*Merkmal*) of a sensation, which expression Ziehen makes use of in the last edition of his *Leitfaden der physiologischen Psychologie*. More to the purpose is the proposal advanced by Ziehen in his above-mentioned work of 1915, p. 219, to call his theory "epigenetic" or the theory of the "central supplementary process." These designations emphasize, to my thinking, the special character of Ziehen's hypothesis. Less acceptable seems to me his proposal to call his theory the theory of the feeling-tone, for the tone of feeling is that very psychic experience which all theories on the subject are endeavoring to explain.

Ziehen rightly rejects the expression "sensory" feeling; still it seems to me that not very much is gained in the one which he suggests should take its place. He speaks of "sensorial" feelings and "sensorial" tones of feeling, and divides these further into "primary" and "secondary" according to whether they are "conditioned exclusively by an external stimulus or by sensations themselves" or "are due to previous connection with representations." My opinion is that the expression "tone of feeling" suffices with the further distinction between the feeling-tone of sensation, of representation, etc.

Concerning pain sensations, in the first place, Ziehen advocates a view which is opposed to that held by von Frey and his adherents. Ziehen, too, considers pain sensations to be supplementary qualities due to the agency of central processes. On these lines, he tries, for instance, to explain the gradual transition of sensations of touch, warmth, and cold, under continuous increase of stimulus, into pain. Needless to say, I reject this opinion. Not only is the arousal of pain through purely central processes incomprehensible to me, but this view is combatted by the fact that analgesic spots are to be found upon the skin of the body and that the mucous membrane of the mouth contains zones insensible to pain. It is, similarly, to my mind, an incontrovertible fact that the warm and cold spots on the skin of the body are, as was first shown by Goldscheider, analgesic.

With respect to the tones of feelings of pleasantness and unpleasantness accompanying other sensations, Ziehen, in a paper
published in 1903 (*Zeitschrift für Psychologie*, XXXIII, p. 216)
attributes their origin to the discharge tendency (*Entladungs-
bereitschaft*) of cortical brain-cells, a process which the author
strictly distinguishes from the "excitability" of these cells. Positive processes of feeling are said to correspond to a great "discharge tendency," negative processes to a feebler tendency. In
the article of 1915 (p. 216) already mentioned, the hypothesis is
made more explicit by the affirmation that the cells of the cortex,
in which the processes released through the peripheral stimulation
develop and to which the sensations correspond, contain, further,
other substances in which a second physiological process is set up,
to which the tone of feeling is said to correspond. This process
is, according to Ziehen, facultative. The conception might seem
to owe its rise to Ewald Hering's theory of the antagonistic
processes in the visual substance.

Ziehen finds that his theory agrees with the following observations: tones of feeling may be absent; they have not been proved
to exist by isolation; they are capable of an increase in intensity;
as regards characteristic, quality, and intensity, they are dependent on the quality, intensity, locality, and duration of the
sensation; there is nothing in the stimulus which bears specially
on the tone of feeling; the tone of feeling can unite with all qualities
of sensation and is influenced to a very much greater degree by
representations than are qualities of sensation. Ziehen emphasizes as a positive fact that "the sensorial tone of feeling varies
exactly like any other sensation in intensity, quality, and locality."
(*Grundlagen der Psychologie*, II, p. 215, 221.) The author concludes from this that sensation and its tone of feeling cannot be
essentially different from one another. This can mean nothing
else but that the tone of feeling must also be considered as a
sensation. It is at this point that Ziehen's theory, in spite of its
deviation in details, ends by agreeing with that of Stumpf.

With regard to the above observations, it is certainly correct
that tones of feeling may be absent. There can be no doubt about
this. There are sensations without tones of feeling. Nevertheless, respecting this, I think, certain particulars are open to discussion. I may mention, for example, that, given an increasing
stimulus, there is observable, sometimes, in the feeling-curve, a
point of indifference or a brief space of indifference, which fact
seems to me to conflict with Ziehen's hypothesis. If I experiment with a sweet solution, for instance, and try to compare the
tones of feeling accompanying the sensation during the con-

tinuously increasing stimulation, I observe at the outset a growing pleasant feeling, then intervenes a point or a brief space in which I perceive neither pleasantness nor decided unpleasantness, and then unpleasantness appears which augments with the further increase of the stimulus.

As for the assertion that a tone of feeling never appears in isolation, the following observations are to the point. In his *Grundriss der Psychologie*, 1893 (p. 233), Oswald Külpe remarks that in his experience there are feelings free from sensations. In 1905 (*Archiv für die gesamte Psychologie*, VI, p. 383 ff.) I myself communicated cases in which apparently unmotivated feelings, arising in a thoroughly dependable observer in a condition of quite normal wakefulness, called forth a sudden change in the general mood. These results testify against Ziehen's theory. Oskar Vogt, in 1897, seems to have observed a similar phenomenon in a subject whom he had placed under hypnosis. More particularly, I cannot admit that tones of feeling are localizable. One is liable to error in this respect. In all cases, however, in which the tone of feeling appears with any vividness, it has, so far as my observations bear me out, no circumscription of locality. This militates against the assertion that sensation and its tone of feeling are of like nature. Then, if they are not of like, they must be of different nature, and this, indeed, is my conviction.

There is not time to go into other sensualistic theories such as the well-known James-Lange theory. I will only remark that the peculiar nature of the feeling-tone of sensation cannot, I am convinced, be explained by this theory either.

We now come to the conception of Wilhelm Wundt. Wundt's theory of feeling developed gradually. His views in these matters gained in limpidity through his polemics with Horwicz, and in depth through the work of his pupils who had turned to good advantage the improvements which the registration methods of expressive movements had undergone in the domain of physiology, principally through Angelo Mosso. Until about 1896 Wundt retained his affirmative position as to the pleasantness-unpleasantness theory, which Stumpf and Ziehen also advocated and with them many others such as Külpe and Titchener, although if we look through his works today, we find indications even in the first edition of his *Grundzüge der physiologischen Psychologie* that this theory was not destined permanently to satisfy him. And, indeed, whoever delves down into his own personal domain of feeling must, I think, come to the conclusion that it is much too manifold to be forced into a system as simple as that of the pleasure-displeasure scheme. Our task would be considerably simplified if we could reduce everything in the domain of feeling to these terms. But the matter is not so simple. If, therefore, in the investigation of complexes of feeling we are confronted by more than can be expressed by the simple pleasure-displeasure system, it is surely patent that this "more" must be contained in the elements of which those complexes are composed. A profound study of this problem gave rise to Wilhelm Wundt's tridimensional system of feeling, which is planned on the analogy of the tridimensional system of light and color sensations.

This theory is so well known that I need not expound it here. Only my personal attitude towards it calls for a few words. I hold the elementary feeling, as it appears in the feeling-tone of sensation, to be essentially different from the sensation itself. In my opinion Wundt's tridimensional system is a grand attempt to emerge from the chaos of all the manifold and contradictory views about the domain of feeling, and to point out a new road for the forward march of investigation. The lasting value of this system lies, to my thinking, in the indisputable demonstration that the old pleasure-displeasure theory is inadequate. Its intrinsic value will remain untouched, therefore, even if, as is probable, the further course of investigation should demand modifications as to detail. The conviction, however, that the problem of feeling can be solved only upon the basis of a multidimensionality of the single feeling will, I believe, permanently hold its ground in psychology. Wundt worked out his system on the foundation of the newly acquired results of the expression method. I recall with pleasure, tinged with sadness, how, many years ago, in the pulse-curves of Sellmann's investigations, he demonstrated to me the correctness of his theory.

Like Stumpf and Ziehen, Oswald Külpe and Edward Titchener are also amongst the opponents of Wundt's system of feeling. Both, alas, have been taken from us by premature decease. In Külpe's case, we cannot see whether he, in the further course of his work, even though not surrendering completely to Wundt, might not eventually have fought his way through to the acceptance of the multidimensionality of the feelings. Certain passages in his works relating to the domain of feeling, as well as personal conversations which I had with this highly esteemed friend, lead me to believe that this would not have been impossible.

Concerning the objections which Titchener has raised to Wundt's theory of feeling, I freely admit, amongst other things, that he is right in maintaining that the tone of feeling varies with the extension of the spatial contents of sensation. In the case of colors I myself have frequently been able to furnish proof of this fact.

But it does not appear to me to follow that Wundt's system of feeling is, as Titchener thinks, "illogical." Since Wundt took into account, in addition to the quality and intensity of the feelings, only their direction, he doubtless did so deliberately. Duration represents the most general condition for every psychic experience, consequently also for the experience of space. There are numerous experiences which contain nothing spatial, but there is no experience of space for which temporal duration is not a *conditio sine qua non*. Duration is, thus, the more general condition. This is the point of view which guided Wundt in working out the new theory of feeling. I am unable to see anything illogical in it.

I must agree with Titchener's further objection that Wundt does not distinguish sufficiently between experiences which we call "calm" (*Beruhigung*) and "depression," but uses those expressions synonymously. I notice this deficiency whenever I study Wundt's theory of feeling. "Depression" is without a doubt, a composite process of feeling to begin with, a mood, if you will, and is certainly different from the experience which we call "calm." When we are depressed, we are not calm. Personally, I use the term "calm" because it seems to me to be the more consistent.

Our time does not allow us to discuss, point by point, the other objections which Titchener raises against the tridimensional system of feeling. I acknowledge, however, that they all seem to me of importance. I must add, nevertheless, that not only Külpe's objections but still more those of Titchener strengthen me in my conviction that the old pleasure-displeasure theory has not a wide enough outlook to embrace the variety of experiences of feeling. Only upon the foundation of the multidimensional system can the problem of feeling, so important for the comprehension of our whole psychic life, be finally solved. To have proved this is Wilhelm Wundt's great achievement. There are, indeed, more elementary feelings than experiences of pleasantness and unpleasantness, whether we call them, with Wundt, "excitement" and "calm," "tension" and "relaxation," or otherwise. The great variety of expressions by which every language indicates the multiplicity of experiences of feeling is indeed proof of it. It is at this point that we must begin afresh. All the results obtained up to the present must be taken into consideration and the elementary feelings arising in every separate field of sensation must be compared with one another by that method, first of all, which Wundt has aptly called the method of impression.

Investigation on these new lines will eventually settle the question whether the terms applied to the several experiences of feeling

are to be looked upon as class-concepts, or whether all feelings
belonging to one category are all exactly like one another. To a
certain degree the question is independent of whether we shall
recognize a unidimensional or a multidimensional system of feeling.
The supporters of the unidimensional system would formulate it
thus: Are there different pleasantnesses and unpleasantnesses or
are all feelings of pleasantness and unpleasantness alike? This
apparently simple question is hard to answer. Without venturing
to give a positive answer, I confess that I incline to the opinion
that the latter is not the case. The feeling of pleasure which I
experience in tasting a sweet solution appears to me, for example,
to be qualitatively different from that which arises in me at the
sight of colors. But, as I say, many accurate experiments are
necessary before this question can be finally settled.

With respect to the method of expression, which obtained its
name from Oswald Külpe, the many carefully controlled experiments which were conducted according to it have so far led to no
uniform results. On the contrary, the discrepancies in the results
of the several investigators have been extraordinarily great. We
conclude from this that not all the experiments were carried out
under the same conditions, and it may be asked whether this be
really possible. We must always remember, when registering the
pulse, the breathing, the blood-pressure, etc., that these processes
are not given to us in order that we may learn from them without
further effort the laws to which the domain of feeling is subject,
but that we possess in them merely motor reactions in the service of the *physical* organism. These very complicated physiological processes are therefore only concomitant phenomena. And
the question with which we are confronted can be this only: To
what degree is a *constant* relation between psychic experience and
its expression demonstrable under perfectly definite psychic and
physiological conditions? If this preliminary question is not
finally settled, we shall not be able to rely absolutely upon the results obtained by means of the method of expression. In the
experiments conducted in my institute upon this question, we
have found that the pneumogram in general reveals more in this
respect than the sphygmogram. Dr. Ponzo, for instance, has
for many years worked at the task of rendering possible, under
the most diversified conditions and under the most absolute exclusion obtainable of all easily arising sources of error, the recognition of the expression of simple will-processes in the breathing-
curve. He decided to begin his work not with the simple feelings
but with simple will-processes, because the latter are more easily
controlled by the expression method, and because their expression

appears more distinctly in the pneumogram. I cannot go into the details here, but in general I may say that, upon the basis of Ponzo's experiments, we are compelled to recognize the subjection to definite laws of the expression of the will-factor in the breathing-curve. This induces us to hope that eventually the expression of simple and of composite feelings may be recognized in a more unequivocal manner than has been possible heretofore. Ponzo's numerous works are, for the most part, published in the *Archivio Italiano di Psicologia.* Personally, I remain convinced that the methods of measuring blood-pressure may also be used for such purposes to great advantage, but my experience goes to prove that the corresponding instruments need improvement for very exact determinations.

I will not enter into the question of the processes in the brain which underlie the feelings. On this subject nearly every psychologist has still his own particular hypothesis. Perhaps we may hope that exact observations in pathological cases may throw new light upon this unexplored field.

Respecting the question discussed by the older authors and again in modern psychology, whether in the development of the living being the sensations or their feelings be primary, I can say only that the experiments which I have performed upon little children lead me to conclude that in human beings both phenomena appear together from the very beginning, and I may add that my microscopic observations of lower forms of life tend to show that, even in these, sensations do not seem to arise without a tone of feeling. All these various observations have led me to look skeptically upon the theory according to which sensations have developed out of feelings.

CHAPTER 7

EMOTION AND THOUGHT

A MOTOR THEORY OF THEIR RELATIONS

Margaret F. Washburn
Vassar College

In what sense, and for what reasons, do emotions paralyze thought; and when and why, if ever, do they aid it? These are the questions which in the short time at my disposal I am not, indeed, hoping to answer adequately, but on which I wish to offer a few reflections. The reflections will be made from the point of view of a motor psychology whose main assumptions I will ask you for the time to accept.

The first assumption is that while consciousness exists and is not a form of movement, it has as its indispensable basis certain motor processes, and that the only sense in which we can explain conscious processes is by studying the laws governing these underlying motor phenomena. The second assumption is that the motor accompaniment of thinking, as distinguished from sensation, consists of slight, incipient or tentative muscular contractions, which if fully performed would be visible or audible reactions to a situation, but which as only tentatively performed are a kind of rehearsal of the reactions. They may also occur unconsciously. Both full and tentative movements may be organized into systems, which may be of movements either simultaneously performed, as when we play the piano with both hands, or successively performed, as when we repeat a phrase; they may also either be steady tonic muscular contractions, such as are involved in maintaining an attitude (these I have called static movement systems), or involve actual change of position (these I have called phasic movement systems). All association of ideas and thus all thinking involves on this hypothesis the organization of tentative movements into systems.

But the word thought may be used in two senses. It may mean reverie or undirected thinking, or it may mean thinking directed towards a problem or purpose. In the first case, each idea suggests the one that follows it, but here its influence ends and our thoughts wander: A suggests B and then is forgotten, while B suggests C without aid from A. In the other case, that of directed thinking, a long series of ideas is governed by the idea of an end, problem, or purpose, and irrelevant wandering thoughts are inhibited. Now the third main assumption that I shall ask you to bear in mind is that the peculiarly persistent influence of the idea of an end or purpose as compared with that of ordinary ideas is due to its association with a persistent bodily attitude or static movement system which I have elsewhere called the activity attitude. I have said of this attitude that "in its intenser degrees it is revealed to introspection as the 'feeling of effort.'[1] . . . . Introspection further indicates that it is not due to shifting innervations but to a steady and persistent set of innervations. It appears from introspection, also, to be in its intenser forms a bodily attitude involving a kind of tense quietness, a quietness due not to relaxation but to a system of static innervations." Through the inherent and characteristic persistence of the innervations involved in the activity attitude as members of a static movement system, the innervations connected with the problem situation may exert the long enduring influence which is characteristic of directed thinking. This theory holds that "the motor innervations underlying the consciousness of effort are not mere accompaniments of directed thought, but an essential part of the cause of directed thought"—a proposition that has recently received support from the results of experiments by A. G. Bills,[2] indicating the impossibility of thought during complete muscular relaxation.

The motor theory under consideration thus bases all thinking on the occurrence of tentative movements, and bases directed thinking on the occurrence of a persistent motor innervation here called the activity attitude. Whatever interferes with tentative movements will inhibit all thinking; whatever interferes with the activity attitude will inhibit directed thinking. The tentative movements underlying thinking are, it is reasonable to suppose, chiefly those of the smaller and more delicate muscles of the body, such as those of the eyes, the fingers, and above all the muscles involved in speech. For it is impossible that the large muscles, say of the arms and legs, should be capable of enough variety of movement to supply the multitude of differing movements needed to form the basis of ideas. In the activity attitude, on the other hand, it is largely the trunk muscles that are concerned, as may be introspectively observed in its intenser form, the feeling of effort.

While the assumptions about thought which have just been outlined may not command assent, we shall all agree in the follow-

[1] *Movement and Mental Imagery* (New York, 1916), pp. 161–2.
[2] "The Influence of Muscular Tension on the Efficiency of Mental Work," *American Journal of Psychology*, XXXVIII (1927), 227–251.

ing statements about emotion. An emotion occurs in a situation of vital significance to the organism; primitively, perhaps, the flight, fighting, or mating situations. In such a situation, the possibilities of response may be divided into several classes. First, there may occur adaptive movements of the striped muscles, adequately meeting the situation: movements of flight, fighting, or mating. Secondly, there may be non-adaptive movements of the striped muscles. Some of these, like human facial expressions, are survivals of movements formerly adaptive, or adaptive under conditions somewhat but not wholly similar. But the most striking instance of non-adaptive movements is constituted by what may be called the motor explosion: the kicks and screams of the baffled child, the curses and furniture abuse of the baffled adult, the wild expansive movements of extreme joy. A motor explosion tends to happen when adaptive response is impossible. Thirdly, there may occur internal changes produced through the sympathetic and glandular systems.

On a motor theory, the question as to when and how emotion will interfere with thought becomes the question as to which of the various things we do in an emotional situation are likely to interfere with the things we do in thinking. Which will tend most to interrupt the tentative movements underlying ideas and the activity attitude underlying directed thinking: adaptive striped muscle reactions, non-adaptive striped muscle reactions, or visceral reactions produced through the sympathetic and endocrine systems?

Clearly, one motor process can interfere with another only when it is physically impossible for the two movements or attitudes to occur together, as for example it is impossible to raise and lower the arm at the same time. Nothing can interfere with a movement but another movement. The motor theory would go farther and say that when one nervous process inhibits another, it must be because the two are connected with incompatible movements. Further, what is true of single movements is true of their combinations: whenever two movement systems are simultaneously stimulated, if one contains a movement incompatible with some movement in the other, the systems cannot be simultaneously performed and will tend to inhibit each other, unless, indeed, they become smaller by dropping out the incompatible elements. The functioning of such smaller movement systems may be regarded as responsible for dissociation, and a tendency toward it as characteristic of those individuals whom we call hysterics.

We may turn, then, to the first type of response possible in an emotional situation, namely, adaptive movements of the striped muscles. Will these be incompatible with thought? It is obvious that one motor process will be more likely to disturb others, the more muscles it involves, that is, the more wide-spread its distribution over the body. Now definitely adaptive movements of the striped muscles, as compared with the non-adaptive motor explosion, will as a rule involve only definitely demarcated groups of muscles, and these will be for the most part the larger muscles—those of the limbs. Thinking, on the other hand, is, according to the hypothesis here adopted, based chiefly on contractions of small muscles capable of a large repertory of different movements. Stratton[3] reports the case of an aviator who, during a tail-spin fall of four thousand feet, made all the movements needed to remedy the trouble with his plane and straighten it out, while experiencing a series of intensely vivid mental images from his past life, beginning with childhood. These images, on the theory here presented, would be based on tentative movements in certain muscles, which were evidently not incompatible with actual movements in the other muscles needed to meet the emergency. Stratton deduces from this and other similar cases that it is only the intenser degrees of emotion which interfere either with coordinated action or with thinking. It is true, however, that the more serious the situation which excites emotion, the more extensive the adaptive movements are likely to be. Thus one fighting situation may require only a short, well-directed attack, while another demands a desperate struggle calling into play all the body muscles, and, by virtue of the alert watching of the enemy's movements needed, many of the smaller ones. Except in extreme cases, however, adaptive movements, it would appear, need not interfere with thought.

What, now, is the relation of thinking to the second type of response in an emotional situation? The motor explosion or non-adaptive striped muscle response has been often overlooked by psychologists. For example, Wechsler[4] divides emotional reactions into "*choc*" or visceral responses and "behavior reactions," which involve orientation to the stimulus, thus ignoring the motor explosion, which is neither visceral nor oriented. Yet it is really an important and interesting phenomenon. As we have noted, it occurs when adaptive response is impossible. This is usually because such responses are repressed either by external force or by internal inhibitions, as in impotent anger. The case

[3] G. M. Stratton, "An Experience during Danger and the Wider Functions of Emotion," *Problems of Personality* (New York, 1925).

[4] D. Wechsler, "What Constitutes an Emotion?" *Psychological Review*, XXXII (1925), 235–240.

of the motor explosion resulting from joy, by the way, is a curious one. People do, of course, all sorts of wildly irrelevant things in extreme joy. Now here adaptive response is impossible not because it is being prevented, but because it is non-existent. There is nothing one can do in joy that has any essential appropriateness to the situation, in the way that knocking a man down has essential appropriateness to anger. Joy represents not a situation where something needs to be done, but the release of energy that has been occupied in long-continued tensions, which, since it has no pre-ordained channel, diffuses itself into many channels.

There is high probability that the motor explosion, in which any and all muscular systems, including those of speech, may take part, will interfere with thinking, if thinking has any motor basis at all. A man in a wildly gesticulating, vociferous fit of rage has no muscles left at liberty to think with. In its milder form, the motor explosion is identical with general restlessness, which also involves a wide range of muscles, although in less violent contractions. And it should be noted that a motor explosion may occur in the form of tentative rather than actual movements. In such a case, I would suggest, it forms the basis of the experience of mental panic. When no adaptive movement is possible, there may occur impulses towards all kinds of non-adaptive movements; these tentative movements in all directions may well produce the effect of making our brains whirl, as we say, and would evidently through their widespread character be antagonistic to clear thought.

Thirdly, will the visceral reactions, those dependent on the autonomic and glandular systems, interfere with thinking? Why should they, on a motor theory of thought? If thinking is based on movements and attitudes of the striped muscles, nothing can interfere with it but antagonistic movements and attitudes of these muscles. And the internal changes produced through the autonomic and endocrine systems do not involve striped muscles. May we not say, then, that visceral changes *per se* cannot disorganize thinking?

Visceral changes have, however, indirect effects upon the external muscles. Cannon has pointed out their important influence upon *adaptive* responses; the pouring of sugar into the blood, the neutralizing of fatigue poisons, the checking of digestive processes—all serve the purpose of producing more powerful reactions of an adaptive nature, for instance, movements of fighting or flight. Such movements, as we have just seen, are not necessarily incompatible with thought. What, now, is the relation of *non-adaptive* movements to visceral changes? Since non-adaptive movements are in themselves useless, and since, as we have seen, they are likely to interfere with thought, have such movements any function, or shall we class them with nature's superfluous products? We *seem* to "feel better" after them! Pascal and Davesne[5] in a recent article suggest that the non-adaptive movements called "tics" are useful in preventing the emotion from invading the "vegetative" or visceral plane, that is, the autonomic and endocrine systems; the more the emotion discharges into motor paths the less it goes into visceral paths. Various writers imply that the organism seeks to avoid the visceral discharge; why should it be avoided? The normal function of discharge into the autonomic and glandular level is to aid the performance of adaptive movements. Should these be interfered with either the visceral discharge is worked off in motor explosion, or it remains in the organic level. And according to Cannon,[6] "if these results of emotion and pain are not 'worked off' by action, it is conceivable that the excessive adrenin and sugar in the blood may have pathological effects." When, then, adaptive movements remain blocked, it is probably for the safety of the organism that the visceral processes should work themselves off in a non-adaptive motor explosion. And so they have indirectly, though not directly, a disturbing influence on thought.

When and how does emotion aid thought? There is time for only a few reflections on this topic.

It is a well-known fact that emotional states may function as the associative links between ideas, thus forming what in the Freudian terminology are called complexes. Thinking of this type, however, is highly inefficient, and emotion cannot be said to do thought any service in thus binding together what might better be left separate. Another type of thinking which may occur along with emotion is, as we have seen, dissociated thinking, made possible by the shrinkage of movement systems so that incompatible movements are dropped out. MacCurdy,[7] in his *Psychology of Emotion*, regards such subconscious and co-conscious ideas as forming the very essence of *affect*, the conscious aspect of emotion. It is, naturally enough, from pathological cases that he draws the evidence for his statement that "the quality of the affect is determined by the sum total of unconscious complexes that are activated, and may therefore have an infinite variety."

[5] C. Pascal and J. Davesne, "Chocs émotionnels, pathogènes, et thérapeutiques," *Journal de psychologie*, XXIII (1926), 456–487.

[6] W. B. Cannon, *Bodily Changes in Pain, Hunger, Fear, and Rage* (New York, 1915), p. 196, note.

[7] J. T. MacCurdy, *The Psychology of Emotion, Morbid and Normal* (New York, 1925), p. 86.

But again, emotion cannot be said to *aid* thought in thus permitting itself to be accompanied by dissociated ideas.

Yet if thought has a motor basis, it must need some energy, and the visceral changes in emotion are supposed to supply an extra amount of energy; they should be able, therefore, actually to aid thought. According to the hypothesis here presented, efficient thinking requires two factors: a varied supply of tentative movements to serve as the basis of ideas, and a persistent, tense attitude of the trunk muscles associated with some of these ideas to secure their influence during a considerable period. Now when the amount of extra energy generated in the visceral discharge is not too great, it may pass over into the tentative movements underlying ideas, so that their number and speed are increased and new combinations of them occur without the long effort of directed thinking. Experience shows that the flow of ideas is heightened by mild emotion. Moreover, a part of the emotional energy may, even in discharging through *non-adaptive* movements, relax an inhibition that has been repressing the flow of ideas. But the most important function of emotion in aiding thought will relate to the activity attitude.

Directed thinking never occurs without a motive. Reverie, the drifting of ideas, may go on while we are indifferent, but if we suddenly begin purposeful thinking, it is because some affective process has been stirred up. And also, of course, because direct, external reaction to the stimulus that thus taps the storehouse of the organism's energy is blocked; if it were not blocked, there would be no need of thinking. Thus we have directed thinking as the outcome of the very type of situation that occasions emotion; but in directed thinking the energy thus set free and blocked finds its outlet in the tense quietness of the activity attitude instead of in the random and uncoordinated movements of the motor explosion. The setting free of energy in the visceral levels, so far from being incompatible with thought, is necessary for directed thought.

Why does this energy sometimes discharge into restlessness and useless movements and sometimes into the attitude of tense quietness? At least three factors seem to be concerned in the decision of this point: the amount of energy released by the situation, and the thresholds of discharge of the non-adaptive pathways and of the activity attitude, respectively. If the situation is desperate and the amount of energy set free is great, the tensely quiet attitude and the tentative movements of thought, requiring so little energy, will be inadequate outlets. But evidently the seriousness of the situation is not the only factor; in less desperate situations it will not always be the weaker desires that produce in a given individual directed, purposeful planning and the stronger ones mere restlessness. With a given amount of energy stirred up by the situation, certain conditions evidently open the pathways to diffuse discharge and block those to the concentrated tonic discharge of the activity attitude. One of these conditions is certainly fatigue. In fatigue all muscles tend to relax, and the activity attitude, which involves steady and continued contraction of certain muscles, is more readily fatigued than is restlessness, which involves diffuse contractions followed by relaxations. Fatigue is involved also in another condition that determines whether we shall think or merely be restless, namely, the lack of ideas. No one can keep on trying to think on a subject of which he has no knowledge. In fruitful thinking, when out of a storehouse of information one relevant idea after another occurs to us, the activity attitude is refreshed by little relaxations along the way and fatigue is postponed.

On the motor theory here suggested, emotion, then, interferes with thought only when the movements made in emotion are incompatible with the movements and attitudes essential to thinking. This will be most likely to happen when the energy set free by the glandular processes in emotion discharges into the diffuse and random movements of the motor explosion. Emotion will aid thought when conditions favor the discharge of this energy into the maintenance of a steady innervation of the trunk muscles, which is the basis of introspectively reported feelings of will, determination, activity, or effort, and which secures the steady influence of the idea of a goal.

DISCUSSION

DR. DUNLAP (*The Johns Hopkins University*): Dr. Washburn's paper has given rise in me to some emotions which I hope will not interfere with my thinking. Before I take up the main point that I want to inflict on you in connection with this paper, I would like to say that I wish that Dr. Washburn's optimistic statement were true. I am afraid it is not. She said, "People cannot keep on trying to think about topics of which they have no knowledge." Would to God that were true! I don't know what would happen to much of our psychology if it were true.

Some of these emotions were aroused by this fact, that I suppose I can say that Dr. Washburn and I are the pioneers in this movement on theoretical foundation of thought in motor processes. My own formulae were put forth before behaviorism had begun to behave, and I have deplored—I suspect Dr. Washburn also has deplored—the extremes to which the motor theory has been pushed in behaviorism. I feel that before the connection between thinking and emotion shall be worked out on the basis of the motor theory—the motor hypothesis of thinking—that hypothesis itself needs a great deal more elaboration and correction.

In the first form I assumed—I think Dr. Washburn still assumes, if I understand her paper correctly, as she did at the start—that all thinking requires muscular contraction. The more I attempt to connect that theory with the actual facts of life and with the learning process, as we know it now from our laboratory work, the more improbable does that become. It is a serious question at present whether that theory can be still held. Experimental work now in progress in several universities bearing upon the particular point as to whether implicit reactions—I do not know whether Dr. Washburn would accept that behavioristic term, but it expresses the older view—can be demonstrated as occurring in typical thought processes. These experiments must tell the tale, before we can go further.

Personally I have had to modify my theory and assume that the thought processes during the learning period, during the period of modification, are motor in full. Muscular contractions are involved. I believe we can demonstrate many of the things Dr. Washburn has pointed out in connection with disturbances of the thought process in the incipient or learning stages. I have a suspicion that after thought has become crystallized, as it were, a great deal of our thought is routine thinking, even when it is highly efficient, that that stage has passed away, and that the muscular contractions are no longer needed.

That is an experimental matter, a matter that will be experimentally determined I am tolerably sure within the next five years, which is of vital importance in this matter which Dr. Washburn has brought up.

There are one or two other things, if I may take a little of your time, which I would like to speak about. One is a minor matter with regard to the illustration which Dr. Washburn used, taken from Dr. Stratton's story of the aviator. I am beginning more and more to distrust all that type of evidence. It is a very good illustration of a very interesting type of evidence. From the point of view of dreams, I no longer believe people dream what they afterwards record. There is very strong evidence in dreams as recalled and in cases of this kind as recalled of illusions of memory occurring. Conditions are exceedingly favorable for a man afterwards speaking as if he did think so and so during that period, when he did not think it. All that is a very interesting type of evidence which requires scrutiny. It does not at all invalidate Dr. Washburn's illustration.

I do want to ask Dr. Washburn whether in the present state of her views she is implying the peripheral doctrine or the central. It is a very vital matter concerning thinking in connection with emotions.

Yesterday I was upholding the peripheral view. Dr. Cannon was upholding the central view if I understood him. Fortunately, I was all pepped up to discuss Cannon's paper last night, but unfortunately for me at least I could not get near enough to the stage to hear what he said. So that had to go by. So I may be forgiven for introducing something which has reference to both Dr. Washburn's paper and what I gathered yesterday and what better eared observers told me last night about Dr. Cannon's paper.

The work which Dr. Cannon has been doing in determining the pathways through which the reflexes, or what I should prefer to call the transits, should go is one of the most important works of its kind that has been carried on for years. That as far as I see has no bearing on the James-Lange theory, on the peripheral theory, or the central. On either theory these transits must occur, and what we call the expressions of the emotions be produced.

This question (whether or not in a pre-neurological state, that is, in our experience when we do not try to associate things with the neurological machinery, whether they be produced as Descartes would have it by the process of discharging from the brain—that is, innervation feelings in the old sense—or whether they be like the perceptual parts of our experience due to the peripheral sensation of setting up complete new transits) is the issue on which we are divided—the innervation feeling, the Cartesian theory, on the one hand, and the James-Lange theory, which as a matter of fact neither James nor Lange believed, on the other hand.

I am not sure whether Dr. Washburn is upholding here what I should call the James-Lange theory, that is, the peripheral view, or the central view. I am interested in that. It is not, of course, essential to the point Dr. Washburn is making, but I am very much interested in whether she is assuming that this discharge of energy—here again is a concept of a very dangerous sort, talking of energy as if there were a reservoir of it somewhere in the body, and all you have to do is to open a spigot to get it here, and if you do not open it, you get your pressure some place else, a dangerous metaphor, but not important in this particular discussion—produces the external disturbance, which I would be willing to admit is not essentially visceral, and if in turn it produces the afferent impulse which leads to it.

With regard to a point which I understand Dr. Cannon to have made concerning the peripheral theory, the very fewness of visceral sensory neurones is a point on which I have previously laid stress in connection with this theory as related to the other fact which I understand Dr. Cannon to bring up, i.e., that the analysis of the emotion into visceral and somatic components, if it can be so analyzed, has been strangely delayed in the light of the fact that the human race has been experiencing these emotions for a good many centuries. These things seem to be connected. The fact that we have not the apparatus receptorally for discrimination viscerally as we have for discrimination tactually and visually and in an auditory way—this fact contributes to the difficulty of analysis or identification.

Secondly, the very enclosure of our viscera within our bodies prevents our making experimental determinations, which we make in our daily lives as children, varying the stimuli, so that we perform in the course of years an exact special localizing analysis through our external senses, which is impossible for the internal organs. That difficulty of analysis and the dependence of that analysis upon the development of refined experimental methods which have only recently, if ever, been developed, the fact that the human race would not be able to analyze these visceral contents, is exactly what we would expect from our psychological knowledge of the nature and conditions of analysis and localization of external factors, so that those factors fit together and fit in with the peripheral hypothesis.

Again—and I won't do any more of this retroactive talking—just one more point. Suppose a person who had never heard any of the instruments of an orchestra separately to be in a room through the window of which he might hear from time to time a splendid symphony orchestra playing. Would that man ever know analytically what that mass of sounds is composed of? No. We have every reason to believe, from what we do know of the psychology of massive experience, that he would never be able to analyze such experience into the sound of the flute, the harp, and so on. But somebody might, without acoustical experiments in the room, without the instruments, explain it to him. We have not been able to analyze this. We cannot stimulate them separately. We stimulate them only in large masses. We have had no experience in the elements, and only in the round-about way can we perform that analysis.

But finally, with regard to that point of view, with regard to the introspective experiments with adrenalin, with regard to certain points in Professor Washburn's paper, what I have been trying to point out unsuccessfully yesterday and today is that an emotion is not just one limited thing. In fact if I were to say what I really think, without trying to exaggerate, not only is there no such thing as an emotion, there is no such thing as thinking, there is no such thing as perception; those are terms of our laboratories. There is no process separated from thinking. We have a much more highly integrated situation, in which, for the purpose of discussion, we omit certain fundamental facts and include others. Just as we say this light is the stimulus, when as a matter of fact it is not, but we use that term for the purpose of our discussion.

Interference of thought with perception, interference of thought with action, is a much more complicated thing—I imagine I am not criticizing Dr. Washburn, for she will agree with me—is a much more complicated matter than we might assume from Professor Washburn's brief discussion, that is, in no case is it true that we have an emotion as one set of processes, that we have thought as another, that we have perception as another. We have a single set of processes of a highly complicated order, in which we can artificially for convenience, and falsely if we are misled, distinguish this factor and that factor, which are distinguishable in thought, but never are actually separate.

DR. WASHBURN: A great deal of what Professor Dunlap has said I agree with, more apparently than he would have expected me to. There was nothing in my paper to indicate any hypothesis as to the basis of emotion as a conscious experience. I did not say that emotion resulted from visceral processes. I said that in an emotion, among the other changes which occur in the body, were these visceral changes. So that all he has to say about the impossibility of analyzing the visceral processes, and so forth, is something with which I quite heartily agree, but which was not germane to the ideas which I was trying to put forward.

The most important point, of course, at least the most important point to me, is the point Dr. Dunlap raised first, the fact that he is becoming convinced by the course of experiments that much of our thinking goes on without any motor accompaniment. Now, I believe I am quite prepared to find that experiments will fail to discover any motor accompaniment in a great deal of our thinking. But it seems to me possible, and in fact altogether probable, almost self-evident, that as the tentative movements in thinking become organized into systems some single slight movement may by association, by the ordinary associative processes, come to stand for, to act in place of, such an entire system.

This is the whole process of symbolizing in thinking. If it is possible in ideas, I do not see why it is not possible in tentative movements. So that a motor process, accompanied by quite a complicated set of movements, may be reduced by habituation to one physiological process represented by only some insignificant movements, which it might be impossible to demonstrate by the very rough apparatus which we still have at our disposal.

PROFESSOR JAMES MELROSE (*Milliken University*): I should like to ask on the same point Professor Dunlap raised and Dr. Washburn has just answered more specifically what is included in thinking as we have heard it used. Watson, for example, divides thinking into three parts: first of all, a mere rehearsal of long habits; secondly, thinking upon matters that are not new; and finally, thinking as applied to the solving of new problems. I wondered if it would not answer the question brought up by Dr. Dunlap if we confined the meaning of thinking arbitrarily to the last point. I wonder if he is thinking in the conception in which Dr. Washburn's paper was presented.

DR. WASHBURN: I intended to refer to all thinking, but, since the last type of thinking is the type of thinking that is most truly thinking and that is not reducible to automatic habits, that is the type it seems to me which presents the most interesting problem, and virtually I would be willing to confine myself to that type because of that fact. That is practically the only type of thinking in which perhaps we really use ideas.

PROFESSOR MELROSE: I have in mind, Mr. Chairman, that it has been, I think, proved by physiological test that in certain types of thinking there is no evidence of a large amount of metabolism, and consequently it would be difficult to find a large amount of concomitant bodily behavior. I wondered if, for example, certain types of thinking upon problems that were strictly theoretical (such as, for example, working upon the plans of a house that you might be intending to construct) would not have a considerable amount of motor activity, although you had no immediate motor problem; whereas, if you were thinking upon some line where for the most part you were thoroughly accustomed to the type of thought, the pattern of thought, and there was no motor action attendant at the time, would you have very much motor activity?

DR. WASHBURN: That would reduce to a place where the thinking had become so organized into systems of motor activity that one very slight movement might act as agent, so to speak, for the whole system.

DR. PRINCE (*Harvard University*): Some facts occurred to me during the reading of the paper, and I wonder if Dr. Washburn will inform me about them and reconcile them with the motor theory of thought?´ These are facts which have grown up in pathological fields. Now we have certain types of paralysis in which all the muscles of the face are involved, particularly those of the tongue and palate, a type of motor paralysis. In that kind of paralysis the person is unable to use those muscles at all, and yet is able to think perfectly clearly. Their mental processes are not interfered with at all. If muscular movements or movements of those small muscles are required, why should it not interfere with continued thought, unless Dr. Washburn means that it is not necessarily action of the muscles, but the effort of innervation?

Let us take the hypnotized subject, a subject that had been under observation for a long time, after coming out from that influence, after the amnesia or the hypnotic state. Now during the hypnotic state I taught her several characters of a shorthand of my own, which she could not possibly have known anything about. I taught her some of the characters. The experiment was one of subconscious perception. I taught her those characters. After she was awake I wrote in that polyglot shorthand of mine a phrase. I haven't a blackboard here on which I could write it or I would see how many here could translate it. I would be willing to give a dollar to a man who could translate it. And then I had the subject write the translation automatically with her hands and the hand wrote it out; mind you, she interpreted those characters or perceived them, thought them out, and wrote the translation with the hands, all of the time discussing with me other matters. Now, there was a matter of a mental process going on during the time of the experiment the subject was conversing with me. And it seemed that two kinds of thinking could go on at the same time. It does not matter whether one type is subconscious thinking or whether it is co-conscious thinking or what it may be. A mental process was going on, which is thinking.

Now, what I want to know is, how it can be reconciled with the motor theory of thinking.

Then take another test, one to which I referrred—the solution of mathematical problems while the person is thinking about something else. You know we have lots of such observations in everyday life, that for example of the mathematician who had the solution of a mathematical problem pop into his head spontaneously while he was thinking of something else. There are a great many such cases. I hypnotized the same subject and told her that when she was awake she was to solve a mathematical problem, to calculate the number of seconds intervening between certain hours. She would not know what the hours were until she was awake. When she was awake she did not know that any experiment at all was being done. So I arranged the experiment—I will not go into the details of it. She subconsciously received the data and performed the calculation. The calculation was made while the person was thinking about something else. Now, you have the facts. I won't take up more time.

CHAPTER 8

THE UTILITY OF EMOTIONS

W. B. Pillsbury
University of Michigan

My intention is to make an analysis of the facts, so far as known, that throw light upon whether we may regard emotion as having any utility in the scheme of man, and, if we answer in the affirmative, to ask what that utility may be. It pretends to offer no new facts but merely to summarize and coordinate those that we have.

The first step in the undertaking is to discover when and under what circumstances emotions occur. For its freedom from presupposition we may assume the behaviorist's attitude and study the conditions from their external side. We may assume that emotion accompanies only those types of behavior which have not been sufficiently automatized to be reflex. If that be true, all of the so-called instincts and instances of learned behavior would fall into one class of trial and error responses. If the situation be a new one, each response would be determined in the first place by the stimuli acting upon the organism and in the second place by the factors that selected one from among the various responses that resulted. In eating, for example, hunger, an internal stimulus, causes random movements that continue until food is found. When the food stimulus presents itself to taste, smell, or sight, the random movements are succeeded by the straight ahead eating movements. These continue until hunger is satisfied or the food is exhausted.

Each type of response divides into these two parts: the initial stimulus that incites to random movements, and the terminal stimulus that puts an end to the random movements. Emotion attaches to both of these initial and terminal situations. If we are to consider its utility, we must keep in mind the two situations and recognize that the emotions developed in each are distinct in function, although in objective and subjective characteristics they may be identical. *The stimulus that arouses any form of response for the first time nearly always has an emotional accompaniment.* If the stimulus is external and intense, the animal or child is either inhibited in all movements (paralysis or death-feigning response), makes a series of uncoordinated movements that may result in flight, or gives vent to more or less coordinated aggressive movements (defense movements). The overt acts are accompanied by incipient movements and contractions of internal muscles and glands that constitute a large part of what we ordinarily call emotion. Classed largely according to the nature of the overt responses, we call these the emotions of fear if the reaction be of the first two types and probably anger if of the third.

When the stimulus is internal, as in hunger, thirst, or sex, the movements are less vigorous although equally random in character. The animal merely wanders here and there until a new stimulus causes the responses necessary to satisfy or remove the inward disturbance. Similar random movements also arise when the animal is in good physical condition without particular external stimuli. These are the play movements. Here the emotion would be named largely from the nature of the internal diffuse movements, rather than from the initiating situation or the external response. In this group, too, we might have a condition of quiescence from slight stimulation, as in Watson's instance of the stimulation of the erogenous zone or in the cuddling of the kitten or child when stroked or lying against a warm or soft object. The emotion in the latter case would be very much like the ones that may present themselves as terminal stimuli. The external response or its lack is also the same.

In this whole group the emotion would seem to have no direct utility. *By emotion in this sense we need mean no more than the sum of accessory internal responses, the contraction of muscles not directly involved in the act, the contraction of the striped muscles in remote or neighboring parts of the body, the contraction of unstriped muscles active in respiration, circulation, digestion, and the secretions of glands, internal and external.* With each type of stimulus some are increased and others are inhibited. They contribute to the mental state we call emotion if we are not behaviorists, and so we may consider them as the emotions if we are speaking as behaviorists. How they help is still largely a matter of speculation. In the active movements, changes in circulation and respiration probably increase the energy of response. The adrenalin secretion has the same effect. Most of the other endocrines are too slow to be effective at the moment of action although their activity induced by earlier excitation may determine the type of response. O'Gonigal has suggested that the thyroids, by their secretions, produce the condition in which strong stimuli will evoke the tetanic death-feigning response, while adrenalin prepares for the defense reactions of anger. Here the condition of the endocrines determines the type of response and so of emotion. The emotional responses connected with the initial stimulus and response further or check the response itself, and are useful to that extent.

The emotions and affections connected with the terminal response are the fundamental determinants of animal and human conduct. With the exception of reflexes, all acts are developed from random responses, and responses continue until an emotional or affective condition puts an end to them. We say roughly that we keep trying until we find something that pleases us and then use that something, or stop. *What shall please is the real determinant of the actions that we call instinctive or learned.* This makes the hypothesis that all so-called instincts are trial and error responses different from ordinary habits in that the situations which arouse the responses are natural and of frequent occurrence and possibly become established with rather fewer responses than in the processes that we call learning. What is inherited, and so the determinant of the instinct, is the factor that selects between the different responses to the initial stimulus. This many speak of as affection, Thorndike as satisfaction, but we must look more deeply into the process if we are to make any pretense of understanding it.

Direct observation of the animal shows that the process of selection consists in little more than changing the random movements into a specific straight ahead one. The hungry rat runs here and there until he finds food. Then he begins to eat. The immediate selection depends upon the acceptance of the odors and taste. Suitable appearance and odor start the eating. If taste confirms them when the substance is taken into the mouth, chewing and swallowing succeed. If not, they are ejected, as Lloyd Morgan reports for his chicks with caterpillars. Similar analysis might be made of the sex-determined random movements. Curiosity would be only slightly different in that the original movements may start with a stimulus that might make possible one of two different reactions. The movements of approach, tentative in character, continue until they evoke movements of flight or use. These then replace the tentative movements. Objectively regarded, satisfaction is usually the substitution of a direct movement for a random tentative one.

The exception is found when the animal merely becomes quiescent in place of acting. This we see in the nestling of the tired animal into a smooth soft bed, or the cessation of movement induced by patting, by contact of the young with the mother or with other members of the species. We also have in this group the cessation of wandering when the social animal comes into a herd or group of its own kind. He wanders here and there when alone, but grazes calmly, lies down, or stands quietly when with others of the same species. The social approbation that is so effective in the learning of the child would have a marked effect in selecting the suitable random movement. This is the important factor in learning its native speech. The paralysis of movement that comes from social disapproval has an equally strong negative influence. At times, passive response may approach a positive character. Tolman, who has presented a somewhat similar analysis of instinct, suggests that the nesting of the bird follows somewhat this·course. Building the nest seems to be in many species rather a random type of activity. The materials are gathered, we may assume, as a result of a general restlessness from internal stimuli, and are put together in a somewhat hit-or-miss way. When the pile takes a shape that will contain the eggs, it serves as a stimulus for laying the eggs; then eggs and nest together stimulate the continued brooding. Each of these types of response or quiescence constitutes the physical accompaniment of satisfaction.

Accepting satisfaction as fundamentally a straight away type of response, we still have the question as to why one situation gives this reaction while others do not. In answer to this we can do no more than point again to hereditary connection. The response is always evoked by a stimulus. All that we can say is that the nervous connections inherited by the animal are of such a character that he must respond as he does. The odor of meat starts the approach mechanism; the odor of hydrogen sulphide, the withdrawal mechanism; the taste of biscuit initiates in rat or chick the swallowing movements; the taste of quinine, the ejecting reactions. All depends upon hereditary connections, and these connections initiate reflexes on the same principle that what we called the initial stimulus evoked the random search movement or the withdrawing movements of flight. *"Why" can only be answered in terms of evolution and natural selection.* That the animal or man does have these fundamental forms of response is the beginning of our explanation of all action and of all learning. We cannot, however, explain why he has them. They must be accepted. The feeling processes can be derived from them; they cannot be explained by the mental states.

If we reverse our question and ask to what the condition of satisfaction corresponds, we can answer only that it accompanies a straight ahead type of response, marked usually by approach and acceptance rather than rejection and flight. These straight ahead types of reactions are also accompanied by characteristic accessory responses, secretions of glands, normal peristaltic reactions, and with slight and well-coordinated contractions of the striped muscles. These serve to color the responses subjectively, and are useful incidentally to the performance of the reactions. It is hard to see that they make any important contribution to the selective activity itself, except as they further the responses. This analysis would tend to put the pleasant affections and emotions in the class of accompaniments of non-inhibited or furthering activities of the neuro-muscular mechanism, while the unpleasant would fall under the head of contractions that were mutually opposing each other, the hindrance group. The difference would lie in that our description does not assume any direction or purpose in the response of the organism as does Stout's old statement. On the contrary, the animal when he makes his first response is driven by stimuli he knows not where, and he is stopped or his activities turned in another direction by new stimuli. Both responses are determined by the innate nervous connections acted upon by the stimuli. *Pleasure, satisfaction, or emotion are to be looked upon as accompaniments not causes.*

Once this new connection is established between the original situation considered as stimulus and the new response determined by the terminal stimulus we have the beginning of learning. With repetition the activities that follow upon the original stimulus become less and less random, more and more direct, until with full learning the train of responses becomes unvarying. We need not go into the complexities of this problem, although learning is one of the functions that has been most frequently explained in terms of the emotional accompaniments.

Learning would not take place without the direction given by the terminal stimulus, but it is the repeated arriving at the point where the terminal stimulus may act that makes learning possible, rather than the emotional accompaniments themselves. The controversies as to the learning mechanism revolve about how the separate links in the chain of acts that attain the end may be forged or eliminated. Each must assume that the separate acts all finally bring the individual to the terminal stimulus. Without that stimulus to set an end to the random movements, no learning and no ordered action would be possible. The pleasant stimulus is more effective than the unpleasant because the pleasant begins a new series of acts which in the end remove the internal stimulus that produces the random movements, while the unpleasant merely drives the animal away and gives no conclusion to the drive. In a series of partial acts, however, the animal learns even more quickly to avoid an opening where it receives an electric shock than it does to take a path that leads to food. This, too, gives a new turn to the tentative movements, more strongly reinforced.

If we admit that it is not the emotional accompaniment but the repetition of the terminal stimulus in succession to the original exciting stimulation that is responsible for learning, we still may ask whether the incidental contractions, the overflow phenomena that James would make the basis of emotion, have any effect upon the formation of the connection. On this point the evidence is conflicting, so far as there is evidence at all. It is probably true that many, if not most, stimuli that initiate a new line of reaction and so stop the random movements are accompanied by diffuse bodily responses. Even most stimuli that give reflexes that may be transferred to other stimuli by conditioning have this accompaniment of non-essential responses. The meat probably arouses other overflow phenomena as well as the secretion of saliva. The sound of the bell need have no such effect. In the light reflex of the pupil, which Cason could transfer to a sound stimulus, there seems to be no necessary emotional accompaniment. There is no reason for assuming that the connection depends upon these added contractions and not upon the simultaneous occurrence of the two stimuli, even if we assume that they always accompany the reflex to be conditioned. It could be interpreted to mean only that any stimulus strong enough to produce a reflex that could be conditioned would also be strong enough to arouse the wide-spread incidental contractions.

Again, after the connection has been established between the exciting situation and the terminal stimulus and response, one tends to arouse the other. How this is brought about is not easy to investigate in the animal. In man, however, and here we must abandon the behavioristic assumptions, the situation at once recalls memories of the old terminal responses, or ways of eliminating the unpleasant present conditions. These memories have their emotional attachments, due in part at least to the actual rearousal of striped and unstriped muscular and glandular responses. The drive, if we may use Woodworth's terms, is not merely the neuro-muscular tendency to make random movements, coupled with the unpleasantness of the present stimulus, but has added to it the memories of old satisfactions with their pleasant emotional accompaniments. Even if there is nothing in the present situation to suggest where the old alleviating stimulus could be found, the memory that it has been found spurs to greater effort for the random movements and keeps one on the *qui vive* for the random thoughts that might solve the difficulty. It also serves to select from the ideas those that are more promising and reserves them for actual trial.

Here again the question arises whether the choice is in terms of pleasure or of emotional and affective phases in general. A better case can be made for this than for the statement that pleasure determines the selection of the original terminal stimulus. The pleasure comes, in fact, with the thought and before the actions begin. If, however, we are to keep to a parallelistic assumption and have only physical processes modify other physical processes, obviously not pleasure but the physical conditions that give rise to pleasure would be the determining and inciting force. The stimulus that arouses the memory, either directly or through the associative paths that evoke the memory, would also give us the overflow innervation of glands, and the preparatory activities of muscles. The hormones from the ductless glands would energize the nervous and muscular mechanism, in general; the activity of the nervous system would prepare specifically for the activities that had previously been useful. To these we must look for the real determinants, although the accompanying emotional and ideational experiences stand out introspectively as the incentives and constitute the drives of our conscious life.

Again, we have the fact that stimuli and situations, by virtue of what the behaviorists call conditioning or the more classic group were content to designate association, tend to become connected with innumerable other experiences and objects, and the emotion that attaches originally to each of these becomes transferred to the first in addition to the innate characteristics and accompaniments. No one would dare to say how much of the emotion aroused by a picture, by a human face or form, or even by simpler objects is an immediate natural or innate accompaniment and how much has been attached to it incidentally. Here the psychoanalyst would translate all to one type, but we need not accept his extreme assumptions to see the importance of transfer. The network of interrelations is so complicated that it almost justifies us in agreeing with our friends of the Gestalt school that we must think of the pattern as making the elements that compose it rather than having the pattern develop from the arrangement of the elements. It is this maze of cross-references that obscures the explanation and makes it impossible to distinguish between the inherited determinants of action and learning, the fundamental feelings and emotions, and the adventitious additions. These again, however, are derived from other inherited affective responses. They merely attached originally to other situations.

One might point out, although there is no space to develop it, that, even in the animal, where we have no introspective evidence, there must be similar neurological organizations that change the latent response in terms of wider interconnections.

We assume no consciousness attaching to them, but in man it is not consciousness but the neural organization that is affective. They would undoubtedly be accompanied by all of the diffuse muscular and glandular reactions that we appreciate in man.

If we come back to our special problem, to what end the emotion as such? We must answer: it is everything or nothing according as we define it. If we look at the matter in the rough, we can assert confidently that all learning, all of what we call instinct, except the vanishing portion that can be ascribed to chain reflexes, is determined by affection or emotion. That alone puts an end to random responses and so selects the particular response that shall be learned. If, however, we ask how the selection takes place, we find that, so far as analysis can be pushed, the actual mechanism of selection is nothing more than starting a specific definite response in place of the earlier random ones. If you reply that this is not affection or emotion but merely a reflex, we must admit it. The only physical accompaniments that could be called emotion or affection are the diffuse neuro-muscular and neuro-glandular discharges, and we know little as to what use these may have. They can be shown in certain cases to intensify the original reaction, and we may speculate that they make more easy the establishment of connections between stimuli, but of this we know little definitely. It is entirely probable that they have an important function and that only our ignorance prevents our describing it. This paper will have attained its purpose if it stimulates investigation of the detailed mechanism by which this effect is exerted.

CHAPTER 9

FEELINGS AND EMOTIONS

Ed. Claparède
University of Geneva

The psychology of affective processes is the most confused chapter in all psychology. Here it is that the greatest differences appear from one psychologist to another. They are in agreement neither on the facts nor on the words. Some call feelings what others call emotions. Some regard feelings as simple, ultimate, unanalyzable phenomena, similar always to themselves, varying only in quantity. Some, on the contrary, believe that the range of feelings includes an infinity of *nuances*, and that feeling always forms a part of a more complex whole, in exhibition or in condition. Certain psychologists regard physical pain and moral pain as identical, while others separate them by calling one a sensation, the other an emotion. Some regard pleasure and pain as two phenomena, antagonistic but of the same kind, while others describe them as entirely heterogeneous. A number of pages might be filled by simply enumerating the fundamental differences.

These differences are increased when one passes from one language to another, since the lack of agreement about the facts is then complicated by lack of agreement about words. What French word is the exact equivalent of the word feeling? Does *Gemütsbewegung* correspond exactly with emotion? And what equivalent does one find from one language to another between the words *Affekt*, *Gefühl*, *passion*, *douleur*, pain, affection, etc.?

If we survey the problems which are presented by affective psychology, we shall bring to our attention the extent of the field to be covered. Some of the problems follow:

1. The specific character of feelings and emotions. What is it which distinguishes them from other psychological phenomena?

2. Variety of affective phenomena. Are there several kinds of simple feelings? How many kinds of emotions are there?

3. Are all feelings located on a single bipolar line running from pleasure to pain, or are certain feelings located outside this line? Or do feelings, indeed, arrange themselves in a figure of several dimensions?

4. What relations exist between feelings and emotions?

5. Genetic origin of feelings. Have they the same origin as sensations, and are they distinguished only by a secondary differentiation, or are they, from the beginning, phenomena distinct from sensations and irreducible to them?

6. What are the physiological concomitants of feelings and emotions? Relations existing between these phenomena and the sympathetic nervous system and internal secretions.

7. Do feelings of the same sort vary in themselves only in intensity, or do they perhaps vary in other directions different from intensity, as, for example, according to "depth."

8. Does a true affective memory exist? (Or do affective memories constitute an *actual* revival of feelings or emotions?)

9. What are the relations between feelings and other related phenomena—need, interest, desire, will, character, temperament?

10. Pathology of affective phenomena. Rôle of the affective phenomena in the production of nervous or mental diseases.

11. Relations between affective and intellectual phenomena. Rôle of feeling in normal thought. Rôle of feeling in the formation of concepts (for example, the concept of "danger," of "beauty," etc.). Affective logic.

12. Biological significance and general functions of affective phenomena. Affective dynamics.

I make no claim to have given here a complete list of the problems which present themselves. Each of the problems enumerated implies a number of others, and, in proportion to the new researches which are conducted, new problems will arise. However, I believe that it will be in the interest of the progress of affective psychology if psychologists can make clear among themselves the fundamental problems which are to be solved.

THE FUNCTIONAL POINT OF VIEW

It is always advantageous, in my opinion, when one wishes to study a psychological phenomenon, to begin the approach from the functional angle; in other words, before trying to analyze it in detail under a strong magnifying glass, as it were, to examine it rather less enlarged, in order to take account of its functional value, its general part in conduct.

If we apply this principle of method to the study of affective phenomena, we ought to commence by asking ourselves: Of what use are feelings? Of what use are emotions? And, if this way of speaking should be found too finalistic, one can say: What are the situations in which feelings and emotions intervene, and what is the rôle played by these phenomena in the conduct of the individual?

It cannot be denied that the functional point of view has shown itself fruitful in psychology. Let us recall Groos's theory of play, which has shown the value of play in development, and the Freudian concepts, which have considered mental maladies from the point of view of their functional significance. I myself have considered thus sleep, hysteria, and also intelligence and will. Without doubt, the functional study constitutes only an introduction to a more complete study. Nevertheless, it has no slight value in making clear the path to follow.

The functional point of view then places the emphasis on conduct. Functional psychology demands less what the phenomena *are*, then what they *do*. It is thus closely related to behaviorism. It is clearly distinguished from it, however, since that which interests it is conduct, its laws, its determinism, and not the method by which one pursues the study of these laws. It is of very little importance to it whether these methods be objective or introspective.

Let us observe another advantage of the functional point of view: it brings to our notice problems which otherwise would not have been raised.

Distinction Between Feelings and Emotions

From the analytical point of view, feelings and emotions are distinguished with difficulty. One needs but to open any book on psychology to see the confusion which reigns in this subject. Let us see if the functional point of view permits a clearer delineation of the two groups of phenomena.

Suppose we ask ourselves: Of what use, in everyday life, are feelings, and of what use are emotions? We are immediately tempted to give to these two questions very different answers: Feelings are useful in our conduct while emotions serve no purpose.

We can, in fact, very easily imagine a man who would never feel an emotion, who would never experience a crisis of fear or of anger, and who would be none the less viable. But we cannot imagine a man deprived of feelings, of that range of affective *nuances* which permit him to estimate the value of things to which he must adapt himself, who would not distinguish between what is good for him and what is detrimental to him.

Observation shows us, on the other hand, how unadaptable emotional phenomena are. Emotions occur precisely when adaptation is hindered for any reason whatever. The man who can run away does not have the emotion of fear. Fear occurs only when flight is impossible. Anger is displayed only when one cannot strike his enemy. Analysis of bodily reactions in emotion points to the evidence that one does not make adaptive movements but, on the contrary, reactions which recall the primitive instincts. (Darwin has also shown this.) Far from being the psychic side of an instinct, as McDougall teaches, emotion represents on the contrary a confusion of instinct, "a miscarriage of instinct," as Larguier des Bancels has said. And, as in emotion, we can prove not only the vestige of the ancestral reaction but also the confusion or insufficiency of the acquired reaction, so we can, perhaps, with more justice define emotion as a "miscarriage of conduct."

The uselessness, or even the harmfulness of emotion, is known to everyone. Here is an individual who would cross a street; if he is afraid of automobiles, he loses his composure and is run over. Sorrow, joy, anger, by enfeebling attention or judgment, often make us commit regrettable acts. In brief, the individual, in the grip of an emotion "loses his head."

Emotion, from the functional point of view, appears to be a regression of conduct. When, for one reason or another, the normal correct reaction cannot be made, then the opposite tendencies borrow the primitive ways of reaction. And these primitive reactions, rudiments of reactions formerly useful, may be contractions of the peripheral muscles as well as phenomena vascular, inhibitive, secretory, visceral, etc. Perhaps some of them have no biological significance (e.g., tears) and result only in the propagation of a nervous impulse which has not found its normal issue. Everyone has noticed that one weeps more easily in the theater than in real life, although in the theater one knows that the scenes in which one is taking part are fictitious, but in the theater the normal reactions are prevented from occurring.

And again, in these cases one can attribute to these phenomena a secondary function of discharge, an appeasement of the nervous system unduly excited.[1]

Peripheral Theory of Emotion

The James-Lange theory is the only one, to my mind, which explains the existence of specific bodily phenomena in emotion. In regarding the bodily phenomena as the result (and not the cause) of the emotion, the old theories made the emotion an

[1] If organic phenomena are the bases for all emotions, it does not follow that all organic phenomena cause emotions. It is probable that many physiological phenomena (internal secretions, vasomotor modifications, etc.) are compensatory reactions of regulation, the function of which is to repair the disturbance caused by the emotion.

entirely enigmatic process. Moreover, facts of great importance speak in favor of the James-Lange theory: the suppression of the emotion by the suppression of the peripheral phenomena according to James's observation; and also the production or the facilitation of certain emotional states by the consumption of poisons, alcohol, coffee, hasheesh, etc.

The peripheral theory of James and Lange raises, however, a very great difficulty. Why, if the emotion is only consciousness of peripheral changes in the organism, is it perceived as an "emotion" and not as "organic sensations"? Why, when I am afraid, am I conscious of "having fear," instead of being simply conscious of certain organic impressions, tremblings, beatings of the heart, etc.?

I do not remember that anyone has sought until now to reply to this objection. However, it does not seem to me that it should be very difficult to do so. The emotion is nothing other than the consciousness of a form, of a "Gestalt," of these multiple organic impressions. In other words, the emotion is the consciousness of a global attitude of the organism.

This confused and general perception of the whole, which I have formerly called "syncretic perception,"[2] is the primitive form of perception. In the case of emotional perception, we know well that it is more useful to know the total attitude of the body than the elementary sensations composing the whole. There must be for an individual no great interest in perceiving the detail of internal sensations. What is above all important to an organism is action; the question then is whether it is aware of the general attitude it is showing to the environment. As to the "internal sensations," their perception results especially from a theoretical interest, and perhaps, before there were psychologists in the world, each internal sensation, each kinaesthetic or muscular sensation was not, as such, an object of consciousness.

Many of the impressions which we receive are interpreted differently according to the direction of our interest. This is particularly true for tactile impressions, which sometimes are perceived as objective, sometimes as subjective. The experiment is very easy to make. Put your hand on the table. The same tactile impression is apperceived, according to the direction of your attention, sometimes as a "tactile sensation," sometimes as "a hard object," a table. If, at that moment, your interest is turned to yourself (for example, in the course of psychological experiment on tactile sensations), you feel your hand, but no longer the table.

[2] *Archives de psychologie*, VII (1908), 195.

It is the same thing in the case of emotion. When you are angry, turn your attention to the kinaesthetic sensations in your clenched fists, to the trembling of your lips, etc., but then you have no longer the consciousness of anger. Or permit yourself to become absorbed in your anger; but then you no longer experience distinctly the trembling of your lips, your pallor, or the isolated sensations arising from the different parts of your contracted muscular machinery.

What the consciousness seizes in emotion is, so to speak, the form of the organism itself—that is to say—its attitude.

This peripheral conception which regards the emotion as the consciousness of an attitude of the organism is, besides, the only one which can take account of the fact that the emotion is immediately, implicitly "understood" by him who experiences it. The emotion contains in itself its significance. As far as we can judge by external observation or by our own memory, a child who for the first time experiences a great fear or a great joy or falls into an excess of anger understands immediately what has happened to him. He does not need experience to understand successfully the meaning of this explosion of his organism, as he does to understand the meaning of impressions which come to him by sight or by hearing, impressions which do not possess any immediate and implicit significance. But what is meant by "understand"? Does not the "understanding" consist essentially in the assuming of an attitude with respect to an object? If this is so, it is not astonishing that emotions should be implicitly understood, since they consist in the assuming of an attitude toward a given situation, this assumption of an attitude being itself due to hereditary and instinctive causes.

These last remarks allow us to understand not only how antibiological but also how antipsychological the "central," classic concept of emotion is: "we tremble because we are afraid, we weep because we are sad, we gnash our teeth because we are angry." This concept is antibiological because it does not allow any significance to the organic reactions and because it makes these primitive reactions, evidently of reflexive or instinctive nature, the result of a purely intellectual perception, of a judgment which can be formulated as follows: The situation in which I find myself is dangerous or terrifying (fear) or it is sad (sorrow) or it is provoking to me (anger), etc.

This concept is also altogether antipsychological. It implies in fact that we can, by a simple intellectual perception of a situation in which we find ourselves, call it "dangerous," "terrifying," "sad," etc. But "dangerous," "sad," etc., are not consciousnesses which are given us by means of the external senses, as are color or temperature. It is we ourselves who color the things or the external situations, by projecting into them the feelings which they arouse in *us* and which they excite by producing a reaction of our organism. A large dog or the dark is found terrifying by a child because they have aroused in him the reactions the consciousness of which is what we call "fear."

To say, as the classic theory does, that a situation arouses fear because we judge it to be terrifying, is either not to explain why we find this situation frightening, or to revolve in a vicious circle.

Indeed, how does an individual "comprehend" that a situation is "terrifying"? To comprehend, we have said, is to take an attitude toward things. To understand that a situation is "dangerous," "frightening," is to take, with regard to this situation, an attitude of flight or of protection. But this attitude of flight or of protection is precisely what is at the basis of the emotion of fear. In other words, to say with the classic theory that a situation makes you afraid because it is terrifying is to say that it makes you afraid because it makes you afraid. It is only revolving in a circle!

FUNCTIONAL CONCEPT OF AFFECTIVE PHENOMENA

We say that the emotion is capable of giving a significance to the situation which it arouses. This assertion demands examination. For, if the emotion is a deficiency in conduct, a poorly adapted act, how can it give a true meaning of things?

It must not be forgotten, however, if the emotion is an objectively poorly adapted act, it represents none the less a total of reaction having a biological significance. To an objective misadaptation may correspond a subjective significance. The attitude taken by the organism is without efficacy on the surrounding environment. It is none the less comprehended by itself; that is to say, it orients itself in a certain definite direction.

I believe that, in order to explain the paradox of an unadapted act which plays, nevertheless, a useful rôle—for one cannot deny that fear, shame, sorrow, joy have great importance in the life of man—it is more simple to make the following hypothesis. The emotion is a mixture of adaptive reactions and unadaptive actions, of which the proportions vary. The more the emotion takes the form of shock, of explosion, the more important is the share of the misadaptation as compared with that of the adaptation.

Considered from the point of time, the two parts of the emotional phenomenon habitually succeed one another. Sometimes the emotion begins with a shock, with unadapted reactions, which little by little readjust themselves toward a useful behavior. Sometimes on the contrary, the useful adaptation delineates itself at first, and if it is hindered in its termination, it is followed by an emotional explosion. Does not the observation of emotional phenomena in everyday life show us the presence of these two forms of affective processes?

That the emotion, when it is an explosive phenomenon, is not capable of influencing behavior usefully, seems to be shown by the following example, taken from among many others.

Here are two individuals passing through a forest at night. One, of emotional character, feels violent fear. The other remains calm. They have to return another time, also at night, through the same forest. The frightened man will take precautions. He will carry a weapon, take with him a dog. The second will not modify his behavior. It is without doubt the affective experience of the first journey through the forest which has later modified the behavior of the first traveler. We can, nevertheless, ask whether it is the emotion, as such (considered as a disorder of the reactions), which has made this modification in the ulterior conduct. We can very well indeed imagine a courageous man who, in passing through this forest, ascertains that this crossing is not without danger, and makes this decision *without feeling the least emotion of fear*. His subsequent behavior will be, however, modified in the same manner as that of the man who was afraid; he takes with him a weapon, a dog. The comparison of the two cases shows that the fear as such has not played the rôle which it seems to have had.

What then has happened to the brave man? The crossing of the gloomy forest has excited in him diverse reactions of attention, of eventual defense; it has determined, in a word, an attitude of "being on his guard." Is it not the perception of this attitude which constitutes the "consciousness of danger"? And can one not say, in the case of the man who is afraid, that it is this attitude of precaution which has modified his subsequent behavior in a useful way? This attitude was blended with the emotion or alternated with it, and one can say that it is not because of the emotion but in spite of it that the behavior has been happily modified.

Do not these reflections lead us to admit, besides the emotions, reactions which are distinguished from them by the fact that they are, themselves, adapted, and as a result capable of orienting behavior usefully. These reactions, these attitudes, and the consciousness that the subject possesses of them, we group together under the name of feelings.

Besides the emotion of fear, we should have then the "feeling of fear," which it would be better to call "feeling of danger" and which would consist of the consciousness of the defensive attitude. Besides the emotion of anger, there would be the "feeling of anger," which it would be better to call "combative feeling" and which consists of the consciousness of the offensive attitude and the attitude of combat. Besides the "emotion of shame"—which seems to me to be a "miscarriage" of the instinct to hide oneself—there would be the "feeling of shame," which betrays the tendency to hide from the sight of others.

For the emotions of joy and sorrow, the corresponding feelings would then be the pleasant and unpleasant, pleasure and pain, as described by current psychology, and also would be only the consciousness of an attitude of the organism, an attitude positive or negative with respect to the present situation. Only, in the case of the pleasant and the unpleasant we have the case of particularly obscure phenomena, which represent surely a very primitive phase of the organic attitude, that phase in which the humoral processes still predominates over the nervous processes.

The concept which I have outlined seems to me to give an account of the various facts, and presents certain advantages, which I shall enumerate.

Reconciliation with the Current Concept of Emotions

Our concept permits of a reconciliation to a certain extent of the peripheral theory with the current concept of emotions.

It is true, as the current concept affirms, that often fear does not arise in us until after we have first had a consciousness of the danger of the situation in which we find ourselves. Only, this consciousness of danger does not consist, as the classic theory supposes, in a purely intellectual judgment. According to our theory, it results in a "feeling of danger." Let us say then that the emotion of fear follows the feeling of danger; it follows if we cannot flee or protect ourselves in an effective way, for the normal unrolling of behavior is then substituted a miscarriage of behavior. In its principle this way of looking at it, however, is profoundly different from the classic theory, since it considers that neither the emotion nor the feeling of danger is awakened immediately by the perception. The reactionary processes always intervene, as indispensable to the development of the affective phenomenon. It is the awakening of this process which warns us of danger. The emotion, then, appears only as a special phase of the reactionary process. The primitive reactions are substituted for the adaptive reactions when these are prevented from terminating in an act. In cases where the emotion appears quickly, as when we jump at a sudden noise, the James-Lange theory in its ordinary form retains its full value.

The following schema shows the theories about emotions, and will make more clear what we understand by them:

Classic Theory	Perception—Emotion—Organic Reactions
James-Lange Theory	Perception—Organic Reactions—Emotions
Modified Peripheral Theory	Perception—Attitude (of flight), Feeling (of danger)—Organic Reactions—Emotion (fear)
Flight without Emotion	Perception—Attitude (of flight), Feeling (of danger)—Flight

VARIETY OF FEELINGS

Our concept also enables us to render account of the infinite variety of affective phenomena, feelings, and emotions. If the whole affective phenomenon is subjectively the consciousness of an attitude and objectively this attitude itself, we can conceive how infinite is the possible range of all of the attitudes. Even attitudes orienting themselves in the same general sense (for example, in the sense of the agreeable) can, nevertheless, differ between themselves in the relation of the quality, since these attitudes can be very different in form.

We now understand why the range of affective phenomena is indeed richer than a thory would foresee which, as that of McDougall, would relate each emotion to a definite instinct. In the first place, these are not emotions, but feelings (as those of danger, of aggression, etc.) which correspond to actual instincts. In the second place, as there are more affective *nuances* than definite instincts, one is obliged to admit that feelings may sometimes have for organic base reactions or attitudes intermediate to two or more instincts.

The concept here presented also permits us to understand that feelings and emotions are distinguished not only by their quality and their intensity, but also by their *depth*. The pain which a pin-prick causes me may be much more intense than the pain which is produced by the news of a shipwreck of a boat full of passengers, but the latter is assuredly a deeper pain. One may suppose that this "depth" corresponds to a supplementary arousal of certain reactionary systems. Perhaps, however, once admitted that feelings of the same kind can differ among themselves in the relation of the quality, the depth resolves itself simply into a question of quality.

The "Transcendental Revelation of Feelings"

A peripheral theory of feeling also explains the kind of immediate comprehension which we have of feelings—a comprehension of which I have just spoken above with reference to emotion. All affective phenomena have for us not only a content but a value. While blue or red has for us no immediate value, no implicit meaning, pleasure and pain have a value, an inborn value. It seems that, in the affective consciousness, we are the beneficiaries of a really transcendental revelation. How can a little infant, just born, or a caterpillar on a leaf know that this is good and that that is bad; and how, receiving only *subjective* impressions, do they behave as if they know the *objective value* of impressions of good and bad? Here we have material for fine metaphysical discussions. For us psychologists, the mystery resolves itself remarkably as soon as we consider that if feeling has, to consciousness, a subjective value, it is because it corresponds, in behavior, to an attitude, to reactions, which have an objective value. The value perceived by consciousness corresponds to the value for life, for conduct. And one cannot go farther in the way of explanation, if one holds to the principle of psychophysical parallelism.

Intellectual Feelings

Our theory of feeling has also this advantage—that it gives a place to intellectual feelings. The term "intellectual feeling" has not a very definite meaning. In his *Psychology of Feeling*, Ribot includes under this name only surprise, astonishment, curiosity, doubt. Other authors add to these the general feeling which we have of the movement of our thought, of its success, or its impotence. To my mind, one can go much farther, and include among the intellectual feelings all those elements of thought which James calls transitive and which are not representations: conformity, implication, congruity, certitude, probability, and those thousands of relations which we have expressed in the words *but, if, and, why, after, before,* the thoughts which we express by the words *future, past, conditional, negation, affirmation,* etc.

William James has very well seen all this. "If there be such things as feelings at all, then, so surely as relations between objects exist *in rerum natura,* so surely and more surely do feelings exist by which these relations are known. There is not a conjunction or a preposition, and hardly an adverbial phrase, syntatic form, or inflection of voice, that does not express some shading or other of relations which we at some moment actually feel to exist between the larger objects of our thought. . . . We ought to say a feeling of *and*, and a feeling of *if*, a feeling of *but*, a feeling of *by*.· . . . . ."

It is very curious that so illuminating a passage of William James, which contains in all its essence a fruitful psychology of thought, should have remained almost a dead letter for psychology. This results, no doubt, from the fact that psychology, under the reign of the associationist doctrine, has remained very definitely closed to biological thought, which alone, to my mind, is capable of rendering it fruitful.

It must be noted, however, that Ribot, in all his work, has insisted on the rôle of movements and of tendencies in behavior. To him, thought brings itself at last to account in movement. But even he has not seen the consequence which can be drawn from this concept, being in part fascinated by associationism. However, in his *Evolution of General Ideas* (1897, p. 94), he rallies to an opinion derived from the linguists—the opinion according to which the prepositions and the conjunctions express movements. "The consciousness of these movements," says Ribot, "is the feeling of the different directions of the thought."

In my *Association of Ideas* (1903), where I have strongly combated associationism, I have revived James's idea and sought to develop it in biological terms. I consider here all intellectual feelings as corresponding to adaptive reactions or to attitudes of the organism. "Cannot the body," I say (p. 317), "be also the source of those numerous ideas which do not correspond, it is true, to anything in the external world which is capable of making an impression on the senses, but which can indeed be nothing other than the consciousness of the reactions of the body with regard to its environment?" I have applied this point of view to the "comprehension" which brings itself back to an adaptation, and have considered the feeling of comprehension as "the consciousness of the more or less complete adaptation which is produced." With respect to the consciousness of relations, "it suffices," I say (p. 369), "to admit a different reaction according as the relation perceived is a relation of identity, of resemblance or of equivalence, of possibility or of necessity, of affirmation or of negation, etc. . . . And, in fact, we do not behave the same with two things when they are different, or similar, or simply equivalent."

We well perceive, when we see someone gesticulating as he speaks, that all thought is doubled by a moving manifestation. One can say that to think is to gesticulate internally, to outline the acts which the thought prepares and coordinates. This concept, I repeat, is the only one which takes account of the rôle of thought, of its dynamism. But the psychology of thought, in developing—with the Würzburg school—towards pure introspection, has lost at the same time its explicative value. For, whatever may be the descriptive value of phenomena, like *Bewusstheiten* or *Bewusstseinslagen*, one must agree that the description of these states does not explain at all how they influence in an adequate way the course of thought and of behavior. This is, by the way, what Binet has recognized in an excellent article, where he also brings together the "mental attitudes" of emotion and feelings.[3]

If one considers all intellectual feelings to be the outlines of actions or of inhibitions, all is clear, since one can understand how movements can influence the one over the other, reinforce, oppose, or modify themselves in their respective directions.

There remains, however, one difficulty—that is to know why, while emotions and ordinary feelings seem to us to be "states of our self," the intellectual feelings appear to be objective.

But is this exact? Very many intellectual feelings, such as certainty, doubt, affirmation and negation, logical constraint, etc., can indeed, according to circumstances, according to the direction of our interest at the particular moment, appear to us as objective or as subjective. On the other hand, are ordinary feelings really always subjective? We know how they easily objectify themselves. The aesthetic emotion objectifies itself in the beautiful, the emotion of disgust in the repugnant, etc. We say that an event (objective) is sad, joyous, shameful, comic, or disagreeable. When we declare that a task is painful, we place the pain in the task or in ourselves according to the context of our thought.

To my mind, the subjectivity or the objectivity of a content of consciousness is always the result of a secondary process, depending on the acquired experiences. In the beginning, our states of consciousness are neither objective nor subjective. They become little by little the one or the other according to the necessity of our adaptation to our physical or social environment.

FEELINGS AND INTERNAL SENSATIONS

The functional concept developed above permits us to state what distinguishes feeling from internal or organic sensations,

[3]A. Binet, "Qu'est-ce qu'une émotion? Qu'est-ce qu'un acte intellectuel?" *L'année psychologique*, XVII (1911), 1-47. Cf. also M. F. Washburn, "The Term 'Feeling,'" *Journal of Philosophy, Psychology, and Scientific Methods*, III (1903), 62-63; E. B. Titchener, *Experimental Psychology of the Thought Processes* (New York: Macmillan, 1909), p. 176.

notably the sensations of hunger, thirst, fatigue, or synaesthesia. Often this distinction is not made, and people generally speak of the "feeling" of fatigue or of hunger.

To my mind, the sensations of hunger, of thirst, of fatigue (and perhaps one might add to these those of pain) have no value in themselves; they are phenomena which derive their value only from attitudes, tendencies, movements, which they instinctively arouse, and it is the instinctive reactions which confer on them their value for the behavior of the individual. But these instinctive reactions are nothing other than the basis of feelings: feelings agreeable or disagreeable, of desire, of need.

The internal sensations are then states, contrasting with feelings which are attitudes. The internal sensations inform us about such and such states of our organism as our external senses inform us about such and such state of the surrounding environment. But it is by virtue of these feelings that we can estimate the vital value of the organic sensations.

If we seek to represent to ourselves in a purely physiological way, in making abstractions from consciousness, the function of the stimulations corresponding to internal sensations, and the function of the attitudes corresponding to the feelings, it is easy for us to see the functional difference between the two orders of phenomena. The stimulations have value for behavior only in so far as they determine the attitudes or the movements of the organism. One can, with different stimulations, obtain identical attitudes (as, for example, in the experience of Pavlov's conditioned reflexes). This shows us that the stimulation of an internal origin has something of the accidental with relation to the attitude while the attitude represents *itself* a vital value, because it is already an outline of behavior.

Feelings express in some way a relation. The relation between such a situation or such an object and our welfare (or, what comes to the same thing, the attitude which we should take with regard to it). The physiological basis of this relation is the attitude itself. Feeling is the consciousness of this attitude. On the contrary, sensations give us only the objects with regard to which we should take an attitude. In the cases of internal sensations, as those of hunger, of thirst, of fatigue, the object which they give us is *our own body*. It is through the relation to its own state that our body can take a certain attitude. We understand that we have here a very intimate relation between internal sensations and feelings, since they have this in common—that they both have their source in our body. But this does not prevent us from distinguishing them very well from the functional point of view.

They are opposed the one to the other, as a reaction is opposed to the object which has aroused it.

I have spoken about the fact that internal sensations correspond to our needs. What is the internal sensation of kinaesthetic nature, such as tension or relaxation, excitement or depression, which Wundt regards as of an affective nature? To my mind, the same observations can be made here that I have made just above. These phenomena are, on the one hand, sensations, or, on the contrary, feelings, according to the context in which we examine them. When we examine them in *themselves*, as states of the organism, they are sensations, objects, which can be agreeable or disagreeable. When we examine them as dependent on the situation which arouses them (an exciting situation, or one calling for a tension, etc.), they become feelings. In other words, considered as evaluated objects, they are sensations; considered as instruments of evaluation, they are feelings.

MENTALIZATION OF AFFECTIVE PHENOMENA

In everything discussed above, I have taken the point of view of psychophysical parallelism. However little satisfying parallelism is, perhaps, from the point of view of philosophy, it is none the less the only position tenable by psychology which would be based on biology.

Although parallelism forbids us to set ourselves the question of the usefulness of consciousness *as such*, it does not prohibit us from setting the problem of the becoming conscious of mental phenomena. This becoming conscious, like the loss of consciousness of a phenomenon, is a purely empirical question. From the point of view of parallelism, indeed, an organic phenomenon accompanied by consciousness differs from a purely automatic phenomenon. To the fact of being "conscious" corresponds a special physiological process. Let us suppose (a rough hypothesis to fix our ideas) that this special process should be a cortical process. We could ask ourselves why, in certain cases, a process which has not been cortical becomes, at a certain instant, cortical (i.e., why a process which has not been conscious is, at a certain instant, the object which has been seized by consciousness).

I formulated some years ago in the following way the *law of becoming conscious*.[4] "The individual becomes conscious of a relation the more tardily as his behavior has earlier and longer implied the automatic (instinctive, unconscious) use of this relation."

[4] *Archives de psychologie*, XVII (1918), 71.

One can, to simplify the language, call this change from the unconscious to the conscious of a given phenomenon *mentalization*.

It is necessary to say one word here about the mentalization, the capture of consciousness, of affective phenomena.

The function of affective phenomena is a function of regulation. This regulation consists in the attitudes which the organism takes with respect to the stimuli (internal or external) which reach it. But we can ask: Since these attitudes are of instinctive nature, why are they conscious? Why do they not all take place in a purely automatic fashion? Why this mentalization of affective phenomena?

Of course, we can readily imagine an automatic regulation and a purely objective valuation of stimuli; we establish this in a large number of organic processes of assimilation, nutrition, secretion, digestion, etc., where substances are selected, rejected, received— all this in a purely instinctive and unconscious manner. But the point in question here concerns those functions which are accomplished in a uniform manner. Mentalization has evidently for its function the enabling of the individual to cope with new circumstances.

The mentalization of affective phenomena has the same source as the mentalization of other psychological phenomena, namely, sensations (which one can also imagine acting under the form of purely physical stimuli). I cannot enter here into this interesting question. Becoming conscious seems to be the result of a misadaptation before which the individual finds himself. In the face of new circumstances his habitual automatisms no longer adapt him, and then it is necessary that he should "be conscious" of the situation in order to be able to adjust to it by new means. In the work of readjustment the mentalization of affective phenomena has evidently the advantage of permitting a comparison of the values considered, of associating feelings with certain representations, of establishing certain concepts (as danger, kindness, etc.), of granting, in a word, to thought its exercise of a rôle of anticipation of movement. Feeling has, for conduct, a functional value analogous to that of meaning (concept): it is an instrument of adjustment. But there are still many obscure points to elucidate in detail.

I have been able in these pages only to touch on the large subject which was proposed. I hope that I have shown by some examples the fruitfulness of the functional point of view applied to feelings and to emotions.

CHAPTER 10

A FUNCTIONAL THEORY OF THE EMOTIONS

D. T. Howard
Northwestern University

The first unambiguous statement of a functional theory of
the emotions with which I am acquainted was made by John
Dewey in two articles appearing in the *Psychological Review* in
1894 and 1895.[1] In 1895 S. F. McLennan advanced a similar
theory as an independent discovery.[2] Although the functional
theory has had some currency in recent times, it has not, I am
convinced, attracted the attention to which by reason of merit
it is entitled. I propose in this paper: (1) to restate the theory in
its most elementary form; (2) to develop certain of its implications; and (3) to suggest how, following the lead of this theory,
we may discover an experimental approach to the study of the
emotions that holds promise of profitable development.

First, then, to state the theory. I am going to borrow for this
purpose the language of J. R. Kantor, who, in the second volume
of his *Principles of Psychology*,[3] gives us an excellent presentation
of the functional theory exclusively, of course, in terms of behavior. I would not be understood to subscribe unreservedly to
all that Kantor has to say about the emotions, but his identification of the emotional states seems to me essentially sound.

"Emotional behavior," he tells us, "consists essentially of interruptive forms of
action stimulated by rapidly changing circumstances and in all cases involves
various slight or intense general organic and visceral processes.

"Probably the most obvious observation made in studying emotional conduct
is that the primary occurrences in such action are the confusion and excitement
which disrupt the behavior that ordinarily takes place when the emotion-exciting
stimulus appears. When we attempt to describe the specific characteristics of
an emotional act we are profoundly impressed with this condition of disrupting
chaos and inhibition of action. We may look upon the emotional person as one
who is practically paralyzed for a moment; he appears to undergo a dissociation
of his reaction systems, so that he remains powerless and helpless until his responses are reconstituted. This reconstitution may be superficially described
as a refocussing of the person toward some definite object. Essentially, emotional
conduct is a momentary condition of 'no response,' since there appears to be a

---

[1] "The Theory of Emotion," *Psychological Review*, I (1894), 553–569; II (1895),
13–32.
[2] "Emotion, Desire, and Interest: Descriptive," *Psychological Review*, II (1895),
462–474.
[3] Chapter XVI, pp. 1–25.

complete cessation of all directed responses to surrounding conditions. In point of fact, it is this disruptive chaos which definitely distinguishes the milder emotional activities from the numerous classes of affective or feeling behavior to which they otherwise display a striking resemblance.

"In detail, it might be pointed out that emotional conduct consists of a definite type of failure to perform an expected form of adjustment or adaptation upon the basis of surrounding conditions and the individual's reactional biography or previous behavior history. Whenever it is possible for the person to make the expected or necessary response to the stimulating condition, there is no emotional disturbance."

Now a theory of this type, presupposing as it does an organism in process of adapting, and a stasis or disruption of the adjustment activities as the occasion of emotion, is intelligible only in the light of evolutionary conceptions. The organism, an individual entity, must be able to adapt itself to the changing circumstances of its environment if it is to preserve its integrity of life and action. We find, accordingly, that organisms which survive and prosper and secure for themselves the fullest range of action and mastery are quick and discriminating in their adaptive reactions, resourceful in the face of difficulties. So much is elementary. But the theory has still another implication which is too often neglected. A distinction is to be made between two types of adaptive reaction. There is a form of organic adaptation—brought to its highest perfection in the social bees and ants—which is reflex, routine, automatic, or predetermined by habit patterns in the nervous system. There is another kind of adaptive reaction that is plastic, built up to meet the peculiar requirements of novel situations, essentially creative and spontaneous. No psychologist may call himself a functionalist who has not grasped the reality and the significance of the latter form of adaptive reaction.

Dewey first insisted upon this distinction, and its implications have been developed by many of his colleagues. Permit me to quote briefly from the writings of B. H. Bode.

"Is that noise, for example, a horse in the street, or is it the rain on the roof? What we find in such a situation is not a paralysis of activity, but a redirection. The incompatibility of responses is purely relative. There is indeed a mutual inhibition of the responses for hoof-beats and rain, respectively, in the sense that neither has undisputed possession of the field; but this very inhibition sets free the process of attention, in which the various responses participate and cooperate. There is no static balancing of forces, but rather a process in which the conflict is simply a condition for an activity of a different kind. If I am near a window facing the street, my eye turns thither for a clue; if the appeal to vision be eliminated, the eye becomes unseeing and cooperates with the ear by excluding all that is irrelevant to the matter in hand. In this process the nervous system functions as a unit, with reference to the task of determining the source and character of the sound. This task or problem dominates the situation. A voice in an adjoining room may break in, but only as something to be ignored and shut out; whereas a voice in the street may become all-absorbing as possibly indicating the driver of the hypothetical horse. That is, the reason why the conflict of responses does not end in a deadlock, but in a redirection, is that a certain selectiveness of response comes into play."

When the individual confronts a situation to which he is not habituated, to which no pre-organized response is forthcoming, the internal conflict or disequilibrium that results immediately arouses a secondary, indirect process by which the stimulus is reconstituted, the disorganization overcome, and a response prepared that is suited to the occasion. Such secondary, reconstitutive activities are what we know in humans as mental, conscious, or attentive processes; they are non-habitual, creative, emergent. In calling these processes secondary, I mean that they involve the preparation and guidance of reactions, and do not themselves involve direct responses to stimuli. Perhaps, also, the statement that they occur upon occasion of the failure of automatic and habitual responses may mislead some into supposing a real disjunction between the secondary and primary activities of the organism. It is probable, on the contrary, that the secondary processes are constantly operative, in waking life, to maintain the organism's equilibrium of action. For the secondary or conscious processes are just the equilibrium-maintaining activity of the organism itself.

The functional theory would hold, then, that emotion occurs upon the occasion of the disruption of these secondary, reconstitutive activities. A conflict is set up with which the equilibrium-maintaining process is unable to cope, and unity of thought and action is lost. Let me illustrate. I, a greenhorn, walk one bright and balmy day through the woods and suddenly meet with a large grizzly bear. The perception of the bear begets, first of all, an impulsion towards response. But, as common sense has it, I "do not know what to do"—I have no habitual modes of response to uncaged grizzlies. The organism is thrown out of equilibrium. A secondary process of adjustment starts up, but explodes under the impact of conflicting reaction tendencies. A disruption occurs—I "go to pieces," "lose my head," and am "unable to pull myself together" or "collect" myself, and stand trembling and helpless with fright. But old Leatherstocking, an experienced woodsman, meeting a grizzly under similar circumstances, calmly sizes up the situation, and reacts effectively. He is so habituated, and has such resources in the way of response patterns, as to be able to devise a new mode of response, if old ones will not serve, to meet the needs of the situation.

All of the grosser emotions can obviously be similarly described. Rage, for instance, is a state of disruption. The individual "flies to pieces," quite literally. He finds himself in a situation to which he cannot adapt himself effectually, which baffles his efforts at control. His mental processes disintegrate under the effort to secure adjustment. In the resultant state of confusion reflex or habitual responses, under the impact of accumulated energy, may fly loose and get out of control—too often with disastrous results, as every prize fighter knows. Anger is thus a sign of failure, an evidence of maladjustment.

In the disruptive state called emotional the victim can be said, in one sense, "not to know what to do." The bear is too much for him. He has no ready-made responses to draw upon, and too little resource in the way of reaction patterns to enable a reconstitutive process to build up an appropriate response. From another point of view the victim can be said to think of too many things to do. For, upon sight of the bear, he tends simultaneously to yell, to climb a tree, to run away, to throw a stone, to grasp a club, and what not. All of these impulses seek motor expression, get jammed in the process, and the result is a state of discoordination. Accompanying this disruptive condition we have those strange visceral and vegetative phenomena commonly recognized as characteristic of the emotional condition. I will not attempt any account of them, since they have been described by many competent investigators.

Some years ago, in an effort to make an objective experimental study of the mental processes, I constructed a rather elaborate apparatus and designed a series of studies from which we secured some results that seemed to us highly interesting. Some of them were not at all anticipated. It was my desire to create for the subject problematical combinations of stimuli, to which he could not have been accustomed by practice, and to which he could not respond in habitual modes. The subject was to react to visual stimuli by pulling levers and pushing pedals. He sat on a stool before the apparatus. At the level of his hands were five long levers, numbered from left to right, 1-2-3-4-5. His feet rested each on a pedal, the left pedal designated A, the right B. In a slot before him, in large type, appeared combinations of the signals —B-4-1-2, A-5-B-4-3-1, and the like. He was to respond by manipulating—all at once—the designated levers and pedals. Immediately upon the completion of a correct response a new signal appeared in the slot, and it was the subject's task to react to a series of 24 such signals in the shortest possible time. The reaction apparatus had one notable advantage: it called for extended visible bodily movements, which could be very readily observed and studied.

In this experiment we have an individual confronted by novel stimuli, and can observe him in the act of reconstituting the stimuli preparatory to making his responses. The mental process, at the perceptual level, of course, is rendered amenable to analysis. The secondary process of reconstitution is visible in the tentative, groping movements of the hands, in the movements of the eyes, in the play of the musculature of the body, in the movements of the lips, and in the furrowing of the brow. It is as if the coordinating activity—which we so often think of as confined to the brain alone, although it never is so confined—had been suddenly projected into the whole organism, and there enlarged upon, as the activities of amoeba are magnified under a microscope. This experiment, properly conducted, will convince the most skeptical that our mental processes are activities of a secondary and indirect type, involving a discriminative reaction upon the stimulus, an inner process of coordination, and the preparation of an adequate response. The preparation of responses, the building-up of the reactions that are to emerge, can be seen as actual operations. The results of our principal studies by my colleagues, Miss Phyllis Bartelme and Professor S. N. Stevens, have not yet been published, but I am hopeful that Professor Stevens' report may soon be in print.

We made one discovery that came as a surprise to us, for it was found that the subject of the experiment frequently lost coordination completely under the stress of the conditions imposed on him. The preparatory process would get under way—and suddenly disintegrate. It is the kind of thing that often happens to people when learning to drive automobiles. The individual "gets rattled," "loses command of himself," and works his controls at random, in a flurry of blind excitement. We observed many instances of such loss of control, in our experiments, before it occurred to us that these states were emotional in character. We had unwittingly verified the functional theory of the emotions.

I do not propose to magnify the importance of the emotional states thus produced. The states which we observed were transient—the individual soon recovered his poise. None the less they had all the characteristics, objectively and introspectively considered, of true emotions. The signs of anger, embarrassment, and frustration were unmistakable. We are now trying to develop the reaction experiment with the specific object of inducing emotional states that can be observed, and have good reason to expect success. Every experimentalist knows that it is difficult to produce genuinely emotional states in the laboratory subject. The reaction method here suggested may prove a valuable instrument of research. I would anticipate two conditions as essential in the use of the method: (1) the reaction must be highly complex; (2) it must be performed under high pressure

I am not prepared to report on the results of our studies of the emotions, for these were tentative and preliminary in character. But I would like to touch upon the theoretical implications of certain of our more assured observations, since they bear strongly upon our whole doctrine of the emotional states. In this discussion we turn to the introspective part of our studies, for we have not hesitated to ask our subjects for observations on what they themselves did and what they experienced. I must first acquaint you, then, with what we called the "blur"—for lack of a better name.

It has been said that the mental processes are reconstructive, having the function of reconstituting stimuli and preparing responses. It was our expectation, therefore, that the conflict or uncertainty visible in the subject's movements would be experienced by him as a vagueness or haziness on the side of the senses. The stimulus as it first appears is unclear and inadequate; the motor reactions incipiently started are confused. In what form was this uncertainty actually experienced by our subjects? We found that it appeared in a variety of forms—which we called "blurs." Many observers reported kinaesthetic blurs—actually experienced in arms and body. Some reported concrete visual fogs or hazes. Let me quote some rather unusual reports of this kind. "There was a definite grayness before me," one subject reports, "as I sought to discover the stimulus. The stimulus seemed to clear up through this gray haze, each part becoming definitely meaningful." Again: "Even those first stimuli, simple as they were, just worried me; that is the only word I can use for it. Why, I could not always see the signals, and I was looking right at them. They come and go just as though they possessed some freak capacity." These are instances of actual visual blurs, reported by competent observers. We had many observations on kinaesthetic blurs, which were frequent and typical. Other blurs might be called intellectual, since they had to do almost exclusively with meaning—vision and kinaesthesis remaining under control.

Our observers reported, also, that the blurs, concomitant with the initiation of the reconstitutive process, cleared up, sometimes suddenly, sometimes gradually, as the adequate response emerged. This was to have been expected, since it is precisely the function of the attentive or reconstructive processes to make things clear —to remove blurs. We secured introspective evidence, very definite in character, to show that the final formation of the response was attended by a heightened feeling of clearness, as if light had suddenly been let in upon a state of obscurity. "When the blur dissipates," one observer told us, "the feeling of relaxation is quite marked." Another said, "The feeling of uncertainty and the lack of clearness passed away when the stimulus was seen in its true relationship, and I was prepared to respond."

I wish now to advance the thesis that in the emotional state, in its true form, what is experienced is an enlargement and irradiation of the original blur. Introspectively, as well as objectively, emotion is a state of disruption. All the sensational, imaginal, and affective elements of the experience are exploded out of their natural patterns, are confused and mixed and meaningless. Some theorists maintain that organic sensations are the characteristic elements in the emotions; others emphasize the feelings. Introspection upon genuine emotional states will, I am assured, in the light of our studies already made, show that none of the sensational or affective elements are definitely in the focus of experience, but that, on the contrary, experience is without focus or margin, a confused and scattered state of consciousness. The affective tones which introspectionists describe—or try to describe—are probably present in all of our experiences. But in the emotional state they are confused and dissipated, and the affective tone of the emotional state—if it can be called a tone—is one of blankness and lostness; a condition in which the thousand colors of feeling lose all definiteness and are mixed indiscriminately in the star-dust of general psychical confusion.

DISCUSSION

PROFESSOR HUGHES (*Lehigh University*): Mr. Chairman, the statements that we have just heard read, it seems to me, refer to one class only of what are generally classed as emotional disturbances. It seems to me that we have plenty of evidence of another class of human responses, human activities, which we can hardly deny are emotional, but which, so far from being blurred, are the clearest and the most effective responses that human beings make. Dr. Stratton, in a recent article, has drawn attention to the experiences of an aviator, who, however great the stress, thinks with unusual clarity. The literature of the world is filled with illustrations of that type. Just why it is that psychologists neglect that type of experiences it would be interesting to consider.

You will recall how Plato defines the act of creative imagination. He does not think the best work can be done in a condition of high excitement.

Perhaps some of us are familiar with Oliver Wendell Holmes's account in *The Autocrat at the Breakfast Table* of how it feels to write a poem like "The Chambered Nautilus." At the same moment the man is in a great state of excitement, stunned, thrilled, and so on, to read his adjectives—still he receives things with clearness, a clarity which is unexampled in his experience.

Francis Galton, in speaking of the greatest geniuses, men of the highest imagination, insists on that great emotional quality in their work. Side by side with energy and intelligence he puts what he calls zeal. The emotional factor in human behavior he looks upon as necessary. That is, as the poet says, the fine frenzy of doing.

Until we find what it is that is common in those two types of emotional activity, I do not think we can proceed so far. Why is it that so many psychologists think that an emotionally disturbed state of mind is one in which we are confused? Of course, if it is a matter of definition and we want to say that emotional states are states in which the image is blurred, let us say so. But we are overlooking a department of human behavior that is as important as anything, the work of the minds of the highest quality of creative imagination who seem to be practically unanimous in their treatment of emotional states. So I think I am compelled to reject Dr. Howard's theory of emotional behavior.

DR. HOWARD: There are a great many experiences, such as the one described, that have at various times been called emotional. I certainly do not want to interfere with the examination of any of these interesting experiences. The states that I have called emotional states are confused states, states of blur. I think the other states ought to be studied, too, but it seems to me their nature is different, just as their description is different.

PROFESSOR McMULLEN (*University of Kentucky*): I would like to ask what the connection would be between what we call latent intelligence and the tendency of emotion to be disturbed? What is the connection between those two: tentative or emotional reaction and the strength of the intelligence?

DR. HOWARD: I can see some kind of connection between the two things all right. Assuredly a person who has a character or a make-up that tends to break down constantly under strain can do intellectual work only under the most favorable conditions. Certainly the operation of the intellect would be greatly hindered in the case of a personality that was dissociated or that constantly tended toward disassociation or disruption, and emotional disturbance after all is just a breakdown of personality—temporary break-down of the kind that we often find permanent in abnormal cases.

DR. REYMERT: It occurs to your Chairman that the question from Professor Hughes has been given at least one intelligible answer, worthy of note: namely, by Bergson, in his treatment of "intuition."

DR. HOWARD: I do think that those states of experience in which things stand out clearly and are perceived clearly, in which memory is clear, and in which there seems to be a general uplift of one's whole conscious life, are undoubtedly very interesting. Just what their condition is I am not sure. I am certain that they are not disruptive states. I should say they are the opposite of disruptive. That man has these splendid high moments in life is true, and he must be completely integrated for that moment in order to experience them. The gentleman spoke of a case of clear perception, clear memory, where the person was working under a strain. Well, clarity of memory or clarity of perception are not emotional necessarily. They carry an affective tone with them secondarily, but to be able to see clearly is not to have an emotion. But in general I think those fine high moments of life, which we all experience more or less, come to us when we are integrated, when we are most of all ourselves, most completely in command of ourselves.

PROFESSOR THOMPSON: In support of Dr. Hughes, I would like to ask this question: Is it not the biological and physiological purpose of emotion to protect the person rather than to confuse him?

DR. HOWARD: I have always been interested in that question, as to the value of emotional states, and the conclusion to which I come is that they have absolutely no value at all, but represent a defect in human nature. I cannot see any other conclusion you can come to.

DR. CANNON (*Harvard University*): I studied a short time ago a large number of bodily changes that occur in times when emotions are expressed by lower animals. I spoke of a redistribution of the blood in the body, a rapid heart, a dilation of the bronchia, a liberation of sugar from the liver, a discharge of adrenalin from the glands. Now every one of those changes are directed—at least, they are serviceable; I will not say that they are directed—in making the organism more effective in the struggle. If an animal is enraged, he is likely to attack. If he is frightened, he is likely to run. Whether one is to be the attacker or the attacked, or whether one is the pursuer or the pursued, work must be done by the big skeletal muscles. And perhaps it is a great and lasting struggle. To say that these changes in the body, all of which are serviceable for struggle, are defects, is going against physiological investigation and examination, it seems to me.

I can account for both of the situations which have been developed this afternoon, the clarity and the confusion. It seems to me that there are parts of the central nervous system below the cortex in which all of these emotions have their pattern—have their natural expression. If the cortical inhibition is removed, the expression is intense—intense to the highest degree. If the cortical control is still there, there is a conflict between the natural discharge of these inpulses and the control from above. Under those circumstances there would be hesitation, there would be confusion, there would be no clear integration of the organism in its responses to influences from the outside. The moment that release comes from the cortex and the lower centers have full sway over the body, obviously the clarity would appear.

James had to confront this matter. It was complained by those who opposed his theory that there was an emotion when no work was being done, that there was an emotion when there was no bodily change occurring. I do not think James met that very well, because he had to assume changes were taking place, and he said there were tensions that were not ordinarily observed. You do not have to do that. There are operations going on in these lower states which are discharging upward to the cortex, but which can discharge down lower in the motor mechanism because the cortex holds control. You see we have a conflict. The moment that conflict is resolved by the release to the lower centers of the higher centers, the bodily centers are integrated and the whole process runs off smoothly, and then occurs what James claims did occur under these circumstances, which directly contradicts what the last speaker said. James declared that it was in the expression of the emotion and not in the confusion that the emotion was felt.

DR. PRINCE (*Harvard University*): There are certain things to explain the interpretation that emotions are serviceable. That is to say, when an intense emotion occurs there is a tendency to dissociation of all other processes that are not serviceable for the moment to carry out the adaptation of the person to the situation. In an attack of intense rage, for example, not only is there the discharge of the visceral currents that Dr. Cannon has described and worked out, but there is a discharge that inhibits all other mental processes, so that there is only one focus of intention, there is only one object, one point of view, to which all behavior is directed, and all conflicting behavior or conflicting emotions are inhibited and rendered unconscious. That is the situation as we find it from observation anyway, whether it is serviceable or not. That is to say, if there is a conflict between anger and love, and occasionally that occurs between man and wife, if the husband or the wife arouses that anger, it discharges in the body emotions of that sentiment. Every other point of view, every other conception of the other party, every other emotion that is presented, is inhibited. There is a large number of data derived from abnormal psychology, where the emotion has dissociated the personality, as to that one factor at least, even to the extent of creating a second personality and affecting the defense reaction. Anger is, in one sense, a defense reaction, and when we have the defense reactions, they are serviceable because they direct all of the activities to that point. It is a question of the interpretation of the phenomena.

DR. WILM (*Boston University*): The conception of the emotion as a predicament has seemed to me to be very attractive. I do not see why we should call it a theory. It is a way of regarding an emotion rather than a theory. It affects those emotions which are disagreeable and upsetting—rather than the agreeable emotions—the emotion of predicament. Therefore I went through this list of emotions to see how many are disagreeable and how many are pleasant and agreeable, and I found the describers give a very large number of disagreeable and unpleasant emotions, and a few agreeable. Nevertheless, the predicament is not quite so obvious in the agreeable. However, there are situations, as in excesses of joy where one is beside himself and so happy that he does not know what to do, which will show the emotions of predicament. And whether beyond those agreeable emotions, whether beyond the predicamentive sort there are things we should call emotion, I suppose is more or less a matter of definition. At least a good many of them can be there cared for. I see no contradiction between outcomes of emotive states, such as have been noticed, the clearing out of the muscles, the removal of fatigue products, and the predicament. I do not think it has been shown by the physiologists, but those combining outcomes are common. They are present. Even there, however, as Dr. Cannon said a little while ago, it is doubtful whether the autonomic and visceral changes are resident in the emotion and belong thereto, because they occur without emotion. But even if they are integral to the emotion, I see no contradiction in conceiving the emotion as a predicamentive state, which may, notwithstanding, in its ultimate outcome have certain benefits in certain cases for the organism.

DR. HOWARD: I would like to say just one word. I agree thoroughly with what Dr. Cannon said, and I think there is no real disharmony when I said that emotion had no value. I meant the disruption itself had no value. I say the extreme gross emotional states have no value.

CHAPTER 11

EMOTION AS A DYNAMIC BACKGROUND

Knight Dunlap

The Johns Hopkins University

In my title there are three words the meanings of which are uncertain. These words are: *emotion, background*, and *dynamic*. No one can predict what anyone will mean by these words, until they have been scrupulously defined. Even with the most careful definition and explanation I could give, many persons would probably understand me to use them in senses radically different from those of my definition. It would be better in some ways if I made substitutions for these terms, using the common symbols for unknown quantities, so that the title should read "*X* as a *Y Z*." But even then, there would come a moment at which the listener would say: "Oh, yes, by *X* you mean an emotion." And then he would proceed to refer everything I might say about *X* to an emotion as he understands the term, regardless of what I mean by it.

I must confess that a great deal of what is said about emotions passes over my head. It is probable that the psychologists who discuss this topic are talking about *something*, and I am willing to admit that they are; but if so, then that "something" is something in which I am not interested, except as a matter of folk lore and mythology. Hypogriffs, satyrs, nymphs, djinn, and all the other creatures of mythology, of course, are *something;* and I am afraid that the emotions most psychologists talk about belong with them.

It is supposed that psychology deals first of all with facts, and second with the laws or principles in which these facts are bound up. Admittedly, the laws or principles are tentative, that is, more or less hypothetical; but, if hypothetical, they are hypotheses about facts. The assumption is that before one can legitimately build a hypothesis he must first establish the facts it is designed to fit. But of recent years I have begun to wonder whether psychologists are really interested in facts at all. Artifacts, or concepts, or conjectural facts seem, at any rate, to interest them much more.

I have been asked recently, "What is a fact?" And I can answer that question. A fact is either an object, a relation, or an occurrence. Here is a grain of corn. That is an *object*. I heat it and it pops open. The heating and the popping are series of *occurrences*. The corn may be said to be bigger than another kernel; it differs from a kernel of a different variety. These are *relations*. Are there any other kinds of facts? If there are, they have not been demonstrated.

Now, relations involve something else, usually objects, although there may be relations between relations. But in these cases the relational complexes always go back to relations between objects. An occurrence always involves objects. Hence all factual matters go back to objects.

The dependence of the psychology of perception and of thought on objects has long been recognized. We start our investigations by defining, or pointing out the objects of perception, and we accept the scholastic dictum that all thought depends upon perception, that we can think only of what we have perceived. That this recognition leads to the creation of a class of clumsy mythological objects (sensations and images), does not alter the case. These fictions were created in a well-meaning but unfortunate effort to adhere to the principle that there can be no perception, no thought, without objects. We have discarded sensation and images only because they are fictitious objects, and we can better refer our perceptual and ideational processes to the real objects of the world in which we live and move and have our being; these objects, on the other hand, we no longer confuse with the mathematical symbols and formulae of chemistry or physics by which we must represent them. For such reality as the physicists' and chemists' objects have is pretty well understood to be derived from the real objects of perception.

The so-called emotions of the psychologist (and the so-called feelings also) remain, however, in the world of myth. They are, so far as I can understand, neither objects, nor occurrences, nor relations, but mystical entities, concerning which a mass of mystical speculation has grown up. These are not the emotions of which the unsophisticated man speaks. They have the same connection with reality as the hypogriff, the demon, and the entelechy.

When the plain man speaks of fear, rage, or grief, he apparently has reference to some facts—moreover, to facts which are, or can be, experienced (and experience is an occurrence, and an undisputed fact). If these emotions are facts, they must be either objects or occurrences "in" objects. (I omit the consideration of the possibility of their being relations between objects, for the sake of saving time.) If they are objects, *where* are they? How can we demonstrate them? If they are occurrences, where are the objects in which they occur?

I shall not attempt to consider the answer that objects or occurrences are parts of the brain or occurrences in the brain. This might have been argued forty years ago, but would merely bore you now. One might as well discuss the question whether the observed grain of pop-corn is a part of the brain, and whether the popping is a brain occurrence.

Scientific psychology assumes brain changes, and change in other parts of the organism as well, as the "basis" of *experiencing* an object or occurrence. But in the field of perception it assumes, in the terms of our modern response hypotheses, that there is an object or occurrence outside of the central nervous system which initiates the response of perception. The principle of parsimony impels us to extend this same principle to emotion and the experiencing of emotion. If we actually experience an emotion, the emotion is something demonstrable; and it is something capable of being a stimulus pattern. If it is not, then we are talking in fables, and we should stop discussing emotion in psychology.

Now, James and Lange more or less clearly faced this problem and suggested the answer. Actual conditions and occurrences in the viscera, and in certain parts of the soma, are manifestly capable of serving as stimulus patterns, and can be experienced. Here are demonstrable facts, which *might* be what we mean by emotions. Since no one else has even remotely suggested any other groups of facts which could be indicated by the term, the problem is really this: Shall we agree to call these experienceable visceral (or visceral and somatic) occurrences, emotions? Or shall we reject these, and apply the term to vaguely mystical entities, in which we may happen to believe? The scientific attitude in this dilemma is clear. We must deal with the facts, and let the fictions alone. The only further question is whether we have a right to use the term emotion for these facts, or shall we find a new term and give over the term emotion to the mystics?

Towards the answering of this question, the speculative and analytical work of James and Lange was really directed. It is not a question of the psychological importance of visceral changes. It is solely a question of whether we shall name them emotions. The work of subsequent investigations, analytical and experimental, has been partly directed toward the same end, and in part to the more definite understanding of just what these visceral changes are. The issue was somewhat clouded by the reappearance of the James-Lange theory in what was supposed to be a new form; namely, with emphasis on the anatomical branches of the nervous system involved in the visceral response. This so-called "auto-nomic" theory, however, is merely an anatomical elaboration of the James-Lange theory or, as we should rather term it, the visceral hypothesis of the emotions.

The experimental work has had the following program. We establish conditions in the animal such that, in popular usage of the terms, certain emotions are said to be present. We then try to determine what visceral or somatic occurrences are essential to these conditions. Having established these, we then ask, per-haps: Shall we call these occurrences emotions, or perhaps elements, parts, or features of emotions?

Such experimental work is necessarily slow, and we have but begun to cultivate it. The results, however, are all encouraging. No phenomena appear, so far, which tend to make it impracticable to call these occurrences emotions (or feelings). In addition, we are deriving some information as to the nature of the processes thus named. For example, the work of Cannon, perhaps the most significant thus far, indicates that the emotions which would be commonly classed together as "exciting" do really have a common element. While it is not finally certain that this common element is the important one, the finding of this community in emotion which would be, by simple observation, classed as closely allied, or largely identical, is distinctly encouraging to the visceral view. Moreover, our suspicion that emotions are not distinct entities, but complexes of many variables shading into one another, there-fore in many dimensions, is strengthened.

I have spoken of objects and occurrences as demonstrable. By that I mean that they are capable of observation in various ways, and in particular by those methods, indirect though they may be, called physical and chemical. We would not be satisfied as to the reality of an apple which could only be seen, not touched, unless the light wave from it could be registered photographically. We would not be satisfied with the reality of a smell, unless chemical tests showed the presence of a stimulus. We would not be satisfied with the reality of movement of an object, an occurrence, unless that movement could be registered. In the same way, we should not be satisfied with any object of experience unless it is capable of physical or chemical registration. The "emotions" of which too many psychologists and most physiologists talk are not facts of this kind. Hence, I have no interest whatever in them. The vis-ceral occurrences are demonstrable. Hence, when I use the term emotion, I mean these things. This is the final *demonstration*.

One more point, and then I am through with this part of my discourse. The physical method does not register the yellow of the unpopped kernel of corn, nor the whiteness of the popped corn. Only the optico-neural mechanism of the animal organism can do that. Neither does the physical and chemical examination of the visceral changes register the peculiar "quality" which is experienced as an emotion. But the concomitance is the same in the two cases, and the methods of demonstration are identical. I am not denying, necessarily, that there may be "imaginary" colors: color phenomena not capable of physical registration. The possibility of "imaginary" emotion, therefore, is also open. This problem is no more important in the affective experience than is the visual, and is not the point at issue in my discussion.

I may now pass to my second term, *dynamic*. I am well aware that this term too has mystical implications, and seems to apply, in the discussions of several psychologists, to frankly mystical conceptions. I am using it, however, in a strictly mechanistic sense.

By dynamic, I mean simply having the characteristic of releasing or affecting responses terminating in muscular activity. On our current response hypothesis, which is the basis of what I have named *scientific psychology*, the effective activities of the organs, muscular and glandular, are in large part due to neural transits beginning in the stimulation of receptors. Any stimulus or stimulus pattern is therefore *dynamic*, since it brings about, or checks, these activities. By calling emotions *dynamic*, I am merely emphasizing the fact that they are stimulus patterns. The only demonstrable stimulus patterns which we could rather uniformly designate as emotions are the visceral ones.

Here we are breaking no new ground. The importance of the emotion as a stimulus to action, as initiating certain types of response, as greatly intensifying certain responses, as powerfully inhibiting others has long been recognized. The psychologists paid little attention to this, so long as they dealt with the dreamworld of fictitious "psychic" content. Now that we have descended from the clouds to deal with facts, we are forced to face this aspect of emotion. But so long as our emotion is a mystic entity, our conception of the effects of the emotion is a mystical one, tied up with superstitions of psychic energy and animistic purposes. As soon as we accept emotion as a visceral occurrence, the conception becomes scientific. Vast numbers of receptors are stimulated by visceral changes. The stimulus to any movement is not merely the stimulus pattern imposed on the receptors of the external senses, but the total pattern of these and the somatic and visceral pattern. Any response is the outcome, not of a limited external pattern, as we unfortunately figure it in many of our textbooks, but of the total pattern. Emotions, therefore, participate in the determination of all our responses at all times. The dynamic aspect of emotion is of enormous practical importance, and merits our experimental consideration.

I come now to my third term, *background*. Here I am using a term which is definitely metaphorical. I am implicitly likening the total stimulus pattern to the limited visual pattern. Just as the totality of objects in the visual field is integrated into a pattern, so the total of visceral occurrences and external objects and persons affecting the external sense is integrated into a pattern. But in these patterns we recognize the fact of *dominance*. Dominance is a concept which is hard to define, but we are more and more using the term in psychology and physiology, and its general significance is fairly definite.

In more conventional terminology, we may point out that, in the visual field, certain details "stand out" or are "focal," while the remainder are the "background." What I wish to emphasize by the use of this figure is that in normal life the emotions are the general background, against which external objects appear. This is, of course, a psychological commonplace. I wish to point out certain problems it implies.

1. Why is an emotion different from an external object? Why should we set *these* occurrences aside from all others of our experience? Why not speak merely of the "visceral sense" as one speaks of the visual sense, the auditory sense, etc.?

2. Is emotion always and necessarily "background"? If not, under what conditions can it become "focal"?

3. Can external objects and occurrences reverse their normal relations, and become "background" for the visceral processes?

The answers I would suggest to these questions come from the consideration of the popular use of the term "feeling" in two different ways. It is applied to emotional concepts and processes on the one hand, and to tactual and kinaesthetic on the other. Most texts treat this confusion as a merely vicious one, and explain it as an unfortunate popular lapse to be corrected. On the contrary, I think it is highly important and significant.

If there is a peculiarity of visceral occurrence—of visceral sense —which sets it off from external perception, then it would seem probable that somatic sensitivity, including kinaesthetic and dermal, would occupy a place intermediate between the two. This I believe to be the case. Visceral content is normally "background." External content is normally "foreground." Somatic content is normally integrated with the background, but may from time to time emerge into the foreground, or even into the focus. Our emotions, in other words, are normally not visceral alone, but include, more frequently than not, the somatic, even the dermal factors.

On the other hand, it is observed that at various times large parts of the external world are as much a part of the background as are the visceral factors. There is thus no organic division, no anatomical one, of perception from feeling. The distinction is one of integration.

As a possible illustration of the change from foreground to background of the external content, I suggest observations on music. The movie houses furnish the conditions for this. Undoubtedly, most orchestral noise in the movie houses is an irritation and a distraction. But occasionally, the movie is really absorbing and becomes focal, while the music becomes a part of the background, as unanalyzed and undifferentiated as the visceral processes commonly are. In such cases it may be valuable addition to the total pattern. Is this because it stimulates certain emotional processes? Perhaps. But is it not itself in these cases *a part* of the emotion? I suspect that the answer to this is largely an arbitrary one, depending solely on how you chance to employ and define the term.

Consider, now, the problem of whether the whole group of external contents may become background, against which the visceral contents become foreground. In such a case, would we say that the external world is our emotion, or would we say the emotion has become focal? Again, a terminological matter. But it is important to consider the possibility of the integrative reversal, for I have a strong suspicion that this is exactly what is occurring in certain types of psychopathic patients. This is another problem which well merits investigation.

What I am trying to point out is that, on the visceral hypothesis of emotion, there is no divine peculiarity of the visceral processes themselves which sets them off as emotions in contrast with the external world—rather, that it is a peculiarity of the habitual pattern of integration which is responsible. Why integration normally takes this pattern type, we may not be able to explain in full, but we can make a good guess. The constancy of presence of the visceral factors (auditory and visual stimuli may come and go, but our guts are always with us) and the difficulty of spatial analysis on account of the enclosure of the organs are, no doubt, contributing factors. But I suspect that the most important reason is a combined hygienic and motor one. The visceral processes work the better, the less we attempt to attend to them, and our attention is needed for control of our environment. (By attention I refer to the type of dominance in integration.) The introspective person is morbid, that is, in an unhygienic condition, and is also inefficient. The outdoor life demands a minimizing of introspection. The sedentary life permits introspection because of the lessened demands of environmental adaptation, and hence it facilitates morbidity. Routine has the same effect. The visceral contents are emotions because mankind has to integrate in that way in order to live effectively.

DISCUSSION

DR. PRINCE (*Harvard University*): There should be a great deal of discussion on this paper. There are one or two points about which I would like to speak and have further elucidation from Dr. Dunlap. But before doing so, I would like to cite this: I like very much his point of view, his critical and analytical approach, and his examination of the grounds. It is said that London University was founded for those who were not willing to accept conclusions until they had examined the ground upon which they were based. I think that Dr. Dunlap's stand is that. He wants to examine the grounds. But there are one or two points which are not quite clear to me, and on which I wish he would elucidate a little further.

I cannot understand why, under his definition of a fact, he does not accept emotion as a fact, that is to say, as an occurrence, and define a fact as an occurrence; and if he admits emotion at all, why doesn't he accept that as a fact? If he accepts emotion as something or other, why isn't it just as much an occurrence as a pain would be? I have a pain now. Or we will assume it. I may not present evidence to you that I have a pain. I know very well that I am subconscious of it. It may not appear to you but I know it perfectly well. Now to me, if I had a pain, it would be a serious fact, and I would class it as an occurrence. Dr. Dunlap was using thoughts. Weren't they facts? I don't see exactly why he takes that position.

Now, what sort of facts they are is a different kind of proposition. And so, another point that I want to bring out. As I understand Dr. Dunlap, he quotes James and others as holding the fact, and also himself adopts the fact, that the emotion is the visceral change. I never understood that James said they were the visceral changes. As I understand that theory, it is the awareness or consciousness of the visceral changes. The bell rings when the visceral changes take place. To identify emotion with the visceral changes seems very much like identifying my perception of the locomotive with the locomotive. But they are two different things. I do not quite understand identifying emotion with a physical change unless you are an idealist. But those points I cannot help but refer to. I think they should have more elucidation.

I also wish that Dr. Cannon, who is here, would tell us something of his experiments bearing upon these things.

DR. CANNON (*Harvard University*): I was very much interested in the emphasis which Dr. Dunlap laid on the visceral changes. Also I was interested in what was said about the relatively small number of visceral changes that had been described as a consequence of the experiments carried on in the Harvard laboratory. After we had shown that there was a stoppage of the movements of the stomach and the intestines, a liberation of sugar from the liver, an acceleration of the heart, a liberation of adrenalin from the suprarenal glands, a dilation of the bronchia, and other physiological changes, Dr. Humphrey said that Cannon had brought so many facts to bear in support of the James-Lange theory that it was very extraordinary that he thought he was arguing against it.

The point that Dr. Prince refers to, I think, is this. We found that the same sort of change occurs in the viscera whether the animal shows signs of aggression and attack or signs of retreat and attempts at escape. We have interpreted these two different sources of behavior as of the nature of rage or anger or fear. Those are two experiences which we testify to, at least to each other, as being very different experiences, and yet, so far as the changes in the viscera are concerned, they are very much alike. It is hard to see how you can differentiate such emotions, such different emotions as these, on the basis of phenomena that are so alike as the visceral changes in the two.

More recently we have found that the same changes occur when the animal is exposed to cold, when the animal is given an injection of dead bacteria and has fever; also when it is given insulin and the blood sugar drops down to about half of its amount. The viscera have the same changes in all these various conditions.

And in the last three conditions I have mentioned there is no emotional state that results from the change. Furthermore, a Spanish investigator who administered insulin in large doses to numerous persons, well and ill, recorded their testimony. Adrenalin brings about in the body the same physiological changes that are wrought by the activity, the impulse, of the sympathetic division of the autonomic system. What did these patients testify? They did not have feelings of emotion. They said they felt edgy, they felt as if they might have an emotion; they had what Meringian has himself called a cold emotion. It was as if they were sitting by and watching something going on, but the emotion as such was not testified to by these persons.

Again, if the viscera are so important as elements of the emotional experience, as a basis for the emotional experience—I may say that James specifically laid a greater emphasis on visceral changes than on the changes of the skeletal muscle—if they are so important, it seems to me peculiar that we are not conscious of peristaltic changes that are passing through the stomachs of you who have enjoyed a good lunch, of the rhythmic contractions in the small intestines, and of the pouring out of bile or the pancreatic juices. All of these visceral changes had to wait for myriads and myriads of generations for observers to be prepared to look into the body and find out what is going on there.

We know of only about one-tenth as many afferent nerves as motor nerves, but the situation is altogether different in the spinal nerve trunk, in which the afferent nerves are more numerous than the motor.

These evidences seem to me may be put together as making out a very strong case against the reverberations, the returns from the sounding board, to use James's expression, as a source of emotional quality.

As I have pointed out, the observations of Henry Head indicate that the afferent nerves from the skeletal muscles are likewise not a source of affective states of feeling at all.

What is there left? We have going on, in the lower part of the brain, processes of a pattern character. That they are of a pattern character is shown by the fact that they establish patterns. When a person weeps he is displaying a very different skeletal muscle pattern from that which he displays when he is angry or when he is glad and laughs. The external pattern is indicative of an internal pattern.

We know, furthermore, that this part of the nervous system works with extraordinary intensity if it is only released from inhibition.

It seems to me that, in this region where such patterns arise and play their rôle in establishing external forms of muscle settings, all you have to assume is that the impulses which are started there outward toward the periphery also affect directly the conscious states or send impulses up to the cortex, where they are experienced as a conscious state of the feeling character, and that these feelings are added on to the experiences which we have as a consequence of the stimulus of external objects. The feeling-tone is obtained from the lower part of the brain and not from the periphery.

DR. DUNLAP: I will say with regard to Dr. Morton Prince's questions, if I gathered them correctly, that what I was trying to show was that I accept the emotion as an occurrence, and, when I try to find out where it is, the only thing I can find is something in the viscera. I was accepting it. That is what I was trying to do.

With regard to James and Lange, it is true that James never accepted his own theory in a full way, and not only held on to psychopathic parallelism, but he also reserved a whole lot of spiritual feelings that he was not willing to subject to the gross bodily condition. You know we have a feeling that our stomachs and intestines are low and vulgar. Curiously our brains, which biologically are not so very superior, we do not think degrade our feelings.

With regard to Dr. Cannon's remark, I want to say my paper has had exactly the effect I had hoped it would have. I shall not attempt to answer Dr. Cannon (I will say that I cannot) but I do feel—I am not going to burden you with a lengthy argument here—but I do feel that Dr. Cannon's results are rather in favor of the visceral theory than against it. The old theory which Descartes proposed, that is, that the afferent currents produced the intellect and the efferent produced the passions of the soul, James thought Münsterberg had knocked out. Apparently James was wrong.

There are many points of argument on that basis. We do have these patterns, muscular and glandular. How are they going to register? Is it a double-handed affair? Or is it experience of the same type where a stimulus pattern introduces a response which ends in another pattern, but in which we experience the stimulus pattern but not the terminal pattern? I am for the sake of parsimony trying to make our theory which works for perception also work for emotion.

Now, with regard to the many points that Dr. Cannon has brought up that I shall not take time to argue—I do not say I can answer them—I think that the matter of interpretation of results is sometimes a thing we want to keep distinct from the results themselves. The uniformity of results from uniformity of visceral conditions in certain of what we call emotional states is a thing I would have predicted on the basis of the James-Lange theory. These emotions with which Dr. Cannon works are exciting emotions. They are much more alike than they are different. We expect to find the similarities first. I say I do not believe that they produce anything. I do not know that adrenalin had anything to do with the case. But where we expected to find overwhelming agreement, we find similarity in that respect. Out of that adrenalin test—I think Dr. Cannon himself has some discussions on that point which will clear that matter up.

So with regard to the numerousness of the visceral receptors. That is an important point we must consider. With regard to the few or many types of visceral process that can be identified with something emotional, that again is something about which we cannot say we have exhausted all the possibilities there are. Dr. Cannon himself will say that. There is still a great deal more to be found with reference to the ductless glands, with respect to the tissues, with respect to other conditions. I am not attempting to answer Dr. Cannon. I cannot do it, but I think there is a strong point there that can be brought out in more detail.

I want to say this. I value my hypothesis, as I said in the beginning, as suggesting experimental means of attack. There has been suggested to me a method of approaching facial expression that I had never thought of before. I had not thought of it until I got this old visceral theory. I hooked it up in intelligent shape to myself and it occurred to me there are certain details of expression—of what we popularly call emotion or feeling—of various types that ought to be more characteristic to the muscles surrounding the mouth, which belong to the feeding system, than to the muscles around the eyes, which do not belong to that system. There is something in the theory. I tried it out. My results are interesting. I have some more stuff on that line that is also going to be interesting. The only defense I am going to make to that theory is that it can suggest interesting things to try out in our laboratories.

DR. WILM (*Boston University*): The most sensational part of Dr. Dunlap's paper to me at least was the denial that emotions or feelings are facts. Now, it seems to me that that is a highly debatable statement. To my mind, to deny that the pain I feel from the pin-prick is not a fact, and a fact distinguished, for example, from the fact of sensation, seems to be a highly untenable and absurd proposition. There are some theories, like behaviorism, that are so intrinsically absurd that only the most learned men may hold them. I may add two very elementary remarks about the reason why emotions and feelings might possibly not be regarded as facts, in the sense at least that they may not be dealt with as legitimate objects of scientific investigation. The first consideration would be that the emotion, as opposed to the antecedents and the consequents of the emotion, is not an object of common observation. And, in the second place, the emotion as distinguished from the condition of the physical correlates of emotion and the physical accompaniments. They are not susceptible of exact correlation. Those are patent facts. But it does not seem to me that those facts would enable one to deny the existence of the emotions as facts.

I think it would be well to refer to Hume's discussion of causation in this connection. It does not seem to me that we have to do more than to note a rough correlation between the antecedents and consequents, in order to recognize the emotion not only as a fact but as a cause. It is undoubtedly true, if you are satisfied with the causation in the relation of antecedents and consequents, that there is a cause relation between emotion and the physical antecedents of emotions and any physical consequents which they may have.

DR. DUNLAP: What I was trying to show was that emotions *were* facts, and any attempt to make anything of them other than facts is necromancy. A man says he has a pain in his toe. As a fact I want to find that fact in his toe. I am afraid I cannot find it in the sphere in which Professor Cannon wants to find it. As far as that goes, I was trying to demonstrate the thing which my critic demonstrates.

CHAPTER 12

CAN EMOTION BE REGARDED AS ENERGY?

MORTON PRINCE
Harvard University

Let me begin by saying that in bringing this question before you I do not intend to dogmatize or lay down any final conclusions. Rather what I want to do is to invite discussion of the problem of emotion and energy as one that needs full and open-minded consideration. For, to my way of thinking, it is one which lies at the root of a number of difficult problems of emotion and particularly that of the part it plays in the mechanism of instincts (if there be instincts) and in many mental processes such as inhibition, repression, and conflicts, and consequently in behavior in general.

"Can emotion be regarded as energy?" I quite well realize that this question is one at which psychologists tend to look askance and balk like timid, nervous colts. They like to put it aside as a disagreeable one for they scent an unpleasant trail that is likely to lead them to epistemology and concepts which cannot be reduced to tabulated correlations of objective data so dear to the present-day psychologist. If he can only correlate something and present us with figures embellished with plus and minus signs in expensively arranged tables (I speak with the feelings of an editor), he feels he is entitled to enter at least the porticoes of objective science and perhaps will be permitted to sit down on equal terms with physicists and chemists and other fortunate devotees of exact methods. It does not matter much what he correlates, or how much energy he wastes, as long as he correlates something.

The concept of emotion as physical or psychophysical energy involves consequences of serious import. It must be obvious that it makes a radical difference in the validity of some of the theories of emotion, and also in our interpretation of the part it plays in the mechanism of the emotional reactions of the organism, whether they be regarded as instinctive or not.

If, for instance, it is energy, a Cartesian concept by the way, then plainly it needs no argument to show that it does not play the rôle of "passive sensory receptions" of visceral functions (to use a phrase of L. H. Horton's), as the James-Lange theory holds, but its discharge must of itself determine behavior of *some* kind.

Likewise, again, in the interpretation of behavior as response to a

stimulus, emotion, if energy, cannot be regarded as an epiphenomenon correlated with neural reflexes, as behaviorists would have
us believe, but must be a factor in the neural discharges affecting
motor and other responses, whether it be only by exploding or
releasing those discharges or providing the energy for them.

Nor, in the responses of those innate inherited mechanisms
characterized by emotion—call them instincts or not, as you
please—can emotion, if energy, play the passive part of an epiphenomenon; it must *do* something; and it is logical to infer that,
as a discharge of energy, it provides the drive for the response of the
mechanism to the stimulus. And, if such be the case, emotion
would have to be regarded as a discharge of psychophysical energy
along neural pathways. This does not mean that those particular
units of energy, alias emotion, must or would as such traverse as
waves, or some other kind of motion, the neural pathways. They
might transmit their energy to efferent neurones, i. e., be transformed into neural energy, just as in the world of physics and
chemistry mechanical energy is transformed into electrical, thermal, and chemical energy, or electrical energy is transformed
into neural and magnetic energy (light, radio, and other waves).

Aside from these considerations I would point out that the
serviceability of emotion to the organism becomes much more intelligible by this concept of emotion and energy, for if, per contra,
emotion is nothing but a conscious correlate of a neural discharge
of energy, or if only a passive sensory awareness of visceral activity,
as many maintain, one may well ask: "What is the good of emotion? 'What price emotion' if the physiological neural discharge
accomplishes everything—is the whole drive? Why could we not
get along perfectly well without emotion, without anger, or fear,
or any other feeling, even if we were only automata?"

But, granting all this, if you are willing to do so, the real question is: What facts have we for the concept that would identify
emotion with so-called physical energy? Facts we have but their
interpretation is not easy, and positive conclusions, perhaps, are
not justifiable.

In the first place, we know that with the excitation of emotion
there *is* a discharge of energy of some kind in different directions.
That is a demonstrable fact. There is the discharge to the viscera,
to the heart, and to the suprarenal glands, for instance. The discharge to the heart could be·measured in foot pounds by recording
the increased work done by that organ. The discharge to the
suprarenal glands might well be measured by weighing the increased quantity of adrenalin poured out into the blood stream.

The discharge to the voluntary muscular system could also be reckoned in foot pounds by measuring the increase of work done. And so with other effects of the discharge. Whether such discharges of energy have their source in the emotions is another question—is the question at issue. It is the simplest explanation and we are forced to ask, why not?

In the second place, the discharge of energy occurs apparently, i. e., so far as it is possible with our present technique to determine, synchronously with the occurrence of the emotion and continues as long as the emotion persists. In other words, the stimulus that sets off the discharge of neural energy synchronously excites or at least conditions the emotion.

Now if it can be safely assumed that the occurrence of emotion is synchronous with the discharge of energy, then this fact gives a knock-out blow to the James-Lange theory. For obviously as emotion, according to this theory, is the "passive sensory reception" awakened in consciousness by the visceral activities *following* the discharge, the emotion must occur still later and *follow* the visceral response. But if emotion is synchronous with the neural discharge, it must precede, not follow, the visceral response. We could not say with James that "we are pleased because we laugh" or "are sad because we weep," because we would be pleased or sad before we laughed or wept. (As a matter of fact, by the way, a hysteric may laugh without being joyous and weep without feeling sad.)

On the other hand, if emotion be a pure, luxurious epiphenomenon, enabling us only to enjoy the pleasure or pain of an experience without in any way determining our response to a situation, it presents nothing incompatible with the fact of occurring synchronously with its correlated energy-discharge. So synchronism is an important problem awaiting solution.

As an epiphenomenon, however, it would seem to be a perfectly useless, in a biological sense, phenomenon, as abhorrent to evolution as a vacuum is to nature. But, it may be argued, this is not true. It may be that emotion as an epiphenomenon may be serviceable indirectly to the organism in warning it of danger or pleasure in the present situation, or in one to come. In that case it might correspondingly in some obscure way originate the stimulation of habit neurograms or patterns of response that will avoid the danger or secure the biological advantages of pleasure. In this sense it would be comparable to a fire-gong sounding an alarm that brings the firemen, or a theater-gong that between the acts advises the audience smoking cigarettes in the lobby that the pleasure of a new act awaits it. But would not even such a stimulation function be equivalent to the discharge of energy?

There is another fact that must be considered though how much weight should be given to it is not wholly clear. It certainly has some significance. We all have a feeling that passion moves us, that it energizes our thoughts and our bodily actions. We have a consciousness that emotion and feeling activate us. This conscious experience is a fact; its significance is another question. The expression, "I was moved by emotion," or "I was overwhelmed by emotion," "I was driven by emotion," is on everybody's lips, meaning moved or overwhelmed, or driven by emotion as a force or an energy. It is the interpretation of "common sense." Common sense, of course, is a dangerous criterion. As a test it is unreliable for it is quite likely, as we all know, to be fallacious. Yet it may be right and sometimes is more likely right than some new-fangled, far-fetched theories of schools.

In this case, the testimony of consciousness and common sense, if it can be shown not to be contradicted by demonstrable facts, acquires some weight as evidence. And I think we must admit that there are no demonstrated facts that contradict the evidence of consciousness, even if it be insisted that there is none which supports it.

It is not without bearing on this point that the notion of "energy" and "force" is derived, as I shall presently insist, from our conscious experience of exerting force, from our consciousness or feeling of exerting energy. If it were not for the reality of this consciousness of force, whether it be delusion or not, in all probability the term would never have come into being; some other term would have been invented by the physicist though it is impossible to guess what it would have been. He derives his concept of energy as something that moves and does things and causes things to happen from his conscious experience of that which, as it seems to him, moves his muscles and energizes his whole being.

At any rate, the conscious experience of passion energizing us as a force is a fact though its interpretation and significance may be in doubt.

But how reconcile the concept of emotion as energy with the physicist's concept of energy? Emotion, the psychologists and the plain man in the street recognize as a state of his consciousness, but if it is of the order of consciousness how reconcile it with the physicist's conception of energy, or rather identify it with his energy, a physical term—which is to say, with what the physicist means by energy? Here is an apparent paradox.

Well, what does a physicist mean by energy? It is not going too far to say that he has nothing in mind, if by energy is meant a concrete entity of a specific nature and quality, like the ether, or electromagnetic waves or mass. It is only a concept which he postulates as an entity to explain why and how things happen. To be sure, he measures and weighs it and tells us what quantity of kinetic energy is involved in the appearance and disappearance of motion. But how does he do this? He does it by measuring the motion and mass moved, as when, for instance, he measures the energy of a great turbine engine by measuring the motion and mass of things moved, etc.—the product of the motion times one-half the mass. Then he tells us such a quantity of energy was used—derived from the coal and expended in motion. He even tells us that mass itself is energy, and makes us a bit dizzy by his formula which now becomes: quantity of energy is motion times one-half the energy!

If asked what energy is, he does not pretend to know or even care to know. It is not necessary for him to know. In fact it cannot be known by his objective methods. It belongs to the *unknowables* of physical science. But, as I have already pointed out, the concept is derived from conscious experience and may be said to be an anthropomorphic term. Things happen *as if* there were an entity called energy. But the physicist will tell you that it is none of his business to determine what it *is*. It is none of his job.

Is it the job of the psychologist? Can he say that it is none of his business, if it is true that the physicist derives his terminology and concept from psychology, and if it is an entertainable hypothesis that emotion is a certain kind of energy, that the two can be identified? Isn't it his job to explain how this can be? I leave it to you.

This brings us back to the remark I made at the beginning about psychologists' fighting shy of the question, feeling that it will lead them astray out of the beaten path of objective methods. But if the notion of emotion's being energy is entertainable, I submit it becomes the business of psychologists to examine what is meant by physical energy and inquire how the apparent paradox of emotion's being—like mechanical, electrical, and thermal energy— a form of this postulate of physics can be explained; that is, explain how they can be one and the same thing. And this would seem to be the business of the psychologist, as emotion is a psychological event and energy a psychological concept. For without the concept of energy of some kind behavior cannot be explained.

The need of this inquiry is further forced upon us, as the answer may make all the difference in the world in our understanding of those fundamental psychological problems about which there is much present-day debate, and which we are called together in this symposium to discuss.

In lieu of an extended discussion of the paradox in question I will content myself with stating my own conception of the answer to the problem.

The postulate of physical science of an entity called anthropomorphically energy is, by all the criteria of matter, *immaterial*. Its nature is unknowable by the objective methods of science. It is inferred from and postulated to explain the happenings of the so-called "physical world"; it is only known, therefore, by its manifestations or behavior—by what it does. It is known from without, not from within.

As kinetic energy it manifests itself in many forms—as mechanical, electrical, thermal, chemical, etc., and perhaps neural energy, and each may be transformed into another form. Many of its forms, it is agreed, are the resultants of the complexities, collocation, combination, number, and organization of its units. The present thesis is that psychical energy is another form.

Kinetic energy is only known through its manifestations, among which are the motions of electrons and of coll cations of electrons (atoms, molecules) and electromagnetic ether waves. But the most advanced and philosophical physicists tend to regard electrons not as little lumps of something called electricity, but as units of energy itself and as such, of course, unknown in their inner nature. Under this concept the whole universe is this mysterious, unknown, immaterial energy.

Now according to our thesis emotions may be conceived as emerging as consciousness out of energy in either one or two ways. (1) They may be discharging complexes of units of energy associated with the electrons of the highly complex atomic structure of the nervous system. That is to say, the discharges emerge (by the principle of "emergent evolution") as emotion because they are the energy itself—energy from *within* not as observed from without, *of the extremely complex organization of enormous numbers of units of neural energy.* Observed from without they would be known only by what they do. Or (2) we can conceive that kinetic *afferent* neural energy, being *immaterial*, becomes transformed into its like, immaterial psychical energy, which in turn, as a link in the chain of events, becomes transformed into *immaterial* efferent energy, thus conforming to the physical law of the transformation of energy.

That which is the unknown and unknowable by the objective methods of science emerges as the known of psychology, as states of consciousness. This, of course, is monism.

The only alternative hypothesis is dualism and parallelism, that is to say, epiphenomenonism and human automatism.

But emotion as an epiphenomenon would be as useless to the organism as the steam whistle, to borrow Huxley's famous phrase, is to the working of the engine. It would be only a symbol in consciousness of what was happening without power to control, direct, or determine behavior, or at best its serviceability would be limited like a fire-gong, if the emotion be fear, to warning of danger, a signal to "look out" for fire but without power to direct how to put it out or escape. Here we stand between two concepts or hypotheses, both of which we find difficult to reconcile with conscious experience.

The difficulty with the first is that our modes of thinking are so horribly and incorrigibly concrete that we find ourselves handicapped in conceiving physical forces as immaterial, as anything like the psychical, and therefore as comprehensible as an entity out of which anything like emotion or other state of consciousness can emerge; or, as an alternative, though the psychical be force, how physical force, even if it be immaterial, can be transformed into the psychical as a link in the chain of events to be transformed again into the immaterial physical.

The difficulty with the second is that it is irreconcilable with conscious experience and common sense that tell us we are something more than physiological automata, and that emotion moves us, determines our behavior, and is not an epiphenomenon nor only a symbol in consciousness of neural processes.

Yet between these two hypotheses we must choose.

Which hypothesis is the more probable I submit for your consideration. For my part, I lean towards the first.

For one thing, it escapes the difficulty, if not impossibility, of constructing emotion and feeling out of sensory elements as the James-Lange theory requires, but it assumes they are definite, psychical states in accordance with the commonly accepted conscious experience of ages—a possibly debatable postulate.

I have avoided speculation as to the locus of origin of the psychical energy, whether at the central brain receptors of sensory stimuli, or at the central motor outlets (synapses) to efferent paths, or in a special locus of pattern neurones in the thalamus or cortex in accordance with the very beautiful experimental studies of Cannon. The first two localizations are purely speculative.

Wherever it may be, the hypothesis enables us to form a constructive notion of the serviceability of emotion and feeling to the organism and the part they play in behavior. "Step on it, step on the gas," you tell your chauffeur. And he steps on the accelerator, and your machine springs forward with increased energy. "Go to it," you tell the young man who has undertaken a job. "Go to it," the coach tells the athlete—the track runners, the football team, the crew—and each and all step on the accelerator of their emotions and spring with revitalizing energy, power, to their task of beating their rivals. Without turning on the energy of their emotions, what a listless game they would play! But they step on the accelerator only when increased power is needed, yet at all times the throttle is partially open, just enough to supply sufficient energy to keep the wheels of activity going and to help in doing the everyday job.

The mechanism by which the throttle of emotional energy is thrown wide open or closed is another problem, but in the organization of sentiments as worked out by Shand and McDougall, we have at least an adequate arrangement. The linkage of ideas to the emotional dispositions (that is, to the innate psychophysiological mechanism of which emotion is the central energizing factor) to form sentiments would provide a serviceable adequate device. According to this theory of sentiments their driving power is derived from some such linkage of the emotions. When, then, the coach exorts his team to "go to it," he calls into being, stimulates, a sentiment of one kind or another, one of winning, and the emotional energy of that sentiment supplies the needed power.

It is not necessary for me to point out how this conception is in line with McDougall's theory of instincts so far as they are "prime movers of human activity." Unless emotion and feeling are energy his theory would, it seems to me, have little weight.

William James, with that almost uncanny insight, a sort of clairvoyance which enabled him to see into commonplace things some meaning which escaped those of lesser vision, called attention to the "reserve energies of men." It was just a commonplace fact until he touched it with his imagination, when it became an intriguing mystery.

The mystery disappears if emotion be energy. Under certain conditions men are known to perform feats of strength and endurance of which they are incapable in everyday life. They seem to tap a reserve of energy! I think that in such conditions it will be found that they are in an emotional state of exaltation, or ecstasy, or some sort of state when all inhibitions of emotion are dissociated, cast off, and the throttle of energy is thrown wide open allowing the driving force of emotion full play.

Other fruitful applications of the hypothesis as well as elaborations of its details could be given if time permitted. As it is, I leave it here as a useful concept to explain human behavior, comparable to that which physical science makes use of to explain the universe.

DISCUSSION

UNIDENTIFIED MEMBER OF AUDIENCE: I should like to ask Dr. Prince upon what theory he says energy is an anthropomorphic term.

DR. PRINCE: In the first place, energy is a concept that was used in psychology and philosophy long before it was used in physics, I take it—as far back as Aristotle. In the second place, I think it is a generally accepted fact by all the physicists—certainly by all the physicists with whom I have spoken, and I was only recently speaking to one of our most distinguished mathematicians and physicists—that it was derived from conscious experience. If you stop to think about it, what does the physicist see in the electron? He sees, if there were such a thing as that, something like that which I feel. That would account for it. I think it is generally accepted by every physicist and every psychologist that I have talked to.

MR. X: May I ask how you would relate the theory to Keith Lucas' theory of all or none?

DR. PRINCE: First, I will say it is something I had not thought of. Secondly, I do not think it alters the situation under observation. We now conceive of the discharge of neural energy, only we do not identify it as an emotion, and you have to ask the same question with reference to neural energy, whether it conforms to the all or none theory. I do not think it alters the thing at all. If it is compatible with the theory of energy, it would also be with this.

CHAPTER 13

FEELING AND EMOTION AS FORMS OF BEHAVIOR

ALBERT P. WEISS
Ohio State University

INTRODUCTION

Changes in Psychology

I believe we all agree that the fundamental assumptions of psychology are changing. Man is being studied not only (*a*) as an organism that reports mental states, but also (*b*) with respect to the biological and social conditions which make him a participating unit in a social organization. These two points of view may be distinguished as (*a*) mentalistic, introspective, experiential, or literary, (*b*) as the biological-sociological.[1]

The systematic difference between the two lies in the fact that the mentalistic approach leads to philosophical[2] or metaphysical discussions; the biosocial approach leads to social, statistical, biological, chemical, or physical discussions.

In order to throw the two points of view in strong relief against each other let me present them in contrast. A definition of psychology stressing the mentalistic set of fundamentals is given by Bentley (1925): "It (psychology) seeks to describe and to understand experience and the activities of the total organism in which experience plays an essential part" (p. 15). As representative of the biosocial set of fundamentals, I give the following: "Psychology studies those movements of the individual from

[1] For linguistic convenience I shall use the term "biosocial" for the compound word biological-sociological, natural-evolutionary, or merely scientific.

[2] The philosophical categories are inadequate for psychology because they are the remnants of classifications of human behavior which were developed before neurological observation had made it possible to describe human behavior. Philosophy represents the unanalyzable complex linguistic responses which are substitutes for personal and tribal taboos, social, political, and religious practices whose origins are lost in antiquity. For those who lack the scientific and particularly the biological training that makes human behavior comprehensible, outworn racial, national, and class shibboleths have been synthesized into an ambiguous, but more elegant, terminology which is more acceptable than the cruder popular superstitions. In practice philosophic discussions lead to heterogeneity in classification, scientific discussions to homogeneity.

infancy to maturity which establish his social status in the social organization of which he is a member."

According to Bentley the psychological problem is largely that of describing human experiences (whatever we may mean by this term). I do not mean to be facetious in the use of the parenthetical phrase. I believe the phrase is necessary because there is not sufficient agreement among psychologists as to just what is to be included under the term. For any given writer, however, it is usually possible to formulate a reasonably clear statement. Bentley, for instance, indicates what he would include as follows: "In experience, for example, appear tones and noises; and as they appear the organism is affected in a specific way and at a particular place by the vibratory movements of the air. These vibratory movements (a part of the physicist's world) affect experience only by way of the ear; more exactly stated, by way of the auditory receptor or sense organ in the inner ear" (p. 33).

According to the biosocial position "experience" is merely a name for our acquired responses. It is an open question whether the study of human behavior (as opposed to the study of human experience) will replace the mentalistic conception. For the present it is only necessary to differentiate the two sets of fundamental "doctrines," mentalistic and biosocial psychology.[3]

[3] In earlier writings I have used the term "behavioristic" instead of biosocial. When, among others, I first began using the term behavioristic about twelve years ago, I used it as the biologists and zoölogists use it; as a description of the *activities* of an organism. Within the last few years, however, it has acquired an entirely different meaning in psychology. That there is a profound change taking place we may all admit, whatever we may think about the permanence of the change. But this change is not as sudden or of the same nature as the flare-up of "behaviorism" in popular psychology. As with biology, psychology is getting farther and farther away from the position assigned to it by philosophy and is taking a place intermediate between biology and sociology. For a time it perhaps will be necessary to distinguish this transition by a name. I have suggested the term biosocial. This would have been unnecessary had the term behavioristic retained the scientific meaning that it has in animal behavior. Unfortunately psychology is not yet scientific enough to have a generally accepted system of fundamental assumptions. We may as well admit this. When we get these, and this is a problem for all of us, we can dispense with both the terms mental and biosocial. There will be only one approach to the study of human behavior. When there is only one approach we shall not need to characterize it any more than it is now necessary to distinguish the scientific approach to physics and chemistry from the older approach of alchemy. Biology is still struggling with a "vitalistic approach," but in America at least the biochemical approach is now regarded as almost self-evident.

Does Psychology Need a Different Set of Fundamental Assumptions?

The introspective method isolates psychology from the biological and social sciences, and we may ask whether it is possible to substitute fundamentals[4] which will place psychology in the system of the natural sciences without losing whatever the introspective technique has to contribute. I believe we must plan our experiments in such a way that it will be possible to weave our results into the fabric of science as represented by physics, chemistry, biology, and a social science which studies statistically the biological and environmental conditions under which human institutions arise.

To be more specific, Titchener (1908) defines feeling "as mental processes of the same general kind as sensations, and as mental processes that might, under favorable conditions have developed into sensation" (p. 292). Meyer (1908) defines feeling as, "the (nervous) correlate of pleasantness and unpleasantness is the increase or decrease of the intensity of a previously constant current if the increase or decrease is caused by a force acting at a point other than the point of sensory stimulation" (p. 307).

These two statements of the concept of feeling rest upon entirely different fundamental doctrines. Professor Titchener rests his analysis upon a mentalistic foundation, Professor Meyer upon a biological foundation. We may ask which set of assumptions will best meet those requirements which are recognized as inherent in scientific method. Simply stated, cannot what is included under the term mind or experience by psychologists and writers in general be more clearly described under a set of non-mentalistic assumptions? Suppose we begin with a shorter review of the problem of feeling as represented by traditional psychology.

THE PROBLEM OF FEELING

Contradictory Views of Feeling

Lagerborg (1906) regards a feeling as a weak and unlocalized sensation. As soon as its intensity is increased it can be localized and is then called a sensation. There are three classes of feeling: unpleasantness, pleasantness, and common feelings. The corresponding sensations are pain, the sexual sensation, and visceral or kinaesthetic sensations. There are probably special pleasure and pain nerves in various parts of the body which may be stimulated

[4] I have outlined such a set of postulates in my *A Theoretical Basis of Human Behavior*.

in two ways: (a) mechanically and (b) chemically by the nutritive processes in the tissues. Heightened metabolic processes produce pleasantness; lowered metabolic processes produce unpleasantness.

Titchener (1924) regards pleasantness and unpleasantness as elementary processes of a different sort from sensations and images, the main difference being that feeling cannot be made the object of direct attention. In combination with organic and kinaesthetic sensation, pleasantness and unpleasantness produce sense feelings of six types: agreeable and disagreeable, the exciting and subduing, the straining and relaxing. He does not offer specific biological correlates, nor does he regard feelings as causes in the modification of behavior. "The explanation of action," he says, "is to be found in the determining tendencies of the nervous system and not in the motive force of feeling" (p. 258).

For Marshall (1894) pleasure indicates the expenditure of surplus stored energy whereas pain indicates an expenditure of energy larger than the possible supply. As mental correlates Marshall (1908) proposes psychical elements of the nature of pain and pleasure.

Stumpf (1906) regards pleasantness and unpleasantness as sensations. Unpleasantness is merely a slight degree of the sensation of pain. Pleasantness is a slight degree of that sensation which in its greatest intensity results from stimulation of the sexual organs, and of which intermediate degrees are given the name of tickling and, somewhat stronger, itching. As the nervous correlate of pleasantness and unpleasantness Stumpf assumes the existence of the algedonic pain nerves suggested by Marshall.

The distinction between pain and unpleasantness is clearly brought out by Professor Calkins in her very apt illustration, "It is unpleasant, for example, but not painful, to mistake an ice-cream fork for an oyster fork at a dinner party" (p. 71). As a neural basis for pleasantness and unpleasantness she proposes the nutritive conditions of the cells in the frontal lobes. Pleasantness occurs when the nervous discharge passes over well-nourished cells; unpleasantness when it passes over fatigued cells.

Pikler (1900) raised the question which has now become dominant in psychology, namely, what is the selective factor in changes of behavior? He holds that all organic life may be regarded as a mechanical process in one definite direction. This process, which is about identical with the vegetative life of an animal, depends for its continuance on the impressions made constantly upon the animal by the physical world surrounding it. A part of the process occurs in the nervous system, another part in the rest of the body. To force this process into its opposite direction results in death.

But temporarily parts of this process may be forced into the opposite direction. From out of the large number of possible movements, that one is selected which does not oppose the forward direction of the general nervous activity going on all the time. The nervous correlate of pleasantness is this relation between temporary nervous activities and the continuous nervous activity. The relation of opposite direction is the nervous correlate of unpleasantness, the relation of equal direction that of pleasantness.

For Meyer (1908) the mental states are pleasantness and unpleasantness. The nervous correlate is the increase or decrease of the intensity of a previously constant nervous process if the increase or the decrease is caused by a force acting at a point other than the point of sensory stimulation.

Fite (1903) asks how pleasure and pain can modify behavior. He extends the limits of pleasantness and unpleasantness beyond a few purely physiological metabolic processes to more complex habit systems, and expresses doubt as to the causal nature of the feelings. For him pleasure and pain are not causes in mental life but mere indicators of the conflict or harmony between acting causes. To express this in the light of recent theory, Fite regards the mental states as pleasure and pain, and the nervous correlate as some effect of the operation of the conflict or harmony between acting causes.

In presenting these theories I have ignored complications such as localization, clearness, recognition, lack of habituation, value, etc. In doing this I have simplified the facts so as to get the maximum of clearness in the present state in the psychology of feeling when expressed in traditional terms.[5] It seems to be agreed that at least the mental states of pleasantness and unpleasantness are characteristic of feeling. The physical or physiological correlates of feeling are given as: sensory processes (Lagerborg, Marshall, Stumpf); relationships between sensory processes (Pikler, Meyer); indicators of physiological condition (Calkins, Titchener, Marshall, Lagerborg); harmony between the causes for action (Fite, Meyer).

No Unified Experimental Program

The difficulty of resolving the lack of agreement into a series of crucial experiments is well indicated by the lack of unity in the recent experimental work on feeling. There seem to be too many questions that are not questions. Even though the problem of

[5] No attempt has been made to exhaust the possibilities. I only wish to show that even where we are fairly well agreed on any introspective findings, we are not agreed on any objective correlate for these findings.

feeling has been before us for many years, the obvious question—
what percentage of an individual's daily activity is pleasant, what
percentage is unpleasant?—has no ready answer. The practical
question—shall I select alternative modes of action on the basis of
an anticipated feeling content, either immediate or remote?—
is still answered as it was by the Greeks, by various ethical codes
which have never been subjected to scientific analysis.

Of course this limitation is not restricted to the mental states
called feelings. It is a limitation wherever mental states are
restricted to the introspective method leading, as it does, to
metaphysical discussions rather than to the analysis of environmental and sensorimotor components.

Feeling "as such" or as Action

It has been urged that biological and social considerations should
not determine the character of psychological investigations and
that the introspective method *does* make it possible to study feeling
"as such" even though the data secured by this method make no
contact with the work of other scientists.

For those who expect an investigation to contribute toward the
development of general scientific laws, the study of feeling "as
such" is not very alluring. Of course, I recognize that isolation
from the other sciences need not result in inactivity. That it does
not is well attested by the novelist, especially the so-called psychological novelist who probably represents the highest degree of
introspective efficiency. However, is *this* science? Or does it
become science by merely restricting the scope of the free literary
associations to the special introspective categories of sensation-
image, feeling, attention? This is, I believe, a personal problem
which each must decide for himself. However, none can escape
the verdict which science eventually will render as to the merits of
this method.

In this connection I wish to call attention to a difference between
introspective observation and scientific observation which is not
generally recognized. Titchener (1924) maintains that psychological observation is not essentially different from other
observation, that the world which the psychologist explores is
"the world with *man left in.*" Now it seems to me that by the
way in which Titchener uses the phrase "man left in" he is introducing a "something more" which is not in the category of
natural science. We find this more clearly stated in the following
quotation: "the experience which we are to have is a mental
experience, and our account of it is to be couched in psychological

language. We are, then, ready for the experience; it comes, and we give it our best attention; we then express it in words; and we try to express it fully and adequately in the words that it itself points to and requires. When the account has been written down, and so made available for other students, we have completed a psychological observation. When a number of such observations have been taken, we have the materials for a scientific description" (p. 19).

We may ask just what is included under the term "experience," and what is the "it" which comes and to which we give attention? That the "it" is not merely a linguistic idiom is clear when we try to answer any genetic question in psychology. To be specific, suppose we ask when does the "it" (say the experience of pleasantness) first occur in the infant? We cannot answer this question in the same way that we can answer the question when does the plantar reflex first appear? Asking the infant to report when pleasantness appears or disappears is useless. To answer the question at all we must select some action[6] of the infant from which we must infer the experience of pleasantness. Here controversy begins. We are confronted with the following questions:

1. Can an infant experience pleasantness?

2. If we agree that he can (and few would answer this with a categorical *yes*), what act shall we accept as an invariable indicator of pleasantness?

a) If we select the act of smiling, very few psychologists will accept this as an invariable sign of pleasantness.

b) Some will refuse to accept any physical manifestation and will refer the problem to philosophy or metaphysics.

c) Some will maintain that it may be necessary to agree upon some physical criterion but that we must not forget that the physical criterion is only a correlate or an indicator, that there is a "something more" of which we must not lose sight.

d) Still others, and this is by far the greatest number, will have no criteria and will simply begin on some kind of an investigation which they claim reveals the "facts" of pleasantness rather than any theoretical principles.

These questions illustrate what I mean by saying that the introspective method leads us to philosophical discussions. None of these questions arise in a scientific investigation. The fact is that traditional psychology has limited itself to observations which, from their nature, are philosophic and not scientific.

[6] That we must select an *action*, some contractile effect in the infant, which produces changes in the light waves or sound waves that act on the eyes or ears of the experimenter, is obvious. A motionless infant cannot become the object of the type of investigation I am describing.

Young (1927) in a very significant experiment on pleasantness and unpleasantness concludes: "Some of the conditions which determine the report in affective psychology are (a) the O's education in psychology which includes the kind and the amount of his information, (b) the O's bias determined in part by his theoretical reflections, (c) the O's understanding of words and his habits of speech, and (d) the suggestions which happen to reach him from various sources" (p. 187).

In other words, introspection is *not* inspection. Introspection assumes an "it," an "experience," an entity of some sort which is not assumed in the natural sciences. However, at this time I merely wish to call attention to the fact that an ontogenetic approach to the study of experience is practically excluded. This does not mean that feeling cannot be studied from the biological and social points of view. However, when we do this we are clearly relinquishing the mentalistic or experiential group of fundamentals and adopting other fundamentals.

Literary versus Scientific Observation

I think that my analysis thus far indicates what an exceedingly difficult task confronts us if we try to make a scientific study of the many things that have been included under the term feeling. We can well agree with Young (1927) that: "The confusion and contradiction found to-day within affective psychology are notorious. Upon the most fundamental matters there is little agreement among psychologists" (p. 186).

Perhaps, however, this confusion arises only because of the traditional introspective approach which yields unverifiable data and which assumes that feeling is "something more" than physical or physiological conditions. This has led us to regard pleasantness or unpleasantness as "something" which determines our actions. Such a theory removes the need for making a careful analysis of biological and social factors. We need only learn how to control our own minds or our mental states by some simple philosophic device such as "reflection and self-analysis" and then be able to produce pleasantness or unpleasantness at will. If we can do this, why make painstaking observations on stimulating and sensorimotor conditions which are at most only indirectly associated with feeling?

The same ambiguity is evident in recent writings in which the term "experience" is used as a causal or *selecting* agent in modifying behavior. From the biosocial standpoint the term experience is merely a name for any change in activity which replaces instinctive or acquired behavior. This is equivalent to saying that the term experience is merely the literary name for the totality of our acquired responses, particularly our social responses.

This, of course, does not explain "how" experience can modify behavior. From the biosocial point of view behavior is modified only by:

1. The growth of the sensorimotor system along lines that are determined by inheritance.

2. The internal stimulating conditions produced by internal biochemical processes.

3. The external stimulating conditions which act upon the sensorimotor mechanism. These can be divided into two classes:

   a) The ordinary physical environment which is common to both human and infrahuman organisms;

   b) The social environment which is specific for human beings. The social environment itself is the product of contemporaneous and past human behavior.

An individual does not respond to all the possibilities which the environment presents, if we measure the possibilities by the different responses of all the individuals who have been acted upon by it. When we say the responses of an individual are *selective*, this means only that he does not make all possible responses. The selective agent is the sensorimotor system as determined by inheritance, by its structure, by its biochemical properties, by the physical and biosocial environment. To say that "experience" acts as a selective agent is merely the literary way of stating the scientific fact that sensorimotor conditions determine our behavior.

To study human behavior scientifically we must drop the literary approach and begin a series of careful analyses of the stimulating and response conditions. The introspective method has made us practically blind to the fact that normal human behavior is mostly acquired and that changes in behavior originate as changes in the physical conditions.

The social environment of speech, language, and other individuals is a *physical* environment, patterns of light and sound waves principally. The individual produces these patterns by muscular contractions and in no other way. In turn his own reactions are produced by the light and sound patterns produced by the muscular contractions in others. Many of these patterns developed long before man was able to isolate their physical components and this explains their non-scientific form. Language, for instance, must always remain incomprehensible to one unacquainted with such things as the vocalizing reflex, sensory structure and function, and sensorimotor interchangeability between individuals.

The scientific approach to the study of human behavior and human achievement is the rearrangement of the literary classification of human behavior into those classifications which give the structural and functional components of human actions. These are physical and biological, and the "something more" upon which the mentalistic conception insists is only a substitute speech response for our inability to isolate all the physical components in a given form of behavior.

THE BIOSOCIAL APPROACH TO THE PROBLEM OF FEELING

Stimulating and Contractile Effects

This approach assumes that all of human behavior can be understood if we know the properties of the stimulating conditions which act on an organism and the properties of the organism itself. Specifically with respect to the problem of feeling, a biosocial analysis requires a description and enumeration of: (1) the contractile effects (reactions) that are to be included under the term feeling, (2) the ontogeny and phylogeny of the contractile effects, (3) the stimulus antecedents of the contractile effects, (4) the social effects of the contractions on other individuals.

If an analysis of a limited number of responses leads to a generalization from which the four phases can be deduced without the specific analysis of each response or response series, we have a scientific uniformity or law.

(1) *The Contractile Effects.* A complete analysis of the contractile effects that are to be included under the term feeling would cover a description of all the reactions, implicit and overt, which have been described under feeling by the various writers. These descriptions need not be in actual anatomical or neurological terms, provided they are clearly understood. Thus a "smile" describes a contractile effect as well for our purpose as would an enumeration of the extents and sequences of the contractions of the many muscles actually involved in producing the smile.[7]

Have we such a list? We have not. However, suppose we ignore this for the present and assume that those contractile effects which produce the stimulus pattern called a smile are an indication of what is called pleasantness. The *verbal* contractile effects which may indicate feeling are of the type that produce the sounds: "it is pleasant," "it is unpleasant," "it is indifferent." There are

---

[7] Landis (1924) has performed a series of experiments in which he recorded photographically the actual changes in the contractions of the facial muscles as revealed by displacements of the skin surface.

many linguistic variants of these phrases. More doubtful reactions are laughing, crying, avoiding, reaching, vomiting, injury, manner of eating, sex responses, etc., according as we try to fit our definition of feeling to one or another writer. I think we all agree that we have no relatively complete list of actions which could be classified under the category of feeling, nor do we have a generalization from which such a list could be *deduced*.

(2) *Ontogeny and Phylogeny of the Contractile Effects.* The genesis, both ontogenetic and phylogenetic, of the contractile effects in feeling has received scanty recognition. Restricting our remarks to the act of smiling, we know that the infant does not smile for about ten days after birth. After the smile does appear it is variable and writers are not agreed that it always expresses feeling. Some characterize it as an automatic reflex at first. Gradually the muscular contractions of smiling follow better-known stimulating conditions but the stimuli again soon become too complex for classification. In adult life the smile may express many different conditions. It may lose entirely its feeling of significance and become a response to a non-affective stimulus such as the smile of a salesman greeting a customer. As to the phylogeny of the smile many animals, apes particularly, show changes which have been called smiles. However, we are not able at present to trace back to infrahuman conditions those sensorimotor structures and functions which are now the smile of the infant. About other activities such as laughing (vocalization) we know even less. We cannot ascribe these gaps in our information as entirely due to the nature of the problem. The paleo-anthropologists, for instance, have worked out a very comprehensive record of the ontogeny and phylogeny of the bones and muscles of the foot. Of course, the genesis of sensorimotor structures is more difficult, but it is a problem of the same sort.

(3) *The Stimulating Effects.* The stimuli which release the contractile effects that express feeling, say the act of smiling in an infant of six months, include such stimuli as the light-wave patterns reflected from parents, nurse, feeding bottle, rattle, toys; the sound-wave patterns produced by the movements of parents, nurse, animals, toys; the internal stimuli from metabolic and nutritional conditions. Besides these direct stimulations, supplementation or interferences between the nervous processes themselves seem to release feeling responses. The list is different for each infant and does not remain constant. To attempt to enumerate all the stimuli which release the smile in a given *adult* would be futile. If this is impossible for even such a simple response as a smile, the task has no conceivable limits when we consider

the many other responses from which writers have inferred the presence of feeling.

If feeling is to be included as a scientific uniformity, it is necessary to arbitrarily establish a generalization which will enable us to classify stimulating conditions according as they do, or do not, produce the contractile effects which are to be included under the term feeling.

(4) *The Social Effect of the Contractions.* One of the most frequent effects of the smile of one person on another is also to release a smile in the other person. Two factors which usually are not isolated should be listed separately:

a) The actual muscle contractions. In a smile these would be certain facial muscles; in a laugh, the contractions of certain muscles in the throat and chest.

b) The effects of these contractions on the medium which acts as the stimulus on the other person's sense organs. Thus, a smile is transmitted from one person to another by the changes which the contractions of the facial muscles produce in the pattern of the light waves which act on the other person's eyes. In transmitting a laugh (assuming that vision is excluded) the change is in the sound-wave patterns acting on the ear of the other person.

We may begin by asking, what kind of response does the smile release in other individuals? The smile of the infant releases fondling, vocalizing, playing, coddling, and in general some form of behavior directed toward the child. The smile of the salesman serves as an introduction which releases the buying and selling responses. The smile of the diplomat is supposed to be noncommittal, should not be reacted to at all. Thus we might continue with all kinds of smiles, the coquettish smile, the smile of derision, sympathy, approval, etc., all of which are different physical patterns which act on others in more or less specific ways. This purely physical transmission of stimuli is overlooked in the mentalistic approach. In some way the mental state of the smile in one person is said to *arouse* a corresponding mental state in another. Any of our so-called psychological novels will reveal many hypothetical effects produced on others by the various kinds of smiles, but little has been done along scientific lines. Again I have limited my analysis to that of the smile. To include the many other ways in which the physical expression of feeling may act as a stimulus which changes the behavior of others would be an enormous task. It is this speaker-hearer relation (as it is called by the linguists) which has been practically ignored in the psychological investigations. The smile has been studied as an individual response or as an individual mental state. Its effect on others has received very little attention.

I shall refrain from even attempting to indicate the ontogenetic and historical phases by which the contractile effects expressive of feeling have acquired their special social stimulating values. The problem is scarcely recognized. But again when we consider the much more intensive biological studies in animal life, such as love antics, dances, plumage decorations, bird songs, strutting, etc., we can see that the subject is not beyond the limits of the scientific method. Our experiments on affection and feeling have been based on the implicit assumption that responses which belong to the literary feeling category are *more* than physical effects, that they are *expressions* of underlying mental states. A complete biosocial analysis of feeling requires a description of all the responses, all the forms of stimulation which release these responses, all the social effects produced in other individuals, and the genetic and historical description of the antecedents of both the responses and stimuli. Until we undertake to investigate feeling in this way we are not attacking the problem in a scientific manner.

Feeling as a Biosocial Category

I think it is clear that if feeling is to be an important topic in psychology we must limit ourselves to verifiable data, drop the causal implication in mental processes, and try to develop a generalization from which we can *deduce* the stimulus-response relations. Without a generalization, an attempt to analyze each response which conceivably can be included under the literary category of feeling presents insurmountable and experimental difficulties.

The most promising approach along these lines seems to be that of Meyer (1908), who has tried to discover some biological condition (a nervous correlate) which seems to conform to most of the literary requirements. However, we should be careful to recognize that there is an ambiguity in the term correlate. If we mean by correlate the biological or sociological manifestation of a psychical entity, we shall not have gained anything. If the nervous correlate is merely a scientific description of what in the past has been described only in a literary manner, we shall be safe; but we may then ask, why use the term "nervous correlate?" Why not merely differentiate the scientific from the literary description?

Normal Interferences and Facilitations in Behavior Series

At any given time, for each individual, the environment releases responses which are determined by the individual's previous behavior history. They represent the daily personal, domestic, professional, and public adjustments which give the individual his social status. The stimulating potential of the environment is always greater than is indicated by the responses which actually occur. But from early infancy the physical and social environment is such that the individual is constantly being trained in a particular direction and this represents his behavior career.

However, at no time is the series of day-to-day activities so uniform, and the environment so unvarying, that abrupt changes do not occur. These changes which are of relatively short duration (as compared with the longer life-history series) may affect the normal behavior in two ways:

a)   A facilitation or supplementation of the normal series so that it requires less energy or less time.

b)   An interference or retardation of the normal series so that it requires more energy or a longer time.

Feeling as a Relationship between Responses

From the biosocial viewpoint we may include under the term feeling this facilitation or interference of new stimulus and response groupings with the system of coordinated activities making up the normal behavior of the individual. Feeling then would be the term used to describe a relationship between relatively temporary and permanent behavior. Pi asantness would refer to a condition in which some new stimulus grouping releases responses that facilitate the general coordination of movements, provided this facilitation arises not as a mere increase in the intensity of a stimulus already acting. The term unpleasantness may be used to indicate the sensorimotor conditions in which a new stimulus releases responses which interfere with the normal behavior career, again providing the interference arises not as a mere decrease in the intensity of a stimulus already acting. This is practically the equivalent of Meyer's point of view as developed about twenty years ago. Since this is readily accessible I need only indicate his main conclusions:

The term feeling should be restricted to pleasantness-unpleasantness.
Pleasantness-unpleasantness does not occur apart from perception.
Pleasantness-unpleasantness is not localized.
Some sensations are usually unpleasant; some are usually pleasant.
Sensory and intellectual pleasantness and unpleasantness are of the same nature, but the highest intellectual activities give the most intensive pleasantness-unpleasantness whereas sensory pleasantness-unpleasantness is rather insignificant in the life of a person of culture.
Emotions are usually accompanied by pleasantness-unpleasantness.
Pleasantness-unpleasantness is not the cause of action and is the latest product of mental evolution.

We may now ask why has not Meyer's clear presentation received more attention? I believe this is due to the general inadequacy of the mental categories as the basis for an experimental program for the study of human behavior. Students well trained in science frequently assert that the difficulty with psychological problems lies in the fact that "one does not know how to get started."

The sensorimotor problems of supplementation and interference are very important psychological problems because they form a part of the general problem of how new actions are selected and acquired. However, the special case of supplementation and interference which seems to fit the literary descriptions of feeling best, is relatively unimportant. The question, "Is it pleasant or unpleasant?" is a relatively unimportant one when the individual is learning those responses required by his social status. Most new adjustments are at first unpleasant, but this does not prevent us from acquiring them. From the biosocial standpoint, then, pleasantness only indicates that the action probably will be repeated. Unpleasantness indicates that it probably will not be repeated. However, these propositions have so many exceptions and are so difficult to state statistically that they do not seem to be very promising as indicators of what actions will or will not become part of the individual's normal behavior. It is the biosocial requirement that determines this.

Conclusion

What traditionally has been included under the term feeling may be regarded as a literary description of the biological factors of facilitation and interference. Nevertheless, the scientific analysis of facilitation and interference is such a general problem that it occurs wherever changes in behavior occur. The special type of facilitation and interference which Meyer gives as the nervous correlate of feeling is a special case of the general problem of the interaction between the structural and functional properties of the sensorimotor system, and the stimulating conditions of the environment.

The mentalistic point of view has failed to distinguish adequately between sensory facilitation and interference on the one hand, and the type of facilitation and interference which may occur between acquired behavior series of long and short duration. In addition the mentalistic conception has only recently recognized the fact that pleasantness and unpleasantness are not causes in the important life-adjustments, and therefore a literary analysis of the feelings of an individual from birth to death does not contribute as much to the development of the laws of human behavior as does a study of the biosocial components of human behavior during the social maturation of the individual. A mentalistic analysis is restricted to relatively new adjustments and exceptional conditions; it does not describe the very prosaic and very uninteresting phases through which an infant enters adulthood and which for the most part are so commonplace that we have ceased, even as scientists, to react to them. From the scientific standpoint feeling is a relatively unimportant category because it does not enter as a causal factor in biosocial adjustment.

THE PROBLEM OF EMOTION

Introduction

The topic of emotion is at present being investigated from many angles. Again we find planless experiments of the "let us see what we can see" type. The simple question—what is an emotion, or what shall we include under the term emotion?— was raised by Landis et al. (1925). They begin with the assumption that a rating scale is the best criterion for emotionality. Part of the instructions to the raters reads: "By emotional stability we mean the ability to resist the cumulative effect of the emotional situations such as might be employed in experimental conditions" (p. 215). The extreme conditions are represented as "going to pieces" and "not going to pieces."

Of course this already assumes that the raters have some definition of emotionality, and the degree of the consistency of the ratings that was actually found shows that they do. However, this may be merely an expression of the fact that the raters have had similar linguistic and social training. From the biosocial standpoint the rating scale is a quantitative expression of the degree of uniformity which exists in the literary terminology of the "emotion" category. With raters representing wide variations in social status, the consistency would be correspondingly less. Even with his relatively uniform group and the results of subsequent experiments, Landis (1926) is unable to convince himself that the literary classification is serviceable. He says, "Any attempt to define 'emotion' in a simple, clean-cut fashion must be a failure since the phenomena generally classified under the term are much too complex and diverse to admit such treatment" (p. 242). I think this means that the literary classification of emotions, developed as it was without a sensorimotor background simply cuts across the stimulus-response uniformities which Landis was investigating. In emotions as in feelings, it is probably more fruitful to differentiate the mentalistic category into biosocial categories.

The plausibility of the James-Lange theory of emotions has led to studies of the changes in bodily processes during those conditions in which the organism was said to be in an emotional state. Among the organic processes that have been and are being studied we find changes in pulse, blood-pressure, blood composition, respiration, knee-jerk; changes in the electrical resistance of the tissues, in action currents, basal metabolism, and metabolic rate, etc.

As one phase of these studies a peculiar condition has arisen. Because of the absence of a generally acceptable criterion of emotion, the tendency is in the direction of defining emotion in terms of these organic measurements. For instance, instead of regarding the psychogalvanic process as an organic function of emotion, we tend to say that the psychogalvanic process is proportional to the emotion. As yet the real problem—how does the psychogalvanic process correlate with the degree of biosocial adjustment which the individual is able to make?—is just being recognized. Whether these organic responses are better functions of the character of the overt responses which determine the individual's social status than are some other easily measurable responses, remains an open question.

The Biosocial Approach to the Problem of Emotion

As I pointed out under the topic of feeling, the biosocial approach is specifically directed toward the description of those movements and the antecedents of those movements which we call human behavior. Thus an individual who is sitting on a chair in a relaxed condition and whose hand is suddenly brought into contact with a number of live frogs, which he did not see beforehand, goes through a series of movements which can be described, photographically at least.

The greater the number of responses that are recorded and the better the stimuli have been controlled, the more instructive will be the experiment. Whether we call this a "fear" response or an "emotion" is quite beside the point. If the stimulus and the response conditions are under the best control, we may classify the subjects on the basis of the behavior records of which a psychogalvanic reading may be one out of many others.

If, further, the action is studied from the standpoint of the ontogeny and phylogeny of both the individual and social stimulus and response conditions, we shall approach the limit of at least knowing something about this one form of behavior.

Specific and Non-specific Behavior

From the biosocial standpoint a very important relationship between responses is one in which we determine the percentage of specific as compared with non-specific activity in performing a given task. The difficulty of defining specific and non-specific can be eliminated by assigning a task which must be done in a predetermined manner before the response series is accepted as biologically or biosocially adequate. If in performing such a task the individual makes many non-specific movements (either implicit or overt), the time will be lengthened. If he fails to make the specific movements necessary to perform the task, the time will also be lengthened. We can now define specific movements as those movements which complete the task in the shortest time, even though they are not qualitatively identical. The particular task can be simple or complex to meet the capacities of the individuals to be measured.

Meyer (1924) was the first, to my knowledge, to formulate this category,[8] and he has designed an apparatus which meets the preceding conditions. The task consists of a combination of relatively simple movements, which the subject learns for the first time. By combining these simple movements into various. tempi and rates, a problem of any degree of complexity can be developed.

It seems to me that the literary classification "emotional instability" best describes an individual who makes non-specific responses for which specific biosocial responses have been established. This conception seems also to be shared by Warren (1919) who says, under the rôle of emotion in mental life: "The emotions, more than any other kind of mental states, represent by-gone conditions of life. They do not fit particularly well into the human world of to-day" (p. 300). "The emotional part of our mental life is to some extent an anachronism. Emotion, if uncontrolled, hampers the proper interrelation between the individual of to-day and the environment of to-day. It is only when the instinctive emotions are trained into intelligent modes of expression that this phase of mental life works harmoniously with the rest" (p. 302).

[8] Meyer uses the terms "useful" and "useless" movements. If we abide strictly by Meyer's definition of useful and useless, no difficulties arise, but I doubt whether in the present state of psychology it is possible to use the terms without a strong "vitalistic" tinge. We are still too much disposed to run into discussions of the "purposive" type which include much more than Meyer would include.

The Elimination of the Literary Category of Emotion

It seems to me that a category of behavior which is defined as the ratio between specific and non-specific movements will eliminate many of the problems that lie hidden in such a classification of the emotions as given by Warren (1919):

1. Expressive (Nutritive): e. g., joy, grief, shock, etc.
2. Reproductive: e. g., love, lust, tenderness, etc.
3. Defensive: e. g., fear, disgust, shame, etc.
4. Aggressive: e. g., anger, hatred, pride, etc.
5. Social Emotion: e. g., affection, cordiality, pity, etc.
6. With Temporal Projection: e. g., regret, surprise, etc.

Of course for special forms of behavior such as aesthetic or ethical, it may be useful to attempt a complete biosocial analysis of some of the separate items given in lists of this type. The stimulus-response conditions of any behavior series can be arbitrarily delimited and, when so delimited, the movements of which it is made up can be classified as specific or non-specific on the basis of some criterion based upon personal, domestic, professional, and public requirements which are relatively constant for a given social status.

If a biosocial approach can eliminate such vexing questions as these—Are there any emotions? What is rage? What is anger, joy, grief? Are there any instincts?, etc.— questions which are now sources of much controversy, a great deal will have been gained. The biosocial approach clearly recognizes the fact that all behavior classifications are human classifications and that classifications or descriptions in biological, statistical, and social terms are superseding those that were developed when only a supernaturalistic theory of human behavior was possible.

Organic Measurements in Emotion

Every response requires a certain expenditure of energy which varies greatly for different stimulating conditions. Under normal conditions the reserve food material in the nervous and muscular tissue is not much above that required for the demand of a basal metabolism rate of about 100 calories per hour. If a set of muscles functions strongly, the available reserve is soon used up and must be renewed. This is done through the blood stream, which carries a constant amount of food in the form of glucose. As this is absorbed by the functioning tissues it is replaced in the blood by the conversion of the glycogen in the liver to sugar. To keep the sugar content of the blood as constant as it actually has been found to be, requires delicate sensorimotor regulation of the glandular system. If this system is not functioning properly the individual makes movements that are too strong, too weak, or biosocially troublesome.

Inadequate functioning of the regulating mechanism[9] would give us another class of behavior which would indicate emotional instability as generally understood. It seems to me that the present interest in the organic measurements under experimental emotional situations is an attempt to learn how this regulating mechanism is related to social interaction.

Conclusion

From what has preceded we may regard the biosocial problem of emotions from two views: (a) as the ratio of specific as compared with non-specific movements in the performance of a given task, (b) the relationship between the internal energy regulating mechanism and biosocial adjustment.

SUMMARY

One of the big problems in science is to answer the question: What does the normal person do and how does he come to do it? The individual himself does not know and the traditional method of asking him does not yield scientific results. We must make a study of the biological and social antecedents of his actions. There are at least four phases to be studied: (a) the actions themselves, (b) the conditions which produce them, (c) the effects of the actions on other persons, (d) and the origin both ontogenetic and phylogenetic of both the stimuli and the movements of which the actions are made up. In other words, we wish to know how the infant becomes the adult and how the adult modifies the infant.

Our present conceptions of the individual and of human behavior were developed long before we had the neurological information that is essential to make *any action at all comprehensible*. As a result, the literary categories that were developed show no connection with the stimulus-response type of categories now developing.

The problem of feeling becomes a study of the facilitation or interference between movements when these conditions arise from stimuli at sensory points other than the ones which are releasing the particular response. This is a special case of the more general problem of how any facilitations and interferences between responses are brought about.

[9] A more complete account is given in my *A Theoretical Basis of Human Behavior*, pp. 369–377.

The problem of emotion becomes that of determining the conditions under which non-specific activity interferes with the development of biosocially specific action, or of determining the relation between the internal energy regulating mechanism and the biosocial adjustment.

Feeling and emotion should be regarded as categories of behavior resulting from the interaction between physical stimulating conditions and the sensorimotor system. To regard feelings and emotions as non-physical forces which modify behavior leads to a type of experimentation the results of which cannot be incorporated into the rapidly developing system of biological and social laws.

BIBLIOGRAPHY

BENTLEY, M. The field of psychology. New York: Appleton, 1925.

CALKINS, M. W. An introduction to psychology. New York: Macmillan, 1908.

FITE, W. The place of pleasure and pain in the functional psychology. *Psychological Review*, X (1903), 633–644.

LAGERBORG, R. Ueber die specifischen Ursachen der Unlust und Lustgefühle. *Skandinavisches Archiv für Physiologie*, XVIII (1906), 7–56.

LANDIS, C. Studies in emotional reaction: II. General behavior and facial expression. *Journal of Comparative Psychology*, IV (1924), 447–509.

———. Studies in emotional reaction: V. Severe emotional upset. *Journal of Comparative Psychology*, VI (1926), 221–242.

LANDIS, C., GULLETTE, R., AND JACOBSON, C. Criteria of emotionality. *The Pedagogical Seminary and Journal of Genetic Psychology*, XXXII (1925), 209–234.

MARSHALL, H. R. Pain, pleasure, and aesthetics. London: Macmillan, 1894.

———. The methods of the naturalist and psychologist. *Psychological Review*, XV (1908), 1–24.

MEYER, M. F. The nervous correlate of pleasantness and unpleasantness. *Psychological Review*, XV (1908), 201–216, 292–322.

———. Special ability tests. *Psychological Bulletin*, XXI (1924), 114–116.

PIKLER, J. Das Grundgesetz alles neuro-psychischen Lebens. Leipzig: Barth, 1900.

STUMPF, C. Ueber Gefühlsempfindungen. *Zeitschrift für Psychologie*, XLIV (1906), 1–49.

TITCHENER, E. B. Lectures on the elementary psychology of feeling and attention. New York: Macmillan, 1908.

———. A beginner's psychology. New York: Macmillan, 1924.

WARREN, H. C. Human psychology. Boston: Houghton Mifflin, 1919.

WEISS, A. P. A theoretical basis of human behavior. Columbus, Ohio: R. G. Adams, 1925.

YOUNG, P. T. Studies in affective psychology. *American Journal of Psychology*, XXXViII (1927), 157–193.

DISCUSSION

DR. BÜHLER (*University of Vienna*): I do not intend to isolate but to reconcile the main standpoints we have today in psychology. When recalling last night's introspective paper and comparing it with what you heard from Dr. Weiss today, the situation seems to be this: we shall have to decide whether in the future we want to be behaviorists or introspectionists. I do not think so. I think I am a behaviorist and a mentalist too, and I think that in the future all of us will be at the same time behaviorists and mentalists. I do not think we have two exclusive standpoints, but I think we must have the one and the other, too. I cannot explain to you briefly the reason for my opinion, but I shall pick out some points from what Dr. Weiss said. First, let me tell you a little story. Last Sunday morning I had a very nice drive around Johns Hopkins; the driver was a psychologist— you know him very well. His little daughter was with us and suddenly she asked the question: "Father, they ask me at school whether you are a behaviorist." Papa shrugged his shoulders and finally said, "Ask Dr. Bühler whether he is a behaviorist or not." "Yes, I am a behaviorist"—and I am willing to be a behaviorist in the field of animal psychology, and in so far as behaviorism is a method to make experiments and use what we can observe in young children or animals. But it is not possible to carry out entire scientific work when you think in terms of the behaviorist only. I state further that Dr. Weiss in his paper used terms, notions, coming from the other aspect, from mentalism. For instance, I have not been able to appreciate exactly and to get his definitions of pleasure and displeasure, but one I think is that "pleasure means that the movement of our behavior will be repeated, and displeasure means that it will not be repeated." All right; let us point out that this definition means that certain behavior will be repeated in the future. Yet he goes on to say that this is not a stern rule, not a definite law, but has many, many exceptions. All right; who gives him the right to say there are exceptions—exceptions to what? If those movements will not be repeated, they will not belong to this type of movements of behavior—to what he calls pleasure. All movements that are repeated belong to this class—the movements of behavior called pleasure. Why say that not all movements—not all behavior is repeated? Let us ask ourselves and our subjects. We all know exactly what pleasure is and what displeasure is. Weiss compares the experiences he has and those of other people with what he calls the law. Some movements are repeated, others are not. He said, "You have not an exact definition of pleasure and displeasure in the field of emotional psychology." Has he an exact definition? I do not think so. You remember there are many exceptions to his rule. Is that an exact definition? Let us take another view. We have a fact; for instance, you remember that Roentgen found his famous X-rays, as he called that phenomenon. He found a certain fact and then by scientific reasoning defined it, and we now know partly what X-rays are. In the same way we define pleasure and displeasure. We are quite sure we have had pleasure and displeasure. Ask a child of three years. It knows exactly that some things have been pleasant and others unpleasant. This is not a definition, of course; but, we first state the facts and then we have to find a good definition. I have tried to show in a new book just published, *The Crisis of Psychology*, that behaviorism as such is a very good aspect, one of the possible and one of the necessary aspects of psychology; but the terms of behaviorism need some facts derived from other aspects, for instance, from introspection. I think we need more than that, another, a third aspect—perhaps in the future we shall call it a social aspect. Everyone of these three aspects is possible as well as necessary. Behaviorism as such cannot carry out the whole program and cannot cover the whole ground of systematic psychology. I think with Dr. Dunlap that in the future we will not have as many psychologies as we have now. The situation now is that we must decide whether we are behaviorists or mentalists, but in the future we will combine these two and maybe more aspects in psychology.

DR. PRINCE (*Harvard University*): I should like to ask Professor Weiss two or three questions. If I understand him correctly, he told us that experience does not modify behavior. I take it that by experience, of course, he means conscious experience, consciousness in some of its forms. I like to get away from the word "consciousness," calling it experience; but I think we ought to call facts by their names, call a spade a spade. Consciousness does not modify behavior. Now I should like to ask if that is not pure dogmatism; is it not a dogma to say that all our behavior is determined in every way by physiological activities? If that be true we are only automatons. Of course it would be a corollary. I should like to ask whether that statement was made by his intelligence or by his nervous system. It seems to me that if you adopt that view, then you are simply going back to the old discussion of whether or not we are automatons, which, as you remember, Huxley discussed many years ago. Is not the whole of the social organization based upon the fact that intelligence or consciousness does modify behavior? Is it not the basis of criminal law or criminal intent? And I should like to ask Professor Weiss that he assume that he had committed a criminal act (impossible supposition we admit, I suppose) but let us say he has committed a criminal act—stolen some oil lands, or committed a murder, or whatever it may be. Suppose he pleaded to the judge that he had no criminal intent, "Why, Your Honor, it was nothing but my nervous system, my neurones that committed the crime." What do you suppose the answer of the judge would be? "We shall punish your nervous system; we shall send your grey matter down there?" He is practically reducing us to mere machines. Now, we may be automatons, but I believe it is very difficult to make the man in the street believe that we are nothing but automatons and that our experiences, that our feelings, are only the symptoms of consciousness, or that behavior takes place in us and that we are powerless to determine that behavior. I find myself in accord with a great deal of what Professor Bühler has said. There seem to be only two aspects of the same question. You have got to consider both aspects. But we can go a certain distance as a method of investigation, using the physiological method. And I say to anyone that uses that method, "Godspeed to you! Go as far as you can go; but you are bound to come up against a stone wall somewhere, sometime, and you have finally got to come to conscious experience." I can trace back, as I see it, to something that went before my presence here today. When I was nine years of age I was first interested in psychology. In a way, everything is related to what has gone before. We cannot isolate any behavior from what has gone before; but that antecedent behavior was conscious behavior, it was conscious experience at that time. And so it seems to me impossible to conceive that our feelings, our consciousness, our ideas, our beliefs, are different. They finally boil down to different aspects of one and the same thing.

CHAIRMAN: I regret that lack of time makes it impossible for Dr. Weiss to answer his various challengers.

PART II

Special Problems in the Psychology of
Feeling and Emotion

CHAPTER 14

DISPLEASURE AND PLEASURE IN RELATION TO ACTIVITY

Karl Bühler
University of Vienna

If a first sign, *D*, means displeasure, and a second one, *P*, pleasure, then psychologists have generally agreed, since Aristotle and Epicurus, that the general direction of human activity is, as a rule, from *D* to *P*. In terms of behaviorism we may say: There is a steering principle to be found in the field of movements we can observe. Think of what physicists call a field in the theory of electricity and magnetism. As the needle in the compass shows a certain directing influence, so also does human behavior. Concerning this scheme let us make the assumption that the arrow has not a static but a dynamic significance—there is a movement, an occurrence, along the arrow, changing the status *D* into the status *P*.

Now, draw the consequences and you have a theory—the theory of common sense applied to pleasure since ancient times, but nobody till Fechner tried to formulate it in exact scientific terms. After Fechner, Freud and I myself in the same year (1920) were concerned with this formula.

There are small differences. Fechner speaks as a pure physicist on this point, and Freud, whose speculations always touch philosophical problems, took the opportunity to find a fundamental definition of libido, and to confess his black pessimism in things of human life. Freud's relationship to Schopenhauer appeared clearly on this occasion. I myself, without knowing Freud and Fechner and coming from biology, used some biological terms.

But beyond those differences there is an agreement in the main point, which I shall now state. Whatever human activity may be, wherever the forces (powers) implied in the movements we can observe are coming from, as far as this scheme is right and the movements are steered along the direction represented by this arrow, there is no reason why the status of *P* once reached should be transgressed and left again by the continuing of the same movements.

Therefore, Fechner says, P means stability, D means instability, in terms of physics. Out of the status of D springs what we call an action (or reaction), and in the status of a relative and maybe temporary stability is to be found the natural end and conclusion of the movements, the changes. In other words, if you substitute the psychological terms tension and relaxation in the scheme, the place of tension is here and the place of relaxation is there.

$$D \longrightarrow P$$
$$T \longrightarrow R$$
$$H \longrightarrow S$$

I do not think there is anything new or astonishing for any psychologist in this formulation. Replace the general terms tension and relaxation by adequate notions drawn from more concrete situations like the food business or sexuality, and the behavior in the status of being hungry comes to stay here and the opposite behavior in the status of satisfaction there; sexual eagerness here, satisfaction there. In zoölogical gardens before and after the mealtime of the big carnivorous animals there is a good opportunity to observe a relatively short and swift transition from the first status to the second, and so to examine and prove this formula. Or think of certain big snakes, like the boa constrictor. Their behavior after the meal is a picture of a long and complete relaxation.

In human beings, especially in those restless products of modern civilization like us, maybe this picture is sometimes a bit faded out. Neurologists know and describe a certain form of neurasthenia in which the patients are entirely unable to relax and digest, as it were, in the right manner. They chase after the enjoyments of life and collect them, like trophies or scalps, only to feel themselves in all the riches of their collection starving with hunger for new ones, or finally prostrated with satiation or disgust. Maybe we restless men of modern civilization are placed in the series far from the behavior of a boa constrictor, and nearer the neurasthenic patients. But I do not think we have overcome and surpassed the general law of this formula. The human child in the first years of its life shows better the naïve and unspoiled status than we adults.

But, notwithstanding, it is observation of the child that has convinced me that the old and venerable formula does not contain the whole truth about the relation between the pleasure principle and activity—neither in man nor in animals. It explains but one side of the facts. There are two others. And psychology does violence to the facts when it confines itself to that one principle applicable only to the first of the three aspects we must consider in our field.

By the way, it was also observation of the child that spoiled Freud's theory of libido for him. He then started anew, and wrote that strange book, *Beyond the Pleasure Principle*, and so startled his followers that for seven years they have not recovered from their fright. Beyond the pleasure principle Freud felt compelled to invent and state the existence of a second powerful factor determining and ruling human and animal behavior, because he once came in direct contact with and observed some facts in a child's playing.

I now have for examination a series of six systematic researches, complementing each other, which we have just finished in Vienna. These six researches concern play in childhood and its development, and they agree with Freud in the main point. Indeed, the facts concerning children's activity in play are not to be explained by the supposition of a general libido and this formula alone.

I found another one. Think of the movements themselves as endowed with pleasure, and we have formulated a fundamental, a central knowledge concerning children's play. I call it *Function Pleasure*. The fact is, certain forms of movements are themselves pleasurable. I postpone the general question as to what forms and why. It is my purpose to enumerate some concrete cases. In the phase of development where the child learns to grasp, the grasping movements of arms, hands, and fingers are endowed with function pleasure—and so in other phases the movements of walking, or talking, etc.

Do not expect me to explain in this short reference the empirical reasons we found for this central statement. But suppose it is true and look with me at some important theoretical consequences:

1. According to the first formula, *P* means relaxation and quietness. Freud drew the radical conclusion: Ergo *P* finally is a principle of death. I do not think that relaxation is equal to death. But there is indeed a problem. One and the same thing, namely, the playing business in childhood, is endowed with pleasure and is characterized by movement (not relaxation). All right, because, according to the second formula, *P* does not play the part of a brake but the part of a motor.

2. Repetition is one of the most impressive characteristics in children's playing. Well, this repetition is the necessary and immediate consequence of function pleasure. Repetition is the simplest way for the *P* of a movement to be prolonged. It is superfluous to state a special principle of repetition as Freud did. Children's

playing is not beyond the pleasure principle, but the first and simple consequence of function pleasure.

3. We know repetition means habit formation. All right. This agrees with the old and good supposition that children's playing produces useful habits and abilities for later life. Certain forms of behavior endowed with function pleasure constitute a method so simple and efficient as to effect the training of restless youth.

4. There is a general direction to be found in the development of children's playing leading to better and higher *forms* of movements. Function pleasure is bound to rhythm, for example, and to other shapes, structures, forms of movements. And therefore we find a selection and performance progressing from worse to better and more effective movements or behavior.

These are, in short, the main steps of a theory of play: beginning with the fundamental statement that the movements of the functions implied in play are themselves endowed with pleasure, and finishing with the other statement that the development we can observe in children's playing business goes all the way from simpler and lower to higher and more complicated forms of movements or behavior, because function pleasure especially is bound to what we call today form, structure, shape, like rhythm and the others. There is a steering principle to be found in the development of children's playing which leads to better and higher forms in behavior.

Now the third formula, the third aspect, in which we find *P* connected with activity. Look at the enjoyment, the happiness in any creative human work. What phase of creative work is endowed with the highest kind of enjoyment of happiness humans are able to experience? I think of inventions and discoveries and how they are endowed with pleasure.

My answer is: This kind of pleasure is bound neither to the end and the following relaxation nor to the process of realization, but to those delicious moments when the invention or discovery overcomes the subject and grows up in him. It is bound to what we call the conception, and conception stays here.

Think of the highest forms of human inventions and discoveries in the fields of sciences, arts, technical inventions, organizations, etc. Psychologically considered, it is always the same process. Or think of the lowest forms we know today, Köhler's chimpanzees. I don't know whether the chimpanzees already enjoy the moment of finding a solution in a new situation or not. But I know exactly, because we have observed the phenomena, that human children do that already in the first years. I think it belongs to the common features in human nature.

The process of growing human civilization can be considered as a complicated texture of accumulated inventions and discoveries. Well, and one of the different powers or leading principles in it is, I think, and was from the beginning, the enjoyment humans find in making inventions and discoveries.

If we, by way of convention, call this side or aspect of human behavior intellect, then the pleasure in creative work is the emotional background of intellect and is correlated with it as nearly and as adequately as function pleasure is correlated with habit formation in children's playing. It would take me too long a time to explain here the details and to discuss the observations, especially on children, upon which this statement is based.

Let me finish the abstract scheme of the theory with two remarks:

1. I think it can be and is to be carried out in the most exact and well-defined terms of modern psychology. I can give an exact definition for the notion of a steering principle in human and animal behavior.

2. As for the correlations and transitions between the three formulae, I think they are nothing less than differentiations or specifications of one and the same more primitive and fundamental relation between movements and what we call pleasure. I am an optimist in things of life and suppose, with Herbert Spencer and many others, that life with its changes and movements of vital processes originally means pleasure.

Jennings found that the natural status of lower organisms is not quietness and relaxation but movement. That statement is not true, except in certain respects, when applied to what we can observe with children in the first weeks of life. It is a fact that sleep and relaxation dominate in them nearly all the movements we find which follow the characteristics of this first formula, except a relatively small group of those events that Preyer called impulsive movements. But out of them, in swift development, springs the important playing of children. And concerning the great development of living beings, I suppose that not what we can find in the differentiated system of behavior of new-born human children but what Jennings found in the system of behavior of lower organisms is to be considered as the first step. I am willing to think those movements are already endowed with pleasure, because I am an optimist. But that belongs to philosophy.

CHAPTER 15

EMOTION AND FEELING DISTINGUISHED

William McDougall

Duke University

There is still much uncertainty and confusion in the use of the terms "emotion" and "feeling," corresponding to the uncertainties and diversities of views as to the status, conditions, and functions of the processes to which these terms are applied. After many years of gradual advance toward clarity of my own thinking on these problems I feel able to offer a scheme which seems to me comprehensive, coherent, and fundamentally correct, however much in need of correction and elaboration in details.

The scheme I offer is founded on evolutionary and comparative or genetic considerations and moulded in conformity with the facts of human experience and behavior. It implies a voluntaristic or hormic psychology, that is to say, a psychology which regards as the most fundamental feature of all animal life the capacity actively to seek goals by means of plastic behavior, of striving expressed in bodily movements adjusted from moment to moment to the details of each developing situation in the manner called by common consent, intelligent.

As I have argued elsewhere, the capacity to strive towards an end or ends, to seek goals, to sustain and renew activity adopted to secure consequences beneficial to the organism or the species must be accepted as a fundamental category of psychology.[1] Whether in the course of evolution such capacity has "emerged" from modes of being lacking all germ of it; whether it can be explained in terms of physics and chemistry, as the psychologists of the Gestalt School seek to show—these are questions for the future. Psychology is not called upon to await affirmative answers to these questions before recognizing purposive striving as a mode of activity that pervades and characterizes all animal life. Nor need we determine whether plant life exhibits in some lowly degree the same essential functions, or whether some cognition, however lowly, is always and everywhere a cooperating function.

It is reasonable to assume that the primary forms of animal

[1] "Purposive Striving as a Fundamental Category of Psychology." Presidential address to the Psychological Section of the British Association, 1924. Reprinted in *Science*, November, 1924.

striving were the seeking of food and the turning away from the noxious, primitive appetition and aversion; and that from these two primitive forms all other modes of appetition and aversion have been differentiated and evolved.

Setting out from these assumptions, my thesis is, first, that all the modes of experience we call feeling and emotion are incidental to the striving activities, the conations of the organism, evoked either by impressions from the environment or by metabolic processes taking place within it or, more commonly, in both ways; secondly, that we may broadly and consistently distinguish feelings on the one hand and emotions on the other by their functional relations to the conative activities which they accompany and qualify, these relations being very different in the two cases.

There are two primary and fundamental modes of feeling, pleasure and pain, or satisfaction and dissatisfaction, which color and qualify in some degree, however slight, all strivings. Pleasure is the consequence of, and sign of, success whether partial or complete; pain, the consequence and sign of failure and frustration. It seems probable that primitive pleasure and pain were alternatives, perhaps not mutually exclusive in any absolute sense but practically so. But with the development of the cognitive powers came the simultaneous apprehension of diverse aspects of objects and situations and, further, the pleasures and pains of anticipation and recollection. The former brought the possibility of the simultaneous excitation of diverse impulses conflicting or cooperating with reciprocal modifications. The latter rendered possible the conjunction of present success with anticipation of failure, and of present frustration with anticipation of success. With these came corresponding complications of the modes of feeling.

The organism that has attained such a level of cognitive development no longer oscillates between simple pleasure and simple pain; beside and between these simple primitive extremes, it attains a range of feelings which are in some sense fusions or blendings of pleasure and pain; it experiences such feelings as hope, anxiety, despondency, despair, regret, and sorrow. And, with the fuller development of mental structure, the adult man learns to know "sweet sorrows," joys touched with pain, "hope deferred that maketh the heart sick," and "strange webs of melancholy mirth"; "his sincerest laughter with some pain is fraught"; his darkest moments of abject failure are lightened by some ray of hope; his bright moments of triumph and elation are sobered by his abiding sense of the vanity of human wishes and the fleeting, unstable nature of all attainment. In short, the grown man no longer is capable of the simple feelings of the child, because he

has learned to "look before and after and pine for what is not."
With the development of his cognitive powers, his desires have
become complex and of long range, and the simple alternation
between pleasure and pain has given place to a perpetual ranging
through the scale of complex feelings. These complex feelings are
known in common speech as emotions. Adopting the terminology
proposed by Shand, I have elsewhere discussed them under the
general title "the derived emotions of desire, prospective and
retrospective."[2]

It would greatly conduce to clarity and precision if, in science,
we should cease to give the general name "emotion" to these
complex feelings. The difficulty of distinguishing these complex
feelings from the emotions proper and the common practice of
confusing them arise from the fact that well-nigh all the strivings
of the developed mind are qualified both by emotions proper and
by complex feelings or "derived emotions," blended in one complex whole or configuration.

To turn now to the emotions proper or the qualities of emotional
experience: As the primitive appetition and aversion became differentiated into impulses directed toward more special goals and
evocable by more special objects and situations, each specialized
impulse found expression in some special mode of bodily striving
with some corresponding complex of bodily adjustments facilitating
and supporting that mode of bodily activity. Without accepting
the James-Lange theory in an extreme and literal way, we must
suppose that each such system of bodily adjustments is reflected
in the experience of the striving organism, giving to each specialized
mode of striving a peculiar and distinctive quality, the quality of
one of the primary emotions; and that, when mental development
reaches the level at which two or more of the specialized impulses
come into play simultaneously, conflicting or cooperating, these
primary qualities are experienced in the complex blendings that
we call the secondary or blended emotions, such complex qualities
as embarrassment, shame, awe, reverence, reproach.

Let me now contrast the complex feelings or "derived emotions"
with the emotions proper, primary and blended, bearing in mind
that all the concrete emotional experiences of the developed mind
are configurations in which are blended qualities of both kinds,
qualities which we abstractly distinguish as the true and the derived
emotions.

1. The complex feelings, like the simple feelings, arise from,
are conditioned by, the degrees of success and failure of our striv-

[2] *Introduction to Social Psychology* (Boston: Luce, 1910), and *Outline of Psychology* (New York: Scribner, 1923).

ings, and, like the simple feelings, they modify the further working of the impulses by which they are generated, strengthening and sustaining them in so far as the balance of feeling-tone is on the pleasurable side, checking and diverting them in so far as the balance of feeling is on the painful side.

The true emotional qualities, on the other hand, are prior to and independent of success and failure; they spring to life with the evocation of the corresponding impulses and continue to color the experiences of striving each with its distinctive tone, giving its specific quality to the whole configuration regardless of degrees of success or failure, actual or anticipated. And they have no direct influence upon the course of striving. As qualities of experience they are merely indicative of the nature of bodily adjustments organically bound up with each fundamental mode of striving; but in the developed mind they play an indirect part in determining the course of conation because, serving as signs of the nature of the impulse at work, they render possible to the self-conscious organism some degree of direction and control of these impulses.

2. The complex feelings, then, are dependent upon and secondary to the development of the cognitive functions. It is perhaps true to say that they are peculiar to man, though possibly attained in their simpler forms by the highest of animals. The true emotions, on the other hand, must be supposed to be of very much earlier appearance in the evolutionary scale. Throughout the major part of that scale they appear as mere by-products of the impulsive strivings of the animals. In man alone they become an important source of self-knowledge and, therefore, of self-direction.

The introspective study of these emotional qualities has been much neglected by psychology, for the reasons that they do not readily lend themselves to experimental control, and that our nomenclature inevitably remains very inadequate. Yet the practice of such introspection brings great increase of facility in recognition of the nature of our conations; and such facility is of more practical importance than any other kind of introspective skill, not only because it greatly conduces to efficient self-direction, but also because it is a principal means to a better understanding of the motivation of conduct in general. It is not difficult to know that we desire (or are averse to) some particular end; the difficulty, theoretical and practical, is to know what is the nature of the impulse in which the desire is rooted, what tendency finds satisfaction in the attainment of such an end.

3. The named complex feelings (such as hope, anxiety, regret) are not in any sense entities and do not spring from special

dispositions. Rather, each of the names we use in describing such feelings denotes merely an ill-defined part of a large range of feeling, the whole of which may be incidental to the working of any strong desire, no matter what its nature and origin. As the subject, moved by desire, passes through this range of complex feelings, each named part is experienced in turn, and in turn passes over into its neighbor quality; there is consequently no blending of such qualities.

On the other hand, each one of the true primary emotional qualities arises on the coming into activity of a corresponding conative disposition, which is an enduring feature of the mental structure of the organism; hence, each such quality is experienced only in association with an impulse or a desire of a specific type; and, since two or more such dispositions may come simultaneously into play, yielding cooperative or conflicting desires, the corresponding primary emotional qualities may be simultaneously evoked and may fuse or blend with one another in various intensities. Let me illustrate these contrasting features with examples. Hope is the name we give to the complex feeling which arises when *any* strong desire is working in us and we anticipate success; if new difficulties arise hope gives place to anxiety or despondency, but cannot under any circumstances be said to blend with despondency to yield anxiety; rather, as the circumstances become less favorable, the feeling rooted in our desire changes by imperceptible gradations from hope to anxiety and then to despondency. Contrast with this the emotion we call curiosity or wonder and its relations to the emotion we call fear. The emotion-quality wonder accompanies always, in some degree, the impulse or desire to explore and to become better acquainted with some object; it is never experienced save as an accompaniment of that tendency in action. The process of exploration leads to the better comprehension of the nature of the object and this in turn may evoke fear, a quality which accompanies always the impulse to shrink from, or the desire to retreat from, the object. But with the rise of this new impulse with its distinctive emotion-quality, wonder is not necessarily driven out or arrested; the impulse to explore may continue to work simultaneously with the impulse to retreat, and in this case we experience an emotion-quality in which we recognize affinity to both wonder and fear, and which we seem justified in describing as in some sense a blend of these two primary qualities.

Note: I seize this opportunity to illustrate the fact that the distinction drawn in the foregoing paper obviates certain objections which have been raised against the view of the relation between emotion and instinct propounded in my *Social*

Psychology. Professor Harvey Carr (in the paper contributed to the symposium) raises against that view (namely, that each primary emotion is one aspect of the functioning of a corresponding instinct) the fact that "the emotion of joy" is apt to spring up on the completion of some instinctive action, that is to say at the moment of attainment of the goal, the moment when the instinctive impulse subsides. This fact would constitute a serious objection, if joy were a primary emotion (as has so commonly been assumed ever since Descartes claimed that position for it). But as I have tried to show elsewhere, joy lacks the distinguishing features of a primary emotion; it must rather be regarded (together with sorrow) as one of the "derived emotions of desire," that is to say, in stricter language, one of the complex modes of feeling. Joy, as Professor Carr points out, has no specific tendency, does not constantly accompany or qualify any one instinctive impulse, the desire for a goal of any one type, but rather may arise upon the attainment of any strongly desired goal, no matter what the instinctive root of the desire. It has all the distinctive marks of feeling, rather than those of emotion.

CHAPTER 16

PHONOPHOTOGRAPHY AS A NEW APPROACH TO THE PSYCHOLOGY OF EMOTION

CARL E. SEASHORE
State University of Iowa

The new approach to the study of emotion which I wish to outline in a few words is restricted largely to the field of emotional expression in music and speech. But the principles observed in vocalization are often such as may be transferred directly or indirectly to other channels of expression.

The technique I advocate on the basis of our experience in the laboratory for the last eight or nine years rests upon the simple assumption that everything that the singer or speaker conveys to the listener in the form of music or speech is conveyed on the sound wave. We may have dramatic singing and gesture and other forms of embellishing action, but these are accessory and can readily be recorded by photographic methods if desired. But the fundamental fact is one which even the psychologists and physicists have been slow to recognize, namely, that what is conveyed from voice or instrument to the ear is conveyed on the sound wave and through no other medium.

This being granted, we have only to take advantage of the marvellous development in phonophotography which has taken place within the last few years. We intercept the sound-wave message with the camera, which records every character of the message on moving-picture film permanently and in minute detail. We may then build a scientific terminology of emotion within these fields in terms of measurement upon this sound-wave record and convert this into psychological terminology.

My purpose in speaking today is not to announce any marked contribution to the advance in phonophotography, but rather to point out how we psychologists may take advantage of the remarkable development of facilities for exact record, reproduction, analysis, and measurement of sound waves.

We may note three reasons why this approach to the study of emotion is full of promise and assurance for the psychology of emotion. These are: (1) that phonophotography furnishes us in this field complete objective records of emotional expressions in permanent form and adequate detail; (2) that music and speech represent perhaps the most highly developed artistic forms of the expression of emotion in the human being and constitute the medium most commonly used for the expression of all stages of affective life; and (3) that basic records of this kind become a common instrument of reference in all studies of physical and mental conditions of emotional expression.

1.   The physical record in a phonophotogram may be reduced to four factors; namely, the wave-form, the wave-length, the wave-amplitude, and the wave-recurrence, each of these giving us in turn timbre, pitch, intensity, and duration of sound.[1] The infinite complexes of rich experience in hearing are all built up from these four fundamental sources.   Each of these four factors of the sound wave has a large range for itself and when we take into account all the possible permutations in combination of these four series of variables we have sufficient physical basis to account for all auditory experience from the stimulus point of view.

The thing I wish to emphasize here is that a complete record of vocalization may be available for physical measurements on these four phases of the sound wave and that theoretically we shall be able to reconstruct from these four fundamental measurements an almost infinite variety of experiences or expressions which are recognized as vocal.   While some of the detail in the building of instruments for a complete record of sound waves yet remains to be worked out in practice, we have theoretically in sight, and in most cases practically, instruments which will record emotional expression in appeal to the ear through voice or instrument in as fine detail as may be significant for psychological analysis.   I know of no other field for the expression of emotional life in which we have or are ever likely to have a tool of investigation so adequate and readily available.

2.   When we regard all mental life as tinged with emotion and when our object is to tease out this particular tinge from the normal, beautiful or ugly, agreeable or disagreeable act, music and speech present an incomparably fertile field.   Our largest interest is, of course, in the problem of determining the laws for the expression of the beautiful.   The expression of the ugly may be regarded as the negative or obverse phase of the same thing. Now beauty in vocal expression may be regarded as a pleasing deviation from the regular, the fixed, and the exact.   Thus, in determining what constitutes beauty in singing, we must formulate

[1] Although the attribute of extensity belongs in this category of attributes of sound I do not give it a separate status here because its physical basis is wave-length, which is the same as for pitch.

the laws for deviation from the regular—true pitch, exact time, fixed rhythm, pure tone, and so forth. This simplifies our problem and makes it specific and concrete. I am using the term "expression of emotion" here in the broadest sense so as to include the affective phase of concrete acts and experiences from the most attenuated affective tone in the everyday act up to the violent emotional expression or experience. The emotion is therefore never regarded as a process in itself but rather as a phase of experience and action almost universally present. We, therefore, speak of the photogram as representing a song or a speech *in toto*, yet the photogram is such as to enable us to deal with the affective aspects in and by themselves in the actual setting of the process as a whole.

3. A phonophotogram becomes a basic record embodying or representing the emotional act. In the study of all factors involved we have, therefore, not that illusive consciousness which introspective psychology has changed, but the overt emotional act as a whole preserved and available for examination from all points of view. The photogram therefore becomes a universal tool of investigation.

On the basis of our own experiments in the laboratory, I may give a number of examples of the manner in which this tool may be used. I cannot stop to give results, but merely indicate principles involved.

a) Comparison of the auditory experience and the analysis of the objective record. The photogram of the rendition of a great singer from a phonograph record has strategic value in that it enables us to go back at any time and compare the hearing of the sound and its objectively analyzed features. Countless problems involving laws of hearing may be solved in this manner. By the introduction of the tone-producing feature the same film may now report both for the purpose of auditory reproduction, as in the vitaphone, and for quantitative analysis as now studied in our laboratory. When such a camera can be taken out to primitive peoples for the making of this double record, a new wonderland may be brought home to the laboratory. And, when distance is annihilated so that the double record may be made instantly in the laboratory from any part of the world over the radio, science seems to approach magic.

b) The motor mechanism in the expression of emotion. With the conditions under which phonophotograms are taken, objective record may be made of any feature in the motor mechanism for the purpose of determining the primary sources of innervation and the order and relationship of the various secondary innervations which enter into the musculature of a given act. For example, with the phonophotogram of the beautiful rendition of a tone, minute photographic records may be made also of the time, the extent, the form, and the spread of the movement in the individual muscles involved which produce that element of beauty. The same amplifying system which is used in reporting the sound may be used in amplifying the reproduction of other inceptive and otherwise unobservable muscular movements. Such studies enable us to give a structural picture of the motor mechanism in a given emotional act.

c) *The neural functions which condition the act.* The principle of amplifying for the recording of sound may also be applied to the photographing of the action current. Thus in the study of the sources and paths of innervation we need not wait for the response of the muscle as an indication of the innervation, but may record directly the origin, the course, and the frequency of the innervations of the given muscle. It has been shown recently that the rate of transmission of a nerve impulse through a simple set of synapses is correlated with mental alertness, and by the same principle there would be reason for assuming that it would correlate with types of emotional response. Although it concerns only the grosser movements of the nerve impulse, the technique of measurement of action currents furnishes a new tool for the determination of the neural mechanism which correlates with a given emotional act.

d) *Causes and conditions of emotional responses.* The phonophotogram as a permanent representation of the original act enables us to tease out under experimental control one after another of the countless subjective and objective factors which condition a particular emotional act, such as its relation to stimuli, specific mental processes, awareness, effort, and dominant drives. The problems and types of approach from this point of view are countless.

e) *The relation of artistic expression of emotion to talent.* The quality and degree of artistic emotion expressed in song, for example, is dependent upon the singer's possession of certain special capacities such as the sense of pitch, sense of rhythm, musical imagery, reflective thinking, and various forms of motor control. Each of these may be studied in turn under control in relation to the actual performances as recorded by a photogram and such studies immediately reveal aspects of general forms of personality traits such as emotional stability, persistence, or introversion.

f) *Objective differences in the expression of emotional qualities.* The differentiation in the expressions of love and anger, the quiet emotion and the violent emotion, and similar qualitative differences in emotional experience may now be approached a step nearer by measurement; for, if fear, anger, love, are expressed through music, the differences among them, so far as the affective quality of the singing is concerned, may be expressed in terms of measurements upon the sound wave.

g) Development or adaptation of emotional expression. Since age groups may readily be studied by phonophotography for this purpose, the development of artistic singing forms the modulation of the expression of feeling; and the actual rise and fall of certain emotional tendencies may be adequately recorded.

h) Racial traits in song and speech. We may now compare the beauty or ugliness of a particular expression of emotion in music or speech of the Hottentot or the Bostonian, the Fiji Islander or the Eskimo, for many of our instruments now available bring all these within our reach.

i) The inheritance of emotional qualities. Likewise, since our objective records enable us to make comparisons within a family and for successive generations in a family group, the study of inheritance of emotional traits, such as a beautiful singing voice or a conspicuous rhythmic activity, may be studied objectively.

j) Learning, the acquisition of emotional skill. The voice has up to the present time been one of the most grossly neglected factors in the judgment of the charm of personality. As interest in art grows we are going to place the development of the affective aspects of human intercourse on a part with the cognitive; and the most important of these is the pleasingness of the human voice. Appreciation of the forms of beauty in the human voice and skill in its control are among the large lessons that cultured man has yet to learn; and, in the present approach, we have a means for laying scientific foundation for a science of the expression of the beautiful through voice.

To this list of ten vantage grounds many more might be added. These are selected as points of view which are actually in operation at the present time in the Iowa laboratory. I might illustrate all of them in a specific case, the study of the vibrato by Dr. Metfessel and others. By such methods the investigator has been enabled to work out a number of laws of the relation of the perception which the vibrato has to its objective existence; what fundamental types of motor mechanism actually operate in the production of the vibrato; what are the primary and what are secondary forms of innervation indicating the seat of control of the vibrato; what types of mental and physical antecedents and motives condition the vibrato; what are some of the characteristic limitations of artistic vibrato as set by limitations upon specific musical talents; what are some of the objective devices in an expression of, for example, love and anger; what is the normal order of development and the mode of origin of the vibrato in an age series of children; how the vibrato of the Carolina negro spiritual compares with that of the trained artistic singer; whether an early vibrato comes through true inheritance or merely as a social or educational factor; how may the vibrato be taught and how a disagreeable vibrato may be corrected.

This illustration should suffice to convey something of the unlimited scope of possibilities which are open to us by the technique of phonophotography in the study of emotional life.

DISCUSSION

DR. DUNLAP: (*The Johns Hopkins University*): The program which Dr. Seashore has laid down is one which should excite our enthusiasm as an experimental program, and it does excite mine. Nevertheless, I am 99.44 per cent skeptical. Many of us have worked in this field in the past. I am still somewhat skeptical, not as to the desirability of the program, but as to the possibility of attaining the results which Dr. Seashore has predicted for us. I am afraid that in exposition Dr. Seashore has confused beauty and expression, which I believe are two different things, and possibly Dr. Seashore seemed to confuse them because of the limitations of his presentation here.

But the beauty of a singer's voice, its power to arouse emotions in the hearers, is one thing. Her voice as an expression of her own emotions is in most cases an entirely different thing. Many of our singers are, you might say, human violins or oboes. They do not feel the emotions which they arouse in their hearers.

Moreover, the mechanism which they have built up for the purpose of working on our organisms in that way is one which is not built up through emotional experience of that type, but through a careful and long training in details of technique, which singers know will have that effect in the mechanical perfection of the human organs.

To a large extent, as we know, those methods of arousing feeling in auditors, these elements of beauty, as we may call them, are conventional. The things which to us are of great value, which arouse deep emotions in us, to other men of the same heredity, who have not been trained in that same thing, arouse loathing and disgust. The vibrato is an example, where the training to that constant trembling of voice may lead us to accept that somewhat jazzy element of singing as something of great beauty, that is, may arouse in us emotions which it did not arouse fifty years ago.

When it comes to the voice as expressing the actual feelings of the vocalizer, then we are entering upon a problem of exceeding great interest, but the problem where my pessimism is deepest.

It is true, as Dr. Seashore has pointed out, that the totality of vocal expression can be reduced to a few elements. In that consideration lies great advantage and significant danger.

Water can be reduced to two elements, oxygen and hydrogen. But you tell your engineer designing a city water system, with all of its complicated requirements, that all he has to do is to deal with oxygen and hydrogen, and you won't convince him that the matters of pressure and purification and the manifold details of engineering practice in regard to water supplies can be solved by a simple synthetic consideration of primary elements.

Our problem with regard to emotions is as much an engineering problem as it is a chemical problem, I believe, and I think Dr. Cannon would agree with that. But important as the chemical consideration is, it is a much more complicated problem than that, and I think we can very quickly assure ourselves of that fact with regard to vocal expression. The voice does express feeling or emotion, whatever you want to call it. Of that there is no question. It is one of those physiological signs. We are long past the day when we were inclined to connect those factors with anatomical signs in a mixed population. But we know all physiological signs must be considered, both with regard to the fleeting expressions of mental changes, and with regard to the permanent tendencies in mental constitution.

But here we are dealing, if my experience is dependable, with factors of great subtlety. If we were to estimate Galli-Curci's voice in the terms of simple factors on the basis of a synthesis and an analysis which we could make of those at present, I am afraid that Galli-Curci, with her well-known characteristic of inability to keep on the pitch, would be rated much below some of our church sopranos. Those elements of superiority in Galli-Curci's voice which enable her to produce her effects —you see I am getting over into expression, but you see now it is the effect of the voice itself rather in beauty than expression—regardless of how Galli-Curci feels when she sings, and from what I have heard, her introspection would be quite worth while in that regard—those elements which give her voice superiority in spite of its grave technical defects are subtle considerations. That has to do with the difficulties of instrumentation and analysis which we get immediately.

I unfortunately did not hear the beginning of Dr. Seashore's paper. He may have overcome this in his opening. But all of the instruments which I know, six or seven different instruments of phonographic registration of vocal expression, are exceedingly troublesome. I suppose nobody in our land knows that better than Dr. Dayton C. Miller, who spent the greater part of his life in attempts at this type of analysis. And a phonograph isn't any more a source of difficulty than the other instruments. We can, it is true, register pitch, we can register duration, we can register amplitude, we can register wave-form. How much these details of average pitch, average amplitude, have to do with emotion is a question. I do not think they have much to do with it.

A person who talks may talk in a voice which has been standardized for many years, but he gives himself away in small matters, and those small matters are the significant matters. Timbre is important but timbre is standardized by our methods of training, and the analysis of timbre from our best phonographic records, as some of you know, is a matter yet for conjecture. If you succeed in analyzing in months a few feet of record and are sure of your analysis, I think you will have the commendation of Dr. Miller.

Our instruments are not at the present time capable of registering timbre accurately. You have to make manifold physical corrections. It is in those slight variations that we find the significant things, so that slight variations over a long period of time, not through a few seconds but over some moments, in pitch and in amplitude are the things which give the other fellow's expression away to you.

Now, those difficulties may be overcome. Maybe sometime in the future we will be able to make analyses which will give us these glittering results. But after considering some of the simpler points and finding the best I can calculate the solution of a single one of these minor points for a single singer (which would be a mile of phonographic records), then consider how long it would take anybody, comparing details over miles of records, assuming he has methods of analysis not yet invented, to get that done in several years, if it could be done. The labor of getting at general principles, you see, would still be left as an exceedingly long task.

The question of instrumentation and analysis is a different thing. I think it is a splendid thing that Dr. Seashore has held up these glittering ideals, in order that our energy, which many people have been putting into attempts to overcome these apparently insuperable difficulties, shall be restored, our courage heartened, and we may go on and perhaps in the course of thirty or forty years—I will be optimistic to that extent—we may have succeeded in getting a start on this program.

Even then, however, valuable and important as the registration of the emotional expressions of the human voice may be, I am not sure but what dependence on that as a very important index of emotional life would not be something like depending upon a record of barometric changes in the state of Colorado over ten years as an index of the agricultural and mercantile productions she might be ultimately capable of producing.

DR. SEASHORE: This is a splendid opportunity to add another specimen to my collection of those who are not willing to go back to fundamentals and what seem to me to be self-evident truths with which I start out and which we must believe in if we are going to do laboratory work. As Dr. Dunlap spoke, I was trying to decide whether he was speaking as a philosopher or psychologist. If he speaks as a psychologist or as a critic of laboratory methods, he has my full support and sympathy. And I am sure he will agree with me that we are at the very beginning of an extremely large program. But I see no reason why we should not see the program.

The paper which I read has been written with some care for the purpose of printing it, and I shall be very glad to have psychologists of that very fine critical type of mind which Dr. Dunlap represents show wherein I have made a wrong forecast in placing the program for measurements of this type before you.

I should consider it unnecessary to mention in this audience that the first principle of scientific work in psychology is that you must isolate one factor, study that under controlled conditions, and limit your conclusions to the factor which is under control. I did not think it necessary to say that in my paper, but if I had said that, I would have taken the momentum away from the thunder which seems to carry the impression that I had a complete explanation of emotional life and experience.

What I am making a plea for is that we scientists shall be willing to settle down and spend generations and ages if necessary in studying one form of one sound wave, in order that we may lay sound foundations. And, of course, the apparatus is not the feature. But even the most excellent apparatus with which Dr. Miller has led the way is very much surpassed at the present time by the newest forms of instrument for recording, and I want to say at this time that we owe a great deal to Dr. Miller for doing just the thing which I have tried to do a stage further by showing what the program is. We do not have to philosophize about it. We do not have to be gloomy or stand in despair. The facts in regard to what is transferred physically from the singer to the listener are objective facts which can be studied by instruments.

PROFESSOR RIEBLER (*St. Lawrence University*): I would like to know whether we might transgress on Dr. Seashore's time and have him put on the blackboard a typical graph of some emotion, rage or fear, say.

DR. SEASHORE: That is asking too much, because that is an awfully long story, and we have just begun to pry into it. But if you had stopped in the first part of your sentence, I could have given you fifty principles somewhat on the order of laws in psychology which must be taken into account in the interpretation of that. The vibrato that is beautiful is approximately, when plotted in terms of pitch and in terms of intensity, a synchronous pulsation of pitch and intensity in which to the present musical ear and musical conventions the most beautiful form is that in which the amplitude oscillation is something between a half and a third of a tone, and in which the intensity oscillation is equally perceptible to the pitch oscillation. This oscillation is smooth at the rate of about six to eight or ten vibrations per second, depending upon the quality of the emotion that is expressed.

DR. PRINCE (*Harvard University*): I did not catch—none of us did, I think—the method of how Dr. Seashore records the nerve pulsation or nerve current respecting the voice. May I ask that question, because I can see that that may be a very important and valuable method for the solution of some problems. Will you explain that please?

DR. SEASHORE: We have just recently perfected the instrument for measuring these things, so that we have no important results to give as yet. I may say in just a word that it is the well-recognized principle of recording the action current, and if, for instance, you want to know how the diaphragm is actuated, the nearest approach is to the muscles which control the diaphragm and record the time intervals, so stated as to be significant for your purpose. We have to begin with the grosser reflexes in studying stuttering and the vibrato, because vibrato is an instability of the voice and stuttering is an instability of the voice. We began with the study of patellar reflexes, thinking that if we could master that, we could transfer to the study of other reflexes which are less accessible.

DR. CANNON (*Harvard University*): How is differentiation made between the action current of the muscle and the action current of the nerve?

DR. SEASHORE: I can answer that only in objective facts; that in this particular thing we took the easiest approach, taking the stimulation—for the patellar reflex, the nerve impulse has to go up to the spinal cord through a reflex arc (how far up that goes we do not know) and then back. And the question arose which you asked, how shall we differentiate the place with reference to the recording. Now, as I understand it, the action current which we record at the present time is a neuro-muscular affair, and the boys who did this measuring went into the anatomical laboratory and dissected a lot of cadavers, in which they knew where the motor impulse which innervates the large muscle, the patellar muscle, is located, and then they put the electrodes just above that point. That is the empirical way of answering that question. I do not think the full answer can be given to your question, but it may be possible to get it.

DR. CANNON: I hardly think that would give the action current of the nerves. The only way that can be got is by having the nerve wholly isolated from surrounding tissues and having the electrodes applied directly to it. The current is so extraordinarily minute that the fluids which surround the nerve would readily carry any difference of potential which might develop as the impulse passes along the nerve, and would not be expressed on the surface by electrodes that are applied to the surface of the body.

DR. SEASHORE: There is no difficulty in getting the response large enough.

DR. CANNON: You can get muscular action current?

DR. SEASHORE: Yes, whatever it is. But it is at that point and it is one step in advance. Say roughly, not to be exact, the patellar response has ordinarily been taken at about a tenth of a second, now the response which we get at this point is less than a hundredth of a second, and while we don't know exactly what it is, it gives a vantage ground, in that we are closer to the time over the circuit which is examined. I admit fully that we do not know just what happens and what it is that we are picking up there where the nerve runs into the muscle.

CHAPTER 17

EXCITEMENT AS AN UNDIFFERENTIATED EMOTION

George M. Stratton
University of California

On an earlier occasion, there was reported the experience of an aviator who, while doing "stunts" at a height of about 5500 feet, found that his elevator-control was stuck, and that his airplane in that respect no longer answered to the "stick." He thereupon kicked the rudder over and sent his ship into a tail-spin, and, while falling, discovered and corrected an entanglement in the wire of his control, and was able thereupon to straighten out the airplane after a fall of about 4000 feet and when within about 1500 feet of the ground.[1] While considering this experience and its indication of the uses of emotion, I ventured to suggest that, along with the particular emotions well recognized by psychologists of the day, a place should be made for excitement. But at the moment there was no opportunity to explain or to justify this thought. Yet because of its intrinsic interest and its important bearing on current theory of the emotions, I shall now return to it, with the hope of doing more justice to what was then confessedly slighted.

In proposing to recognize excitement in this manner, it will of course be clear to the reader that the way has been prepared by others. Excitement appears in one of the "dimensions" of simple feeling in the well-known account by Wundt. For Ladd and Woodworth[2] a feeling of excitement is unquestionably real, and they describe some of its forms of expression. Excitement is mentioned or briefly spoken of by Bain,[3] Woodworth,[4] Warren,[5] and others. But while it is recognized by some as a feature common to various emotions, there is a reluctance to admit it to a

[1] "An Experience during Danger, and the Wider Functions of Emotion" in *Problems of Personality: Studies in Honor of Dr. Morton Prince* (New York: Harcourt, Brace, 1925), p. 47.

[2] *Elements of Physiological Psychology* (New York: Scribner, 1911), pp. 501 ff., 531.

[3] *The Emotions and the Will* (4th ed.; London: Longmans, 1899), p. 13.

[4] *Psychology* (New York: Holt, 1921), p. 126.

[5] *Human Psychology* (Boston: Houghton Mifflin, 1919), p. 284 f.

place of importance along with sadness, joy, anger, fear, love, and the rest.　Thus it is notably absent from James's classical survey of the instincts and emotions;[6] and from the accounts of the emotions and instincts by Shand[7] and by McDougall.[8]　Nor does it appear in the tabulation by Warren.[9]

I

Before I attempt a fuller account of this important psychophysical process, let me give a few instances to show what I mean by excitement.　My dog "pointing" at a squirrel-hole in the hills, standing stock-still, but uncommonly ready to be startled by some slight sound I make, perhaps by my dislodging a small stone which rolls down the slope, or by a single light clap of my hands—this, I believe, might be called excitement in the dog. And in the reports to me by cattlemen, as to the effect of the sight or smell of blood, several of them rather shrewdly, I am now led to believe, resisted the temptation to call the cattle's response anger; they preferred to call it excitement.[10]　Some of the behavior of birds described by W. H. Hudson, I should feel might most safely be regarded not as fear, nor as anger clearly, and certainly not as love, but rather as excitement.

In human beings, the emotion is to be found fairly clearly in the experience of public speaking, after one has passed through his initial anxiety and, getting well under way, finds his audience becoming attentive and ready to indicate its interest.　He warms to his theme, his misgiving vanishes, and there may come over him a condition clearly emotional and yet difficult to identify with any of the recognized emotions.　I doubt that it is always vainglory, a rejoicing in one's adequacy and progress; there seems often to come, rather, a lessened self-consciousness and a more complete absorption in the work at hand.　And when a person is hunting or fishing, he experiences fateful moments, when the greatest trout of the day hesitates between striking and flight; or when the twigs snap deep in the forest, as though the expected deer was at last about to emerge.　The heart's action, the breathing, here is no longer calm; the entire receptive and effective system is so keyed that the slightest sound, the slightest seen-movement, is apt to cause a start; the attention is preternaturally

---

[6] *Principles of Psychology,* (New York: Holt, 1890), II, p. 409 ff.

[7] *Foundations of Character* (2nd ed.; London: Macmillan, 1920), p. 27 ff.

[8] *Introduction to Social Psychology* (Boston: Luce, 1910).

[9] *Human Psychology* (Boston: Houghton Mifflin, 1919), p. 299.

[10] "Cattle, and Excitement from Blood," *Psychological Review,* **XXX** (1923), 380 ff.

alert; according to the impressions of the moment, action is ready to be set off instantly along one or another course.

Excitement would also be exemplified in tense moments while reading a novel, when observing a decisive football game or game of baseball, and by the behavior of those students who, in a conflagration in Berkeley a few years ago, rushed to the help of the townspeople whose houses lay in the path of the fire. Houses were entered, all manner of household things were salvaged, pianos were carried out to the street, smoking roofs were scaled, life was risked for anything or for nothing. Such men were not afraid, nor angry, nor in love; neither were they sorrowful nor rejoicing, nor were they calm. They were in a highly emotional state. The plain man would probably have said that they were excited, or would have urged them not to get excited. And I do not see but that he is right in recognizing their condition as emotional and yet as being not that of any specialized emotion.

There can accordingly be no shadow of doubt, it seems to me, that we here have a principal form of psychophysical behavior as real and as definite and we might say as important as fear, or anger, or joy, or sadness. But its definite character, if one may risk a bull, lies in its indefiniteness, in its being more nearly general than any of these others, in its being less specific.

Excitement differs from joy or sorrow in its external behavior and in its internal course and quality, as well as in the situation which usually calls it forth. It goes less clearly to one or the other extreme of rejoicing or of wailing. It is easily distinguished, for example, from the elation of the victor and from the depression of the vanquished. In either of these two emotions, pleasure or unpleasantness comes to a high pitch and occupies a prominent place in the total complication. Excitement, on the other hand, while it may be pleasant or unpleasant, is mildly so, and it may be mixed or perhaps neutral. At the moment, the pleasure or unpleasantness is hardly at the front; what is more prominent in excitement is the tension, the expectation, the readiness for instant adaptation to novel openings in the situation; there is a distinct looking for something yet to come. In joy and sadness, the situation has shown itself with relative fullness, the tension is gone, and one is glad or sad in what has come to pass or is foreshadowed. In excitement the mind and body are extraordinarily alert; and for the normal organism, one may assume, alertness is pleasant. But this is a pleasure had in the very living itself, and not in some particularly favorable turn which the events of life have taken.

Excitement is also distinct from anger, fear, and affection. For these three emotions have characteristic impulses fairly general and unspecialized; and with the impulses there are connected with each of the three emotions movements which are of wide variety and are fairly unspecific. But connected with excitement there is no special impulse nor even a general impulse which is characteristic of this emotion. In anger there is the impulse to injure another person or to destroy his resistance to one's purpose or interests. In fear, there is an impulse to hide or flee or to reduce by some manner of defense an impending injury. In affection, there is an impulse to remain near and to enjoy the endeared object and to benefit that object. But in excitement there may be no clear impulse to any definite form of action. The excited man is active; he is apt to be in motion; but the fact that he is excited tells us nothing as to the end to which his movements will be directed. His whole being may or may not be dominated by a purpose. He may be on the *qui vive* and with no impulse but a most general one of being ready for anything that may occur. Or he may have a very special impulse—to make a fortune by an impending change of the market, to rescue a drowning man, to get to a fire. But what the impulse is or is to be, cannot be deduced from the excitement itself; all will depend on circumstance. Excitement can support and strengthen any particular impulse you please. Or, as I said, it can be without particular impulse. In this respect, then, excitement is unlike anger, fear, and affection. But in this very respect it is like joy and sadness, which also are marked by far less specific and characteristic impulses to action than are anger and fear. Yet it is unlike joy and sadness in the several respects already indicated. Excitement thus appears as the least specialized, the most generalized of all the emotions.

II

The relation of excitement to the other relatively simple emotions might be represented by the accompanying diagram, in which there are conceived to be four limits of emotion; namely, the most generalized and the most differentiated or specialized, and the most pleasant and the most unpleasant.

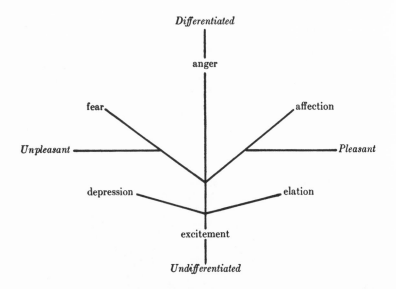

One should not assume that these analytic findings indicate that in evolution and development the causal derivation is precisely as this diagram represents. What the evolutionary and developmental connections may be is a matter to be determined by further observation and experiment. It would not be surprising, however, if the order in evolution and development should be found to correspond to what is here suggested.

The relation of excitement to the other emotions may be further clarified by a word. One might well ask whether excitement always stands clearly apart from the others, or whether it mingles with them. The facts seem to me to warrant us in holding that:

1. Excitement may stand alone; it may arise with the full qualities, even if without the full strength, of excitement, and may, without leading to any other emotion, slowly or swiftly pass away.

2. Excitement may be the precursor of any one of the other emotions; before there is joy or sadness, before there is fear or anger or love there often is—although there need not always be— mere excitement. A man's manner may stir me before he awakens in me fear or anger or any other emotion; there may be an initial stage marked by quick interest and alertness, as though on the

verge of something fateful, but without as yet any clear reaction
of alarm or resentment or of friendly attraction. When the
situation becomes the definite occasion for one of these, then the
mere excitement has gone and a less generalized emotion is in
its place.

3. Excitement may be the successor of other emotions. When
fear is relieved by the sudden disappearance of a menace, as when
one has killed a rattlesnake faced suddenly in the mountains,
there is no instant calm. The alarm is gone, but the waters
continue to be troubled as after a squall. This persisting disturbance, when the specific emotion is no longer demanded by
the situation, this continuing agitation seems to me emotional
and to be identified as excitement.

Some would perhaps add a fourth assertion, that excitement
is an accompaniment or essential constituent of all emotion, being
present in every case of fear, anger, love, elation, or depression,
as well as in the more complex emotions. I have no stout objection to this, although my vote would be against it. In the end
it is a matter less of fact than of words and of prudence in limiting
a concept. To include under the one term "excitement" both
the generalized emotion, and also the commotional aspect of all
the specialized emotions would hardly tend to clarify; we had
better continue to designate this common aspect of the specialized
emotions by a separate term, such as emotionality, or agitation,
or affect, or by Woodworth's "stirred-upness." We shall then
perhaps be less tempted to believe that each emotion is a mere
compound attained by agitation plus specific impulse plus pleasure
or unpleasantness, and so on; whereas, instead, each emotion
is an organized whole.

III

As for the situations which arouse excitement, something of
their character has already become clear. Excitement is our
response to a situation which we recognize as calling for somewhat
more than an easy and routine handling. The situation which
arouses excitement may require no adaptation beyond our powers;
but it does require an adaptation not covered by our resources
immediately available, by our forces at the front; there is need of
our reserves. Moreover, it is not enough that the situation has
this unusual character; it must be *recognized* as having it. A
rattlesnake in the open and within a foot of one's hand or face
would for most of us call for an unusual act of adaptation; but
unless one is aware of the snake's presence, there is no emotion.

But, further, if the situation, including the recognition of it, is of a relatively clear character and such as calls forth what we might call one of the stock impulses—to flight or hiding or attack or affectionate embrace or wailing or glad shouting and laughter, together with the feelings and judgments usually connected with one of these impulses—then, instead of excitement, there is joy or fear, or the like. For excitement, the situation must be other than this. It may be either (a) unresolved as yet, not developed enough to indicate its meaning for us, as when a hunter hears a crash in the underbrush and cannot make out what it is; or (b) so complicated that it tends to stir incompatible impulses which cancel one another and leave the individual bewildered, as was the case with many persons when the World War burst upon us; or (c) relatively clear, and arousing unmistakably a particular impulse but not what I have called one of the stock impulses. Thus to face a difficult examination, or to see one's neighbor's house in flames, or to be stopped on the street by a policeman with a summons, for the first time in one's life to appear in court for jury duty—any one of these may arouse a particular impulse but no primal or stock impulse; the whole reaction, inner and outer, is of mild or intense excitement. In a great business crisis, a man may, as at no other time in his life, be brought to commotion, while also not confused.

Following all these directions of the evidence, then, it has seemed to me that our thinking would be clarified by recognizing this peculiar state of mind and body. In excitement we have a form of emotion, which perhaps exists at an earlier date than do the other forms, and which certainly is less differentiated than any other form of emotion. It may exist itself, or it may be the precursor or successor of any of the other emotions usually recognized by psychologists. It has its own situations which call it forth, and which can be as adequately described as are the situations which arouse joy or sorrow, fear, anger or love.

CHAPTER 18

HOW EMOTIONS ARE IDENTIFIED AND CLASSIFIED

Robert S. Woodworth
Columbia University

Among psychological theories which have won acceptance
because of the neat way in which they introduced order into a
large and confused field, few can rank with William McDougall's
doctrine that specific emotions are the affective phases of specific
instincts.[1] With instinctive avoidance behavior goes the emotion of fear, with instinctive aggressive and pugnacious behavior
the emotion of anger, with curiosity and exploratory behavior
the emotion of wonder, and so on through a list of the most
"powerful instincts," each including one of the primary emotions.

Considered as an attempt to find a one-to-one correspondence
between characteristic modes of overt behavior and equally
characteristic affective states of the organism, this theory presupposes that it is possible to identify the several emotions independently of overt behavior. Otherwise we have only a "spu-
rious correlation." If fear is recognizable and definable only as
the emotional state that goes with avoidance behavior, it is no
great achievement to discover that fear goes with avoidance.

If we turn to the dictionary for definitions of the several emotions, we read that fear is "the painful emotion characteristic
of the apprehension of evil; agitation and desire to avoid an
object"; that anger is an "emotion of displeasure or antagonism
excited by injury or insult"; that wonder is the "emotion excited
by novelty." Apart from non-specific characters such as pain
and agitation, these attempts at definition go outside of the
organism altogether for something to serve as the differentia of
any given emotion. McDougall himself does no better. He makes
no serious attempt to give an introspective description of each
of the primary emotions. Indeed, it is very doubtful if a purely
introspective description—with no reference to the external
situation arousing an emotion or to the overt behavior attending
it—could be made so characteristic as to enable the reader to
identify the emotion which was being described. Warren has

---

[1] W. McDougall, *Introduction to Social Psychology* (Boston: Luce, 1910), p. 46.

gone further than most authors in attempting to describe the emotional states as such.[2] He says of a certain emotion that its hedonic tone is unpleasantness, usually present in a high degree, that its characteristic organic sensations come from the lower viscera and the region of the heart and lungs, and that there are kinaesthetic sensations of trembling, etc. Of another emotion he says that its general hedonic tone is unpleasant, that its characteristic organic sensations come from the upper digestive tract, the heart and lungs, and the circulatory system generally, and that there are intense kinaesthetic sensations of muscular tension from the face, hands, and legs. It is safe to assert that these emotions would not be recognized from the introspective descriptions, aside from the indications of overt behavior admitted by way of the account of kinaesthetic sensations.

Now we have to admit that introspective study of the emotions has not been carried far enough to warrant our denying that each emotion could be defined as a purely affective (and sensory) state. But certainly psychologists are not yet in a position to point to a well-defined list of such states, along with a well-defined list of modes of overt behavior, and then to call attention to the remarkable one-to-one correspondence that exists between the two lists.

The behaviorists, though looking with contempt on any such attempt to characterize emotions in terms of feelings and sensations, still regard the concept of emotion as usable, provided the emotion is defined as intra-organic behavior, consisting largely in the action of glands and unstriped muscles.[3] But when Watson comes to his admitted list of three primary emotions, fear, rage, and love, he describes and identifies them in terms of external stimulus and overt behavior, with practically no reference to the glands and smooth muscles. So he says of fear in infants: "The responses are a sudden catching of the breath, clutching randomly with the hands (the grasping reflex invariably appearing when the child is dropped), sudden closing of the eyelids, puckering of the lips, then crying." Of rage he says, "If the face or head is held, crying results, quickly followed by screaming. The body stiffens and fairly well-coordinated slashing or striking movements of the hands and arms result; the feet and legs are drawn up and down; the breath is held till the child's face is flushed."

Indeed, at the present time it would be as impracticable to present an identifiable picture of each of these three emotions in

[2] H. C. Warren, *Human Psychology* (Boston: Houghton Mifflin, 1919), p. 297.
[3] J. B. Watson, *Psychology from the Standpoint of a Behaviorist* (Philadelphia: Lippincott, 1919), pp. 195–202.

terms of the activities of glands, smooth muscles, and internal organs in general, as it is to present an identifiable picture in terms of sensations and feelings. Cannon[4] finds the same internal changes in fear and rage, as well as in states of "being all keyed up" for strenuous activity, which states cannot properly be called either fear or rage. All serious and thorough experimental efforts to discover a characteristic bodily expression for each emotion have failed. Shepard[5] found that "feelings cannot be classified on the basis of vasomotor and heart rate changes. . . . In short, all moderate nervous activity tends to constrict the peripheral vessels and to increase the volume and size of pulse in the brain." Landis,[6] introducing into the laboratory a variety of often drastic emotional situations, was unable to find differential patterns of response, either from the vascular organs or from the muscles of facial expression, while Brunswick[7] found the same lack of characteristic patterns in the field of gastro-intestinal reactions. Similarly, the students of the psychogalvanic reaction have not reported different types of response for different specific emotions. The present state of the question is thus summed up by Landis:

"When an organism is in a situation which results in a disturbed or wrought-up condition, then the situation plus the reaction gives us a name or word which characterizes the whole as a specific emotion. The reaction of itself is not sufficient to differentiate the emotion; the character of the situation is involved in this differentiation. That is, the same bodily responses in different situations will be called by different names on other than the emotional attributes of the entire situation."

Experimental studies of internal bodily activities, we might say, afford plenty of evidence of emotion, but little or none of the emotions as characteristically different states of the organism. This conclusion should, indeed, be accepted with some reserve, since laughter seems an exception, and since a strong sex emotion, unhampered by embarrassment, has perhaps not yet been examined under laboratory conditions. In short, we may not have succeeded, thus far, in bringing the whole range of emotion under careful observation. But, at any rate, we have to admit that many distinctions which we unhesitatingly make in everyday speech, such as that between fear and anger, do not rest on any known intra-organic difference, either introspectively or objectively observed. We seem to be driven back to where the dic-

[4] W. B. Cannon, *Bodily Changes in Pain, Hunger, Fear, and Rage* (New York: Appleton, 1915).

[5] J. F. Shepard, "Organic Changes and Feeling," *American Journal of Psychology*, XVII (1906), 557–558.

[6] C. Landis, *Journal of Comparative Psychology*, IV (1924), 497; Landis and Gullette, *ibid.*, V (1925), 243; Landis, *ibid.*, VI (1926), 238.

[7] D. Brunswick, *Journal of Comparative Psychology*, IV (1924), 286.

tionary left us. Unable to separate the emotions in intra-organic terms, we needs must seek a basis of distinction in the external situation.

Such a search, indeed, does not appear very promising at the outset, since emotion would seem to be nothing if not intra-organic, and since it would seem very unlikely that we could successfully classify external situations as fear-situations, anger-situations, amusing situations, satisfactory situations, without reference to the responsive organism. The same external situation may be any one of these, according to the native characteristics and past history of the organism in question. The response of the organism must certainly be considered. And it will not be sufficient to take into account the visceral or other internal response of the organism, for we do not know that the internal response differs in fear and anger. Any valid basis for distinguishing between fear and anger must take into account the *overt* response of the organism. The overt response in fear we may call avoidance, and in anger attack. Fear we distinguish from anger, accordingly, by the overt behavior of avoidance in one case and attack in the other.

This tentative conclusion is so far sound, I am sure, that no valid distinction can be drawn between fear and anger that does not include this difference in overt behavior. But several difficulties at once present themselves.

There may be, there often is, a cold-blooded or unemotional avoidance or attack. This difficulty can be readily met, however, much in the manner of Allport,[8] by agreeing to limit fear to instances of emotional avoidance, and anger to instances of emotional attack, and then referring the, perhaps undifferentiated, emotional part of the total response to the viscera, while the distinction between the two "emotions" lies in the overt behavior.

There may be anger or fear without overt attack or avoidance. We speak of a controlled desire to attack or escape. Probably there are minimal movements of attack or escape, and, at any rate, the distinction is still in terms of the overt behavior "desired," whatever that means in terms of the dynamics of the organism—some kind of set, readiness, or adjustment, probably.

A third difficulty is less trifling than it first appears. We have been talking as if, however ill defined might be the difference between fear-situations and anger-situations, or between the intra-organic responses of fear and anger, at least the overt responses of avoidance and attack were perfectly easy to distinguish. As a matter of fact, this distinction cannot be made in

[8] F. H. Allport, *Social Psychology* (Boston: Houghton Mifflin, 1924), p. 91.

purely motor terms. There are no muscles of attack, no muscles of avoidance. Movements are not classified on any such basis, since the same movement, as flexion of the arm, may be an avoidance reaction (if the hand is pricked or burned), or may be "hauling off" preparatory to striking a blow, or preparatory to throwing a kiss. Almost any movement can be a movement of avoidance, or can be something quite different, according to the situation; just as almost any situation can be a fear-situation, or something quite different, according to the response.[9]

Avoidance can be defined only in terms of the *relation* of situation and response, in terms of the change in the situation produced by the response. Let us first attempt to define this change or relation without assuming any "desire," adjustment, set, or orientation of the organism—in short, without assuming anything intra-organic that characterizes one "emotion" as distinct from another.

We might try to define avoidance as any motor response that separated the organism from the exciting stimulus. Of course we should have to break up the total situation to the extent of specifying which element in it was the effective stimulus, since every movement towards one object is inevitably a movement away from some other object. Every movement could be classified as either an approaching or an avoiding reaction, unless we felt we knew enough about the organism to specify which element in the objective situation was getting this response. But even a movement away from an object, aroused by that object, is not always avoidance. The dinner-gong sounding in the living-room provokes a general exodus, which is not an avoidance of the gong, but a "conditioned" approach to the dining-room. In view of the prevalence of substitute stimuli and substitute responses, avoidance reactions would have to be sorted out by a study of the life-history of the individual.

When such an ontogenetic classification has been carried out, the question remains whether the manifold "avoiding responses" have anything in common at present, or are only historically connected. Just as the words "radius," "radium," and "radio" have little in common except their derivation from a common root, so the various forms of behavior classed together under the head of avoidance might have nothing in common, except the fact of a common origin. At this point, I recognize that my argument becomes perceptibly weaker, but I cannot seriously doubt that common sense is dimly viewing some real intra-organic fact

[9] Cf. the discussion by Grace A. De Laguna, *Psychological Review*, XXVI (1919), 418–420.

when it says that certainly, no matter what be the origin of an individual's fear or avoidance, and no matter what the avoiding movement may be, avoidance always means that the individual is trying to get away from something, or trying to keep away from it. Common sense here introduces a teleological note, in speaking of "trying to avoid," but it is a genuine note, which demands to be included harmoniously in our psychological system. We make a start towards a mechanistic, or at least causal, formulation of this teleological notion by speaking of an "adjustment to avoid," for there can be little doubt that this term means something genuine in intra-organic dynamics.

The avoidance adjustment probably represents some pattern of neural and other intra-organic stresses, the attack adjustment another such pattern, the satisfaction adjustment a third. They have to do with the external situation and the overt response, and, since they cannot be objectively observed, they have to be identified in terms of external situation and response. Even if we observe them introspectively as different desires, we still need to identify them by reference to external stimulus and overt response, since desires can be distinguished only by such objective reference. These adjustments cannot be called emotions; they are too external in their reference. If we follow the lead of McDougall and Watson, and distinguish emotion, as some form of internal activity, from overt behavior, then the several distinct "emotions" are not emotions at all, but adjustments for different types of overt behavior.

CHAPTER 19

THE DIFFERENTIA OF AN EMOTION

HARVEY A. CARR

University of Chicago

Since the time of Lange and James, the somatic conception of the nature of emotion has been the orthodox doctrine. For purposes of exposition, the various activities of an organism may be divided into two classes: (1) The first class, which may be termed the intelligent activities, are those which are primarily concerned with the adaptation of the organism to its objective environment. In an emotional situation, they would embrace the apprehension of the nature and significance of the exciting situation, danger for example, and the overt reaction of the organism to that situation on the basis of this appraisal. (2) The second group embraces the vital, the vegetative, the autonomic, or the somatic activities which are primarily concerned with the maintenance of the structural and functional integrity of the organism. They are concerned with the intake, transformation, distribution, and assimilation of energy and the elimination of the waste products involved in its consumption.

An emotion, according to the orthodox doctrine, represents an instinctive and biologically useful interaction between these two classes of organic activities. The stimulating situation of danger, for example, also excites a distinctive set of changes or alterations on the part of the on-going somatic activities whereby the reserve stores of energy are released, mobilized, and distributed to the reacting mechanisms involved in flight, and the waste products involved in this greater expenditure of energy are more quickly eliminated. In other words, the vital or somatic activities are readjusted so as to promote a more vigorous, sustained, and effective response to the stimulating situation.

Certain essential features of this somatic readjustment are obvious. In danger, for example, the heart beats faster and more vigorously. The flow of blood is accentuated. A greater volume of blood is distributed to the reacting mechanisms—a fact which is evidenced by the reddening and flushing of the skin in certain areas and the anaemic condition of others. Some authorities assert that, as a consequence of the action of a certain ductless gland, the composition of the blood is so altered that it contains a higher percentage of a readily available form of energy. Respiration is deepened and quickened, and the waste products are more quickly eliminated. The sweat and sebaceous glands are excited; the skin becomes damp and moist in some regions and dry in others. The circulatory and secretory changes alter the temperature of the skin; the angry individual may feel warm or hot in some areas, and cold and chilly in others. All of the digestive activities may be considerably affected. The whole somatic mechanism is temporarily thrown out of gear. In any profound emotional seizure, this somatic disturbance may reverberate throughout every inch of the organism. For example, our whole being seems to seethe and boil with rage. According to the orthodox conception, it is these various readjustive activities, in so far as they are experienced, that constitute the emotional experience.

An emotion may thus be provisionally defined as a somatic readjustment which is instinctively aroused by a stimulating situation and which in turn promotes a more effective adaptive response to that situation; and it is assumed that this greater efficiency is sufficient to increase materially the chances for the organism's survival in those primitive conditions of life that obtained while this instinctive reaction was evolved.

I am not so much concerned with the truth of this group of definitive characteristics as with their completeness or adequacy. Does any one or all of them differentiate an emotion from other similar experiences?

I wish to call attention to the fact that the two groups of activities—the intelligent and the somatic—are continually interacting in a mutually helpful way. The intelligent activities are frequently adapted to alleviate various somatic conditions such as hunger, thirst, intra-organic pains, digestive disturbances, fatigue and lassitude, etc. Likewise the somatic or vegetative activities are continuously being altered and modified in an appropriate manner in response to all pronounced variations in the organism's reaction to the external world. The heart beats faster and more vigorously, the respiration is altered, the face becomes flushed, the perspiratory activities are stimulated, and digestion is affected when we indulge in any vigorous type of muscular activity, whether it be chopping wood, playing tennis, doing gymnastic stunts, or running after a train as well as running from that which we fear. With the change to other types of activity such as studying, lecturing, writing, arguing with our neighbors, or attempting to be agreeable to our family, we find that these somatic activities are altered accordingly. Interaction is a continuous affair and not an intermittent phenomenon.

An emotion, as we commonly use the term, is an occasional experience. Somatic readjustments to behavior situations are continually occurring, while the emotional type of readjustment occurs relatively infrequently. The emotions are thus special cases of a more general phenomenon. There are non-emotional as well as emotional somatic readjustments to behavior situations, and any definition of an emotion, to be adequate, must differentiate those experiences from the non-emotional class of somatic disturbances. What is the differentia of an emotion? How does it differ from the non-emotional readjustments that are continually occurring? Do the definitive characteristics that have been enumerated do so?

The emotions do not differ from the non-emotional reactions in their compositional character. If we take any standard description of the somatic readjustments in anger, the account can be approximately duplicated almost word for word in describing the somatic changes that accompany any unusually vigorous and prolonged muscular effort. The two do not differ in intensity. While it is true that extreme fear and rage represent a more intense type of reaction than do most of the non-emotional readjustments, yet they may be approximated at least by the somatic disturbances involved in such strenuous forms of exercise as football and the quarter-mile dash. On the other hand many of the emotional adjustments, such as love, sorrow, pity, awe, and the milder forms of fear and anger, are no more intense than the somatic reactions involved in many of our daily activities.

The alleged instinctive character of an emotional response is not a differentiating characteristic. It is assumed that each emotional readjustment is an instinctive response to the stimulating situation, i.e., the character of the somatic response and its relation to the exciting situation is a function of the inherited structure and disposition of the organism. Yet the same statement may also be made for the non-emotional reactions. The circulatory, respiratory, and secretory mechanisms function just as spontaneously and automatically in the case of vigorous muscular work as they do in fear, anger, and joy. One can hardly assert that the reaction was learned in one case and not in the other. Both types of readjustment are equally expressions of the innate endowment of the organism.

Neither can the emotional readjustments be differentiated on the basis of their adaptiveness and biological utility. To my mind, not all of the emotions are adaptive and biologically useful, while some of the non-emotional reactions are.

The biological utility of the emotions is a necessary postulate of the assumption that the various emotions represent distinctive inherited mechanisms that have been independently evolved in phylogenetic development. The concept of natural selection assumes that each instinctive reaction was selected and perpetuated only in so far as that mode of reacting tended to preserve and perpetuate the life of the reacting individual or of the species to which it belongs. If the emotions are a group of instinctive reactions, each of these must possess such a survival or biological value for the conditions of life that obtained at the time of its origin. For example, fear is said to promote a more effective flight, and thus tends to preserve the life of the individual.

The biological utility of the emotions, to my mind, has been somewhat overemphasized. This a priori postulation has considerable difficulty with the empirical data. I am somewhat skeptical of the various attempts to specify the survival value of grief and sorrow. These reactions may have a considerable social value, i. e., they may be cultivated and utilized in the interest of certain social ideals, but this fact will not account for their origin. A biological value assumes that these reactions aid the individual to survive by promoting a more effective response to the situation which excites them. Grief and sorrow are usually awakened by the loss of highly desirable conditions, and I fail to see how grief promotes a type of response to such a situation that materially increases the chances for survival. Joy is awakened by the sudden and unexpected attainment of a highly desirable end. Inasmuch as it is aroused after the attainment of an end, it can hardly promote a more effective way of dealing with that end. Even the survival value of anger and fear is usually overrated. Fear is conducive to a more vigorous flight from danger, and anger promotes a more impetuous and energetic attack, and surely these behavior characteristics will tend to preserve the life of the organism. An enraged animal not only fights impetuously and energetically but also somewhat blindly and rashly—a mode of attack that is hardly suitable to all occasions. A frightened animal may flee precipitately but heedlessly, while a paroxysm of terror may interfere with effective flight, and induce a series of futile and abortive attempts at escape. Fear may paralyze as well as invigorate one's actions. In order to promote survival, perhaps Nature would have been wiser to have endowed organisms with less emotion and more cunning and intelligence. Some writers have classed the paralysis of fear with the death-feigning instinct of animals, which promotes survival because the immobility of the organism renders it less noticeable to its enemies. But the abortive attempts to flee in a paroxysm of fear differ materially from the clear-cut and decisive reaction in feigning death; such attempts merely court instant destruction rather than survival.

Not only may we doubt the survival value of some of the emotional reactions, but we may also call attention to the adaptive character of the non-emotional readjustments. The heart beats faster, breathing is accelerated, the face becomes flushed, and perspiration is accentuated in any vigorous muscular activity, and this somatic readjustment functions in turn to invigorate and prolong that act. Obviously such a device must materially increase the organism's chances for survival.

In passing I wish to take exception to the conventional doctrine that the emotions represent a group of instinctive reactions, each of which evolved independently of the others and was biologically selected and perpetuated because it possessed some distinctive utility. Two general objections may be urged against this doctrine. As has been indicated, the biological utility of many of these emotional reactions may be seriously questioned, and the doctrine likewise necessitates the assumption that the various non-emotional readjustments represent a large group of instincts. We are thus confronted with the hypothesis of a multiplicity of separate instinctive mechanisms to account for the phenomenon of continuous interaction. According to this conception, there will be almost as many instincts as there are instances of interaction. The situation, to my mind, can be better conceived in much simpler terms. As we have said, the two groups of activities are continually interacting in a mutually advantageous manner. The biological utility of such an arrangement is obvious, for the organism is a reactive and biological unit and all its separate activities must be intimately organized and related to each other so as to maintain and perpetuate life. From the standpoint of biological selection and development, we are here dealing, in my opinion, with a unitary phenomenon—a single biological device—and not with a multiplicity of mechanisms, each with its own phylogenetic history. This conception frees us from the necessity of assuming a utility for each emotional reaction and for the non-emotional readjustments as well; for any biological device, according to the principles of natural selection, needs to be useful only in the large majority of cases. So long as the two groups of activities interact in a mutually adaptive manner in the great majority of cases, the fact that they may influence each other at times in a non-adaptive manner and even in a harmful way on occasions will not seriously prejudice the survival of the organism. The unitary character of this biological device is not inconsistent with a considerable variety in its functional manifestations, for what happens in any case will depend upon the nature of the processes that interact. In other words, the manifestations of this interaction will continually vary with the state of the organism and the ever varying behavior situations with which it is confronted.

We may conclude that the conventional definitive characteristics of an emotion are inadequate because they do not differentiate the emotions from the non-emotional adjustments. The two do not differ in nature, intensity, innateness, adaptiveness, or biological utility. The somatic adjustments are essentially alike whether an individual runs from that which he fears or energetically speeds after that which he desires. These vegetative processes function in much the same manner in the fleeing deer and the pursuing pack. In both cases they promote vigorous and sustained action, and they are equally useful from the standpoint of survival.

We do distinguish the emotions from the non-emotional adjustments, however, and it is at once obvious that they must differ in some respect, or else we should not be able to differentiate them as we do. What is the differentia of an emotion? Why do we term the somatic reaction an emotion when we flee from danger, but do not call it an emotion when we run just as energetically to win a race?

The distinction proposed is that of the orderly and coordinated character of the non-emotional adjustments as opposed to the relatively uncoordinated and somewhat chaotic course of events in the emotional reactions.

In our ordinary activities of lecturing, constructive thinking, or chopping wood, we react to the situation in a relatively orderly and methodical way, and the somatic activities nicely adjust themselves to this orderly progression of events. The whole process exhibits a high degree of adaptive coordination and harmonious functioning.

On the other hand, an individual is unable to respond immediately to an emotional situation in an intelligent manner. How can we react to an overwhelming and irreparable loss except to grieve about it? Joy comes with the sudden and unexpected attainment of a valued end, and naturally there is nothing more that can be done except to revel in our enjoyment. A surprising situation is one to which we are temporarily unable to adapt. Dread is awakened by the sense of impending danger whose nature, time of occurrence, and location may be unknown, and as a consequence the individual is at a loss to know what to do. An effective way of dealing with a suddenly encountered danger is not always readily apparent. Because of the caution with which we are endowed or which we have acquired in the vicissitudes of experience, or perhaps because of the inhibitive influence of our moral ideals, most of us are not accustomed to rush immediately to the attack when angered or enraged. An emotional situation is one for which there is no appropriate response or one to which we are unable to respond for the time being.

An emotional stimulus is a very effective one and, being denied any motor outlet, it necessarily discharges into the somatic mechanisms—the only available outlet at the time—and tends to awaken a vigorous appropriate adjustment. These somatic activities function in turn as stimuli and release impulses that are normally incorporated into the organism's adaptive response to the exciting situation. Lacking this normal outlet, these impulses are necessarily drafted back into the somatic mechanisms and thus interfere with their orderly functioning. Because of their vigorous stimulation and because of the lack of a motor outlet, the somatic activities become disrupted and react to the situation in a relatively disorganized and chaotic manner. In dread and terror, our heart jumps and beats irregularly, we gasp for breath, and alternately turn hot and cold in rapid succession. In grief we breathe convulsively and sob hysterically, and our whole being quivers and seethes and boils with rage. In any profound emotional seizure, such as a paroxysm of fear or rage, this somatic disturbance may be such as to render the individual temporarily incapable of either flight or attack. The emotions may paralyze as well as invigorate action. The descriptive statements that have just been employed are certainly not applicable to a harmonious and coordinated type of action. The emotional experience is essentially one of inner turmoil and commotion.

Occasionally an individual may react to a sudden emergency in a prompt and a highly efficient and capable manner. In this event they usually experience no fear, and humorously report that they had no time to be afraid. Again these individuals may be overwhelmed with a severe attack of fear after the emergency has been successfully encountered. In other words, an immediate, effective, and well-coordinated response prevents the arousal of an emotional reaction.

An emotion gradually subsides and finally disappears as the organism begins to respond to the situation in an orderly and methodical manner. Our anger soon cools and wanes as we settle down to the fight, and terror no longer holds us in its grip as our precipitate and hasty initial efforts gradually become organized into an orderly and effective flight. The athlete is likely to become excited as he prepares for the race, but this emotional excitement soon subsides as he settles down to a rhythmical pace.

The somatic reaction does not disappear in these cases. It merely loses its tumultuous and chaotic and emotional character as it becomes adjusted to the demands of orderly action.

To summarize, we may say that the somatic activities are continually being excited to react in an adjustive manner to the behavior demands of the organism. The emotional reactions are those that are awakened when the organism, temporarily at least, is unable to respond in an orderly and efficient fashion to a highly stimulating situation, and for this reason they partake of the nature of a somatic disturbance. The non-emotional reactions, on the other hand, represent a relatively coordinated and orderly type of somatic readjustment, and hence we may suggest that, contrary to orthodox opinion, it is these non-emotional adjustments that exhibit the greater degree of adaptive utility.

CHAPTER 20

PLEASANTNESS AND UNPLEASANTNESS AS MODES OF BODILY EXPERIENCE

L. B. HOISINGTON
Cornell University

In the year 1924 J. P. Nafe published, so far as I know, the first descriptions of the affective experience.[1] The work up to that time, and there is a vast body of it, had dealt with problems about affection and had given us "facts" about pleasantness and unpleasantness, "facts" of correlation, but not one word of description beyond the qualities of P and U which the workers assumed on empirical grounds from the outset. All these "facts" about affection, all the correlations, still hold at the level at which the work was done, at least so far as the published reports of Nafe are concerned; he worked at a different level, viz., description.

Since method and procedure are important, it will be worth our while to turn to the reasons for Nafe's success where others had failed. He offers one reason in the introduction to his study; the reason, namely, that others had used too strong stimuli, thus making their observers into feelers rather than observers of feeling. Let that pass. A more important one, in my opinion, is that since Nafe himself had no notion of what to "set" the observers to look for, he could not instruct them specifically; all he could do was to ask for a complete description of experience in the hope that such reports would reveal the unique in affection. Hence, the general instruction in spirit, if not in words, came into use—at least at Cornell—for the first time. It came out of necessity, bred and born of ignorance. The observers, fortunately, were as ignorant of what to look for as the experimenter to instruct, so they could not set themselves a specific problem from the general instruction; all they could do was to describe experience as a total as it ran its course freed, very largely, from bias and previous determination. Experience became clearer and description more nearly complete.

What of Nafe's results? There are just two that need concern us here. The first, and in some respects the most important, is that the affective experience is in its essential character a kind of

[1] J. P. Nafe, "An Experimental Study of the Affective Qualities," *American Journal of Psychology*, XXXV (1924), 507 ff.

pressure. However varied the pleasantnesses and unpleasantnesses of everyday life, whatever modes of experience go to make up the total at such a moment, the bright or the dull pressure, as the case may be, is essential. After the event it is easy to see that it must have been so; that these experiences must be bodily pressures, as, indeed, Yokoyama had insisted.[2] The particular quality or qualities were not apparent for him; it remained for Nafe to make them specific. That his results will stand the test of time, I have not the least doubt.

At this point I should like to say a word about the use of the term "pressure" as a descriptive symbol. The affective experience, especially pleasantness, receives the name "pressure" partly by courtesy, partly from the fact that it is a bodily experience, partly because it resembles pressure more than it does any quality from the other modalities, partly because the observer does not as a rule coin new terms, but not at all because the quality of the experience is like the pressures of ordinary life. Practically every observer demurred at the term "pressure" but nothing better suggested itself. I am sure we shall have some other word to denote these experiences; I wish very much that I had such a term for the purposes of this paper.

The other result which I shall mention is that these pressures were non-localizable in the state of specific object perception. This explains the former idea of lack of clearness as a special mark of the affective life. It may mean either that we must take experience at its loosest if we are to report the separate qualities, that as experience becomes more highly integrated the qualities lose their individual character in the closely patterned total, or it may mean that with specific object reference the affective quality drops out. For reasons which I shall give presently, I am convinced that the latter alternative is the correct one. This means that we are not pleased or displeased with this or that object as such, but with this or that kind of experience.

The net result of Nafe's work, for our present purposes, is, then, that the essential affective quality is a bright or a dull pressure which arises only under the condition of non-specific object reference.

Last year, in the Cornell laboratory, Horiguchi attacked the problem of the localization of the affective experiences. Although this study is as yet unpublished, I wish to offer such of his results as bear upon our topic. He found not only the localization but some further characteristics of these bodily experiences. The ob-

[2] M. Yokoyama, "The Nature of the Affective Judgment in the Method of Paired Comparison," *American Journal of Psychology*, XXXII (1921), 357 ff.

servers who had not served in Nafe's work, as well as those who had, were better prepared for the task of affective description than were the observers at the time of the earlier study. They knew better how to come observationally passive to the work; how to take an attitude even less favorable to the perceptive formation; in brief, how to shut themselves off from the world of objects and allow the bodily experience to run its course fairly free from and unhindered by other experiential formations. Do not misunderstand me—I do not mean that the pressures of affection come to observation only when *no* meaning is present; they come with what I have, in another place, called *immanent* meaning as opposed to *transcendent* meaning. The former refers to the experience as such; the latter, to some object outside or beyond the experience. But I am not at all sure that we can put it as strongly as that, for, as we shall see, the affective modes of experience may come with a situational meaning which is transcendent in that it refers beyond the experience but not to a particular object as such; it is our way of living the object. There are, moreover, degrees of specificity of the immanent meaning. The more the observer escapes a definite "set" or determination that always comes to observation in terms of muscular pressure, the more do the various bodily experiences which constitute the warp of mental life come immanently into being. This is only another way of saying that, as we free ourselves from the dominance of particular instructions and laboratory "set," we approach nearer to the condition of everyday experience; we get a truer picture of mind in its functional dependencies with some hope eventually of its inherent laws. Of course I presuppose observers capable of painting a word-picture of experience in its totality as a total when under no other determination than that to observe.

Horiguchi found that dull pressure localizes in the region of the abdomen, well inside the body. It is a fairly compact, fairly limited mass which comes, very positively, at its meaningful best, as muscular. That is, it carries a definite muscular reference; it means that some muscles of the abdominal region are in a state of contraction. It is true the observers in this study first came upon the affective pressures as unlocalized, just as Nafe reports them. But then they sat back, as it were, and allowed them to go where they would. Only the sitting back was not absolute; the attitude was not one of complete passivity. The affective pressures were prominent immanently, which proves that the observers had an observational "set." As such, of course, the dull pressures had no muscle or body reference. They came, nevertheless, to the same general localization. They did possess a directional reference, and this came to point to the place where the abdomen would have been if it had been there for perception.

The course of the dull pressure from a wholly unlocalized bare experience to a definitely localized muscular one—and it often came to specific perception—was not an even one. There always was a momentary break or instant of experiential confusion just at the passage from bare dull pressure out there in a fairly determinate direction to dull muscular pressure there in the body. It is true that, after the break, experience showed more than it did before, as if some new feature had entered which carried the muscle reference. Just the same, I am sure that this instant of non-identification and of addition does not prove disparity so far as the dull pressure aspect is concerned. Even here, however, the perceptive reference does not transcend the experience; the reference is to a trait of the experience. This ability of the unpleasant affective experience itself to become, through an accretion, the object of perception is no doubt one reason why so many writers have found it much easier to deal with unpleasantness than with pleasantness.

In some respects the bright pressure of pleasantness presents a very different picture. It localizes in the region where the upper parts of the body, the neck and the shoulders, would be if they were perceived but they never are under these conditions. The bright pressure never takes on transcendence; it never means muscular pressure nor does it belong to the body; it is all the body there is. This detachment makes the bright pressures very elusive and, in a sense, difficult to observe. It really is no wonder we should find in treatises on affection the phrase, "and similarly for pleasantness," following an elaborate discussion of unpleasantness. To put it figuratively, I should say that the reaction in the case of pleasantness is a more or less complete surrender to the luxury of living and does not involve any ordinary or useful response of a particular muscle group, while the reaction in the case of unpleasantness is one of rejection and withdrawal or constriction and involves what may be a useful response of a definite set of muscles although the mechanism is probably different from that for ordinary muscular response. If you remember that this is figurative, the picture will stand.

In another phase of his work Horiguchi asked for reports on the affective pressures and their localization in ordinary everyday cases. For some time the only report was "failure." Logically two possibilities presented themselves: either the pressures reported by all observers were, despite the approximation of the experimental atmosphere to that of ordinary life, artifacts of the experimental situation and the observational attitude; or the observers were guilty of some observational blunder. Success finally came. The task was easy from the first in the case of the unpleasantly toned moods.

In these the dull pressure aspect is undeniable, even for the naïve, with general localization almost, if not quite, as obvious. The story of the way by which we attained success gives nothing really new; it merely throws a known truth into a new and bolder relief. If I take a concrete instance, the facts pertinent to our purpose will appear more clearly. The one who made the observation was somewhat irritated, annoyed, provoked by a statement made by another. As long as the observer looked for unpleasant experience directed specifically upon the offender he did not find it; as soon as he became simply annoyed, without specific object reference, the dull pressure was there—localized fairly definitely in the abdominal region.

An instance of a pleasantly toned experience would show the same failure of the affective pressure to come for observation as long as specific object awareness obtained. That is, if the observer looked for the bright pressure and at the same time perceptively fixated the object that served as stimulus, he did not find it. If, on the contrary, he surrendered himself to the pleasurable experience as such without the specific perception of an object, to just pleasurable existence, the bright pressure was there with the same general though vague localization as found in the experiment.

Now we have to face anew the question of just what happens when, in the older terminology, we attend to an affective experience. The question as we should put it now in empirical terms is: Are the object consciousness and the affective life incompatible? In experiential terms: Can the qualities that go to make up the perceptive pattern and those which enter into the affective pattern be present in experience at the same time? If there is nothing in the nature of the qualities nor in the manner of their arousal which precludes their simultaneous appearance, it may be that the two types of pattern preclude each other. I mean that the pressures of perception as well as those of affection might both be present in experience provided neither the one nor the other, especially the perceptive, became too highly focal. In stimulus terms, being focal would mean, I presume, that the muscular action correlated with the same is highly specific and relatively strong. An alternative to this question might be, as I put it before: Do the various varieties of experience form such an intimate whole that they lose their identity? Our answer to these questions will come with the next approach.

The last set of results I shall consider are those from a preliminary study of the humorous, the comic, and the witty. This study carried on last year by E. Frances Wells and myself is also as yet unpublished. We made no attempt to define the above terms and nothing in the instructions or in the situation indicated the possibility of such a division. With this aspect of the work I am not here concerned, except to state that the main difference is one of degree on the one hand and of temporal course on the other.

In comedy and wit there is a fairly sudden shift in experience which carries one, in the first moment at least, completely away from specific perception. To be seized by the comic is to be wrenched suddenly out of the world of specific meanings and hurled into a world of sheer enjoyment. We do not enjoy or laugh at the concrete; we enjoy and laugh at the enjoyable. Lest this appear to be pure tautology let me state it in a different way: Up to a certain moment experience shows the qualities and pattern of perception together often with the strain of expectation or searching, then comes the complete break-up of the perceptive and expectation experience and the infusion of something at least like the affective pressure plus all the stir from laughter—a moment of just enjoyment.

Humor is a state in which neither the perceptive nor the affective-like aspects of experience come dominantly to the fore. The perceptive aspect reduces to something like the situational consciousness as opposed to the object consciousness, and the affective stands as a diffuse pleasant-like background as opposed to specific pleasure. Both approach the attitudinal level of organization. I have no intention to present a picture of humor; that will come in its proper place. I mention it merely as another instance of the bimodal character of bodily experience and of the relation which the two modes bear to each other.

I do not claim we have to do in this work with simple affection. I am as sure as one can be in a field where ignorance is still master that we are in the face of one of the integrations which involve the same fundamental mode of experience as constitutes the essential character of affection. I do not believe that there is a fundamentally different mode of bodily experience, if there is such, for every one of the different kinds of mental activity as found in empirical and common-sense classifications. The number of unique modes of reaction with their correlated experiences is very small, and each one of these or combination of them in various patterns and integrations gives us our functional variety.

If the results so far presented will stand, and I can see no reason to reject or even to suspect them, we must be ready then to conclude that there are at least three, or perhaps four, modes of bodily experience. But before I proceed to the exposition of these, two other topics need a word. Perhaps nothing has received more emphasis during the past few years than the part played in our mental lives by the bodily experiences. In Bentley's terms, there are no bodiless minds or soulless bodies. It requires no superior insight to see that the one and only source of experience, beyond that immediately aroused by some stimulus which acts upon a particular receptor, is that from our bodies. I also take it, although this will not be granted by all, that the experience correlated with the stimulus serves as nothing more than a cue, a starting-point, for the various mental acts, or experiential patterns of everyday life. That which completes, which renders functionally adequate, which makes meaningful all our perceptions, thoughts, memories, imaginations, volitions, and what-not is that which we bring to the cues offered by the stimulus experience. We should know this from the work on imaginal overlay if we had nothing else. But the evidence is plentiful and convincing almost anywhere we turn. So much so that today it is the fad, if such a term is not derogatory, to evolve theories and systems which emphasize the importance of bodily experience. Since the only part of experience which we can acquire and carry about with us and which we continually possess is this bodily experience, it is logical, if experimental work did not yield the same result, that it should play the formative rôle in our mental acts.

The other topic is one on which we have very little evidence. It is the question of the quarter in which we shall seek the laws which will eventually lead us to a real understanding of mind in its functional character. Many of the so-called laws of psychology, at the present time, are laws of stimuli—at least they refer in one direction to the stimulus. I take it that such laws can never afford us the understanding we seek, if any generalization with a heterogeneous basis deserves to be called a law within a special sphere. Others seek for these laws in the physiological mechanism —laws of physics and biology, we say. What we call them does not matter if they will lead to the goal of our desire. The question is whether these laws, once they are known, will be likely to lead to a workable comprehension of any empirical mental function such as, for example, memory. At present, I can see no promise from this quarter whether we take the muscular and glandular activities physically or biologically. The one other source, as I see it, to which we may turn is the patterns or totals of experience. If we can—and the outlook is hopeful—discover the laws which govern the formation of experiential totals, we may have placed in our hands the means whereby we can understand the functional moments of mental life. Some may contend that we shall need a combination of the laws drawn from these diverse sources but that, to me, is a surrender which I am not willing to make until after further trial.

Our problem now is to determine what we have by way of bodily experiences and how these experiences go together to give us the familiar integrations of ordinary life. I said a moment ago that there are at least three or perhaps four modes of bodily experience. So far as I can make out after long observation, I would say that muscular pressure, i. e., the pressures and strains correlated with the contraction of the skeletal muscles, constitutes one mode; what, for want of a better term, I call bright pressure correlated perhaps with a state of non-contraction of the skeletal muscles forms a second mode; and dull pressure correlated apparently with contraction of the visceral muscles forms the third. The proposed correlations for the affective modes do not preclude the possibility of special end-organs or of special means of stimulation. The bright pressure mode corresponds at times with what we call in common-sense terms a state of high muscular tonicity. The tentative nature of the correlations does not affect the positive evidence for the modes themselves. I am not sure whether the first group will stand as a single mode, or whether the general bodily tensions will make up one mode and the experiences from more special muscular activity another. If this is the case, there would be four modes. At any rate we can be pretty sure that the pressure-strain aspect of experience is the essential mode for what we call perception, thought, memory, and imagination, as well as the attitudes. The general bodily tensions give the attitudes with all that they imply for the above classes of mental activity. In so far as they give rise and direction to the subsequent experience they belong to the energetic aspect of mind. Volition may very well prove to be a more complex experience which involves a combination of modes. I have no experimental evidence on the point at this time. I use the above as well as following common-sense classificatory terms without prejudice, the implication being that psychological description will scarcely support them. The brighter, livelier experiences of the second mode are essential for pleasantness, humor, comedy, well-being, happiness, joy, and the like. The dull heavy experiences of the third mode are peculiar to unpleasantness, the "brown" moods, unhappiness, sorrow, grief, and their kind. With either of the last two modes combined with a high degree of the first we get the emotions, provided the pressure-strain is not specifically patterned. This, as far as I can observe, is our bodily equipment.

What about their integration? I can do little better than to speculate at present. What I have to offer is, by the nature of the case, inference rather than observed fact. This, however, seems certain, that a highly focal state of the perceptive pressure-strains precludes the affective modes from experience. The perceptive and the affective modes are not otherwise exclusive, which proves that the two types of muscular response are not, as such, incompatible. Whether the two affective modes are, as types of muscular response, simultaneously impossible, it is much more difficult to say. The slight evidence we have indicates that they are not; that the incompatibility of pleasantness and unpleasantness is rather a matter of experiential organization.

I cannot concede that the affective moments in mental life are moments that lack pattern. By the term pattern I mean the collocation of qualities, extents, and what-not that constitutes the totality of experience at any one moment and that reveals differences in obtrusiveness or dominance in the organized whole. I do not mean that experience, as I have used that term to denote the describable as opposed to the value side of ordinary experience, comes as a mosaic of separately demarcated qualities. Every quality, as we know them in terms of previous experience under special determination, gives its color to the whole so that we have a blend or fusion which is more than, or at least other than, the qualities if taken separately. Thus experience presents totals, patterns, configurations, in which there is a focus and a background. This definition of the pattern, as similar as it is to the configuration of Gestalt psychology at the level of transcendent meaning, has long been current in the Cornell laboratory. The patterns of the affective moments do not present the same degree of focus as do the perceptive and thought patterns, but they are as characteristic in their type of pattern as is perception. It is as if they belong genetically to the more primitive situational consciousness and that the perceptive pattern is a more modern type built out of a mode of experience which came in with differentiation of muscular activity.

Be all this as it may, the earlier experimental findings do not stand or fall with our interpretation on this last point. What we have then, to put it into brief form, are: first, three modes of bodily experience, two of which enter respectively into the patterns of pleasantness and unpleasantness; and, secondly, experience admits but a single pattern at any one moment. Finally, we have the suggestion that a discovery of the laws of experiential organization will reveal the secrets of mental activity.

DISCUSSION

Dr. Cannon (*Harvard University*): I come to you as a physiologist and not as a psychologist, and I hope you will make concessions to my weaknesses. There are several points, however, in Dr. Hoisington's paper that I should like to call attention to, and they are primarily based on observations which Dr. Henry Head of London has made on some very interesting cases of hemiplegia which he studied during life and also after death. Now the extraordinary feature of these cases is that there is a difference in the experience of feeling on the two sides of the body, when the same stimulus is applied. On the normal side a warm test tube is felt as anyone else reports it; on the other hand, the same test applied to the affected side gives a very pleasant experience of warmth, so reported. A hot test tube and a cold test tube feel very different to the two sides. On the normal side, they are felt as anyone else would feel them; on the affected side, as very pleasant experiences. Now it is very difficult for me as a physiologist to see how these feelings would be different on the two sides of the body. Certainly we cannot divide the liver into right and left sides, nor the alimentary tract, etc., so that so far as the viscera are concerned, on the basis of this difference, they may be ruled out. So far as skeletal muscle is concerned, this is also a poor case. Dr. Head found that bodily posture was entirely without feeling-tone. There was no report back from the muscles which gave any feeling of one sort or another, but utter indifference. These matters are very interesting in the discussion, and I hope that Dr. Hoisington will comment on them.

Dr. Hoisington: Well, it seems that Dr. Cannon said just what I tried to tell you, i. e., that the central muscles have nothing to do with affections. As far as the two sides are concerned, what you have in one case is an affected side which will not respond the same as the other side which has functioning skin.

Dr. Cannon: You have perception on both sides; the experience is the same on both sides.

Dr. Hoisington: What is the exact nature of the experience?

Dr. Cannon: It is a motor affection . . . from the thalamus along the motor tract.

Dr. Hoisington: Well, I don't know why it should be more effective on one side, if they really perceive it as an object the same as they do on the other side. I should rather not have very much attention called to the correlation as such. It is not the aspect of this paper. I know nothing about it and I do not think very much about it myself. It is not what we can observe. I should suspect that probably correlations of a chemical nature will be found, and probably involving the blood-vessels rather than muscles at all; but I don't know.

Dr. Cannon: May I ask whether the localization in the abdomen is regarded by the observer as indicating a definite change there?

Dr. Hoisington: Not as affection, no; only when it goes over to the perceptive aspect does it take on the meaning of a definite change.

Dr. Cannon: May I point out that it is not at all necessary for a change to occur in the abdomen to have it referred there. The reference would often be to the periphery and not to the optic thalamus because we naturally refer things out to the periphery.

Professor Dekker (*Battle Creek College*): I should like to ask a question with regard to the technique of discovering these pressures. I think I understood the definition of a pressure that the speaker gave, but I do not understand the technique of discovering the exact pressure or of measuring these pressures.

DR. HOISINGTON: The technique is largely one of attitude. What we have to do is simply to get the observers into the "set"—or rather out of the set—so they can simply sit there and let the experience come along; and then you apply some stimulus that would, under ordinary circumstances, arouse an affective reaction. It is pretty difficult to say anything about the technique, because this is all up to the observer. Simply get him into such a state that he is not looking for something specific but simply allowing experience to go its way—though of course observing. As soon as you get him into this state, the bright or dull pressure will show up. Everyone who has done that has found it.

PROFESSOR AYRES (*Taylor University*): I should like to ask this question: Are we to understand that the bright and dull pressures are mutually exclusive? And if so, how does the author of the paper deal with what was brought out yesterday concerning melancholics who are happy only when they are unhappy?

DR. HOISINGTON: I should deal with that most summarily! I should say it simply isn't true. We have not done very much work in an effort to find out whether as modes of reaction, the two things are exclusive. All I can say is that the slight evidence we have is that they are not incompatible. It is a matter of organization. I take it for granted that the matter of incompatibility of pleasantness and unpleasantness is an established fact. I know there are people who deny it, but after all, you can't get everybody to agree on everything!

CHAPTER 21

PLEASURABLE REACTIONS TO TACTUAL STIMULI

Robert H. Gault
Northwestern University

The title of this paper has been suggested to me by experience of a year ago with certain deaf subjects in the Vibro-Tactile Research Laboratory.[1] Instrumental aids were being employed by means of which they were enabled to feel in their fingers the movement of spoken sentences and of continued discourse—verse or prose. A small receiver, closely similar to the instrument used by telephone operators and in radio sets, was being held in the hand of each subject. His finger or thumb was held lightly against the diaphragm and thus he felt vibrations that corresponded to the voice of the speaker at a distant microphone.

We were attempting to make these cases familiar with the pattern of spoken language by means of its character as felt, in the expectation that the kinaesthetic elements of language could be built into them by this means, and that these elements would be effective in improving the subject's manner of speech and of reading from the printed page, and in facilitating his reception of speech.

Several examples of verse and prose were selected for reading through the instrument into the fingers of six subjects simultaneously. Each example was chosen because of its strong motor quality. No two selections of verse were in the same meter. Among them was Southey's:

> "How does the water
> Come down at Lodore,
> From its sources that well
> In the tarn by the fell?"

And there were Clement C. Moore's verses:

> "'Twas the night before Christmas, when all through the house
> Not a creature was stirring,—not even a mouse."

After some drill two of the six subjects began to show signs that they enjoyed Southey's verses especially, in relation to other

[1] The activities of this Laboratory are being carried on under the auspices of the Carnegie Institution of Washington.

examples. They began, when these lines were being read, to make signs meaning "pretty." After a week of training, when the signs I mentioned had first been noticed, it was not unusual for them to ask that a reading be repeated.

At first it seemed likely that the strong rhythm of the verses was the basis for the reaction of pleasure. But when we substituted a verse from Stevenson, in the same meter:

"How do you like to go up in a swing?"

we did not find evidence of the accustomed reaction. When this line and those from Southey had been equally employed as stimuli—along with others to be sure—the latter continued to be the more thrilling, and even then, our records show, subjects now and again asked us to repeat the Lodore verses and gave other evidence of their satisfaction with them.

Evidently it is not rhythm that occasioned the choice between them. Possibly it was difference in predominating vowel quality that accounted for the phenomenon.

We set out to examine this hypothesis. For the purpose, on the side of instrumentation, we employed a Western Electric loud-speaker with which we had been supplied through the courtesy of Bell Telephone Laboratories. An oval diaphragm 2″ x 3″ was fixed to the body of the instrument and at its center it was at-tached to the armature. In practice this instrument was held with its vibrating part, not against the tip of a finger, but solidly against the chest wall, over the sternum. The instrument was operated by a high-grade microphone through a Western Electric amplifier.

We selected but one subject to assist in our preliminary examina-tion of the pleasurable reactions I have mentioned. In the labora-tory situation I have described he felt the speaker's voice as a complex of vibrations, not only upon the skin of his chest but throughout the bony wall of his thorax. If he had had any effective residuum of auditory function, the arrangement might easily have enabled him to hear the stimuli by way of bone conduction to the inner ear. But I feel justified in saying that he could not hear in the condition I have described. Four audiometric tests had been made upon him—one of them in the Sound Laboratory at the Bureau of Standards. At the Bureau his hearing for simple tones was described as zero in one ear and 10% in the other. The remaining three reports closely corresponded to this. Such a condition is believed to make it utterly impossible for him to get any auditory cues in such a situation as ours.

I should say that the subject was thirty-five years of age and a successful teacher of mathematics by profession. He was not plagued by that elusive thing that we call temperament; he had an abundance of good common sense and, judging from daily contact with him in the laboratory, one would say that he was above the average in point of intelligence. He came to the laboratory daily and remained there approximately forty minutes. During thirty or thirty-five minutes each day he was steadily occupied with our exercises. The sessions continued day after day from March 16, 1926 to May 26.

This subject was not in the group in which we first observed a preference among verses. We first undertook, therefore, a few exploratory experiments to find whether he would express any preferences as other subjects had done. For the purpose we chose four stanzas: Southey's "How does the water come down at Lodore," etc.; Moore's "'Twas the night before Christmas," etc.; Stevenson's "The friendly cow all red and white," etc.; and Stevenson's "How do you like to go up in a swing?" etc. (This verse is in the same meter as Southey's above. But succeeding ones are different, as—"Up in the air so blue.") No two of the stanzas are alike as to meter, throughout.

We then went about it to read these stanzas by pairs into the subject's chest: the first and second, first and third, first and fourth, second and third, and so on till each one had been recited with every other in a pair. I should say in this place that the subject had no idea before or after or during a session what stimuli were being employed. Now and again the members of a pair were reversed so that each member was recited first in approximately 50% of instances. At once after the recitation of a pair the subject was asked whether either member occasioned a reaction of pleasure and if so which one was the more pleasurable. We tried not to suggest to him that one or the other *must* be found to possess this quality. At the outset, in conversation with him, we discussed the preference for certain verses that had been exhibited by other subjects—preferences that have already been referred to in this paper.

I told him I was not convinced that there was any pleasurable reaction from this work that could be counted upon to extend over a considerable range of experience within the laboratory or outside of it. By this means I sought to dispose him not to indicate a pleasurable reaction merely because he thought I was looking for it.

On the first day, March 16, he was given ten opportunities to compare each of the stanzas I have referred to with every other one.

Number one was preferred to number two *eight* times. It was always preferred to number three, and nine times in ten it was found more pleasurable than number four. Number four was seven times reported as more pleasurable than number three, and two was always more pleasurable than three.

On the basis of that day's experience, therefore, it was possible to rate the stanzas as follows on the ground of their pleasurable quality:

1. "How does the water come down at Lodore"
2. "'Twas the night before Christmas"
3. "How do you like to go up in a swing?"
4. "The friendly cow all red and white."

I repeat that the subject had no knowledge, either before or after, as to what verses were being read. He knew only that they were verses.

Subsequently, on March 24, he had thirty opportunities, under the same conditions, to choose between the Lodore verses and Stevenson's stanza beginning: "How do you like to go up in a swing?" In twenty-seven cases, or 90%, he chose the former. On the following two days he was given the opportunity to choose again when all four stanzas were in the repertoire—thirty judgments on each pair. The order of preferences was exactly what we found on the sixteenth. There were ninety opportunities to react to each of the four stanzas. The first was preferred in 54% of the instances; the second in 24%; the fourth in 16%; and the third in 6% of the cases. Approximately the same result was found two days later.

This appears to make it fairly certain that the subject had a real basis of comparison. More than one variable factor occurred in the situation. There were rhythm, predominating vowel and diphthongal qualities, and varying distinctness of feel correlated with these qualities and with the tactual character of consonantal elements. It seems clear enough from the observations I have mentioned that somewhere in the complex there is a factor, or more than one, that accounts for the pleasurable experience that follows upon the tactual stimulation.

For the purpose of making more systematic observation we began on March 25 substituting the consonant-diphthong compound "Ray" for each syllable in the stanzas that theretofore had served as stimuli. Thus the Lodore verses became:

Ráy Răy Ray Ráy Răy Răy Ráy Răy Răy, etc.

and Stevenson's "The friendly cow" became:

Răy Ráy Răy Ráy Răy Ráy, etc.

In twenty-six out of thirty cases the former was preferred to the latter.

"The night before Christmas" became:

Ráy Răy Ráy Răy Răy Ráy Răy Răy Ráy, etc.

This arrangement of feet practically tied with /ᴜᴜ. In thirty reports sixteen favored /ᴜᴜ and fourteen favored ᴜᴜ/. Each of these had an advantage over the changing meter of Stevenson's "swing" verses:

/ ᴜ ᴜ / ᴜ ᴜ / ᴜ ᴜ /
/ ᴜ ᴜ / ᴜ /
/ ᴜ ᴜ / ᴜ ᴜ / ᴜ ᴜ /
/ ᴜ ᴜ / ᴜ /

In the one case it was an advantage of eighteen to twelve, and in the other of twenty to ten. Throughout six succeeding days, during which the subject was held to these exercises without varying the stimuli, he almost consistently reported as I have indicated. He knew nothing of the nature of the stimuli excepting that "Ray" had been substituted for each syllable in the verses that had earlier been employed. He said he felt more sure of himself in his reactions to the substituted stimuli than to the original words. This may be due to the fact that in this case the successive tactual stimuli were of uniform intensity (barring variations in the speaker's voice) whereas in the other instance there was variation of intensity from word to word due to the fact that no two vowel qualities get through the instrument with equal effect. This would contribute to consistency in the case of the substituted stimuli. On the other hand the subject may have remembered, as soon as he recognized a movement, that he had formerly preferred it to others. This, too, would make for consistency, and I am unable to estimate its force. I had seen enough to afford reasonable assurance that this subject at any rate did have real preferences for tactual rhythms. Several times he told me he believed all rhythms were enjoyable even at the outset. Even then, as the record appears to indicate, some were more enjoyable than others. As time went on, however, differences in pleasurableness seemed to be accentuated progressively. He spoke of it as "learning" to enjoy one thing more than another. Naturally he could not describe the process of learning. It is impossible, on the basis of these preliminary observations, to say anything with respect to a nativistic or an acquired pleasurableness in relation to rhythmic tactual impressions.

The observation we first made in this connection—the greater pleasurableness of Southey's verses on the Waters of Lodore as compared with the first verse of Stevenson's "How do you like to go up in a swing?'"—suggested that, since the meter is the same in the two cases mentioned, the predominating vowel qualities in the two examples may account for the difference in the reaction. In the first two Lodore verses there are ten syllables and the same number occur in Stevenson's first verse. In the Lodore verses there are six vowels that I call "long and broad" and four "short and thin." These terms are roughly descriptive of their tactual quality.

For the purpose of examining this guess I undertook to find whether there is a difference in pleasurable quality when the meter remains constant but the vowel or diphthong changes from time to time. Accordingly, I set Row Row Row, Ray Ray Ray, Re Re Re, Raw Raw Raw, Rou Rou Rou, Roy Roy Roy, Roo Roo Roo, and Ri Ri Ri—each group of syllables into dactylic feet; fifteen syllables or five feet in succession. From April 10 to May 25, inclusive, each of these groupings was compared for pleasurableness with every other. In the course of this period other exercises were interspersed to break the monotony. There were fifty reports upon each pair of nonsense verses.

TABLE 1

DISTRIBUTION OF PREFERENCES

I.	Row — 25	VIII.	Roy — 28	XV.	Rou — 29	XXII.	Raw — 42
	Roy — 25		Rou — 22		Roo — 21		Re — 8
II.	Row — 25	IX.	Roy — 30	XVI.	Rou — 32	XXIII.	Roo — 29
	Rou — 25		Raw — 20		Ri — 18		Ri — 21
III.	Row — 40	X.	Roy — 35	XVII.	Rou — 34	XXIV.	Roo — 33
	Raw — 10		Roo — 15		Ray — 16		Ray — 17
IV.	Row — 42	XI.	Roy — 35	XVIII.	Rou — 41	XXV.	Roo — 33
	Roo — 8		Ri — 15		Re — 9		Re — 17
V.	Row — 43	XII.	Roy — 37	XIX.	Raw — 31	XXVI.	Ri — 34
	Ri — 7		Ray — 13		Roo — 19		Ray — 16
VI.	Row — 44	XIII.	Roy — 37	XX.	Raw — 37	XXVII.	Ri — 30
	Ray — 6		Re — 4		Ri — 13		Re — 20
VII.	Row — 47	XIV.	Rou — 26	XXI.	Raw — 38	XXVIII.	Ray — 28
	Re — 3		Raw — 24		Ray — 12		Re — 22

In the course of all these laboratory exercises each of these vowels or diphthongs combined with R was felt upon the chest of the subject 350 times in company with one other. That number of times he expressed a preference for one or the other of the pair. The total data enable us tentatively to rank the stimuli I have mentioned on the basis of their pleasurable quality. The figures in Table 2 indicate the number of times each was chosen while being compared with others 350 times.

TABLE 2

RANKING OF STIMULI ON THE BASIS OF PLEASANTNESS

		Total preferences
1.	Row	266
2.	Roy	236
3.	Rou	209
4.	Raw	202
5.	Roo	158
6.	Ri	138
7.	Ray	108
8.	Re	83

It is bound to occur to anyone who studies these figures that the order of preference indicated may depend principally upon the relative intensity of the stimuli. One or another may be more satisfactory or pleasurable or agreeable than another merely because it is felt as more intense and hence more distinctly than another. It is appropriate to say here that the subject declared that the vibration of the instrument is felt more distinctly when his fingers rest upon it, but that the more pleasurable experience occurs when the apparatus is upon his chest. And the intensity of the stimulus upon the skin is a function not only of the voice that goes into the apparatus but of the nature of the instrument. And here I have to make what may be a damaging confession: I do not know the quality of my own voice. It has never been subjected to harmonic analysis. In the course of the day-after-day work that brought to pass the material I have presented here I had no means of checking the inevitable variations of my voice from day to day. All I can say is that I tried to keep it uniform.

With the cooperation of two normally hearing subjects I have attempted to rank in the order of their intensity the vowel and diphthongal qualities I have employed here. For this purpose the subjects were placed in a situation in which they could not hear either the voice of the speaker at the microphone or the sound emitted by the instrument. Instead of placing the instrument against his chest each subject rested his thumb ball against it. Each one had twenty-five opportunities to compare every stimulus with each one of its associates. Table 3 gives the combined order of the stimuli on a tactual intensity basis:

TABLE 3

RANKING OF STIMULI ON A TACTUAL INTENSITY BASIS

		Times chosen
1.	Rou	260
2.	Raw	240
3.	Row	200
4.	Roy	206
5.	Ri	162
6.	Roo	140
7.	Ray	110
8.	Re	82

Correlation between *pleasantness* ranking and *intensity* ranking: 21

I believe it is true of this subject at least that he does get a thrill out of some of these vowel and diphthongal qualities—from some of them more than others.

It has been interesting now and again to observe his description of the sensory experience. After several days of practice he reported that at the beginning of the campaign he never got away from the sense of an object vibrating locally against a small area upon his chest. "But now," he said, "I am not conscious of feeling it locally. I feel it nowhere in particular, especially after a sitting has got under way." Neither do you and I *hear locally*. Hearing is all over us just as pleasantness is (excepting perhaps when the stimulus is extremely intense—then it *hurts* our ears).

Work of this nature suggests the well-authenticated case of the totally deaf Eugen Sutermeister of Berne, Switzerland, who enjoys the feel of the orchestra. Our subject, indeed, enjoys the chapel organ, especially when it is playing "Lead Kindly Light." He catches himself now and again moving his head or hands or feet in rhythm with the organ tones.

I do not know that these observations suggest anything in relation to a theory of the pleasurable reaction. The reaction is undoubtedly there and it has to come to pass in an unusual situation. I do not believe that the observations can be used to support a nativistic hypothesis, for my subject did not at once get a thrill out of any movement or tactual quality. Practice was required upon the particular stimuli at hand. Even so he believes that the great variety of tactual exercises that were distributed over an entire year before these experiments began prepared him for enjoying the thing in hand.

Note: Although we have not followed the matter up, it appears probable that the subject of these experiments can enjoy singing when he receives it as he received rhythms and vowel and diphthongal qualities in the course of this work. He was able, roughly, to follow the pitches of the voice of the experimenter while he sang and to indicate a primitive scale by marking with a pencil upon a sheet of paper. He consistently preferred the time of "Old Black Joe" to five others, even though he never knew beforehand what was about to be sung. The syllables "Row" or "Ray" were always substituted for the syllables of the song that was being sung.

PART III

Physiology of Feeling and
Emotion

CHAPTER 22

NEURAL ORGANIZATION FOR EMOTIONAL EXPRESSION

WALTER B. CANNON

Harvard University Medical School

In this paper I shall restrict myself primarily to a consideration of a typical reaction system of the more highly developed organisms, that which is commonly called an expression or outburst of *anger* or *rage*. Later I shall consider some bearings which the facts may have on the nature of emotional excitation.

The complex of bodily alterations that appears in rage has many features resembling the simple reflexes, such as sneezing, coughing, and sucking. First, its occurrence in the early months of even so highly developed an organism as the human infant indicates that its neural pattern, like that of the reflexes mentioned above, is congenitally inwrought in the central nervous apparatus. Second, as in the reflexes, it is a prompt response to the appropriate stimulus. Again, it is a constant and uniform response—so much is this so, indeed, that there is no mistaking its character, whether it be manifested by the diverse races of man or by the lower animals. It is like the reflexes, also, in being a permanent mode of reaction; throughout life the characteristic display of the rage-response may be suddenly evoked in all its elaborateness. Further, it is a response to a fairly definite stimulus—an inner stimulus which arises when there is a hampering or checking of motion or an opposition to one or another primary impulse. Finally, the rage-response is like the simple reflexes in being useful. Elsewhere (1) I have called attention to the wide range of bodily adjustments which occur in an enraged animal—the more rapid heart-beat, the redistribution of the blood, the increase of red corpuscles in the circulation, the deeper ventilation of the lungs, the dilatation of the bronchioles, the liberation of sugar from the liver, the secretion of adrenin with its favorable action on fatigued muscles—all of which may properly be regarded as rendering the organism more efficient in struggle, in such struggle as may be necessary to overwhelm the opposition and to allow the natural impulse to prevail. Thus, as should be clear, all the main features of the simple reflexes—the inborn prompt, constant, uniform, permanent, and utilitarian nature of the response to a definite type of stimulus—all these features of the simple reflexes are reproduced in the characteristics of an outburst of rage.

Much evidence exists which indicates that, whereas delayed responses—uncertain, temporary, and readily modifiable—involve the cerebral cortex the prompt, uniform, and stereotyped reactions to stimuli have their central locus in lower levels of the brain and spinal cord. It becomes a matter of interest, therefore, to inquire regarding the seat of the neural mechanism which operates the action complex of rage. Does this mechanism have its locus in the cortical neurones or in the more primitive parts of the nervous axis?

In the brain-stem there is a group of centers which, in the lower vertebrate, lacking a cerebral cortex, carry on elementary functions for maintaining existence. In higher forms these centers, though normally held in check by the dominant cortex, are capable of energetic response when conditions demand urgent and impulsive action. If the cortical government is set aside the subordinate activities become prominent. Goltz's (2) and Rothmann's (3) hemisphereless dogs and de Barenne's (4) cats deprived of the neopallium illustrate this point. These animals under various conditions reacted commonly with signs of rage. Goltz's dog exhibited a typical outburst of fury when taken from his cage to be fed—barking loudly, snapping in all directions, and resisting vigorously. Trifling stimuli, such as pulling or pressing the skin, called forth similar excesses of emotional response. The behavior of Rothmann's dog was of the same type. Gentle scratching of the back was the occasion for snarls and growls, and the presence of a fly on the dog's nose would send him into a fit of rage. With de Barenne's cats, pinching the toes or skin produced energetic movements of defense and such reactions as are characteristic of the angry cat—spitting, growling, and erection of the hairs of the tail and back. Again very slight disturbance proved an effective stimulus for this response; even the act of lifting the cats from the floor would evoke it.

These various instances of a typical rage-reaction appearing in animals deprived of the cerebral cortex may be interpreted as examples of "release phenomena," to use the term introduced by Hughlings Jackson (5)—phenomena resulting from the activity of lower centers in the cerebrum that appear readily on slight stimulation when the dominance of the superior centers is removed. It seemed reasonable to expect that these lower centers might display their typical activity after removal of the cortex in an acute experiment. Decortication would eliminate an essential condition for sensation and therefore the use of a depressing or disturbing anaesthetic could be dispensed with. Accordingly Britton and I (6), using cats as subjects, undertook an investigation of some of the immediate effects of decortication. A stylet, pressed through the upper, inner quadrant of the left bony orbit and then to the bony tentorium on the opposite side of the skull, was swept downward and outward and withdrawn along the floor of the brain case. A similar operation was performed through the right orbit. Thus the cerebrum was substantially decorticated and almost all of the ganglia at the base of the brain remained intact. As soon as recovery from anaesthesia was complete, a remarkable group of activities appeared, such as are usually seen in an infuriated animal—a sort of sham rage. A complete list of these quasi-emotional phenomena which we observed is as follows: vigorous lashing of the tail; arching of the trunk, and thrusting and jerking of the limbs in the thongs which fasten them to the animal board, combined with a display of claws in the forefeet and clawing motions, often persistent; snarling; rapid head movements from side to side with attempts to bite; and extremely rapid, panting respiration. These activities occur, without special stimulation (apart from the operative trauma and confinement to the holder) in "fits" or periods, lasting from a few seconds to several minutes. During the intermediate quiet stages a "fit" could be evoked by slight handling of the animal, touching the paws or jarring the table. Besides these changes which involved skeletal muscle there were typical and more permanent effects produced by sympathetic impulses: erection of the tail hairs, which recurred again and again after they were smoothed down; elevation of the vibrissae; sweating of the toe pads; dilatation of the pupil to a size during activity that was threefold the size during a preceding quiet period; micturition; a high blood-pressure; an abundant outpouring of adrenin; and, as Bulatao and I (7) found, an increase of blood sugar up to five times the normal concentration. Because of the resemblance of some of these apparently spontaneous reactions to pseudaffective reflexes which Woodworth and Sherrington (8) were able to elicit in decerebrate cats by stimulation of sensory nerves, we used the term "pseudaffective" in designating the preparation. The animals may manifest this pseudaffective state, or sham rage, at short intervals for two or three hours before the arterial blood-pressure falls too low for continuance of activity.

The pseudaffective phenomena observed by Woodworth and Sherrington, and also by Bazett and Penfield (9) in "chronic" decerebrate preparations, were disturbances of an otherwise fairly continuous rigidity. In decerebration the cut passes through the mid-brain (M, Figure 1); thus the diencephalon and all parts of the cerebrum anterior to it are excluded from action. Obviously that part of the neural organization which *directly* sends forth the rage-response lies posterior to the section through the mesencephalon, i. e., in the remnant of the mid-brain or in the medulla. In these decerebrate animals, however, spontaneous exhibitions of sham rage are rare; relatively strong stimulation is required to evoke them, and, when evoked, they are likely to be isolated items of the total reaction and may be associated at times with inconsistent elements, such as violent clawing accompanied by purring. This is in marked contrast to the intense and complete manifestation of fury which may be shown by decorticate animals. The difference in behavior of the two preparations must be referred to some part of the brain-stem lacking in the decerebrate, but present in the decorticate animal. In other words, although various parts of the rage-response can be activated by afferent impulses in the bulbospinal animal, the integration of these responses in an energetic and typically widespread outburst of rage appears to be controlled by a superior center. Britton and I left untouched almost all of the basal gray matter of the anterior brain-stem. Where among these basal ganglia does the dominating center reside? This question has been the subject of an investigation by one of my collaborators, Dr. Bard.

The method employed by Bard was that of ablating various amounts of the brain-stem after decortication, and studying thereafter the behavior of the preparation. He found that typical sham rage, accompanied by vigorous discharge of sympathetic impulses recurs in spontaneous fits or outbursts after both cerebral hemispheres, the corpora striata and the anterior half of the diencephalon have been removed completely (along dash line, Figure 1). The additional removal of the posterior half of the diencephalon promptly abolishes the spontaneous activity; but since it persists after much of the dorsal portion of the region has been cut away (along dotted line, Figure 1), the dominating center, we may infer, is situated near the base, probably in the subthalamus. Its size in the cat is less than a fourth of a cubic centimeter. In recent years considerable evidence has accumulated, pointing to the thalamic region as the central station of the sympathetic system. Isenschmid and his collaborators (10) have localized there the mechanism for temperature regulation—a mechanism controlling heat-production and heat-loss via sympathetic channels. And Karplus and Kreidl (11) have observed that local stimulation of the same region in anaesthetized animals causes a sympathetic discharge. Bard's observations bring strong support to the conclusion that in the subthalamus there exists an integrating center for sympathetic activities. Thus in the diencephalon, in a part of the old brain, which is common to all members of the vertebrate series from the fishes to mammals, is localized the neural apparatus for integrating the complex reaction system of rage, not only the external expression, but also the internal mobilization of the bodily forces for the violent physical efforts in which rage typically culminates.

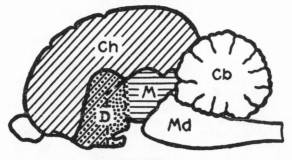

FIGURE 1

DIAGRAM OF THE MID-SECTION OF THE CAT BRAIN

Ch, cerebral hemispheres; *D*, diencephalon (dotted); *M*, mesencephalon; *Cb*, cerebellum; *Md*, medulla. The parts distinguished by slanting lines can be wholly removed without destroying the rage-response.

Besides the central neural organization there are the peripheral effector organs. They are in two divisions—the skeletal muscles and the viscera. The skeletal musculature is so played upon that a characteristic picture is presented. I have described above the appearance of the infuriated cat. Darwin's (12) description of rage in young children is not very different; during a violent outburst they scream, kick, scratch, and bite. In adult men the display is not commonly of this puerile type, but it is likely to include the crouching body, the moist and frowning brow, the firm lips, the clenched or grinding teeth, the growled threats and imprecations, and the tightened fists or the seized weapon ready for attack.

Important visceral alterations accompanying fury I have recounted above. They are profound and widespread. They are called forth by discharges through the sympathetic division of the autonomic system. The neurones of this division are so arranged, as I have noted elsewhere (1), that they discharge impulses diffusely to smooth muscles and glands in all parts of the body. Among the glands is the adrenal medulla—a gland of internal secretion. Thus at the same time with the diffuse emission of sympathetic impulses there is liberation of adrenin (13). The adrenin, which is poured into the blood stream, necessarily has a general distribution and therefore a diffuse action. Everywhere that it acts in the body, it has the same effect as the nerve impulses—i. e., the humoral and the neural agents cooperate. Indeed, this cooperation of the ubiquitously distributed adrenin and the nerve impulses confirms the concept that the sympathetic neurones are arranged for diffuse effects—otherwise any special action by the neural agent would be covered by the general action of the humoral agent.

The sympathetic system is called into operation in various circumstances—during marked excitation of the cerebrum as in fear or rage (1, 13), on exposure to cold (14), when the blood sugar is too greatly reduced (15), in asphyxial states (16), and in very vigorous muscular effort (13). Because the system is activated in quite different conditions and also because it operates as a unit, it induces changes which are useful in one circumstance but may not be useful in another. In the rage-reaction, however, as noted above, all the known changes may be readily and reasonably interpreted as rendering the organism especially capable of enduring prolonged and extreme physical effort.

Although activation of the sympathico-adrenal system is a prominent feature in an outburst of rage, it is not an essential feature. Recently Lewis, Britton, and I (17) have succeeded in removing completely both sympathetic trunks, from the superior cervical to the pelvic ganglia, in cats, keeping the animals healthy and vigorous in the laboratory for many months, and noting that in appropriate circumstances they exhibit almost all the superficial signs of rage. Thus, one of these animals, which had given birth to kittens, showed her teeth, drew back her ears, lifted a front leg ready to strike, and growled and hissed, when a barking dog approached her young. The hairs, however, did not bristle on any part of her body, and vigorous struggle resulted in no increase of blood sugar. In animals with the adrenals, liver, and heart wholly disconnected from the central nervous system the rage-response occurs, as Lewis, Britton, and I (18) have shown, quite as in normal animals, even to the appearance of a bushy tail, without, however, any discharge of adrenin or noteworthy acceleration of the heart. In these cases there is no reason for supposing that the peripheral operations have disturbed the established pathways in the central neurones. If the central neurones are connected with the muscles of the tail hairs, the hairs stand, otherwise they lie flat; if the nervous connections reach to the adrenal glands, adrenin is discharged, otherwise not. In short, the central neurones discharge in their fated manner; and the activity or absence of activity in effector organs depends on the presence or absence of connections with the spinal cord.

Thus far I have given an objective account of physiological facts related to a typical emotional expression—that of rage. Do not these facts have implications pertinent to other emotions? Do not they help towards an understanding of the nature and functions of emotion in the behavior of the organism? May I venture to suggest that they do, and attempt to present some reasons for that suggestion.

A fundamental fact which I would emphasize is that the neuro-muscular and neuro-visceral arrangement for the display of rage has its central control congenitally organized in or near a phylo-genetically ancient part of the brain, the optic thalamus. The thalamus is not like the cerebral cortex in being a region where new relations with the outer world are registered and old relations are modified; it more nearly resembles the spinal cord—a region under superior dominance, where afferent impulses are received, regrouped, and redistributed either to the higher levels, or to neighboring motor neurones which promptly discharge to effector organs in stereotyped reaction patterns. The typical postures and attitudes which result from action of the thalamus are more complicated than those produced by spinal reflexes but are not essentially different. The physiological organization which es-tablishes the reflex figure of rage I have detailed because it may serve as a prototype for other primitive emotional responses. The expressions of fear, joy, and grief are similar in character; in their essential features they are not learned, and they are exhibited so early in the human infant that they may properly be classed with rage as being natively inherent in the brain. There is good evidence that central control for the expression of these emotions, like that for rage, lies subcortically and, specifically, in the thalamic region. Bekhterev (19) has reported that whereas "painful" stimulation excites cries in an animal freshly deprived of its cere-bral hemispheres, gentle stimulation ("petting") may evoke signs of pleasure, e. g., purring in the cat and tail-wagging in the dog. These responses disappeared, in his cases, after removal of the optic thalamus. In human beings indications of a subcortical management of emotional expression are to be seen in the effects of anaesthetics. During the second (excitement) stage of ether anaesthesia, there may be sobbing as in grief, or laughter as in joy, or lively and energetic aggressive reactions as in rage—all without refined or even definite adjustments to the environment. The surgeon may open the chest or perform other operations of equal gravity, while the patient is pushing, pulling, shouting, and mut-tering, and yet the events leave no trace in the cortex which yields later a memory of what has happened. A peculiar effect of nitrous oxide anaesthesia has led to its common name, "laughing gas," though an experienced anaesthetist has informed me that under its influence quite as many patients weep as laugh; in either event, when cortical functions have been so deeply abolished by this gas that the patient has no experience from an ordinarily painful procedure, there is a release of the typical expressions of gladness or sorrow. Pathological cases support these indications of a sub-cortical source of emotional behavior. In certain forms of hemi-plegia the patient is incapable of moving the face on the paralyzed side; but if he is suddenly affected by an occasion which is gay or sad, the muscles which have been dissociated from cortical government act properly to give the face the expression of joy or sadness (19). The clinical studies of Head and Holmes (20) have brought evidence of a more precise localization of centers for emotional acts. They noted that such unilateral damage to the brain as isolates parts of the thalamus from the cortex has a most remarkable consequence in the excessive responses to "all po-tentially affective stimuli." The prick of a pin, painful pressure, excessive heat and cold, all produce a more vigorous unpleasant feeling on the abnormal than on the normal side of the body. At the same time, pleasurable warmth may evoke an unusually vivid pleasant response. And they conclude that since the affective states are increased when the thalamus is freed from cortical con-trol, "the activity of the essential thalamic center is mainly occupied with the affective side of sensation." Similar testimony to residence of the neural mechanisms for affective expression in the brain-stem is afforded by anencephalic monsters—the so-called "frog-babies," born without cerebral hemispheres and often having little more than the medulla and cerebellum. Even with such a poor remnant of the brain as that, noxious stimulation will cause whimpering and drawing down of the corners of the mouth as in distress and grief (21). In all these instances of absence of cortical function, primitive emotional reactions are as perfectly performed as are the reflexes of coughing, sneezing, sucking, and swallowing, i. e., they are complicated automatisms. In all these complicated acts the nerve impulses run their appointed course according to phylogenetic patterns and without individual in-struction or training.

A second point on which I would lay emphasis is the intensity of the rage-reaction which we observed in pseudaffective animals. Many years ago Hughlings Jackson (5) made the suggestion, recently supported by Head (22), that the nervous system is or-ganized in a neural hierarchy, such that primitive reactions, which might otherwise disturb the more discriminative responses of higher levels, are by these repressed. When the cortical govern-ment is set aside, the subordinate activities, released from inhibition, become prominent. Then only slight stimulation is required to produce extreme effects. Thus may be explained the violent and persistent display of sham rage by our decorticate cats while fastened to a holder, the vigorous snapping, snarling, and resistance of the hemisphereless dogs when taken from their cages, and the excessive responses to mildly affective stimuli by human beings with thalamus freed from the cortex. The extraordinary intensity of these exhibitions seems to indicate that the neural apparatus for emotional expression is set and ready for energetic discharge, and that if only the superior control is weakened or inhibited, appropriate stimuli evoke an intense and powerful response. If external conditions should be such as to call forth an emotional response, therefore, a definite innervation of effector organs from the cortex would not be required; withdrawal of cortical dominance would be the main condition for prompt and vigorous action. But the cortical government may not release the excited neurones in the thalamus. Then there is conflict between the higher and lower controls of bodily activities—there are opposing tendencies with accompanying confusion. The cortical neurones, however, can check only some of the bodily activities, those which are normally under voluntary control. It cannot check the stormy processes of the thalamus which cause shivering and forcible emptying of the bladder and rectum. In states of conflict these phenomena become prominent.

A third point—since cognitive consciousness is associated with the functioning of cortical neurones, it follows, as a corollary from the facts cited above, that the neural mechanisms for the primitive emotions operate in a region outside the range of such consciousness. This consideration, together with the readiness of these mechanisms, when released from inhibition, to exhibit a major response to a minor stimulus, explains, I think, some of the most characteristic features of emotional experience. We have emotional "seizures"; we laugh, weep, or rage "uncontrollably"; we feel as if "possessed"; what we do in the stress of excitement is "surprising," "shocking"—something "surges up within us" and our actions seem no longer our own. These common bywords are explicable in terms of a sudden and powerful domination of the bodily forces by subcortical neurones. Under favoring circumstances, with only a momentary lifting of the normal inhibitory check, these neurones capture the effector machinery and drive it violently into one or another of its variegated attitudes.

And finally, it seems to me that the facts presented above suggest a new source for the peculiar feelings which we experience in an emotional upset. We are familiar with James's (23) idea

that the feeling of the bodily changes, which occur spontaneously
in an exciting situation, constitutes the emotion; and also with
the similar idea of Lange (24) that consciousness of cardio-vascular
disturbances is the essential element. Elsewhere I (1) have pointed
out that any high degree of excitation in the central nervous
system, whether felt as anger, terror, pain, anxiety, joy, grief, or
deep disgust, may rouse the sympathetic system to activity and
affect in a stereotyped fashion the functions of organs which that
system innervates. May I recall that the central station for
the sympathetic system is a small, compact center in the diencephalon, and, furthermore, that when strongly aroused, that
system tends to act as a unit. The responses in the viscera,
therefore, are too uniform to offer a satisfactory means of distinguishing states which, in man at least, are very different in subjective quality. For this reason I urged that the differential
features separating one emotion from another could not be
found in diverse afferent impulses from the viscera. Furthermore,
as Marañon (25) has shown, injections of adrenalin into human
beings in amounts which induce the visceral changes characteristic of emotional excitement do not in fact produce an emotional experience; the subject merely becomes reminiscent of
other times when these changes were noted—he reports them and
remains calm. In addition, the afferents from the viscera, especially from cardio-vascular organs, are too meager to yield us any
rich sensation based on the happenings within them. There remain as support for the James-Lange theory the positions and
tensions of skeletal muscle that are peculiar to the various emotions. But forced laughter does not bring real joy, nor forced
sobbing real sorrow, as it appears to me they should do if the
peculiar *quale* of the emotion were derived from the innervated
muscles themselves. Furthermore, Head (26) and his collaborators report that in thalamus cases the quality of feeling-tone,
though markedly intensified in relation to other sensations, notably
those resulting from certain tactile, auditory, and thermal stimuli,
is entirely absent from such sensations as underlie an appreciation
of posture. The theory of a peripheral source of emotional experience has little or no positive factual support. To produce an
effect in the cortex, however, it is not necessary that afferent
impulses arise at the periphery; they may be started anywhere
in the afferent path. May not this happen in emotional excitement? The neurones of the subcortical centers in the cerebrum
act in different combinations in the different emotional expressions,
as proved by the reaction pattern, typical of the several affective
states, which they induce. May not the "feeling" be due to impulses, not from the effector organs, but from the lower neurones

in the special combination which fixes at the moment the peculiar facies and bodily postures of the reaction system? These neurones, as we have seen, are organized in the basal gray matter, in the old brain. They do not require detailed innervation from above in order to be driven into action. Being *released* for action is a primary condition for their service to the body; they then discharge precipitately and intensely. We know that intense activity in one part of the nervous system extends to other parts by "irradiation." The phenomenon occurs in the gray matter of the cerebral cortex; it may occur likewise in the gray matter of the basal ganglia of the old brain-stem. Here, within or near the thalamus, the neurones concerned in emotional expression lie close to the relay on the sensory path from periphery to cortex. We may assume that when these neurones discharge in various combinations they not only innervate muscles and viscera but also affect afferent paths to the cortex by irradiation or by direct connections. Only in this way, I think, can we account for the phenomena observed when in human beings the optic thalamus is freed from cortical control by a unilateral lesion. All the emotional aspects of experience are greatly intensified on the injured side; in a case described by Head (26), though a tuning fork or a bell had no unusual effects, stirring music produced such intolerably intense feelings (referred to the affected side) that the patient was obliged to leave the room. Thus as an accompaniment of each emotional expression there could surge up from the old brain to the cerebral cortex impulses characteristic of the neurone pattern then prevailing. The quality of the emotion might arise from the obscure and unrelated source of the intruding impulses, from the sense of extraneous control of the bodily forces, and from the different combinations of the excited afferent neurones—each combination specific for a particular emotion. In other words, for the theory that emotional experiences arise from changes in effector organs is substituted the idea that they are produced by unusual and powerful influences emerging from the region of the thalamus and affecting various systems of cortical neurones. This view accords with the pertinent physiological facts now available. It can be applied to the "subtler" emotions, which the James-Lange theory had difficulty in explaining. It offers interesting suggestions for the study of emotional expressions experimentally in lower animals and in human beings under the influence of various drugs and in pathological states.

BIBLIOGRAPHY

1. CANNON, W. B. Bodily changes in pain, hunger, fear, and rage. New York: Appleton, 1915.

2. GOLTZ, F. *Pflüger's Archiv für die gesamte Physiologie*, LI (1892), 570.

3. ROTHMANN, H. *Zeitschrift für die gesamte Neurologie und Psychiatrie,* LXXXVII (1923), 247.

4. DE BARENNE, J. G. *Archives néerlandaises de physiologie,* IV (1919), 114.

5. JACKSON, J. H. *British Medical Journal* (1884), 591, 660, 703.

6. CANNON, W. B., and BRITTON, S. W. *American Journal of Physiology.* LXXII (1925), 283.

7. BULATAO, E., and CANNON, W. B. *American Journal of Physiology,* LXXII (1925), 295.

8. WOODWORTH, R. S., and SHERRINGTON, C. S. *Journal of Physiology,* XXXI (1904), 234.

9. BAZETT, H. C., and PENFIELD, W. G. *Brain,* XLV (1922), 215.

10. ISENSCHMID, R. *Handbuch der normalen und pathologischen Physiologie,* XVII (1926), 1.

11. KARPLUS, J. P., and KREIDL, A. *Pflüger's Archiv für die gesamte Physiologie,* CXXIX (1909), 138; CXXXV (1910) 401; CXLIII (1912), 109; CLXXI (1918), 192; CCIII (1924), 533; CCXV (1926), 667.

12. DARWIN, C. The expression of emotion in man and animals. New York: Appleton, 1897.

13. CANNON, W. B., BRITTON, S. W., LEWIS, J. T., and GROENEVELD, A. *American Journal of Physiology,* LXXIX (1927), 433.

14. CANNON, W. B., QUERIDO, A., BRITTON, S. W., and BRIGHT, E. M. *American Journal of Physiology,* LXXIX (1927), 466.

15. CANNON, W. B., McIVER, M. A., and BLISS, S. W. *American Journal of Physiology,* LXIX (1927), 46.

16. CANNON, W. B., and CARRASCO-FORMIGUERA, R. *American Journal of Physiology,* LXI (1922), 215.

17. CANNON, W. B., LEWIS, J. T., and BRITTON, S. W. *Boston Medical and Surgical Journal,* CXCVII (1927), 514.

18. CANNON, W. B., LEWIS, J. T., and BRITTON, S. W. *American Journal of Physiology,* LXXVII (1926), 326.

19. BEKHTEREV, V. *Virchow's Archiv für pathologische Anatomie und Physiologie,* CX (1887), 345.

20. HEAD, H., and HOLMES, G. *Brain,* XXXIV (1911), 109.

21. STERNBERG, M., and LATZKO, W. *Deutsche Zeitschrift für Nervenheilkunde,* XXIV (1903), 209.

22. HEAD, H. *Proceedings of the Royal Society of London,* B, XCII (1921), 184.

23. JAMES, W. Principles of psychology, II. New York: Holt, 1890. P. 449.

24. LANGE, C. G. The emotions. Baltimore: Williams & Wilkins, 1922. Pp. 63–72.

25. MARAÑON, G. *Revue française d'endocrinologie,* II (1924), 301.

26. HEAD, H. Studies in neurology, II. London: Frowde, Hodder, & Stoughton, 1920, p. 620.

DISCUSSION

DR. REYMERT: In opening the discussion of Dr. Cannon's paper, I want to say that we, as psychologists, are extremely fortunate in having a physiologist like Dr. Cannon with us. His works, as we all know, have exerted a great influence upon contemporary psychology, and his latter findings now will most likely bring about some revisions which will have to be made in certain psychological conclusions and investigations. The paper is now open for discussion.

DR. WEISS (*Ohio State University*): I would just like to ask Dr. Cannon this question which was raised in part also as a response to Dr. Dunlap's paper. I agree, of course, with the findings that Dr. Cannon has presented. Now there is this, I think, which would be of extreme importance to psychologists: that is, what is the criterion of emotion and how many different kinds of emotions are there? That, I think, is somewhat unclear to some of us.

DR. CANNON: That is a question of very great importance and, I think, of fundamental importance. It seems to me that this conception that I have tried to bring before you tonight, that these patterns exist in the cortex early—I do not mean in the cortex, but in the brain early, in the thalamus early—allows us to make studies of the various reactions which the animal exhibits—and when I say the animal I mean human beings—in the first days of existence, and that possibly by such careful examination, such as Watson has already started, we can get a notion of how many emotions there are to start off with.

Now my notion is, and I am sure that there are others who have had the same idea, that these primitive responses become associated very much as responses become associated in cortical operations, so that we have all sorts of complicated combinations of emotional reactions that are dependent upon previous experiences. I have an emotion or an emotional feeling that is fairly intense and has been so for many, many years when I hear sleigh-bells, and it goes back to a time when I saw Henry Irving play "The Bells." I was a boy at the time and was immensely stirred by the terrific tragedy which he represented on the stage. Since then I cannot hear sleigh-bells without having a queer feeling inside of me, which I interpret as emotion. An association has been established between the sound of those bells and the experience which I had at that time, so that a recurrence of the sound of the bells brings back the emotions.

It is a very different matter to explain that emotion. At the time I had it I think it would have been an easier emotion to define if I had been introspective or had been watchful at the moment. These complications come as a result of experience. I am talking now to a lot of psychologists. I am only a physiologist, and I am not expert in psychological theorizing and speak upon some of these matters haltingly, but that would be my way of answering Dr. Weiss's question.

DR. WEISS: The results of some investigations which we are now conducting on new-born infants, beginning at birth up to about ten or twelve days, indicate that there are practically none of these emotional disturbances present at that early stage. You can take young infants, wind them tightly in a cloth, and they go to sleep. Hold their noses, which is usually an easy way of getting a strong emotional response from an adult, and they wiggle a bit and go to sleep. That is as far as we have been able to find with our experiments on young infants. We do not get the emotional responses, that is, the skeletal responses, except those organic responses. We do get those. But we get those also with other things, that is, not only with what we would call emotional stimuli, but we get it when we try to elicit a palmar reflex or a blinking reflex or an auditory reflex. We are likely to get any one or all of these things. So, as far as the new-born infant is concerned, I think there is very little opportunity there, as far as our researches go, to try to establish the fact that we have such a thing as a primary emotion, unless we eliminate all skeletal posture. If we consider the organic responses, we can see them. There is evidence of emotion. But we get those organic reactions without emotional stimuli.

DR. CANNON: May I ask any mother here to hold up her hand if she has heard the first cry of her baby? There have been persons who theorized about that first cry and they supposed that the first cry was due to the fact that the child suddenly found after being in heaven that he was in a very much worse place. I am quite sure that that expression of emotion, that cry, is heard almost immediately or very soon after birth, and I am sure that anything in the way of stimulation will bring that out.

CHAPTER 23

EMOTIONS AS SOMATO-MIMETIC REFLEXES

VLADIMIR M. BEKHTEREV
University of Leningrad

The psychology of feeling, as it is called, rests upon two different theories. One maintains that the primary source of feeling is the internal experiences of the psychic sphere, which call forth, secondarily, corresponding changes in the viscera. The other is the well-known James-Lange theory, which considers feeling a secondary phenomenon, usually following physical changes, especially changes in cardio-vascular activity and muscular tonus.

Researches which were carried on in my laboratory by Dr. Sreznevski (Dissertation, 1906) prove conclusively that the James-Lange theory is not corroborated by the results obtained from emotions physiologically aroused. During fright, for instance, there is at first an acceleration of the functions of the reproductive-associative system, followed by retardation, which occurs before the changes in the cardio-vascular system, due to the influence of a sudden external stimulus which calls forth the fright. This shows us that the James-Lange theory does not explain all the phenomena of feeling and emotion, and leads us to conclude that neither of the theories are tenable. We must consider other possible explanations of emotional states.

We also know facts of a different sort. For instance, opium or hasheesh and a few other poisons which affect the intellectual processes bring about a euphoric state; the penetration of the organism by the toxins of hydrophobia is followed by strangely expressed fear or fright, which is augmented by the presence of certain external stimuli, as water or glittering objects. These poisons evidently act upon the nervous system by way of the blood, poisoning the central as well as the peripheral synapses. It is also possible to arouse emotional states artificially. It is well known that the subcutaneous injection of adrenalin is usually followed by a state of anxiety, together with the phenomena of hyperthyroidism (tachycardia and tremor). This shows clearly that anxiety is associated with hyperthyroidism; the state of euphoria, with athyroidism. There is very interesting work on this subject by M. Laignel-Lavastine.[1]

[1] "Les psychoses thyroidiennes," *Progrès médical*, XLIX (1922), 158–163; *Questions neurologiques d'actualité*. Vingt conférences faites à la faculté de médecine de Paris, 1921. (Paris: Masson, 1922.)

There are also pathological states of euphoria, some of which develop independently, and some in connection with manic depression. Thus we see that the basis of these states designated as feelings and emotions is alterations in the composition of the blood. Hence, the ultimate source of these states must be found in the functions of those organs which can quickly alter the chemical composition of the blood. Such are the organs of internal secretion. Cannon's well-known experiment proves this point. When a dog approaches a cat, there is a marked increase in the amount of adrenalin in the cat's blood. The question is: How are these organs innervated? Investigations which have been recently carried out in our laboratory and later corroborated elsewhere prove conclusively that each of the glands of internal secretion receives nerves from the automatic system—afferent as well as efferent. We have demonstrated this in the case of the testicles and some other glands. It should hold true for the others as well. Thus the glands may be controlled through either the parasympathetic or the sympathetic nervous system.

When one remembers that the sympathetic system controls vasoconstriction, and the parasympathetic system vasodilation, it is clear that excitation of the sympathetic nervous system should be accompanied by weakening or inhibition of the glandular functions, and excitation of the parasympathetic nervous system by strengthening or acceleration of them. Individual differences in degree of sympatheticotonia or vagotonia are merely expressions of different degrees of excitability or reactivity in various types of nervous systems. This excitability is naturally reflected in the activities of the glands, which, in turn, stimulate the vegetative nervous system.

But, in addition to this nervous control of the endocrine functions, there is a chemical control. The glands can, and undoubtedly do, react to the chemical composition of the blood (chemical reflexes). Thus there is established a sort of equilibrium between the various glands, due to the direct effect of the chemical composition of the blood upon the chemical elements of the glands themselves.[2]

If the nervous control of the glands explains the relation of mood to the development of innate and acquired reflexes, then the chemical control through the blood may explain the relation of changes in mood to the composition of the blood and, consequently, to the state of the viscera in pathological cases.

If we take into consideration the facts that the basis of emotional

[2] Dr. Bielov, one of the men working under my supervision, has established the law of the mutual interaction of the glands by study of the brain.

states is the secretory activity of the glands, and that certain glands are innervated chiefly by the sympathicus (e. g., the sexual organs, etc.), while others are innervated chiefly by the vagus (e. g., the pancreas), it is clear that the relations between the two systems determine various degrees of emotional excitability. The predominance of one gives the more excitable type of person; the predominance of the other, the less excitable type; a good balance between the two systems, the intermediate emotional type.

The facts thus far presented compel us to realize that the functional changes in the cardio-vascular, respiratory, and other somatic organs during emotional states may be dependent upon changes in the secretory activity of certain glands, brought about by reflex stimulation through the central nervous system or by changes in the chemical composition of the blood. Every case involves the chemical excitation of the nerve cells which determine the emotional states. As for the functional changes in the reproductive-associative system, which precede those of the cardio-vascular system in fright, they must be due to inhibition of cortical processes. In some emotional states, on the other hand, there is an excitation of cortical processes rather than inhibition.

As for the various changes in cardiac function, we must consider the following cases: (a) strengthening of heart action, (b) weakening of heart action, (c) acceleration, (d) retardation, (e) strengthening and acceleration, (f) strengthening and retardation, (g) weakening and acceleration, (h) weakening and retardation. If we consider that other variations in heart action are possible, and remember also that these changes are accompanied by changes in the blood-vessels—dilation and contraction in certain parts of the body—and changes in the respiratory system—deep fast breathing, deep slow breathing, shallow fast breathing, and shallow slow breathing—then we will understand what a large variety of objective changes may occur in the cardio-vascular and respiratory systems. We must also consider the phenomena of excitation and retardation of the mimic reflex activities which accompany these changes. We must take account of the reflexly produced secretions which stimulate the nervous tissues. This will lead us to an understanding of all the various phenomena which occur during the so-called emotional states.

At present we cannot establish the correlations between all the various objective changes in the somatic sphere and specific subjective states. We may, however, recognize certain facts. For instance, the state of fear is correlated with acceleration and strengthening of heart action, contraction of the peripheral vessels, increase of blood-pressure, a violent rush of blood to the head, strengthening of the respiratory movements, and an increase of adrenalin in the blood, according to the results of Cannon's experiments.

Heroic ecstasy is correlated with a strong increase in heart action, active dilation of the vessels of the brain and periphery, and strengthening of the respiratory movements. Grief or sorrow is correlated with weakening of the heart action, accelerated pulse, slight dilation of the vessels, and slow shallow breathing; joy, with increased heart action, moderate dilation of the peripheral vessels, deeper breathing, etc.

It is understood that all these states are accompanied by a number of phenomena which involve the receptors of the striated muscles in addition to the other changes in the conditioned reflex activities. These phenomena include a great variety of external mimetic activities which we will not describe in detail. Emotions, as they are called, consist of these external mimetic movements together with the above-mentioned somatic and conditioned reflex changes. Reflexology regards them as specialized somato-mimetic reflexes. On the basis of the general character of the reflexes we may distinguish: (1) general somato-mimetic tonus, which corresponds to what is called *mood* in subjective psychology; (2) various somato-mimetic reflexes (*emotions* according to the subjective terminology), which may be exciting, depressing, or mixed; and (3) somato-mimetic disturbances or *affects*, as the psychologists designate them. The psychologists usually study the feelings and subjective experiences which accompany these states by the use of the very unreliable introspective method. Consequently, this domain of science has been only slightly developed to date.

Since the subjective experiences and the nerve impulses in the brain which accompany them constitute one and the same process, one may analyze one's own somato-mimetic reflexes (excluding their external manifestations associated with the exciting stimuli), by using proper instruments and keeping at the same time a record of the subjective experiences felt. This is the method of self-analysis or the automatic method, which Shumkov and I have employed.[3] It is quite consistent with the objective, biosocial method of observation (which excludes the external stimuli associated with previous life-experiences and constitutional condition), and may be utilized to insure greater completeness in the study of a subject of such complexity and delicacy as somato-mimetic reflexes.

[3] V. Bekhterev and G. Shumkov, *Monatsschrift für Psychiatrie und Neurologie*, LXV (1927). Flechsigfestschrift.

To turn to the phylogenetic development of the somato-mimetic reflexes, we must point out that Darwin explained that human mimicry is deeply rooted in the biological world. Here we come upon the same law of evolution which applies to all other phenomena of the plant and animal kingdoms. According to Darwin, expressive movements have developed phylogenetically from movements which originally had different meanings. Some of these movements, which were originally useful to the individual, have been retained although they have ceased to be useful. For example, the expression of hatred in man is characterized by the lifting of the upper lip and baring of the teeth, which, Darwin says, represent movements preparatory to fighting, intended to frighten the enemy. Although man does not use his teeth in fighting, the expression of hatred is retained. The setting of the jaws and clenching of the fists in anger have a similar origin. Darwin himself did not consider this principle of useful habits adequate to all types of expression. He supplemented it by two other principles: the principle of "antithesis" and the principle of actions which are dependent upon the structure of the nervous system. These two supplementary principles have been rejected by later critics, and, therefore, need not claim our attention, but the first, the retention of originally useful habits not now useful, is recognized by the majority of authors. Even this principle, however, cannot serve us as a guide, as I have explained definitely in my work, "Biological Development of Mimicry" (*Vestnik Znaniya*, 1910).[4] As a matter of fact, what could be the use of scaring the enemy by baring the teeth, raising the hair on the neck and on the body in general (in order to appear larger and more fearful), when the enemy himself employs the same methods of inducing fear. My interpretation of the movements in question is entirely different. They are "vitally necessary," because they prepare the individual for the fight, because the strength necessary for the attack can be developed in no other way. One cannot fight unless the body assumes the proper position at the appropriate time, unless the muscles are tense preparatory to the development of maximum strength, unless the heart and blood-vessels are prepared to furnish an increased blood supply.

Neither can an adequate defense be developed without corresponding preparations: raising of the hair on the neck and body, the reptile's raising its collar to defend itself against the bites of the enemy, the paling of the superficial vessels to prevent an

[4] See also: V. Bekhterev, "Die biologische Entwicklung der Mimik," *Folia Neuro-biologica*, V (1911), 825–860; "Le rôle biologique de la mimique," *Journal de psychologie*, VII (1910), 385–408.

excess flow of blood from wounds received during the fight, increased heart action, etc. The "muscular concentration," which enables the organism to defend itself or to attack at any moment, could not exist without initial muscular preparation—flow of blood to the muscles and increase in tonus.

Thus we have to deal with general movements which serve the general needs of the organism. The same principle applies to the movements associated with the specialized sense organs (eyes, ears, nose, and tongue). These are movements of accommodation to insure better reception of the external excitations according to the needs of the organism, defensive movements to protect the organs from superfluous and harmful excitations, and muscular readiness which makes possible a better orientation during the given excitation. These movements, which are not only useful but necessary, constitute the very essence of complex activities. They are the ultimate source of the somato-mimetic reflexes or expressive movements. These reflexes, which were produced as the initial stage of certain acts, came to be the mimical language of the animal kingdom, facilitating the exchange of reactions among various individuals. Thus, even at this stage of development, they are just as necessary as they were originally when they constituted a part of the complex activities of the individual. This is my point of view.

We have still to say a few words about sexual mimicry. In dealing with this subject, the great naturalist again emphasized the subjective by interpreting the various expressive phenomena including the displays of the male which occur during the period of mating as attempts to attract the female by their beauty, originating consequently in the process of sexual selection. We know, however, that it is not the females who select the males, but the males who select the females and fight for possession of them. From the point of view which I have set forth above, sexual mimicry is simply the result of the increased activity of the sexual glands preparatory to mating. It serves also to increase sexual excitement in the individual of the opposite sex. This is essential to successful mating, which insures the preservation of the race.

This conception of sexual mimicry furnishes a natural explanation of such phenomena as the reddening of the bare buttocks of monkeys, the reddening of roosters' combs, the spreading of wings and tail feathers of birds, which Darwin regarded as sexual displays intended to attract the female. The secondary sexual characteristics, which are dependent upon the hormones of the sexual glands, also function as sexual stimuli in mating.

The biological method supplies an account of the phylogenetic development of mimicry, but not of its ontogenetic development. Since man's greater perfection and sociability have led to the acquisition of a large number of new and more refined emotional states, we cannot dispense with an ontogenetic study of the subject. We must also keep in mind the comparative method of studying the genetic development of emotions in animals and in man.

Reflexology regards emotional states as somato-mimetic reflexes, in which the subjective and objective aspects represent one and the same indivisible process. The objective method of studying the emotions of other people, which is used in reflexology, permits investigation only of the external bodily and internal somatic changes. These changes, which vary with the nature of the emotion, serve as a preparation, an orientation, for the defense or the attack, or mating, and are consequently quite useful.[5]

The present development of reflexology makes it possible to approach the study of the various somato-mimetic expressions of the human being in a purely objective way. We may be certain that the objective reflexological or bioconscious method of study will lead us to a better understanding of the human being. We approach the subject with the help of this method.

Let us consider the *autogenesis* of the somato-mimetic reflexes. What is the essence of the reflexological method? It is the study of the external expressions of a person under the assumption that these expressions are reflexes conditioned by corresponding excitations. These reflexes are determined by brain processes, for every subjective state presupposes a brain process.

In the case of man the sources of excitation are to be found not only in the biological but in the social environment, especially the latter. It is these social excitations that make man a biosocial being. The reflexological investigation is completed only when the very genesis of the phenomena is explained. The fact that the majority of these reflexes are somatic shows that the vegetative nervous system plays a very important part in their development. Since this system innervates the striated muscles, as recent investigations have shown, it is probable that changes in the muscles—degree of tonus, tremor, etc.—are dependent upon it.[6]

[5] Although gestures are closely associated with emotions and especially with speech, they must be distinguished from mimicry. They are indeed a complement of speech. They do not occur in animals, except, perhaps, in a very rudimentary form. Gestures are incomplete movements which orient, point, defend, attack, and describe. Thus they supplement the intonation of the voice in giving to speech a very vivid demonstrative quality.

[6] We do not include gestures because they are dependent upon the excitation of the pyramidal tracts of the nervous system.

At present the cerebral mechanism of these reflexive somato-mimetic phenomena can be made more or less clear. First I must point out that, as early as the eighties, I proved experimentally the significance of the visual center in the development and execution of these movements, which I have designated as "expressive."[3]

The function of the visual center is shown not only in the external mimetic movements, but also in the various internal somatic changes, as these same experiments have demonstrated. More recently these facts have been confirmed by a number of clinical observations. Studies made upon the encephalon by pathologico-anatomical dissections prove conclusively that the striated system, which is intimately connected with the visual center functionally and anatomically, plays an important part in mimetic phenomena. The main center of the vegetative nervous system is, as we know, the gray matter in the region of the lower part of the third ventricle, the region of tuber cinereum. It is, therefore, probable that the optic nerve sends its fibers in the direction of this center of the vegetative nervous system. In this way the changes in the vegetative nervous system which accompany the somato-mimetic reflexes are brought about. The cortex of the brain also belongs to the general mechanism of the somato-mimetic reflexes. This rôle of the cortex was first demonstrated in our laboratory. We know that the respiratory functions play a part in the somato-mimetic reflexes. For instance, a dog's rate of respiration increases when a cat is brought near it. At the end of the last century, we used this reflex, which is undoubtedly conditioned, to localize the respiratory center in the brain. Dr. Zhukovski (Dissertation, 1898), who experimented with dogs in my laboratory, found that the somato-mimetic reflex in question is eliminated when the cortical respiratory centers, which lie outside and in front of the sigmoid convolution, are removed. This may also be demonstrated with the somato-mimetic erotic reflex. If a male dog is near a bitch during the period of mating, the erection of the penis takes place. But if the cortical sexual centers, which have been located during the course of these investigations in the rear portion of the sigmoid convolution near the center which controls the tail, are removed, erection no longer occurs under the same conditions. (See Dr. Pussep.) The same holds true for the maternal reflex secretion of milk at the sight or cry of the child. Experiments upon milking sheep, which were conducted in our

[3] See my work: "On Expressive Movements," *Russki Vratch*, 1893; "On the Function of the Visual Center," *Vestnik Psikhologi*, 1885; and "Die Bedeutung der Sehhügel auf Grund von experimentellen und pathologischen Daten," Virchow's *Archiv für pathologische Anatomie und Physiologie*, CX (1887), 102, 322.

laboratory by Dr. Nikitin, have shown that the electrical stimulation of certain centers located near the facial center brings about an abundant secretion of milk. Experiments have shown that the same effect takes place at the sight of a lamb or even at hearing its cry when it is outside of the building. The reflex is eliminated when the centers in question are removed. Analogous phenomena have been observed in the case of other glandular secretions.

These facts show clearly that the conditioned reflex phenomena of the vegetative nervous system, which enter into the complex of somato-mimetic reflexes (emotions), are controlled by centers located in the cortex of the brain, which influence the vegetative (vago-sympathetic) nervous system by way of the subcortical vegetative nervous centers.

We must remember that the somato-mimetic reflexes may be divided into two groups—the innate and the acquired. The innate reflexes begin to develop soon after birth without previous experience. Such are the mimetic satisfactions after eating: the cry, the smile, laughter, etc. They are touched off by reflexogenic stimuli— external and internal—and transmitted to the centers by afferent channels. The acquired reflexes originate by an associative process; they are conditioned upon the innate somato-mimetic reflexes. For instance, the smile which was originally induced by favorable internal biological stimuli and appeared later as laughter under the influence of external cutaneous stimuli (such as tickling in certain regions) may, with time, begin to appear in response to visual and auditory (verbal) stimuli, as a result of the association of certain social stimuli with the biological and reflexogenic cutaneous stimuli mentioned. Like all conditioned reflexes, this latter case involves the transmission of the visual and auditory impulses to the visual center by way of the cerebral cortex and thence to the cerebral center of the vegetative nervous system. As for the somato-mimetic (emotional) expressions of the secretory activity of the glands, they, too, are directly dependent upon the vegetative nervous system, and therefore involve a similar mechanism. Furthermore, experiments performed in our laboratory by Pines and others prove that the glands of internal secretion (suprarenals, thyroid, sexual glands, and evidently all the rest) are innervated both by the sympathetic and the parasympathetic systems.

Thus we have to deal with conditioned reflexes, which accelerate or inhibit the activity of the glands of internal secretion, thereby altering the composition of the blood which nourishes the ganglia of the nervous system, thus exerting an influence upon the nervous system itself.

The question is: Which of these somato-mimetic states are to be regarded as the innate or inherited reflexes which supply the basis for the development of conditioned reflexes? Dr. Watson regards the emotions of love, fear, and anger as innate (*The Pedagogical Seminary and Journal of Genetic Psychology*, June, 1925). But all three may be acquired emotions of the conditioned reflex type. There are specific stimuli for each of them. Fear, for instance, is aroused by a sudden noise or by the sudden loss of support. The innate anger reflex is aroused by inhibiting the movements of the body. Stroking of the skin, especially erogenous zones, or patting is the stimulus for the emotion of love. We note here that the sexual glands, which exhibit their hormonal function from the day of birth, play a very important part in love.[8] The stroking of the skin really excites the activity of these glands and so leads to the erection of the sexual organs. Our observations show that stroking of the abdomen when the sexual organs are turgid, results in erection even during the first year of life. But love in its mature form is the result of a number of external stimuli —cutaneous (caressing), visual, and auditory—which are associated with the original stimulus and so excite the hormonal function of the sexual glands.

The three emotional or somato-mimetic reflexes mentioned by Watson are not the only ones which belong to the innate or inherited group. In addition to them we must recognize: (1) the reflex which denotes biological satisfaction, characterized by general dilation of the peripheral blood-vessels, especially those of the face, and smoothening out of the facial wrinkles; and (2) the reflex which denotes biological dissatisfaction, characterized by increased muscular energy, increased tonus of the vessels, and later by the phenomena of muscular unrest. Very much later in the course of development the superabundance of the sexual hormone is indicated by sexual excitement and changes in the face and eyes. Other somato-mimetic states are aroused by ordinary reflexes which act as external reflexogenic stimuli. We know that gentle stroking of the skin causes dilation of the peripheral vessels, that stroking near the sexual region, especially the abdomen, excites the sexual organs, as noted above. Repeated manipulation of the armpits and the soles of the feet with fairly gentle, short strokes causes irregular respiratory movements, contraction of the facial muscles, and characteristic defense reactions, which result in laughter or even hilarity. Lastly, gross stimuli which prick or injure the skin arouse violent and lasting

[8] The influence of these glands upon the uterus before birth is not taken into consideration here.

defense reactions, accompanied by the rush of blood to the face and shedding of tears.[9]

Restraining movements arouse the muscular activity of attack, characterized by increased muscular energy and tonus, violent contraction of the muscles, corresponding changes in facial expression, strong heart action, and a rush of blood to the surface of the body, especially the face.

The acquired somato-mimetic reflexes, which develop as a result of the relations between the individual and his environment, are later superimposed upon the innate, inherited somato-mimetic reflexes. It is easy to trace the development of these conditioned mimetic reflexes in a baby. For instance, satiety is followed by a general quieting, relaxation of the limbs, reddening of the face, and consequent smoothening of the features, which gives a peculiar expression of physical satisfaction with time. But, even very soon after birth, the mere placing of one's arm under the back of the crying, hungry child (an act which usually precedes the process of taking him into the arms for nursing), suffices to produce the quieting effect—the moving limbs relax and the folds of the face smooth out.

The smile and other somato-mimetic movements are developed in the same way. The gentle touching of the child's cheek with two fingers (the thumb and the index finger) very soon after birth causes a contraction of the cheeks which resembles a smile. After this stimulus has been repeated many times, a smile may be induced by merely bringing the fingers near the face without actually touching it. Very much later the conditioned secretion of saliva at the mere sight of food originates in the same manner; similarly the secretion of tears and the secretion from the nose in response to external stimuli which do not involve touching the skin, as well as the cardio-vascular reactions which belong to the complex of somato-mimetic reflexes.

If we trace the development of somato-mimetic reflexes in babies and animals, it is easy to see that all of them originate as conditioned reflexes superimposed upon the ordinary reflexes which appear shortly after birth. All the various somato-mimetic expressions of adults gradually develop in the same way as life-experience goes on. Similarly, conscious stimuli bring about the further development and differentiation of those somato-mimetic conditioned reflexes which give greater expressiveness to human conversation. On the other hand, social stimuli inhibit the

[9] The shedding of tears is itself a defense reaction, for the tear serves to protect the eye just as the secretion of saliva serves to protect against acid stimuli.

manifestation of those somato-mimetic reflexes which are contrary to the social interests of the individual. Finally some of these reflexes acquire a symbolical character by undergoing various modifications, and so become a mimical speech. The development of somato-mimetic reflexes in adult life takes place just as it does in childhood. For instance it has been shown that mere concentration upon work produces a change in the circulation, and that muscular work is preceded by the dilation of the blood-vessels of the muscles (Leber). Analogous phenomena are observed in those somato-mimetic reflexes which involve a state of tension of the striated muscles, as anger.

As we have already seen, the experiments performed with milking sheep in my laboratory show that the mere sight of the approaching lamb or even its cry causes the secretion of milk. The same thing happens in women. After a woman has nursed a child a fairly long time, the mere thought of nursing causes the breasts to fill with milk (Greving). Needless to say, the visceral phenomena, which play a part in the complex of somato-mimetic reflexes, develop as conditioned reflexes.

We now know that all the conditioned reflexes of the internal organs are developed by the vago-sympathetic system. Such are the contractions of the throat, oesophagus, stomach, and intestine, the changes of pulse and blood-pressure, changes in size of the blood-vessels, perspiration, secretion of bile and gastric juice, micturition, and defecation. In general, the endocrine glands react upon the conditioned stimuli, thereby causing an abnormal excitation of the sympatheticus or vagus. Cannon has shown experimentally that stimulation of the nerves of the suprarenal capsules causes a hypersecretion of the thyroid gland just as does a small does of adrenalin. On the other hand, it is known that the somato-mimetic state may bring about not only glycosuria but also suppression of menstruation and sudden disappearance of milk.

Such states generally disturb the equilibrium between the vegetative and endocrine systems. According to Ken, traumatic syndrome causes a poisoning which originates in the tissues, especially the traumatized muscles (histamin). Shocks which cause no organic injury may also be classed with emotions (Ballet, "*Les commotions sont des émotions*"), for the *Ashnerov* symptom, the disturbances of the heart rhythm, and the vasomotor changes which they involve are directly dependent upon the increased excitation and disturbances of the vegetative nervous system.

Cardio-vascular phenomena also belong to the conditioned reflexes of the somato-mimetic type. For instance, a state of gladness arouses faster and stronger heart-beats—an effect which is produced directly by the increased sympathico-vagotonia, the sympathicus predominating. In fright the heart-beat is weaker and interrupted, the pulse is irregular and may stop altogether. In this case vagotonia, which occurs as a conditioned reflex, is highly predominant. The peripheral vessels dilate in gladness; they contract in fright. In conclusion we may say that the success of the reflexological method shows that the somato-mimetic reflexes may be studied experimentally.

The emotional or somato-mimetic reflex was aroused artificially many years ago. In the preliminary experiments made by Dr. Czaly an electrical current was used. The strength of the current was such that, when applied to the sole of the foot, it aroused not only the defensive reflex—jerking away the leg—but also reflexes of the cardio-vascular and respiratory systems. It was shown that, when the electrical stimulus is associated with an indifferent external stimulus, the subject gives a conditioned cardio-vascular reflex, which can be differentiated just as a conditioned motor reflex can be. Further work done by Dr. Schneierson upon conditioned motor reflexes aroused by electrical stimulation of the fingers has shown that, in some sensitive subjects, this stimulation is accompanied by a somato-mimetic reflex, which may also be produced by the indifferent conditioned stimulus—in this case auditory.

These investigations supply experimental proof that the somato-mimetic states originate as conditioned reflexes.

As early as 1913 I began publishing a series of papers, in which I showed that even general neurotic cases and cases of sexual abnormality may be analyzed by the reflexological method.[10] Pathological somato-mimetic states of a persistent, annoying nature originate like other reflexes of the laboratory type. As a rule an external stimulus of a given nature, which arouses a definite somato-mimetic state under certain conditions, establishes the reflex in persons of a pathologically excitable constitution. With time it becomes a habitual conditioned reflex.

We have also developed a therapy for such annoying somato-mimetic states,[11] including a special conditioned reflex therapy,

[10] "Concerning Phobias and Their Cure," *Russki Vratch*, XIV (1915); "On the Development of Phobias," *Psychological Review*, XXIII (1916), *et al.*; "Sexual Abnormality in the Light of Reflexology," *Voprosi Izucheniya i Vospitaniya Lichnosti*, nos. 4 and 5, 1922, *Archiv für Psychiatrie und Nervenkrankheiten*, LXVIII (1923); "Sexual Perversion as Conditioned upon the Sexual Reflex," *Pedagogitcheski Sbornik* (Leningrad: Yefron, 1925); "Concerning the Perversion and Inversion of Sexual Desire from the Standpoint of Reflexology," *Polovoi Voprosi* (Moscow: Gosisdat, 1925).

[11] V. Bakhterev, *Russki Vratch*, XIV (1915).

which has been applied successfully to the more elementary phenomena of general neuroses (anaesthesia, paralysis) as well as to complex annoying acts.[12] It has been applied to such childish states as those characterized by kleptomania, in which the emotion of satisfaction is associated with the annoying act of theft. This method of conditioned reflex therapy, which involves the association of the defensive reflex aroused by reflexogenic stimuli (electric current) with the words, "Do not take," (Osipov, Oparin), has proven quite satisfactory, for stubborn kleptomania in children has been completely eradicated after several of these sittings held at weekly intervals. Our results are closely related to the investigations of Watson in America. Watson was able to develop the somato-mimetic reflex of fear of a white mouse in children by striking a metal bar with a hammer. The reflex was thus aroused by a number of animals (irradiation or generalization of the reflex).[13]

The author regards the above method as the most helpful of the many methods used to suppress the somato-mimetic emotional reflex. Experiments have been performed which involve the introduction of the object of fear while the child is eating breakfast. The object (a rabbit) was brought near to the child on several successive days, until finally the child would drink milk from one hand and caress the rabbit with the other.

There is no reason to doubt that the strictly objective biosocial or reflexological method of investigation, which originated here and has been developed in America, has placed the problem of emotions as somato-mimetic reflexes upon an experimental basis, and has given a great impetus to the development of an exact understanding of these complicated states of the human being.

DR. WALTER B. CANNON (*Harvard University*) requested that the following questions be submitted to Dr. Bekhterev:

1. What is the basis for the statement that the vegetative nervous system determines the tone of skeletal muscle?

2. What is the evidence that the adrenal gland is innervated by parasympathetic fibers, and that the sex glands are innervated by both sympathetic and parasympathetic nerve supplies?

[12] V. Bekhterev, "On the Therapeutic Significance of the Conditioned Reflexes in Hysterical Anaesthesia and Paralysis," *Obozrenie Psikhiatri, Nevrologi, i Eksperimentalnoi Psikhologi*, XI–XII (1917–18). "On Conditioned Reflex Therapy," *Sanitarno Meditsinski Vestnik*, 1925.

[13] J. B. Watson, *The Pedagogical Seminary and Journal of Genetic Psychology* XXXIII (1925).

CHAPTER 24

EMOTIONS IN ANIMALS AND MAN

HENRI PIÉRON

University of Paris

I

In the lower organisms, the protozoans, which are the least differentiated, reactions to stimuli show only slight variation, and reduce practically to the avoidance of certain excitations and attraction toward certain others. These positive and negative responses may be characterized as affective reactions of a primitive sort.

In the more complex organisms, where part-responses appear, we can distinguish diffuse affective reactions of avoidance and attraction on the one hand, and stereotyped reactions to certain stimuli, the adapted ·reflexes, on the other. But, when one watches the development of reactions which become gradually stereotyped with repetition, one ascertains beyond all doubt that these reactions originally constitute a part of a complex affective response and play a definite rôle in a general activity of avoidance and attraction. This may lead one to believe that the same holds true for reactions which have become congenital, and so, to affirm the primacy of the affective reaction, from which the reflex would be derived through the process of mnemonic automatization, with repetition.

In animals at the higher stages of evolution, the reaction systems are extremely numerous and complicated, the reflexes are multiplied, and it is very easy to witness the development of less stable automatic reactions in the form of conditioned reflexes. Under the given conditions, a general competition is set up between possible modes of activity, and prediction of results becomes very difficult in default of knowledge of the precise resistance of the action systems, a resistance which depends upon numerous factors, both past and present. The analysis of the behavior of the higher animals and man shows an elaboration of action, which strives to provide the best means of attaining a certain end, affectively determined.

Thought, which is theoretically reducible to a complex play of more or less stereotyped mental reactions of the conditioned reflex type, *functions only under the affective impulse, which alone prescribes the ends of action.* From the amoeba to man, action is always essentially affective, even when it occurs in the preparatory form which it may assume in the most highly trained animals, the purely mental form of thought.

Modern psychology, of a biological spirit, is called upon to recognize this fundamental rôle of affection in governing the interests, *even in the play of intellectual processes.* If we think of the facts physiologically and trace the play of thought to the activation of complex associative circuits, then we will identify the intellectual sphere of man with the nervous pathways of the cortex as a whole, the circuits provided by the new brain, and we will attribute to the affective sphere, localized in the old brain, the regulation of nervous activity along these pathways, the regulation of the functional dynamism of the nervous impulse.

A network of railroads furnishing numerous and well-distributed pathways is not sufficient; the trains must also be steered and hurtled along the pathways in a number and with a speed suitable to needs. The intellectual sphere is built up just as is the network of railroads; but the regulation of the functioning of the network, sensitive to the variable needs of traffic, is comparable to the affective regulation of thought.[1]

Nervous functioning in all its forms, including the mental form, requires a certain specific expenditure of energy, connected with the *nervous impulse.* What is the precise nature of nervous energy? Does it obey the laws of thermodynamics? These are problems which have not yet been definitely settled. But one does not need to await their solution before utilizing a concept which is indispensable to all general theory of psychophysiology. In the neurones there are reserves of energy, accumulated in the course of normal metabolism, which are expended during functional activity, but their utilization is dependent upon certain liberative stimulations. *It is the affective sphere, acting as regulator, that gives rise to the stimulations, which release the more or less copious discharges into the nervous pathways of thought and action.*

To the intellectual sphere belong the qualities, the modalities; to the affective sphere, the general direction and the quantity.

Now the idea of emotion seems to be associated with a quantitative aspect, a certain level, of the affect. The difference between the moderate interest taken in a theatrical performance and the keen emotion which it arouses, whatever may be the precise nature of the feelings involved—pain, fear, pity, pleasure, or enthusiasm—

[1] Cf. H. Piéron, *Thought and the Brain* (London: Kegan Paul; New York: Harcourt, Brace, 1927), Part IV, "The Affective Regulation of Mental Life," p. 229 ff.

is essentially a quantitative one. But at what moment during the continuous increasing of the affect has one the right to speak of emotion?

Evidently there is a conventional element in the application of the terminology in this case, as in all our classifications, in which we are compelled to establish more or less arbitrary cleavages in a continuous series. The examination of cases which we agree to speak of as emotion leads us to suppose that the word is employed whenever the behavior of the individual reveals either violence or disorder. A child injures one of his comrades, the latter replies by slapping him in the face, and the response is affective; but, if he gets red in the face, stamps his foot, trembles, and slaps violently, then he is in a rage, he is prey to an emotion. Between the slap given calmly without any other noticeable manifestation of the affect and the scene of the rage, all sorts of transitions are possible. Where should we draw the line? In the search for a criterion, let us appeal to the emotional expressions found in animals.

II

An animal is threatened; he gives a defense reaction, a stereotyped reflex, or a more plastic and better adapted response. This reaction is generally connected with an affective orientation of behavior tending toward flight or aggression. There is no reason for invoking the existence of an emotion. But, in addition to the defense reaction, the animal displays processes which are foreign to this reaction and, like it, are aroused by the threatening stimulus. This is the emotional reaction.

I lift a rock which has been left exposed by the ocean; I perceive a poulp, an *Octopus*, covered with little stones, motionless; I try to seize it, and the animal moves away hastily, or, if I take hold of it, grasps my hand in its tentacles so as to bite me with its horny beak. These are the adapted defense reactions which the animal has at its disposal. But, at the same time, its chromatophores are frantically displaying continual changes of color, which pass over its skin like shivers,[2] and its pupils become abnormally dilated. These manifestations, which are foreign to the defense mechanism, reveal a violent emotion.

The toads (*Phrynosoma cornutum*) studied by Redfield,[3] also

[2] These displays of tegumentary coloration have sometimes been regarded as a defense reaction belonging to the class of "terrifying attitudes," such as have been noted among the snakes, the lizards (*Varanus*), the spiders, the mantes, etc. But, in reality, the paling or darkening of the tegument cannot be regarded as possessing a terrifying value in itself.

[3] A. C. Redfield, "The Reactions of the Melanophores of the Horned Toad," *Proceedings of the National Academy of Sciences*, III (1917), 202.

showed chromatophore reactions under the influence of certain emotional stimuli—paling by contraction of the dark pigment cells and also by an ordinary mechanism which might be considered an exaggeration of the secretion of adrenalin and the characteristic hyperglycemia found in the higher animals, such as the cat and man, during emotion. These occur along with visible changes, many of which also involve the skin, as horripilation.

Intense reactions which play no part in the functional activity of the animal constitute a criterion of emotion. But hasty reactions which are unsuited to the present circumstances may be indicative of the emotional state. If a person hurts himself on a table and begins to pound the table or to break a plate, we do not hesitate to say that he is angry. An ant, coming upon a spot of soil near its nest, which has been saturated with the odor of foreign ants, sometimes begins to strike the ground violently with its mandibles, instead of being content to flee or to explore carefully the neighborhood of the suspicious place.[4] In this case it well shows that it is a prey to anger. The same is true of animals which, if held still so that they cannot bite their enemies, take to biting themselves in their anger.

We will now consider some cases which border on the limits of the emotional level of the affect. The reactions shown are indeed defense reactions, but they are of an exceptional nature and do not normally occur under conditions where they would be necessary for the conservation of life, except when the affective shock is present. I borrow examples from my researches on autotomy.[5] (Autotomy appears to be like a reflex set off by the violent excitation of the nerve of the claw. Leon Fredericq has asserted, in his classic monograph,[6] that this is the only possible mechanism of autotomy in the crab.)

We know that many of the Arthropoda (crustaceans, insects) amputate their own limbs under certain conditions. For example, let us take a crab, and cut deeply the meropodite (third joint) of one claw; the claw breaks off and falls into our hands. Let us now tie a crab to a stick by a wire attached to one claw, and leave it alone after placing food near it but out of its reach; after one or

---

[4] I have verified this fact in the course of my researches upon the olfactory recognition of ants: *Comptes rendus de la Société de Biologie*, LXI (1906), 385, 433, 471; and *Comptes rendus de l'Académie des Sciences*, CXLIII, 845.

[5] H. Piéron, "Le problème de l'autotomie," *Bulletin scientifique* XLII (1908), 185–246. Cf. also *Archives internationales de physiologie*, V (1907), 110–121.

[6] *Archives de biologie*, III (1882), 235. *Archives de zoologie expérimentale et générale*, II (1883), ser. I, 413. Cf. also the article "Autotomie" in the *Dictionnaire de Physiologie*, II (1895), 952.

more days we will find it there, still tied, unable to free itself, dying on the spot.[7]

Now let us release a poulp, the most dangerous of its enemies, near to the tied crab, and we will see the latter amputate its limb and escape. In such exceptional cases the reaction is set off by what we believe may be termed an emotional shock, an emotion of fear.

This has been verified with *Carcinus maenas*, in which autotomy is obtained only by the reflex to strong stimulation of the nerve, except in this case.[8] With other crabs, less intense emotions are sufficient to set off autotomy. In the Grapsidae, for example, sudden seizure is sufficient to cause the abandonment of the claws; and if the animal is tied among the rocks, a sudden movement of the hand, as though to seize it, brings about the immediate autotomic liberation, which only the sight of the poulp can cause in *Carcinus*.

A crab, held upon its back by forceps, suddenly removes its claws when I pick its carapace with the point of a scalpel, as a result of the painful shock, which sets up an emotional state.

Autotomy of a tied claw occurs also in the pagurians, when one makes a swift movement as though to seize them. They react by retreating into their shell.

Some Diptera (the tipulids) remain caught by the legs without self-amputation, and one may hold them by the extremities of the legs without their flying away, whereas the grasping of the femur causes immediate reflex autotomy. But the tipulid completely abandons its leg the moment that it is seized, or when it is held by the tibia and a grasping gesture is made.

I have further verified the same facts with various Orthoptera. An oedipod (*Oedipoda coerulescens, Oedipoda minata*) tied by the tibia will die without freeing itself unless its femur is pinched, but it amputates its legs immediately and takes to flight when a mantis, its dangerous enemy, approaches it.[9]

[7] In most cases a specific mechanism, functioning by performed anatomical structures, brings about the self-amputation of the member at a definite place; sometimes there is a simple pulling out of the member, breaking at the weakest point (*autospasie*); finally, certain Orthoptera (phasgonurids) amputate their anterior legs with their mandibles, a mechanism which Rabaud and I have noted and termed "autopsalize." Piéron and Rabaud, *Comptes rendus de la Société de Biologie*, XCI (1924), 362.

[8] The fact has been noted before by Parize, *Revue scientifique*, II (1886), 379. It has been systematically studied by a pupil of Fredericq J. Roskam, who verified my results, *Archives internationales de physiologie*, XII (1912), 474.

[9] H. Piéron, "Les formes élémentaires de l'émotion dans le comportement animal," *Journal de psychologie*, XVII (1920), 937.

III

The emotional level of the affect is first reached when the reactions to a given situation show an abnormal, exceptional intensity. In anger, or when the presence of danger causes an overexcitation of the instinct of self-preservation, the muscular strength is increased by considerable amounts; weights which would have seemed impossible to lift are lifted, forced marches are accomplished, the speed of running may be considerably increased. Fear, they say, gives wings.

It is very evident that changes are not produced in the muscles, but that the nervous excitations for the muscular contractions attain exceptional levels of intensity, compensating for the decreases in functional capacity of the muscles due to local fatigue.

The mental abilities, power of attention, rapidity of elaboration, etc., may also be noticeably augmented in pressing danger. A violent emotion may reinforce memory, and give rise to indelible associations.[10]

The emotional exaltation, the excessive discharge of nervous energy, which is expended in mental elaboration or in motor execution, is highly favorable to the protection—to the defense of the individual. But there is another side to the story. These exceptional expenditures are followed by an exhaustion which demands a long period of recuperation and may have pathological consequences, especially when emotions are frequently repeated.

Moreover, this excessive discharge of nervous energy is useful only in so far as it finds utilization in the situation in which the individual is placed. A stag, threatened by a pack of wolves, manages to gain upon his pursuers by his swiftness, and utilizes all the energy which his emotion generously discharges for the force and rapidity of the movements of running. An angry man vanquishes many enemies, thanks to his ten-times increased strength. But here is a cat in a cage, threatened by a dog, and prey to a violent emotion, although it does not need to fight; here is a man prey to a violent anger because he is injured in an anonymous letter, although he does not know on whom to lay hands. In such cases the expenditures of nervous energy represent a pure waste, exhausting for no purpose. The threatened cat mews, hisses, bristles, crouches to leap; the injured man cries out, strikes the table, grits his teeth—all that in vain.

[10] In my book, *L'évolution de la mémoire* (Paris: Flammarion, 1910), I noted this fact in the case of a lizard which, after biting a particularly nauseous caterpillar, consistently refused thereafter to touch a caterpillar; he had acquired then and there an experience which remained fixed.

But all the nervous energy which emotion discharges is not utilized by motor reactions; part of it finds its way into the vegetative system. The sympathetic and parasympathetic nerves receive stimulations, which are translated into changes in respiration, the heart-beat, the state of the blood-vessels, the tonus and contractility of the smooth muscles, the secretory activity of the glands, etc.

Finalistic biases have lead to an interpretation of these secretory, circulatory, and visceral reactions as useful elements in the activity of defense. A case in point is the conceptions of Cannon, from which Watson has derived the idea of emotion as "visceral and glandular instinct."[11]

But, when we see that these vegetative reactions sometimes end in death,[12] that they usually paralyze the defense mechanism, and that they lead to pathological states which are often serious, we become skeptical as to the value of finalistic interpretations.

The phenomena of cerebral vasoconstriction from emotion involve the loss of the use of the legs and fainting, which may also result from a syncope due to excessive inhibitory action of the vagus nerve upon the heart. The relaxation of the bladder sphincter and the colic pains resulting from exaggerated peristaltic movements of the intestines do not facilitate the useful defense reactions. Although the increased secretion of adrenalin by the suprarenals, along with the hyperglycemia involved, which is indicated by a certain amount of glycosuria, may be regarded as favorable, the other glandular activities which may take the form either of functional acceleration or of inhibition[13] certainly cannot be invoked in support of finalistic conceptions.

In reading Darwin, we smile at the childishness of his detailed utilitarian explanation of the expression of emotion. Apparently the muscles of the face simply participate in the arousal of general

[11] J. B. Watson, *Psychology from the Standpoint of a Behaviorist* (Philadelphia: Lippincott, 1919), p. 195.

[12] Certain birds which are subject to tachycardia and palpitation of the heart die without being wounded, when handled, and I have seen a kitten, which was kept tied for a physiological experiment, die without suffering an injury. On this question, see the observations and researches of E. Martin and Roja Villanova, "La mort subite ou rapide par choc émotionnel," *Journal de médicine de Lyon*, VII (1926), 543.

[13] G. Dumas and Malloizel have promulgated what they have called "the polyglandular expression" of emotions, *Journal de psychologie*, VII (1910), 63. Anger in the dog causes an increased secretion of urine and saliva. In fear, the inhibition of the salivary secretion makes the throat dry, and the digestion is disturbed by the sudden suppression of the gastric juice, while the cold sweats instance the excitation of the perspiration.

motor activity under the influence of an intense, diffused nervous excitation, as the analysis made by G. Dumas well shows.[14]

Of the vegetative reactions, there are some which may be useful, there are some which are unquestionably harmful, while a large number are indifferent. At any rate, they do not fit into a finalistic systematization, but, on the contrary, taken as a total, they appear to confer upon emotion an actual pathogenic value.[15]

Emotion may give rise to true hemoclasic shocks, with all the consequences of these shocks, especially in certain individuals. Benard and Joltrain have produced experimentally a characteristic hemoclasic crisis in a patient suffering from exophthalmic goiter and having fits of asthma as a result of a fright, by using an unexpected detonation close by as an emotional shock.[16]

IV

It seems to us, therefore, that emotion is associated with an affective discharge of abnormally intense nervous energy. A part of this energy is utilized for the useful, adapted reactions, which may be accelerated and reinforced to an exceptional degree. But a more or less considerable part is expended in useless motor reactions (like the reactions of the facial muscles), and even finds its way into the vegetative organs, where many different reactions are produced,[17] varying accordingly as the excitatory or inhibitory systems are stimulated, and where injurious or even pathogenic processes are aroused.

The overflow of the excess discharge of nervous energy into the visceral organs has been explained by Lapicque in the light of his general conception of *chronasie* and the shunting of the nervous

[14] G. Dumas, "L'expression des émotions" in *Traité de psychologie* (Paris: Alcan, 1923), I, 606.

[15] At the present time, we know of well-certified cases of various diseases, in which emotions played the essential pathogenic rôle: cases of jaundice, nettle-rash, eczema, asthma, diabetes, glaucoma, scurf, (including the *canities brusques*), exophthalmic goiter (with persistent tachycardia and tremors, etc.).

[16] *Bulletins et mémoires de la Société Médicale des Hopitaux de Paris*, 42nd year (1926), 1155.

[17] Many medicines have opposite effects depending upon the size of the dose or the phase of the action. The intensity and duration of emotion also play a part. In Italian soldiers sentenced to be shot and warned of it the day before, Gualino has noted tachycardia and increased blood-pressure, soon followed by a large decrease in heart rate and of arterial pressure, *Rivista di psicologia*, XVI (1920), 42. Finally, there may be variations due to the functional condition of the organs at the time of the emotion. Thus Sinelnikov has demonstrated that emotion arrests movements in an active segment of the intestine and instigates them in a quiescent segment, Pflüger's *Archiv für die gesamte Physiologie*, CCXIII (1926), 239.

impulse by the syntony of the neurones.[18]   The impulse in one neurone arouses an impulse in the neurones with which it is connected the more easily when the specific vibration rate of the latter is near its own.   When the impulse is not very intense, the neurones simply respond synchronously with the neurones of equal *chronasie*, as is the case in the reflexes.   If the intensity of the impulse increases, neurones which are more and more dischronous come into play.   When emotion arouses particularly intense impulses, the torrent of excitation overflows the paths of the adapted reactions and produces a general diffusion of this excitation.   The visceral overflow of the emotional excitation takes place more easily in some individuals than in others, and circumstances also have an effect.

It is when the normal utilization of the excessive discharge of energy for the defense reactions is impossible, and especially when motor activity is impeded, that the emotion comes to be diverted to visceral reactions.   In this connection I would mention a fact which seems to establish well the existence of a certain mutual compensation between motor reaction and visceral reaction.

During the war my colleague, Derrien, and I studied the influence which the lumbar puncture exerts, through its psychical effects, upon the amount of sugar in the blood and the cerebro-spinal fluid.[19]   When the puncture involved an emotion, repeated blood tests showed increased glycemia, accompanied by increase in the amount of sugar in the cerebro-spinal fluid, whereas, in the absence of emotion, there was no variation.   For example, in two paretic patients, the glycemia (measured in grams per liter) was 1 to 1.24 gr. before the puncture, 0.95 to 1.20 gr. after it; and, in two imbeciles, 1.31 and 1.01 gr. before, 1.30 and 1.02 gr. afterwards.   These patients had remained indifferent.   But here are two emotional soldiers, who are restless, cry out, and writhe when punctured; in one the amount of sugar increased from 0.98 to 1.08 gr., in the other from 1.06 to 1.26 gr.   Finally, here are three restless soldiers, who, due to their military discipline, offer no resistance, suppress all agitation, inhibit their motor reactions, and try to conceal their emotion—their glycemic reactions are especially high, due to compensation; in one the amount increased from 1.0 to 1.25 gr., in the second from 1.25 to 1.46 gr., and in the third from 0.85 to 1.27 gr., an increase of 50% in this last case.

[18] L. Lapicque, "Essai d'une nouvelle théorie physiologique de l'émotion," *Journal de psychologie*, VIII (1911), 1.

[19] E. Derrien and H. Piéron, "De la réaction glycemique émotionnelle," *Journal de psychologie*, XX (1923), 533.

V

The pathogenic action of emotion, connected in part with the nervous exhaustion resulting from the excessive discharge of energy, especially when a subject is submitted to a regular emotional *surmenage*, to repeated violent shocks, is dependent chiefly upon disturbances in the endocrine equilibrium, hemoclasic shocks, and functional disorders of organs which eliminate poisons, such as the liver,[20] that is to say, vegetative reactions. It is normal, therefore, that this pathogenic action should be particularly marked when the visceral expression is strongest, when the normal defense reactions are consequently rendered impossible, and when the discharged nervous energy cannot be used in motor activity. These conditions were found peculiarly combined during the trench warfare of 1914–1918, and that explains why there have been so many diseases of emotional origin among the soldiers who have experienced violent bombardments.

In particular, there very frequently occurs an "emotional syndrome," which A. Mairet and I identified very early in the course of the war by distinguishing it from the purely shock syndrome resulting from accidents in the air (involving functional neurone troubles and hemorrhages from the small capillaries of the medullar and cerebral regions.[21]

The essential elements of this syndrome include: (1) emotional anaphylaxis, a state of hyperexcitability taking the form of restlessness or of fear, often going to the extent of delirious hallucinations at the beginning, and revealing itself for a long time by persistent nightmares; (2) extreme mental fatigue, evidencing nervous exhaustion from emotion, with aprosexia, fixatory amnesia, slowness of speech, easy confusion; (3) finally, headaches aggravated by mental effort. In the pure shock syndrome, the most noticeable symptoms are inertia, staring, indifference, sometimes accompanied by anger reactions. There is also considerable retrograde amnesia, anaesthesia, and vertigo.

The emotional syndrome often occurs entirely apart from any pathological tendencies, individual or hereditary (in ten out of thirty-five cases of pure emotional syndrome in which I was able

---

[20] In the frightened cat Buscaino has found changes in the blood, the liver, the suprarenals, the thyroid, the ovary or testicles, etc., "Richerche biochimiche in animali normali ed in animali emozionati," *Rivista di patologia nervosa e mentale*, XXIV (1919), 2.

[21] A. Mairet and H. Piéron, "Le syndrome commotionnel dans les traumatismes de guerre," *Bulletin de l'Académie de Médicine*, LXXII (1915), 654, 690, 710; "Le syndrome émotionnel, sa différentiation du syndrome commotionnel, "*Annales médico-psychologiques*, LXXIII (1917), 183.

to obtain adequate information regarding the history of the individual and of the family), thus proving, from the nervous and mental point of view, the pathological nature of repeated emotions in conditions where the normal defense mechanisms are not generally called into play.

SUMMARY

Thus it seems to us that emotion may be described as an extreme level of the affect, tending toward the pathological as a limit. It consists essentially in an abnormal discharge of nervous energy, a discharge which exceeds the amount which can be used for the normal reactions of the individual, and which occurs even when there is no occasion for reaction. It consequently involves a diffusion of excitatory impulses into the viscera, which, on the whole, seems to be not only useless, but harmful, and even pathogenic, adding its own ill effects to the nervous exhaustion which results from the excessive expenditures of discharged energy.

These expressions of emotion are found only among the higher animals, whose associative nervous centers are well developed, the different species varying considerably in emotional susceptibility. It is in the Hymenoptera, the Cephalopoda, and at least the higher Vertebrata[22] (all of which have associative areas either in suboesophagal nervous ganglia, or in the brain) that we find the characteristic expressions of emotion, which take the form of agitation, of cutaneous, cardio-vascular, and visceral manifestations.

It is probable that these centers contribute a reserve of nervous energy releasable under the influence of intense affective shock, and that it is the sudden expenditure of this energy which brings about the overflow into motor and visceral organs. In man, when the susceptibility to emotion is high enough so that there is a strong power of affective mobilization and a high degree of instability in the reserves of energy, the cortical reservoir seems to constitute a real danger, just as do large ponds established along a water course, which accumulate the available energy and may cause disastrous inundations if the barriers begin to give way before a sudden onslaught.

[22] Certain birds which fall victim to the fascination of snakes owe their death to an extreme emotional state, which involves intense visceral reactions, along with motor inhibition, such as are produced in man by extreme terror.

PART IV

Pathology and Psychoanalysis of
Feeling and Emotion

CHAPTER 25

FEAR OF ACTION AS AN ESSENTIAL ELEMENT IN THE SENTIMENT OF MELANCHOLIA

PIERRE JANET
University of Paris

In order to understand the true psychological character of the feelings it is necessary to analyze the often complex attitudes which characterize and even constitute, more often than we think, our diverse feelings. One of these most important attitudes may be called "fear of action"—the fear of acting. This attitude may be observed in its typical form during the crises of melancholic depression, prolonged or transient; but in the exaggerated and slightly ridiculous form, it shows us the caricature of what we often enough are experiencing ourselves while we are sad. These pathological feelings tell us about the veritable nature of sadness and its dangers.

I

One of the things which strike even an inexperienced observer when he speaks to a patient who is in the grip of melancholy is that the ideas, the particular opinions he expresses with regard to the surrounding things and any events of which one speaks to him are always pessimistic and catastrophic appreciations.

From the very first, all things and people have lost their agreeable qualities and all charm; nothing is beautiful, nothing is pretty. A sick woman of this type used to recognize the beginning of her spell by the bizarre detail that the landscape she could see from her window did not look pretty anymore, whereas from experience she knew that it should be pretty. This is the feeling of devalorization, the feeling of emptiness of which we shall not speak now. These feelings develop rapidly, and the objects become ugly, deformed, adulterated, and dirty. "Everything in the house is ignoble, ugly, and dirty; everything is sad and lugubrious." Let me point out to you the feelings of a young man driving an automobile on a rather long ride. At the start he is proud to show his ability; he admires the landscape and invites his companions to do so; soon he stops speaking and makes a sombre face, since the landscape has become "ugly" and, above all, "lugubrious." "It is," he thinks, "as though we are rolling and rolling through one cemetery after another."

All events of which we speak to these patients are valued in the same way, especially when future events are concerned. These events will be horrible in every respect; they will have sacrilegious, immoral, cruel consequences; they will afflict all those we love with terrific sufferings. "We are going to be robbed, massacred; if people come to see me, it is to rob me of my civil position, to steal the gold in my teeth, to tear out my eyes." "If the sun rises tomorrow there will be disaster, for sun and moon hurled against each other by God will smash each other, and the débris will fall upon the earth, burning and annihilating us; the whole world around me suffers and dies."

To study these facts I choose two particularly typical examples, whose mechanism we shall then discuss. A girl, twenty-seven years old, who figures in my books as Flora, when very exhausted has one of those asthenic spells during which the periods of melancholic feelings often and unexpectedly befall. She is at a sanatorium, isolated and at rest. I think to please her in announcing that her brother's wife, of whom she is very fond, has borne a child, and that they intend bringing her the baby to have a look at him and kiss him. "Don't do that," she answers. "The automobile will dash into the trees by the street; my mother, the nurse, the child will be crushed, oh! what horror!" Another time I ask her: "Are you willing to see your mother and sister?" She: "It would be very painful for me to see them in mourning." I: "But the ladies are not in mourning." She: "If they must come and see me, my father and my brother will be dead, and then they will come in mourning." And then she adds intelligently: "I cannot help this; it is a kind of catastrophic vision that is putting all things together. I lose my foothold, people wish me bad luck, mother scares me, everything is gloomy, the street looks gloomy, even the sun looks gloomy." Another example is just as typical: Daniel, forty years old, is busy selecting a country home for his family; a particular house does not displease him and he is willing to rent it. However, immediately one thought invades his mind. Now he knows what in that house was appealing to him: the rather beautiful, monumental entrance door would look fine when draped in black above the coffin of his wife. Another day he hesitates to go home, because he would find the staircase crowded with bearers ready to carry down the coffins of his children.

Undoubtedly these two patients are not entirely delirious, and these ideas present themselves as something like obsessions, the absurdity of which they are able to see, at least for some moments. But there are others who would assert far more foolish ideas with all signs of deep conviction. The woman of whom I have just spoken is sure that the stars would smash each other, and she already sees the beginning of the catastrophe. Another woman whom I used to call Sophie[1] asserts that she sees before her, in the alley through which we are going to pass, the corpses of her parents, on which we necessarily must step. I will not expound here on the different degrees of persuasions, but only on the content of those catastrophic ideas.

These ideas seem to refer to things and events external, but, let us not be mistaken, they are nothing but an extension of pessimistic appreciation; at the bottom of all this there is a fundamental object to which above all this appreciation refers, and that is the patient himself and his own deeds. The patient, in spite of appearances, is not unaware of this disorder of things. When that woman tells us that she sees the stars like fireballs shoot against each other to be crushed into chaos by God, she sadly adds: "I should not like, however, to destroy the work of God." I: "But this does not concern you; if the stars are blinded, and God drives them against each other, it is their business and not yours." She: "Why yes! I don't know just how, but I *am* mixed up in it; however, it is my fault, because I have soiled my hands with evil." At the bottom they all accuse themselves. Flora feels sure that she plays a part in the smashing of the automobile, for she adds: "If they came to visit another person, the car would not run into the tree." When I suggest to Daniel that I go up the stairs, instead of him, to see whether the hearse-drivers have finished their sinister job, so that he may come in, he replies, "It would not be worth while; if you go, there won't be any coffins there." Briefly, they play their part in those catastrophes; it is their own action that produces them, and *they objectivate in their persuasions a feeling they have in relation to themselves and to their actions.* It is indeed always the pessimistic appreciation of their own action which is essential.

It is, by the way, easy to verify this statement. The patients mentioned above, or others whose delirium is not so far advanced, show their unfavorable beliefs are not always relating to the external object, but that they refer directly to the actions. We find a great number of persuasions of this kind which attribute to the act the most horrible characteristics. Acts are considered abominable and sacrilegious from the religious point of view. "I am insulting God and all that is holy if I make one step. If I wash

[1] *De l'angoisse a l'extase* (Paris: Alcan, 1926), I, 337.

myself I lose my heaven. I do horrible things to the dead if I advance in this alley. In stepping forward I should walk on my father's corpse. I make my brother stir in his grave if I pant, if I breathe." One poor fellow, a very good musician, stops playing his violin, declaring: "Whenever I play the violin I have the feeling that I annoy God." And he adds: "When I do anything *whatever* (no matter what) I have the feeling of acting against God's divine will."

Of course this feeling of sacrilegious doing may be toned down, and the act appears as simply immoral and cruel. Daniel, for example, has bought toys for his children, but does not give them to them; for months he keeps the packets unopened. He says: "If I give my children these toys, I make them suffer deadly tortures; their destiny is tied to these parcels and if I open them I put the seal on their death warrant." By the way, the poor man sometimes has the same feeling with regard to anything he does. He has ordered new shirts, but does not wear them; he even tries to take them back to the merchant, since he is convinced that he will wear them at the burial of his children, and that he would expedite that burial.

To a great number of patients, all acts they perform are crimes. One woman says that, if she talks about her people, if she mentions only their names, she betrays them, delivers them up to the police, hurls them into the abyss of misfortune. Or, "This book must be immoral," says another, "since, opening it, I have the same feeling I used to have when I was secretly reading forbidden books in boarding school. While eating my breakfast at the restaurant I have the feeling of robbing poor people." They feel the necessity to take refuge in similes in order to explain this feeling of aversion, of culpability: "It is as though I'm throwing needles in the soup, putting poison into the bread, bombs into the chimney; it is as though I am beckoning to men, inviting them to come up to my room."

On the same level with criminal acts we should place as a bit less serious, but just as significant, feelings of untidiness and uncleanliness. Many persons, especially girls, have the feeling of becoming dirty in an ignominious way, as soon as they move or do anything whatever.

Finally, underneath the feeling accompanying an act is simply that of doing something dangerous, and, especially, awkward. One patient says: "I obey you, I walk with you, I keep quiet, and yet this is the thing I should not do; it is clumsy, stupid. Oh, if I only could do once what I should do!"

"If I am with a friend I feel in advance that I am going to hurt him in saying one word to him. As soon as one word falls from my lips I think I have lied. Whenever I have a passion I feel something in me that remains cold and finds it dirty. If I touch an object I make it fall on somebody's head."

And always there is the feeling of doing something stupid and foolish, of looking like a ridiculous fool, and of being crazy. One patient said: "How must I act in a pseudo-reality, with a pseudo-purpose, and pseudo-liberty? Deep in me, I always have the feeling of acting like a fool."

These feelings are not without importance; they are the starting-point for many frenzies and obsessions; they determine a great number of bizarre manias troubling the conduct of neurotics, even though it be only the washing of the hands and the mania of the endless recommencements of acts. They are especially the veritable starting-point for the pessimistic and catastrophic appreciation mentioned above. When I speak to Flora of her mother's visit and of the baby she will bring along, I conjure up in her mind the picture of that visit and of what she will have to do to receive her parents or to caress the baby. She cannot help picturing these acts as horrible things. Daniel is expected to select a country house, to sign a contract. They are acts that look dreadful to him. When one believes, one is always ready to objectivate, to give external reality to what one believes. If the attitude we must show during a visit, or in making a decision is something feared, it is the whole visit, the whole decision that will be feared, and those patients speak to us of external catastrophes in regard to those events in which their conduct is involved.

Let us not be too severe toward these poor patients; their exaggerated ways show us a caricature of what often enough we think ourselves. Don't we know about persons who see everything in black, who expect lamentable things to happen as soon as we want them to act, simply because they are disgusted, frightened at the very thought that they have to perform that act? Persuasion in relation to things and external events is only an objectivation of the appreciation of that act; these objects and events are, in fact, only a particular expression of the acts themselves.

This is, indeed, the general idea which results from the first and superficial observations of the catastrophic ideas. To consider a thing horrible, dangerous, also means to be afraid of it. And since, at the bottom, it is their own action which assumes those characteristics, *it is their own action of which they are afraid*. Amiel, who was a patient of this type, said again and again: "I am afraid of the objective world; that's why I am afraid of action. It is the instinctive fear to act, the fear to make a decision which is paralyzing me." When we see everything in black and imagine everything to turn out badly, it is because we don't feel strong enough to react and to force things to turn out all right. When we are afraid of the future, it is because we are afraid of what we must do, in other words, we are afraid of action.

II

In order to understand the fear of action, which is so important, let us first remember the important fear of a living being, of a man, an animal, confronted with an object.

We know an object is characterized by what we think to do with or on account of it; an object is, first of all, a comestible object, a sexual object, an object to be talked to, to be given orders, to be asked for something. It is the act that determines the nature of the object, and we recognize the object (only?) if we begin the characteristic action, i. e., eat the apple, write with a pen. This act may be reduced to a minimum and may manifest itself only by outlines of actions which we call *desire*. The perception of an object is only a characteristic act suspended entirely in its first stage; that is, in any notion of an object there is the beginning of characteristic action. Or, all action implies an essential condition; it is necessary that the object be in reach of our senses, our limbs. To eat a fruit or to write with a pen requires that the fruit enter our mouth or that the pen be in our hand. The fundamental act characterizing an object, the *use* or the perception of an object, consists in taking it, touching it, and in every object there is a tendency toward the act of approaching it.

What happens when we are afraid of an object? A radical change takes place: the characteristic act is stopped, completely inhibited. If for some reason or other the fruit we want frightens us, seems to be spoiled, rotten, or poisoned, we don't want to eat it, we stop eating it and even wanting it, for wanting a fruit is the beginning of the act of eating it, and this act is then stopped even in its germ. If the mountain path that invited us to a walk frightens us, we stop our promenade, we become disgusted with it. If a man to whom we want to speak, from whom we want to ask something, frightens us, we stop talking to him, and we have not the slightest desire to have anything to do with him.

The essential condition to stop all action with an object, all relation with a man, is that of his not being any more in reach of our senses or our actions, and that of our not being in reach of his. It is the absence, the removal of that object. *Presence* and *absence* are fundamental psychological facts which are not often enough mentioned by psychologists. To make this absence real we have an act at our disposal: dismissal, removal; as, at the same time, to determine presence, we would use the acts of bringing together.

In a general way, we accomplish this removal by a special conduct that is the reverse of the preceding conduct. Instead of approaching it, we walk, or run, in an opposite direction; this is the act of flight thoroughly characteristic of fear. In particular cases we may effectuate this removal by more precise acts which are exactly the reverse of the acts the object invited us to perform. Instead of eating the fruit, we spit it out; instead of asking the man something, we give him all we have that he might spare us; instead of caressing the dog, we hit him, or kill him, which again is a kind of flight. *To stop the characteristic action of the object and to do the reverse act, to flee from the object instead of approaching it,* these are the essential attitudes of fear.

How can these attitudes of fear in the fear of action apply to actions instead of objects? This is usually not understood very well. In all fear of action there is, first of all, a check of action. It has been stated repeatedly that in the case of melancholia there occurred a check of action, but this inhibition has hardly been explained.

The action does not disappear because it becomes impossible; it is checked by the patient himself who does not want to eat, to walk, or to speak any more. In all the -phobias which are more precise, more localized cases of fear to act than melancholia, the patient stops working, walking, speaking, eating. He stops this or that action and knows what kind of action he stops, whereas the melancholic checks a much larger number of them and, what is more essential, does not know exactly which ones they are. I wish to emphasize one characteristic of this check of action; that is that it not only refers to the entire action to be performed, but also to the outset, to the slightest beginnings of that action. Now, since the desire is nothing but the beginning of the action, more or less complex on account of the efforts added to them, these patients check their desires and, as far as it is in their power, suppress them. The neurotic not only refuses to eat but claims he need not eat because he is not hungry and has no appetite. In those bizarre diseases called "ereutophobias," the fears of blushing in public, which are morbid exaggerations of timidity, stop the patient from joining people, and he loses the slightest desire to do so. Many forms of asceticism are fears of action and melancholias. This suppression of desire is a very important moment since it is responsible for the fact that those patients are not able any more to imagine any satisfaction, any consolation, and that the future appears to them like a black hole. "I have no wish any more but what appears immediately repugnant and criminal."

But the fear of an object determines a more serious reaction, that of the removal of the object by destruction or by flight. Are we able to run away from action, from the motion of our limbs? Are we able to flee from ourselves? Yes, in a higher degree than we think. First, we can run away materially; we can leave places where the acts are expected to be done; we can keep away from persons to whom we should speak. This determines the escapades, the bizarre conduct of individuals who run away from their family, their household, their city, to go no matter where provided they can stay elsewhere. There are even, as I have described them, escapades from situations, when an individual wants by all means to drop out of human society, to break an act of association or engagement just to save himself, to shirk actions he would be obliged to perform in that situation. There are other ways to avoid action. In human society the greatest number of our actions are not dictated by circumstances, but by other men who demand them or order us to do them. The act of eating is provoked by a person who comes to tell us that dinner is served; speech, by individuals who ask us questions, who invite us to speak. A good means of shirking action is resistance against other people's orders; if we never obey orders or invitations, which are sugared orders, we suppress a great number of actions. This is the case with all patients who offer resistance to any request. In the asylums, melancholics may be very quiet in their easy chairs if we don't ask them to do something, but they will become very obstinate and stubborn as soon as you advise them to have breakfast. Negativism, which has been discussed very much at random, is not exclusively a symptom of the so-called "dementia praecox"; it is a general characteristic of all cases of melancholia, of all those depressions in which the fear of action is involved.

The resistance toward orders may complicate itself in various ways; many patients I have described not only resist orders given to them but also protest against other people's actions; they even fight orders they are giving to themselves, which causes the most bizarre act of dividing themselves into two persons (*dédoublement*).

Yet there is, in the flight from action, an attitude still more curious and interesting, a phenomenon I suggest calling "inversion of acts and feelings." In the case of an act necessitated by circumstances, which the individual is perfectly able to perform, we notice the development and sometimes the accomplishment of an act completely contrary. This is a phenomenon which a Swiss author, Ch. Baudoin, has communicated and well described under

the title of "converted effort." He described in this connection
the inexperienced bicyclist who is turning exactly in the direction
of the obstacle he wants to avoid, or the person with a touch of
dizziness who wants to walk straight and who throws himself into
the abyss. The cases of complete execution of this inverted action
are fortunately rather seldom. However, what is frequent and what
I have described a hundred times is the inversion of the very
beginning of the action, the inversion of the desires. "I detest the
things I love, and passionately love what I loathe; it is absurd,"
they repeat very often. The mother who wants to bathe her baby
with kindness and precaution has a desire to boil or drown it. I
have spoken repeatedly of those poor modest women who make up
their mind to practice perfect chastity and yet are convinced to
be the most dissolute women. One of them, whom I have described
under the name of Hermine, has been upset by the loss of her two
boys killed in war; she has sought consolation in religious and moral
exercises. This was the time to be more moral, to behave well.
"Flirtations of love and intercourse with a husband are good for
happy people; we must give them up or at least renounce the
pleasure they might give us." So she puts much energy into the
renunciation of all frivolous entertainments. "I have always been
used to keeping straight, to being severe toward myself." The
result came soon enough: obsessions of immorality, apparent
temptations, and fictitious impulses toward unclean conduct. The
poor woman no more dares to board a bus or a train since she has
horrible desires, and fears to be impelled to throw herself on the
neck of any man. These strange inversions are found in many
pathological symptoms under different names, as, for instance,
ambivalent feelings, monstrous desires, mixtures of love and
disgust—making it sometimes difficult to recognize the real
tendency of the patient.

Unfortunately, I cannot enter into the very interesting discussions of these inversions of acts and feelings. I only remind
you that the opposed actions are interrelated like the antagonistic
muscles of our limbs, and that the flight from an act carries us
away to the opposite extreme which is just the act opposed to the
former. These facts show us above all the nature and importance
of the flight from action, which adds itself to the check of the act
in the fear of action.

III

How can we understand all these kinds of absurd conduct?
And yet it is necessary to understand them a little first, if we want
to try to cure or to prevent them. I should like to collect these
troubles in a number of laws which I am studying now under the

title of "regulation of action," and which, if I am not mistaken, give me the best explanation of the feelings. Here are a number of reactions which are found in everybody and which, in a certain form, are perfectly normal: I mean the actions of retreat, of recoil, which we combine under the name of reactions of defeat.

In psychology we are not very much engaged in the problem of the development of action, its beginning, evolution, and end. It is especially important to understand the end of action, for action does not stop of its own accord. Pathology has shown us a great number of troubles characterized by the indefinite continuation of actions, although they have become useless or even dangerous. With a normal individual, the end of actions is characterized by reactions of internal regulations. One of the most important of these regulations of the end of the act is the attitude of triumph, of which I have spoken extensively in my latest essays. It is the reaction of triumph on successful action, a real or illusory success, which plays the greatest part in the feeling of joy. But this shall not interest us today. The reaction which leads to the fear of actions and which creates the feeling of sadness is the inverted reaction characterizing the acts as recoil, retreat; it is the reaction of stoppage.

An act is always performed on account of a certain stimulation produced on the surface of the body, a stimulation which is either to be eliminated or to be preserved. Its purpose is to adapt us to these modifications of the external world, be it in making them disappear or in transforming us so that they become insensible. When the act fails to effectuate these modifications, when the disturbance from the external world continues, is it good to continue indefinitely the action which has been started in order to rid us of it? Certainly not; the persistence of the same fruitless act would allow the danger to subsist, and, on the other hand, exhaust us completely. It is necessary first to stop this useless act and then to employ the forces it was spending uselessly in a different way, in performing another act that perhaps leads to better results. This reaction of stoppage is rendering the greatest service; it is the starting-point of changes, of attempts, and of progress.

When we study these regulations of action, effort, fatigue, triumph, we always run into a great psychological difficulty, the determination of the starting-point of the reaction. Why, at a certain moment, is the action interrupted by this reaction of checking? One can hardly speak of a real check or a real success; these are external facts, hard to appreciate, which influence the attitude in a more indirect way by the changes of the action which they impel. We must admit that performance of the action changes independently of the external results, that the act becomes too easy or too difficult in the course of its performance, and that these modifications of the act determine the diverse regulations.

However this may be, the melancholic attitudes and in particular the fears of action present themselves as checking regulations which stop the first action, replace it by another, and, above all, invert it in substituting the opposite action.

But what strikes us is the fact that in our patients these reactions of check are enormously exaggerated. Here we have a perpetual failure, which, by the way, is the background of melancholic delirium. In question is an immediate failure which stops action at the very outset after the perception of the least circumstance that calls for action.

Why, then, such exaggeration of the reaction of failure, which should intervene but moderately and only from time to time? A first reason is of greatest importance: that is a considerable weakening of the psychological forces, a reaction to this weakened condition, an attitude of misery. Let us take account of one very important thing which the old psychology has not sufficiently emphasized, namely, the fact that actions, moral life itself, require large expenditures of forces. The philosophers who, as disciples of Descartes, fixed inner thought as the starting-point of psychological life imagined that spiritual phenomena were independent of strength and weakness. We, on the contrary, consider that action is the essential psychological fact and that thought is nothing but a reduced reproduction of it. To our mind, it is extremely important whether a man be strong or weak, whether he can march several kilometers or only a hundred steps, whether he can speak an hour or only five minutes. It is probable that different acts require different expenditures, that certain acts are expensive, and others economic. Actions performed in company cost more than those performed in isolation; acts superior, more perfect, more exalted in the psychological hierarchy, will doubtless bring their money later, but will be very expensive at the start.

In such conditions, exhaustion, the psychological misery, is disturbing action; it determines sluggishness, irregularities, interruptions which we are able to account for in an imperfect way. But the reflexes of regulation of the action of which we have spoken are irritated, and particularly the reflex of the reaction of failure. It seems as though the organism divines that an act that makes so little progress cannot end well, that it is too deficient to arrive at its goal, that it will find too much resistance, and that it would be best to regard it right now as doomed to failure. The driver of an automobile who hears too much squeaking and rattling thinks the best thing to do is to give up right now. The organism is doing the same, and the act, deficient on account of weakness, is stopped, modified, inverted. It is that stopping of action, when it is repeated too often, which is the fear of action.

It is easy to prove that all those melancholics with pessimistic judgments, victims to the fear of action, are psychologically weaklings. The acts they are able to perform even when their fear of action does not stop them are little, not numerous, slow, and imperfect. Besides, we notice in those patients all the physiological signs of exhaustion, all the disturbances of the functions which result especially from an exhaustion of the functions of the central nervous system.

In an almost experimental way, we can ascertain the appearance of the fear of action and of the inversion of the feelings after the performance of a somewhat prolonged action. After enjoying the playing of his violin, L—feels what he calls a "bad, ugly, abashing fatigue," and he thinks he is annoying God. After excessive worldly distractions Sophie believes she walks on the corpses of her her parents. After a little longer visit Flora is falling back into her catastrophes and buries everybody. The young man who invited friends for a ride in his automobile is very proud and happy at the start; then he stops speaking and concentrates on his effort; finally he is invaded by the "lugubrious." They must put him to bed, and for two days he remains in a state of melancholic depression. This explains to me a rather curious characteristic of the spells of anguish I have observed in several persons. It is at the end of an effort, when the subject may stop struggling, when he begins to relax, that anguish and fear of action appear. A girl works excessively in school all year, but at the beginning of the holidays there come distress and the inversions of action. With another they come after an examination; with a third, in the evening, at the end of a day's work, when he is ready to go to bed. During the school year, before the examination, during the day, an enormous effort supported more or less the insufficient strength. When the effort stops and the subject relaxes, the exhaustion becomes evident, the actions offer to stop, and reaction of failure with its retinue of fears and sadness begins its work. It is likewise remarkable to observe melancholic reaction after a great joy or after a period of excessive joy. After joy, I have noticed epileptic spells which are also a manifestation of the exhaustion of the superior functions. We must remember here the spells of distress, with their feelings of the "lugubrious," fear of action, inversion of feelings which overcome certain minds in midst of joyfulness and great exaltation. This happens because joy is an expenditure of great effort; it, therefore, brings exhaustion and thus calls forth melancholic reaction. Briefly, fear of action is often analogous to fear of giving out in individuals who are feeling half-ruined and therefore are afraid to engage themselves beyond their resources.

But whatever may be the importance of this real exhaustion in individuals who are afraid to act, there are always personal dispositions that play a great part. They are weaklings who do not know how to make an effort, who very soon quit struggling. They are thrifty and miserly, not only with their money but also with their strength, individuals disposed to economize with exaggeration and to perform the least possible actions. They are timid people, long since accustomed to being afraid of everything. "It is those fears which always make me indolent," said one of them. And, I add, they are the people who have the habit of melancholic reaction. "Emotivity," which we try to explain as very doubtful visceral modifications, is just a habit which calls for the regulation of stoppage far too early, at the outset of action, at the very perception of the circumstance that might call for action. There are people who, in a struggle, never admit being defeated and fight until they are victorious. There are others who fight for a certain time and then quit. Finally, there are those who declare themselves defeated before any beginning of fighting, as soon as they smell an opponent. In the study of these anticipated reactions we find the explanation for emotion.

We observe the gradual completion of the emotional reaction, and, so to say, the education of melancholia and the fear of action. When the patients have several spells of melancholia in succession they seem to learn their job as melancholics; they have much finer fears of action at the second and third spells than at the first one. They finally arrive at the fear of life, which is a completion of their fear of action. It brings about a general and continuous state of sadness, suppresses all action, makes one indolent, and may even lead to highly absurd feelings and actions.

Let us understand! We have studied this fear of action in patients showing it in its exaggerated form; and don't let us forget that the disease only magnifies facts which exist in everybody. Doubtless, veritable melancholia is a disease, but sadness in its most simple form is, after all, identical with melancholia and contains the same fear of action. There are families and, one might say, entire populations who are going through periods of discouragement, of sadness, and of recoiling from action. Let us also remember that those spells of sadness should not be called poetic, and that they must not be cultivated. Sadness is always a sign of weakness and, sometimes, of a habit of living weakly. The investigations of pathological psychology have shown us the evil of sadness, and, at the same time, have evidenced a very important thing: the value of work and of joy.

CHAPTER 26

A THEORY OF THE ELEMENTS
IN THE EMOTIONS

Carl Jörgensen
Copenhagen

It is a fact that anxiety can arise in mind without any connection with sensations, impressions, ideas, or any cognitive elements at all. In medical pathology the states named "angina pectoris sine dolore" refer to such conditions of physiological anxiety as arise from functional heart disturbances without the pain with which angina pectoris is generally accompanied but even if no pain and local sensations are being felt at all, anxiety may arise in full strength. In psychoses and neuroses, anxiety arising without any object is often described; the patients are frightened, but do not know why. Indeed, this is a sentence heard nearly every day in the practice of neurologists: "I am so anxious, though I have nothing to be afraid of." Certainly there exist not only psychologists, but even also psychiatrists, who deny that emotions can arise without connection with a cognitive element (Isserlin).[1] Now, it is not the first time in the history of science that systematic thinking and convictions have made a fact disappear. I myself have seen the indefinite, isolated anxiety so clearly that I cannot doubt its existence. It is met with not only in heart disturbances, but is sometimes also caused by irritation of the pleura or peritoneum and, as mentioned, is found in neurosis, where organic disturbances are completely missing.

From my viewpoint of psychology there are two decisive points. First, I think it of the greatest importance whether emotions can arise without any connection with cognitive elements or not; second, I cannot agree with a psychology that will deny or close its eyes to the fact that emotions can really do so, for it is evident that *anxiety* can arise and exist without any intellectual background.

I have been glad to see that experimental psychology in recent years has arrived at similar results.[2]

[1] "Psychologische Einleitung," *Handbuch der Psychiatrie,* ed. Ashaffenburg (Leipzig: Deuticke, 1913), II, 179.
[2] A. Wohlgemuth, "Pleasure—Unpleasure: an Experimental Investigation on the Feeling-Elements," *British Journal of Psychology, Monograph Supplements,* No. IV (1919).

Concerning anxiety arising from the heart, or peritoneum, or pleura, it must be stated that on the one hand it is an emotion, but on the other it appears, similar to our sensations, as a sensitive element with its own stamp, its own individuality, its own quality, just as all sensations do in accordance with Müller's Law concerning the specific energies of sensations. I do not think that all conditions of anxiety should arise from heart, or pleura, or peritoneum, but I am tempted to think that all anxiety, including that which arises from intellectual elements, appears in the mind with its own specific quality.

I am tempted to think that something similar can also be said about other emotions. For instance, anger seems to me to contain a similar nucleus of specific quality. It is no explanation to say that anger is a state of displeasure combined with certain conditions in the environment. First, anger is not always disagreeable, and second, it can arise quite "spontaneously." This state of anger arising apparently without any cause—conditioned only by the internal physiological state of the individual—is well known in all asylums in cases of mania. The reader doubtless also knows persons who in everyday life present primarily a condition of anger, and secondarily an attempt to find an object to which the anger can be allied.

If attention is paid to the phenomena of spontaneous conditions of feeling and emotions, it will be seen that there is a great range of such states, which often appear with such a peculiar stamp that it is easy to describe the condition and name it joy, sorrow, want, shyness, etc. If the physiological basis of emotional life were made up of a series of different, specific elements which, in excitement, produce the states known as emotions, falling back to a light tone when in a state of repose, as is commonly observed in neurological elements, we would seem to have a simple explanation of most of the phenomena within emotional life.

Regarding the many difficulties which the understanding of emotional phenomena even today presents to the psychologist, a hypothesis of this content has seemed to me worth trying.

I do not, however, undervalue the difficulties that attach to the practical elaboration of such a theory. Even if we had full security concerning the chief point, namely, that emotional life is built up in the manner named, yet in the finding of the fundamental qualities themselves we would encounter several difficulties. We are facing an analytical problem like that of a chemist searching for chemical elements.

While pointing out this reservation regarding the fundamental elements which I have found, I venture to recommend a series of six elements to be considered as the fundamental elements of our emotional life. The number is small, and it would be easy to propose dozens or hundreds of fundamental elements, but obviously we must credit the emotions with as few fundamental elements as possible.

The elements to be considered as fundamental are the following:

1. Fear (*anxietas, angor*)
2. Happiness (*laetitia, gaudium*)
3. Sorrow (*tristitia, dolor*)
4. Want (*desiderium, cupiditas*)
5. Anger (*ira, furor*)
6. Shyness (*verecundia, pudor*)

Whether it is justifiable to consider these six elements as fundamental and indivisible or not must be passed over at present. Concerning the names chosen for the elements, they are to a certain degree fortuitous, and can only be so, as one and the same emotional element often gets a different name in the language, whether it appears in an intense, perhaps eruptive form, or in a milder one.

1 is the nucleus, the specific energy in dread, terror, fear, anxiety, apprehension. 2 is rapture, joy, happiness, satisfaction. 3 is grief, despair, pain, sorrow, despondency. 4 is hunger of the soul, want, desire, longing. 5 is furiousness, anger, grumbling, and, if present, the emotional element in "strength." 6 is shame, shyness, embarrassment, bashfulness.

Mixed emotions appear when two or more fundamental elements are simultaneously in action. If we distinguish only three degrees of intensity for each of the fundamental elements and combine two, three, or six elements, it will readily be seen that these mixed emotions run into many thousands. Rich though a language may be, it is destitute in comparison with the number of different emotional states that exist. On the other hand, it is quite interesting to try an analysis of the more commonly mixed emotions. In hope, for instance, we easily recognize the quality of 4, 3, and 2; in envy, of 3 and 4; in sadness, of 3 and 2; in bitterness, of 3 and 5; in reverence, of 6 and 1, etc. In the case of love, hate, pride, etc., we must remember that each such word covers both veritable emotions and the dispositions towards producing these emotions in regard to certain objects.

After this brief exposition we should discuss a problem or two. Perhaps the reader will ask why loathing has not been listed among the fundamental qualities. Perhaps we really ought to do so. No doubt there are mixed feelings of 6 and 5, shame and anger, which may appear as loathing. Nevertheless, it is possible that loathing is to be regarded as a fundamental element; I dare not decide the question. I only mention it here to demonstrate the practical difficulties which are not wanting in our theory.

Again, the reader may ask if pleasure and displeasure, those two states which have virtually dominated the psychology of feelings since Spinoza, are not to be listed among the fundamental elements of emotion. To this I must answer "no"; they are not to be considered veritable emotional elements.

Regarding the emotions of fear, happiness, sorrow, want, anger, and shyness, it may be remarked that states containing one or more of these elements may at one time appear agreeable, at another disagreeable. It is also worth noticing that states of fear, sorrow, and want, though generally disagreeable, often seem pleasurable, especially in case of slight intensity. A discussion of the possibility of explaining these facts must be passed over at present. I think, however, that the classification of feelings as pleasurable and displeasurable is to be compared with a division of all colors into light or dark colors, though white and black are not fundamental elements in the conception of colors. Or to divide feelings into pleasurable or displeasurable is like furnishing a row of figures with positive or negative signs. Pleasure and displeasure are peculiar accentuations with which the different emotions are equipped, accentuations which point out their relation to volitional life. *Displeasure means the aversion that lies within or arises from an emotion, just as pleasure means the accepting tendency that lies in or arises from an emotion.* The two phenomena belong to a boundary area between emotional and volitive life.

A question which has often been discussed in psychology is that concerning the line of demarcation between sensation and emotion. Regarding this, I doubt that any such sharp distinction really exists. Psychologists have dwelt on the phenomenon of pain, which in one aspect is kindred to sensations, in other aspects to feelings and emotions. I myself think that bodily pain is a sensitive element with a quality of its own, but in the row of sense qualities it gets its place in the end that nears emotions. Just the same is the case with sensations such as hunger and libido. On the other hand, an emotion like anxiety nears sensation. Briefly, it is partially fortituous in the list of sensory elements to draw a close distinction between sensations and emotions.

In the problem in question the standpoint of Wundt is often quoted. In the demonstration of his conception that feeling cannot be a sort of sensation, he points out that a passage from red to green or from the deepest tone to the highest is a passage through differences, while the passage from displeasure to pleasure shows a zero-point, and thence a phenomenon of opposition (*Grundriss der Psychologie*). This opposition between pleasure and displeasure, *Lust* and *Unlust*, may be right. But the whole way of looking upon the matter fails when we recall to mind that phenomena of pleasure and displeasure cannot be identified with feelings.

In the above exposition I think I have pointed out the principal points in my way of looking upon emotional phenomena. However, I should like to add a few words concerning the opposition it will no doubt meet with among psychologists of today. This opposition will not be due to the fact that the prevailing theories of emotions, such as the pleasure-displeasure theory in its various shapes from Spinoza to Lehmann, or the physiological theory of James-Lange-Ribot, should have satisfied the claim of empiric psychology to a useful hypothesis. In this regard the hypotheses at our disposal have shown several deficiencies. Some oppositions may arise from the difficulties which naturally attach to the theory put forward. In spite of the many phenomena which are explained in a simple and natural way, many questions remain open, and many analyses still remain difficult. The greatest opposition I think, should arise from the fact that this theory on a superficial view may seem like the "faculty psychology" of the Middle Ages. The reader who, when reading the above, has been reminded of the psychology of Suarez or of Thomas Aquinas, may certainly have had "a bad taste in his mouth." Now, I am unable to recognize my indebtedness to the psychology of the scholastics; even when Descartes reduced the eleven emotions of Thomas to six, or when Spinoza reduced them to two, it was a speculative more than an empiric psychology, and there is no relation between the psychology of these authors and mine. I recognize, however, my debt to Johannes Müller, to his law of the specific energy of sensations. Without this law I do not think my conception could have been carried through.

Concerning the utility of the theory brought forward, I should like to recommend it also in studies of temperaments. No doubt the above-named six elements, though present in all normal men, show a different strength in different individuals, and, hence, there arises a different tendency towards reacting on given situations. Likewise there arise differences in the spontaneous, affective tone which the different individuals present. A greater or smaller tendency to anxiety, to happiness, to sorrow, to want, to anger, or to shyness naturally leads us to twelve types differing in the affective aspect of temperament. When two or three fundamental qualities are well marked, whilst the other elements are relatively failing, other temperaments appear.

It lies outside the range of this paper to go into details regarding these problems; only a single observation should be mentioned here, namely, that a temperament charged with sorrow and anger (3 and 5) renders its possessor an invalid. Such a psychic constitution is as fatal to the conduct of the individual as a congenital heart failure or idiotia. An individual suffering from "psychopathia tristomorosa," as this constitution may be named, is an invalid in human society.

CHAPTER 27

FEELINGS AND EMOTIONS FROM THE STANDPOINT OF INDIVIDUAL PSYCHOLOGY

ALFRED ADLER
Vienna

It is obvious that the style of life does not solely rule an individual. The attitudes do not alone create the symptoms, nor do they alone build up the whole neurosis as a security for not going on. To this must be added also feelings which do not hinder the person's strivings on the useless side.

This is a new view in psychology and is presented in contradiction to other conceptions. Individual psychology does not consider the part of mind and psyche as separate but rather as a whole. What we see in this view is no longer physiological or biological and cannot be explained by chemical or technical examination. We presuppose all the right physiological results, but we are more interested in the goal. Our interest is not that anxiety influences the nervous sympaticus and the parasympaticus, but what is the end and aim?

We are very interested in where a feeling has arisen, but we mean the psychical rather than the bodily roots, striving towards totality. We do not believe that anxiety arises from suppression of sexuality nor as the result of birth. We are not interested in such explanations, but we know and understand that a child who is accustomed to be accompanied by the mother uses anxiety—whatever its source may be—to arrive at his goal of superiority to control the mother. In this we are not concerned with a description of anger, but we are experienced enough to see that anger is a means to overcome a person or a situation. We believe that only such a viewpoint is a psychological one, and not other views such as the description of feelings, emotions, and affects, or such as, for example, that of inherited instincts. It can be taken for granted that every bodily and mental power must have inherited material, but what we see in mind and psyche is the use of this material toward a certain goal.

In all the cases we have described up to now we have seen the feelings and emotions grown in such a direction and to such a degree as was essential to attain the neurotic goal. The anxiety, sadness, and all the characteristics have run the way we could predict, and have always agreed with the style of life. We have also seen that dreams have a similar purpose to arrange the feelings and that they are influenced by the neurotic goal. They give us a remarkable insight into the workshop of the soul. A person who accomplishes his goal of superiority by sadness cannot be gay and satisfied in the accomplishment. He can only be happy when he is unhappy. We can also notice that feelings appear and disappear when needed. The patient suffering from agoraphobia loses the feeling of anxiety when he is at home or ruling another person. We come to the point of view that all neurotic patients *exclude* all the parts of life in which they do not feel well and strong enough to be the conqueror.

Character is much more fixed. For example, a coward is always a coward, even though he shows arrogance (against a weaker person) or courage when he is shielded. If he locks the door with three locks, protects himself with watchdogs, guns, and policemen, and insists he is very courageous, nobody could prove a *feeling* of anxiety. However, that he is cowardly in character is proved by the fact that he sought protection.

The realm of sexuality and love is similar. The feelings belonging to them appear always when a person has a desire to approach his sexual goal. His attention and concentration have a tendency to exclude contradictions and conflicting tasks and thus evoke the right feelings and functions. The lack of these feelings and functions—such as impotence, ejaculation praecox, perversions, frigidity—are all established by not excluding other tasks and by contradictions. Such abnormalities are always influenced by a neurotic goal of superiority and a mistaken style of life. In these cases we always find the tendency to expect and not to give. There exists a lack of social feeling, courage, and optimistic activity.

As we have shown, social feeling is of the greatest importance in treatment and education. This feeling is the inevitable supplement of the organic weaknesses of human beings. From the biological side we cannot think of a human being without thinking of social feeling. The new-born animal needs to be supported for a certain length of time, as does the human child. The pregnant animal needs much care before, during, and after birth as does woman. Mankind could not persist without cooperation and social culture. This culture demands common efforts for education. To accomplish the three questions of life it is necessary, as we have seen, to develop sufficient social feeling. As far as we can see, only the possibilities for the development of social feeling are inborn.

There is no use in trusting social instincts because these can be destroyed or increased. The most important factor in the development of social feeling is, as we have shown, the mother. *In his mother every child has his first contact with a trustworthy fellow-creature.* This is the first change in the behavior of a child and the first circuitous expression of his desires and organic drives. His interest includes himself and his mother. The goal of all his strivings is, as before, to overcome the difficulties of life and to gain superiority.

We can presuppose that such a helpless being striving for satisfaction has a feeling of inferiority. This feeling of inferiority becomes later the stimulus among all individuals, whether children or adults, to establish their actions in such a way that they arrive at a goal of superiority.

The first concretization of this goal is the spoiling mother. This goal cannot be fixed permanently. She must, therefore, in this phase try to give the child freedom so that he will be able to establish a style of life which will enable him to seek for superiority on the useful side. The mother must then use a second function, which is to spread the interest of the child to other persons and situations. In this way she makes the child independent so that he feels a part of the whole environment and at home in the world. In this way the mother creates inevitably, in connection with this social feeling, independence, self-confidence, and courage. The goal of such a child will be to become a fellow-man, such as a friend, a useful worker, a true partner in love. Whatever place he may occupy, the degree of his social feeling, courage, and optimistic activity will be influenced by his goal to be superior as a fellow-man on the useful side of life. We cannot emphasize too much the fact that all the feelings of an individual are dependent upon the content of social feeling in his individual goal of superiority.

We can now understand why all actions on the useless side of life among problem children, neurotics, criminals, suicides, sexual perverts, and prostitutes are caused by a lack in social feeling, courage, and self-confidence. We can understand it better when we realize that all the questions of life are social, such as kindergarten, school, companionship, occupation, love, marriage. All these questions demand a well-trained and automatized social feeling. For example, if a boy terrified by illness and death wishes to overcome this fright by being a doctor, he has selected a more social goal than another boy in the same situation who wishes to become a grave-digger.

A lower degree of this automatized social feeling is the same as too great an interest for one's self. Therefore, we can add at this point—what we have pointed out before—that, as a rule, we find this lower degree of social feeling among individuals with a great feeling of inferiority, and this appears in the style of life of spoiled or hated children with imperfect organs. We can conclude also that feelings are always in connection with the whole. They are never independent expressions and never in themselves real arguments for action. They will, nevertheless, always be used in this way and influence our secondary decisions from time to time.

The most important single factor in individual psychology is what we have called a feeling of inferiority. This forms the background for all our studies. We can ascertain this feeling of inferiority only from the actions of an individual. In the beginning of life it is very varied, for we see many expressions of it in order to overcome the urges and the feeling itself.

We find from these expressions that they are connected with the strength or weakness of the organs and the environment. These react upon each other and influence the degree of the feeling. The remarkable part of this is that neither the inherited material nor the *milieu* are responsible for this; neither is it the result of both together. The degree of the feeling of inferiority is due to both of these plus the reaction of the child. We cannot expect that a child, normal or abnormal, reacts from a stimulus in an absolutely right way. Living material as opposed to dead material always reacts more or less in a mistaken manner.

In a study of children in their earliest years we discover three types:

1. Children with imperfect organs. They need more time and more effort than others to integrate.

2. Spoiled children. They are not free to function alone and they develop in the direction of always wishing to be supported. They are attacked on all sides because of this behavior, fall in an inimicable environment, and are, therefore, under strain.

3. Hated children (illegitimate, not wanted, ugly, crippled). They have the same difficulties as the second type, but are without the aid of a supporting person.

After some time these strained efforts, particular interests and attention become mechanical, and this living machine has its own life-plan of how to accomplish the three questions of life. The tension among these children gives them a greater impetus, and forces them to seek a higher goal of security and superiority than the average.

After this goal has been established, the characteristics, attitudes, and feelings are fixed and agree wholly with the purpose to attain it. The impressions, perceptions, and expressions are now selected and seen in this perspective through a prejudiced mind. Such an individual views everything he experiences from all sides until he can assimilate it to his style of life. This is equivalent to how he wishes to solve the three problems of life. Because these three types have a greater feeling of inferiority, they have less social feeling and a greater visible interest for themselves. We thus come to the conclusion that feeling of inferiority and social feeling are connected with, and belong to, the life-plan with which they must agree.

It is not a contradiction if the surface view does not appear so. I once met a very rich old lady, who dominated her whole family. She had no interest for society and only associated with her own relatives. She had great fame as a benevolent woman. This feeling of pity does not seem to agree with her unsocial life. One day I visited her and found her crying. Before her stood an old man weeping. I asked her, "Why do you cry?" She answered, "Look at this poor old man. He has five starving children. He cannot pay his rent and must leave his home unless he pays the £10 due. I can give him only £5." I replied, "You must not cry; let me add to your great gift my small gift of £5." She thanked me and said, "I have always known you are a good man." I replied, "Oh, I am only a quarter as good as you are." As we can see, this feeling of pity and sadness has only agreed with her desire to feel superior over this poor man.

If we judge a feeling separated from other expressions and the style of life, we recognize only the physiological factors. For a psychological understanding we must know the goal towards which the feelings run.

A patient of mine, a second boy in a family, developed a feeling of guilt. The father was very honest, as was also the older brother. The older brother was very much beloved and the second boy strove to overcome him, as is usual with second children. He was seven years old when he deceived his teacher in school by telling him he had achieved a task alone, although his brother had done it for him. After concealing his guilty feeling for three years, my patient went to the teacher and told him how he had lied. The teacher merely laughed at him. He went to his father and discussed this matter with him with a great feeling of sadness. The father enjoyed this love of truth and praised and consoled his son. But the boy always felt depressed, thinking in his compulsion neurosis that he was a liar in spite of the fact that he had been pardoned.

Considering the circumstances, we cannot help the impression that this boy wished to prove his great integrity by accusing himself for such a trifle. The high moral atmosphere of the home gave him the impulse to excel in integrity because he felt inferior to his brother in schoolwork and in attractiveness.

Later in life he suffered from other self-reproaches as a sinner, because he masturbated and was not wholly honest in his studies. This feeling always increased before he took an examination. As we can see, in going on he collected difficulties so that he felt himself much more burdened than his brother and, therefore, had an excuse for not being superior.

When he left the university he planned to do technical work. However, his compulsion neurosis increased so greatly that he prayed all day to God to forgive him, and so he was unable to work. He was put in an asylum and was there considered as incurable. When he had improved, he left the asylum and asked permission to be readmitted if he should have a relapse. He changed his occupation and studied the history of art. Before he was to have an examination in this, he visited a church. It was a holiday and the church was very crowded. He prostrated himself and cried, "I am the greatest sinner." He was thus the center of attention.

He again went to the asylum, where he remained a long time. One day he came to lunch naked. He was a well-built man and could compete in this point with his brother and others.

His feeling of guilt was a means to make him appear more honest than others, but on the useless side of life. His escape from examinations and occupations was a sign of cowardice and a too great feeling of inferiority. For these reasons he made a purposive exclusion of all activities in which he feared defeat. His prostration in the church and his shocking entrance to the dining-room were also cheap expressions of his striving for superiority.

We conclude rightly that in the same way his feelings of guilt also meant an effort to be superior.

PART V

Feeling and Emotion in Children

CHAPTER 28

"ERNSTSPIEL" AND THE AFFECTIVE LIFE

A CONTRIBUTION TO THE PSYCHOLOGY OF PERSONALITY

WILHELM STERN

University of Hamburg

I

I have introduced the concept of *Ernstspiel* to define an actual characteristic of the behavior of the period of puberty. But the meaning of the concept is much more general. *Ernstspiel* behavior occurs at all stages of life in very different situations, and constitutes the common basis for a multifarious group of facts.

In the first place, the concept of *Ernstspiel* must itself be cleared up. It is a "personality" concept, that is, one which is defined by the relation of a single factor to the total life of the individual. One and the same performance may be "serious," "playful," or "*ernstspielhaft*," according to its place and significance in the life of the individual. We speak of the behavior of the individual as "serious" when it is deeply rooted in the living structure of the personality and its real connection with the world. What one does "seriously," what one takes "seriously," is consequential and has consequences. Indeed, it should have consequences; one is responsible for it, because it concerns his own self entirely, and he wants to be taken seriously, that is, he expects that the world will take the particular event or the particular act in its context, and always consider that context as a factor in the account.

With "playful" behavior, it is entirely different. Play, taken in its pure form, moves in a world apart, which seems to bear some similarity to the real world, to be sure, but has no "serious" connection with it. The freedom of play is contrasted with the constraint of the serious. The simple limitation of each period of play, which begins suddenly and ends equally suddenly, running its course, as it were, upon a plane apart from real life, is contrasted with the intricate involvement of serious activity with the subject and with the world. Lastly, the immanent sufficiency of play is contrasted with the transcendence of serious conduct—the regard for the past and the future, for preceding conditions and after-effects.

But, in this rough contrast, we have merely made a first approach to the real problem. For if play activity were so absolutely sundered from the normal continuity of life, appearing and disappearing phantom-like, then, to be sure, it would be a regular foreign body, a senseless appendage to the otherwise meaningful structure of the personality. Schiller observed that this is impossible when he expressed his famous dictum: "Man is thoroughly human only when he plays." As a matter of fact, all the newer theories of play have really assumed no other goal than to correct the notion that play behavior is apparently devoid of meaning. In children's play this "meaning" is found either in the future of the playing individual (preliminary training theory of Groos); or in the past, since atavistic impulses may work themselves off harmlessly in play (recapitulation theory of Stanley Hall); or in the present, since play represents a disguised and often very misleading symbol of unconscious excitations of the sexual or self-assertive impulses (Freud, Adler). In all these theories and others, each of which contains only a part of the truth, the conception is peculiar in that it implies that everything that the person does belongs intimately somehow to his mental structure, and consequently has a "serious" significance.

Does this mean that a distinction between play and serious is untenable, since all play is "serious"? It does not for two reasons.

If we grant that all behavior and experience of the individual has a relation to the total, then this "interrelated totality" may have many degrees of intensity. The individual is "stratified." This means that his separate moments have different depths, that they are more or less focal, persistent, immediately essential. But perhaps it may not be understood that this theory assumes a personal nucleus, the real "essence" of the individual, to which everything else is opposed as pure froth, unconnected with the nucleus. The stratification itself is the distinguishing characteristic of the personality; the superficial is just as necessary a part of the total structure as is the profound. The chronic and the unchanging belong to its vital stream just as do the acute and the changing; that which is inextricably embedded in the total is as much a part of the multiplex unity as that which is less intimately connected with it but never entirely separated from it.

Now playful behavior *per se* stands at one end of this opposition. It has a relatively superficial character, is more transitory, more isolated, less deeply rooted than the especially serious phases of life.

Certainly play always retains its serious relation to the totality, as we have already seen. But—and this brings us to a second difference from the really serious—the serious import of play must be sought *behind* real play itself, in another stratum, somehow more deeply laid than the one in which play, as such, occurs. The immediately given content of play proves to be incomplete and, therefore, *lacking in significance.* Indeed, the conscious content of play—the experience of freedom, caprice, unrestraint, the immanent satisfaction and seclusion—appears nothing less than delusive. In serious activity, on the other hand, there is the agreement of the apparent and the real; the behavior *appears* to be what it is; the consciousness of the consequences involved and the responsibility for the serious act are appropriate reminders that this activity is of real concern to the individual and his society.

But this is merely an ideal picture of serious behavior. Now we must bridge the gap to play from this side. The completely serious, the careful fitting of behavior into the system of consequences to the individual and the world, is merely a limiting case. Even in the most thoroughly serious there somehow lingers a trace of the playful, of protest against that forced constraint, of inner aversion to the confining structure. The absolutely serious would reduce man to the lifelessness of a lofty monument, would eliminate the tension between the more superficial and the deeper factors, thereby denying the whole dimension of *depth* to the life of the individual.

Thus we see that, between the two poles of pure play and pure serious, there lies an unlimited number of modes of behavior which are fusions of the playful and the serious—these are *Ernstspiele.* But we wish to reserve this expression for a very definite type of individual manifestations, using it as a technical psychological term. A primitive *Ernstspiel* is exhibited where play cannot yet be distinguished from the serious, because the individual is still much too vague, too undeveloped, too superficial. Thus, in the early years of childhood, one can scarcely distinguish clearly between what is serious activity and what playful. To the child everything that he plays is *very serious;* and, on the other hand, *his serious doings are no more thought of in terms of consequences than is his play.*

But, first, we wish to consider the really developed form of *Ernstspiel,* in which both the serious and the playful, now clearly differentiated, are present and are recognized, and in which there occurs a characteristic synthesis with intense strain coefficient. *This tension exists between the significance of life to the individual and the nature of his mental experience.*

Consequently, in *Ernstspiel*, the conscious experiences of the serious are present, and they seek straightway to maintain themselves against the non-serious, more or less playful, personal significance of the act. The period of puberty furnishes an abundance of examples of this; indeed, one may well say that nothing characterizes this period more acutely than this struggle, the attempt to take seriously that which is not seriously meant. When young people find their societies, have their love affairs, and begin to carry out their great creative technical, literary, and scientific schemes, they think that they are far removed from childish playthings; but the real import of all this activity lies not in the immediate aims which are taken so seriously, but in their play-like significance, for the whole thing is a preparation for the really serious problems of adult life, a preliminary trial. Various types of life are investigated rather superficially, certain possible experiences are merely touched upon and abandoned, until the young person finally finds, in this school of *Ernstspiel*, the kind of individual behavior and experience best suited to him. More examples will be given in the next section.

II

We have already spoken of *Ernstspiel* as *behavior* of the individual. Now we shall speak of it as a *mode of mental experience*. Up to this point we have been concerned with "personality"; we now turn to psychology in the narrower sense.[1]

Here we separate the intellectual realm of ideas and thought processes from the realm of feeling and volition. The first may be dismissed with only a few words, since it does not belong to the subject of this paper. The mental equivalent of the serious, in the intellectual sphere, is the consciousness of reality; that of play is the experience of unreality, of appearance. From a purely intellectual point of view, there is not a vague wavering between the two in *Ernstspiel*, but a clearly defined consciousness of reality.

---

[1] The *Ernstspiel* problem clearly shows how unsatisfactory is a purely objective theory of behavior such as behaviorism, reflexology, etc.; they are not fair to the phenomenon of "human personality." Since the characteristic mark of *Ernstspiel* lies in the tension between behavior and mental data, it cannot be fully explained from an investigation of behavior alone. On the other hand, a pure consciousness psychology is equally inadequate, since it, too, is unfair to that tension. I seek to avoid both of these one-sided views by setting up a "personalistic" psychology, which treats impartially of all the functions and modes of behavior of the individual—physical, mental, and psychophysical—and under which psychology in the narrower sense is subsumed as a discipline. A more detailed treatment of this concept will be contained in a book on "personality psychology," to be published soon.

The youth who falls in love with a maiden thinks that he is doing this with all seriousness. Thus, in *Ernstspiel*, the intellectual illusion is complete.[2]

But this holds true only for an isolated observation of the constituents of thought and idea, and such an isolation carries with it the danger that we will overlook the most essential. For the consciousness of reality and of appearance is certainly not purely intellectual; indeed, we not only think of reality and un-reality, but we take an affective and volitional attitude toward them. Only in this way do we confer upon them their complete content. This brings us to the very core of our problem: *how is Ernstspiel behavior represented in the affective life of man?*

The series of increasing seriousness runs from pure play through *Ernstspiel* to the completely serious. Does this mean that the feelings associated with this series become continuously stronger? By no means! Often enough the intensity with which a playing child goes about his play is not strong, and, on the other hand, a very serious performance may be accompanied by very weak feelings. Nevertheless, there is something like a scale of feeling which corresponds to the degrees of seriousness, but it varies in a dimension different from the scale of intensities of feeling. It seems to me, therefore, that this is the chief result of our study: *in the affective life there are gradations in various directions; in addition to the gradation of affective intensity there is also a gradation of affective seriousness.* There are feelings, which, in spite of their intensity, are non-serious or semi-serious; and there are feelings, which, in spite of their serious coloring, are of low intensity.

It is very difficult to characterize what we have called the "degree of seriousness" of a feeling. One has to resort to description and explanation by use of examples. The non-serious feeling has a certain instability and transitoriness at all intensities. The fact that the play-like activity has no consequences has its effect upon the accompanying feelings; they lack that conscious background, peculiar to the serious feeling, which reaches from the present experience into the past and the future of the individual, as in remorse, repentence, expectation, anxiety, and hope. They lack also those *nuances* of consciousness which lead from pure feeling to willing, as in the experience of responsibility, being prepared for a decision, and the definition of comprehensive terms. The intermediate portion of this scale is occupied by the "semi-

[2] In this way *Ernstspiel* is differentiated from "aesthetic" behavior, in which there exists that characteristic wavering between surrender to the illusion and conscious dispelling of the illusion. Cf. Conrad Lange's well-known aesthetic theory of "conscious self-delusion."

serious" feeling, which corresponds to the behavior of the *Ernst-spiel*. In this case, those conscious backgrounds of which I have just spoken are not entirely lacking, but they are not very prominent; and, consequently, the resulting affective total always has very little stability.

We give examples:

1. A youth of fourteen years falls in love. He concentrates the first erotic impulses aroused in him upon a chosen person, a young girl, or a juvenile leader. The supreme happiness completely overwhelms him; throughout each waking hour he thinks only of the object of adoration. It seems to him a self-abasement to consider possible an attenuation of this feeling or a complete cessation of it. All of his childish feelings now seem insipid, compared with the ardor of his present affective experiences. And yet this feeling is only "half-serious." The fact that his love affair does not go further than adoration from a distance, that the inhibitions which prevent advances and the realization of the love desire are not overcome, indeed that these inhibitions are themselves created only so that he may revel in ideal feeling as such—this shows that the feeling was not very firmly rooted in the dynamics and volitional system of the young person. This is also corroborated by the fact that the feeling may dwindle away after a more or less brief time as though it had never existed. Half a year later the young person may scarcely be able to conceive that he had been so madly infatuated with this or that one; the feeling has been replaced by love for another person or by an interest of an entirely different sort.

2. A scholar, who is usually entirely absorbed in his scientific interests, may be dragged into politics at times when political tension is running high, and, due to his intelligence and eloquence, may soon rise to be spokesman of a party. He is now in an electoral assembly; he stands upon the speaker's platform, speaks enthusiastically and inspiringly, pledging all the intensity of feeling of which he is capable to the political ideal, and is completely permeated with the purity of his motive, the clarity of his argument. This exuberance of feeling is enhanced by the emotional expressions of the audience, which he moves at will. But, after the assembly, he goes back to his quiet study, and it is not long before this emotional intoxication has disappeared; indeed, it now seems entirely strange, apart from himself, unreal. He looks back upon that excitement much as he does upon a theatrical performance, during which he has lived through a dramatic suspense. Yet there was none of the aesthetic pretense characteristic of theatricals in his participation in the electoral assembly.

There he believed that he was taking his actions and his feelings completely seriously. It is only afterwards that he discovered, from his altered affective attitude, how superficial that seriousness was, how slightly that strong rush of feeling affected the deeper strata and the permanent nature of his affective life. The feelings with which he meets his scientific problems may be less intensive and less turbulent, but they have an entirely different degree of seriousness.

3. The actor is engaged in "play," as his professional name indicates. But among actors we can easily distinguish two types: those who merely "play" their parts in the strict sense of the term, and those who "live" their parts. The virtuosos belong to the first group; the true artists to the second. The feelings of the actors in the first group are entirely non-serious; they are the feelings of *another* person whom the actor impersonates without actually experiencing them as his own feelings. It is different with the second group. In its best representatives, both men and women, the temporary identification with the individual impersonated is complete. The joy and despair, the hope and anxiety, yes, even the good and the evil that the artist acts are actually *his* joy and *his* despair, yes, even *his* good or evil. The state of complete mental exhaustion in which many actors and actresses find themselves at the end of the performance is an indication of the powerful intensity of these merely second-hand emotions. Yet these emotions may be characterized as only "half-serious" even in the most extreme cases. They may result in exhaustion, but not in volitional determinations. They may be acutely violent, but never last on chronically. The mere fact that the same actor can play such diverse rôles is an argument against the complete seriousness of it, for the completely serious is connected with the indivisible totality of the personality.

4. Lastly, we must take account of those cases in which the tendency toward *Ernstspiel* is an essential part of one's constitution. Indeed, there is a type of person in which the *Ernstspiel* is characteristically the predominant behavior, and the half-serious affective life is the predominant content of consciousness. Upon the basis of our preceding examples, we may say that it is the eternal "puberile,"[3] who has not completed the transition from the hybrid state of youth to the complete seriousness of adulthood. It is the dramatic nature which sometimes plays a part in real life, not under pretense, but in complete naïveté.

[3] This term, formed in analogy to "infantile," seems to me indispensable as a designation for the perseveration of the characteristics of puberty in subsequent stages of life.

Ibsen has immortalized the *Ernstspiel* type of person in Peer Gynt, and Cervantes in Don Quixote. With people of this sort the affective life also seems to have a peculiar shallowness and unsubstantiality, although in each particular case it exhibits undiminished intensity. This is most clearly manifested in cases where the limits of the normal are overstepped, and the human *Ernstspiel* type tends toward the abnormal, doubtlessly just because of his inability to adapt himself to the complete seriousness of existence. Hysteria, which is characterized by the pathological self-importance of the particular ego and his petty concerns, and consequently by a tremendous "super-seriousness," also shows that correlate of greater violence and, more especially, fragility and artificiality. But, in normal life, the finest example of the *Ernstspiel* type of life is the great humorist, in whom fixed determination and compelling importance never absorb the individual so completely that he cannot turn upon them playfully and snap his fingers at them. Yet that half-seriousness which we have so often noted before predominates in this vital feeling as well.

CHAPTER 29

THE DEVELOPMENT OF CONSCIENCE IN THE CHILD AS REVEALED BY HIS TALKS WITH ADULTS

David Katz
University of Rostock

I

For about two years my wife and I have been recording, word for word, chats which we have had with our boys, who at the time of writing are aged six years, nine months, and five years, three months, respectively. Up to this time we have had about three hundred chats, some long and some short. These chats have all been entirely spontaneous, far removed from anything which might be considered an examination or a test. These dialogues, which might best be characterized as chats, were taken down at various times of the day and on various occasions. As a rule, the child opened the conversation, and this was continued until the child ceased talking or seemed satisfied with the conclusions suggested by the parents.

We have up to this time in child psychology very thoroughly pursued the development of speech up to the point of complete mastery, but there is almost a total absence of studies that reveal just what the child accomplishes with finished speech after it has acquired the mechanism of speech, the magic key to all higher knowledge. That the most important perceptions are awakened in the child in his talks with adults is a fact. This is true of the preschool period as well as of the child in school.

I made it one of our tasks, in analyzing the talks with our children to study the socialization of speech and to learn to recognize the peculiar psychic attitudes such as assent, pretext, refusal, questions, etc., which develop in them during these talks.

We are trying to apply an unlimited examination method to the entire field of child psychology. This has hitherto not been done. The dialogue, not the isolated sentence response, is in reality the only natural point of departure for the analysis of speech. We are also trying to give the socio-psychological point of view its rightful consideration in these studies, as should be done in all child psychology.

These talks furnish an inexhaustible source of knowledge for the proper understanding of the child world in all its ramifications.[1] From our extensive publication, which is devoted to an analysis of nearly one hundred and fifty talks, we have selected some ideas on the development of a child's conscience as revealed in his dialogues with adults.

The so-called confession talks, which occasionally were carried on when the children were lying in bed and were in a communicative frame of mind, proved to be of special interest in this connection. This procedure stimulated the child to recall consciously the experiences of the past day and to develop in him definite attitudes toward purposeful behavior. We were enabled to incite a critical attitude in the child toward these larger and smaller acts of conduct of the past day in various ways. Sometimes it became necessary to reopen a discussion about some naughty bit of behavior of the child, because at the actual time of the transgression it was difficult, if not impossible, to admonish the child in any effective way. For instance, the child might have been emotionally disturbed, or strangers might have been present, or the child might have been in a precarious position, such as at an open window, near the stove, or at play, at which times a severe admonition was hardly proper.

By no means did the adult questioner always try to lead up to a specific case of misbehavior, but more often the dialogue was of a very general nature. The questions asked were by no means directed altogether toward the transgressions of the day, but also emphasized the good and kind deeds done by the children. A child needs such a comparison in order that it may learn to distinguish between good and bad. However, we were more eager, in seeking out the kind deeds, to prevent a feeling of depression or inferiority in the child. A child should not be led to think that he is a sinful, oppressed creature, but should experience the joy that follows naturally the recollection of a kindly deed.

The more children become accustomed to the quiet evening hour in which the day's experiences are reviewed, the more shrewdly the questioner needs to proceed in order to obtain an unrestrained report of the day's events.

We have found that these confession talks have a very profound influence on the life of the child. The older boy, Theodor (hereafter referred to as T), from the very beginning gave evidence of being mature enough to participate in these confessional talks; however, the younger, Julius (hereafter referred to as J), gave

[1] D. Katz and R. Katz, *Gespräche mit Kindern: Untersuchungen zur Social-psychologie und Pädagogik* (Berlin: Springer, 1927).

such evidence only after some time had elapsed. By and by, we found it possible in the evening to review the events of the day with the children at perfect ease, while during the day they would have balked at any attempt on our part to have them discuss the same questions.

It may be taken for granted that these evening talks frequently afforded the child an opportunity to relieve his mind of distressing experiences or incidents which were deeply impressed on his conscience.

After some time this conversational period had become so fixed that the children could not be induced to go to sleep until they had been given an opportunity to pour out their hearts. Even though conscience is not externally aroused, eventually it does become aroused, and from this moment it may frequently happen that a child who is denied the opportunity of confiding in someone might fall asleep in a state of depression, feeling that he had done a wrong.

We are, in any case, convinced of the great significance of the confessional talk from the psychological point of view, even though we cannot take time to discuss the specific confessional moments in these heart-to-heart talks. According to our experiences, these confessional talks undoubtedly work toward the establishment of desirable motives. They likewise have proved themselves to be builders of will-power. By our talks we mobilize the good qualities of the child, we enable him to be critical toward himself, and this means more than an external coating.

There are doubtless those who object that it is unwholesome for the psychic development of the child to direct attention to his inner life too early, that being occupied with self so constantly is detrimental to natural reactions, which develop more rapidly under conditions where there is a minimum of reflection on the inner life. Our experience has shown that such fears are entirely groundless.

II

We now present several confessional talks in detail. T and J are the children, and M the mother. The letters (*a*, *b*, *c*, *d*, etc.) refer to the order in which the items are discussed, following the dialogue.

TALK NO. 1

EVENING OF DECEMBER 6, 1925—IN BED

M: Did you do anything wrong today?
T: I ran around on the floor and Papa scolded.
M: Well, you shouldn't have done that.

T: But I was also naked and barefooted. (*a*)
M: Did you do anything else? Did you put your finger in your nose?
T: Yes, I also leaned on my elbows when I was eating. (*b*)
M: Did you eat everything on your plate?
T: No. Baby Julius did not do it either. (*c*)
M: We should always eat everything on our plates. Did you finish any work that you started today?
T: Yes. I finished the work on my fireplace. That was not hard. First I pasted on the black and then the gold. (*d*)
M: Are you going to make a fireplace for Tony P. tomorrow?
T: I do not know yet whether I will. (*e*)
M: Have you done something good today?
T: Yesterday there was constant knocking at the door which caused me to wet my bed; I said to Aunt Olga (nursemaid), "Aunt Olga, you have a lot of work." (*f*)
M: Did you do anything else that was nice for Grandmother?
T: I picked up Grandmother's spectacle case from the floor. (*g*)
M: And what did you do for Aunt Olga?
T: I picked up the black yarn. (*h*)
M: Were you not angry with Grandmother today?
T: I struck her. (*i*)
M: Yes. That is bad. And Aunt Olga?
T: I struck her too. (*j*)
M: And Ella (maid)?
T: No. (*k*). Mamma, I will tell you something about Baby. (*l*)
M: Theodor, think, isn't that tattling?
T: Yes, that is tattling.
M: One should not tattle.
T: Mamma, there is such a thing as tattling but one should not do it. (*m*)

Discussion: (*a*) T is not satisfied to relate his misdeeds in a general way, but he feels impelled to add the details also. (*b*) The question of M was directed toward a specific misdeed, but T refers to several other items. (*c*) The fact that J has not cleaned his plate is used by T as an excuse for his own conduct. There is apparent a general, ever recurring tendency to minimize the misdeed by incriminating others in one way or another. Apparently the same misdeed committed by several people is originally regarded as being of lesser consequence. (*d*) Great care was taken to see that all tasks begun were completed. Insistence on this principle was intended to train the child in perseverance and steadfastness. An unfinished task was regarded exactly as a misdeed.

T had pasted together a very attractive fireplace and he remembers all the steps of the process and is very proud of them. (*e*) It speaks for T's feeling of responsibility that he is not willing to make a rash promise. He wants to think about the matter.

(*f, g, h*) Examples of good deeds of previous days that are also readily recalled. (*i, j, k*) Striking is one of the greatest misdeeds that children know of. T, however, admits this rash act, even twice. Ella was not struck by either of the children; both are very friendly toward her, for she knows how to busy herself with them far better than Olga. (*l*) T evidently believes that by also reporting on the misdeeds of J he can relieve himself of further responsibility; tattling, however, will not be tolerated. (*m*) T's discrimination here is very fine. There is such a thing as tattling all right, but one should refrain from it.

TALK NO. 2
EVENING OF DECEMBER 8, 1925—IN BED

J: Mamma, ask me some questions.
M: What shall I ask you?
J: If I slapped anyone.
M: Did you slap anyone?
J: No.
M: Were you bad?
J: No.

Discussion: J's request to be questioned is not due to an inner urge to confess, but to a desire to be treated exactly like his older brother. Since M in the evening busies herself with T by asking him questions, so little J craves attention of his mother. However, he has not grasped the idea of the confessional nature of the dialogues. This fact stands out frequently in the talks. The basis of this desire is, we think, the child's natural striving after recognition. When J demands to be asked if he had struck any one (a question that is answered negatively), he is not doing this to secure approval, as we might imagine and therefore call his attitude naïve and comical, but he is seeking to follow the model of the talks that were carried on with the older brother.

TALK NO. 3
EVENING OF DECEMBER 9, 1925—IN BED

M: Did you do anything bad today?
T: I struck Aunt Olga.
M: Why did you strike Aunt Olga?
T: Because she smashed our depot. Shouldn't she have built it up exactly as it was? (*a*)
M: Were you rude toward your grandmother?
T: (*After considerable silence*) I do not know. (*b*)
M: Have you done anything else bad? Were you disobedient?
T: What is disobedient? (*c*)
M: Disobedience is, for example, when Aunt Olga calls you and you do not come.
T: Mamma, I had run away from Aunt Olga and Papa would not have me near him, so I came to you.
M: Were you disobedient this forenoon?
T: (*Long delay*) No.

M: Did you finish up the work you started?
T: Yes. I finished the fireplace.
M: Did you pack everything back?
T: Yes, I packed up the tool-chest.
M: Did you eat everything on your plate?
T: Not all, but I ate all the dessert. (M *turns to* J)
M: Were you bad today?
J: No. (*d*)
M: Did you permit yourself to be washed?
J: (*Embarrassed laughter*) No. (*e*)
M: Did you eat everything on your plate?
J: Yes. (*f*)
T: (*Comes in tripping, blinking his eyes*) He did not eat everything on his plate. I struck Grandmother with a stick today. (*g*)
M: That is naughty. You dare not do that.
T: But Grandmother was so cross. She took the board for the playthings and broke it in two. (*h*)
M: You must not say anything like that about Grandmother. She did not break the board on purpose. (*Long silence*)
T: Mamma, why did you ask us then? (*i*)
M: I want you to see what is wrong so that you will not do it again.
T: But, Mamma, then we will not ask for one day and see what will happen then. (*j*)
M: I do not ask you every day. Sometimes when I go away, I do not ask you.

Discussion: In this talk it may be clearly seen that, without doubt, it is far from T to conceal his misdeeds in any way. He really tries conscientiously to tell everything that he remembers in thinking over the occurrences of the day. (*a*) When T demands that Aunt Olga restore the thing that she had broken up, he is insisting on that principle of conduct that everything which one breaks up, either purposely or accidentally, must be restored. The boy rightly demands that adults shall respect this principle the same as children, and Aunt Olga's refusal to do this resulted in T's striking her. To be sure, this does not excuse T, and his striking her should not be excused, but his act may thus be explained. (*b*) This is an honest answer. He is unaware of any wrong. When the transgression is later recalled to mind, he spontaneously repeats that he did strike Grandmother. (*c*) It is indeed striking that T does not understand the word "disobedient" especially since it has been used in the playroom so frequently, but it is more than likely that he fails to grasp its meaning because the word is used here in a more or less isolated form, entirely removed from definite concrete acts, in which connection he was accustomed to hearing it. (*d, e*) J does not yet readily admit his transgressions spontaneously but repeatedly answers only after some hesitation. Perhaps this is due, in the first place, to the difference in the ages of the children rather than to a difference in their characters.

That there is a tendency toward conscious falsehood in J we

deny. On the contrary, in his answers there is more often the wish that he might not have done many of the things that depress him, and the desire that by denying his blamable attitude the wrong might become undone. We believe such inclinations to be more conspicuous in J because he is gifted with a vivid imagination, which makes him regard things as real that are but children of his thoughts or desires.

(h) One should not take T's severe rating of his grandmother too seriously. A child has only a very limited vocabulary with which to express human characterizations whether good or bad. These are very often undifferentiated and are sometimes very brazen, just as they would be in the case of uneducated people. For illustration, if an adult were to say, "It was not quite right," the child might say that it was "bold" or "rough stuff." In view of this natural inability of the child to characterize human acts fairly, it would be wrong to use drastic methods in dealing with such a situation, but one should not allow him to slip through easily.

(i, j) It is evidence of an encouraging independence of thinking when T inquires as to the reason for the evening question period. We find something of the tactics of the experimentalist when he suggests that the questioning might be omitted some evening in order to determine if this form of inquisition is entitled to be considered as of positive value.

TALK NO. 4

EVENING OF DECEMBER 10, 1925—IN BED

M: Did you do anything wrong? Did you strike anyone?
J: You must ask, "Did you strike Grandmother?" (a)
M: Did you strike Grandmother?
J: No.
M: Did you strike Aunt Olga?
J: No.
M: Did you strike Papa?
J: No.
M: Did you eat everything on your plate?
J: Yes.
M: Were you disobedient?
J: Yes.
M: What did you do then?
J: I ran away from Aunt Olga. (b)
M: On the street?
J: No. In the room. I wanted to get a pillow but Aunt Olga would not let me.
M: Perhaps you went to an open window?
J: Yes, I was there. (c)
M: Should you go to the open window?
J: No.
M: Why should not one go to the open window?

J: Because you might fall out. (*d*)
M: Don't do it again, Julius. Did you do anything else wrong today?
J: Yes, I cried. (*e*)
M: Why did you cry?
J: I wanted to come to you. (*f*)
M: Did you do anything good today? Perhaps you handed Grandmother a chair?
J: There was a chair and Grandmother sat down in it herself.
M: Perhaps you picked up Grandmother's handkerchief for her?
J: No, Theodor did that.
M: Did you clean up the playroom?
J: Yes.
M: Did you put the chairs away?
J: Yes.
T: Mamma, I struck everybody today and I bit the baby. (*g*)
M: Why did you strike at them?
T: They would not let me come to you from the playroom.
M: Why did you bite the baby?
T: Well, Mamma, you know he changed the locomotive and the cars around, and you know that won't do. The car is shorter and the locomotive is longer. (*h*)
M: Well, is that so bad that you had to bite him?
T: No. You must always explain it. You must have a school. (*i*)
M: How do you come to think that?
T: Yes, you must always say, "Theodor, don't bite." Mamma, I also pinched Baby's fingers in the drawer. (*j*)
M: What, today?
T: No, at another time.
M: Did you do it on purpose?
T: Baby held his finger in the drawer and then I closed it quickly. (*k*)
M: Perhaps you were at an open window?
T: Yes. (*l*)
M: Do you dare to do this?
T: No. (*m*)
M: You know you must always watch out so Baby will not go to the open window. You know you are the older brother. You straightened up your things?
T: Yes.
M: Did you finish up the work that you began?
T: Yes, I made Papa a chain and some stars. (*n*)

Discussion: (*a*) J is not satisfied with a general formulation of the question as to whether he had struck anyone; he asks that it be directed especially to Grandmother in order that he may have the satisfaction of denying any culpability. One might suppose that J, who should certainly know that he had not struck his grandmother, was eager to place himself in a favorable light, but we think that the situation should be explained differently. The concreteness and visual nature of the child's imagery demands concrete and visual questioning.

Only on the basis of such questions is J able to distinguish. Consequently the type of questions demanded by the child is not altogether without reason, however humorous they may sound to an adult. For safety's sake, M asks if there had been any other victims, but he denies that there were any others.

(*b, c*) New evidence of the fact that J's report about the transgressions is not like T's, spontaneous, but follows only after very definite questioning on the individual happenings of the day. Therefore, much more than in T's case, it is advisable to let his confessions be followed by exhortations and descriptions of the disastrous consequences his misdeeds might entail.

(*d, e, f*) The fact that J cried belongs to the other deeds only to the extent that J finds it necessary to mention it, because his attempt to leave the playroom and to go to his parents presumably did not occur without conflict with Aunt Olga or Grandmother. The remaining answers of J's show that it was not made very easy for him to do some good turns, nevertheless he can name a few.

(*g*) T blurts out the chief transgressions of the day almost spontaneously. We should not think of these cases of striking too seriously. As a rule, in the case of adults there is usually more of a threat to punish (strike—*hauen*) than punishment itself. Children tend to such threatening, especially when they make an attempt to get out of the playroom to see their parents. Fisticuffs between the two children are the common way to defend their personal interests; left alone, they not infrequently use even their teeth as efficient weapons.

(*h*) Such a misdeed to change around the locomotives and the cars! Yet T finally understands that this should not be regarded as a real misdeed and, therefore, requests M to give him an explanation as well as a warning to keep him away from similar misdeeds. This, then, is what he calls having a school, for in school we have the opportunity to learn most.

(*j*) T is so engrossed in confessing that he even mentions a mean trick perpetrated on little J many days previous.

(*k*) T, doubtless, did not intend to pinch J's finger and to hurt him, but this was rather a result of a careless act on the part of T, and the latter could not resist the temptation to close the drawer quickly.

(*l, m*) When one lives in an upper flat, one feels constantly that the safety of the children is threatened when the windows are open. Consequently the opportunity, in the evening talks, to warn the children about falling out cannot be passed by.

(*n*) The close of the talk recalls a kind deed that was done for Father, which brought joy to the child.

III

Space will not permit further illustrations of these confessional talks. However, we shall attempt to summarize their psychological and pedagogical significance.

How does the child become embodied in the moral ideals of his environment? Most surely more through becoming accustomed to reacting to definite situations than through instruction. However, we are not speaking of these habit methods only, but we shall show how, by taking these confessional responses as an integrated whole, we proceeded to show the child the difference between good and evil. It was the first attempt of this kind that has been made, and we expect our readers to object, here and there, either to the principles of our method or to details in the formulation of our questions. It need not be said that we welcome criticism whole-heartedly. We ourselves found it necessary to make certain modifications in the form of the confession talks. For example, in the instance of such a direct question as "Did you do anything naughty today?"—a question that might easily suggest to the child that he is a sinful creature—we changed to the form "What did you do today?" or, "Did you do something good today?"

However, we should reject any suggestions to do away altogether with such questions of conscience. In the case of our children such questions have proved an invaluable aid in proper training. We did not notice even a trace of hypochondriacal reaction, which might be expected from early introspection or constant watching of our own doings.

To a rather high degree, the self-defense of our soul sees to it that psychic phenomena, as in our case introspection and its motives, are not mobilized by external stimuli exclusively, if the time of their maturity has not yet come.

No better proof of this statement can be cited than the one furnished by J in the first talk. You will recall that he does not at all grasp the significance of this catechizing. He wants to be questioned, but only because the older brother is questioned. He answers negatively the questions which he himself propounds. In the later talks, by giving proper answers to meaningful questions, he proves that he is mature and has grasped the significance of the whole procedure. In one of the first confessional talks with him, T's answers exhibit a full understanding of the procedure, and in Talk 3 he even rises above the situation by reflecting on the purpose of these evening talks. The suggestion that the talks be omitted sometime to see what might happen implies an experimental attitude on the part of the child toward the will and its motives.

As in the case of all recurring activity of the mind, so confession requires a kind of practice. This is clearly shown by the results in the case of T. There is certainly little connection between these results and his advance in age in the course of the investigation. In support of this contention it should be noted that the account of the day's happenings seems to come more spontaneously and more to the point day by day, so that it becomes more and more unnecessary to ask special or even general questions. In the course of time the reports were entirely deliberate. J does not arrive at this stage, not even after a longer practice. In his case the perfecting lies simply in the continuously growing understanding of the questions as well as in his correct answers. T's ability to ponder over his doings is constantly growing. Of course this ability to remember sometimes fails him, which, by the way, would happen even to adults. However, a progress in this ability is unmistakable.

The fact that these evening talks constantly become more and more of a necessity for T is not to be ascribed merely to repetition. Here we have a noteworthy awakening of conscience. Were it not in the nature of conscience to be thus awakened, not all the chats in the world could arouse it. Of course T does not expect a chat every evening. It depends entirely on whether anything of a depressing nature occurred to him during the day. Nevertheless, the particular incident that would ordinarily serve to awaken a response might be entirely forgotten. The relief which such confessional talks give to the child is always noticeable. This longing of the burdened soul for a confession to a second person manifests one of its most elementary desires. In other words, sociopsychologically, in such cases man is badly in need of an understanding neighbor.

What can be said about the relative significance of good and bad deeds as manifested in these confession chats? We get the distinct impression that bad deeds are much more readily recalled than the good. It seems that good deeds lack the characteristic urging motivation that occurs in the recollection of bad deeds. Even in adults, conscience more frequently plays the rôle of accuser than the rôle of commender.

What do children regard as violations of the social order? In classifying the misdeeds of children we might well have categories called: (1) antisocial acts, which manifest themselves in conduct involving attempted or accomplished bodily injury; (2) injury to things; and (3) harm to his own person. To be sure, the child is unconscious of any such classification or of the magnitude of his transgression. His attitude toward his misdeeds is entirely different from that of the adult. For example, a very minor injury to objects may, under certain conditions, arouse in the child greater pangs of conscience than had he inflicted bodily injury on someone. Indeed, we can almost say that everything that seems "bad" to the child is about equally bad. It will be recalled that the bodily injuries, either threatened or actually carried out, were inflicted upon each other or upon the grandmother or the servants. Only rarely are the parents made to suffer. No serious consequences arose from the children's spatting with each other nor from striking the grandmother or the servants. It requires a far more intimate acquaintance to provoke such "love taps." In fact we never noticed real rows between our children and those who were guests. Occasional visits do not call for frictions so easily as constant living together in a family.

In addition to the antisocial acts we include as misdeeds all violations of the family social rules, disobedience, insulting remarks, running away from the table at mealtime, playing in the street, etc. Cases in which injury to things was admitted in our chats were very rare. This is probably due to the spirit of freedom which is developed in the playroom, where the child is not held strictly accountable for his abuse of playthings and furniture.

What are the good deeds of which the child boasts in his chats with parents? Doing a kindness for his grandmother or aunt, greeting a child on the street, making a paper chain for Father or a fireplace for a little friend, cleaning his plate at the meal. To be sure, no heroic deeds, but after all the opportunity for kindnesses is greatly limited for children so young.

A great many pedagogues have emphasized the significance of habit-forming in the development of will to do good. In our evening chats we always saw to it that the child made a resolution to do better in the future. It is impossible for us to furnish experimental evidence or numerous proofs that our procedure exerted a fine influence; however, we are nevertheless convinced that this is a fact. We felt that the task of educating the child was made much easier by our procedure. However, even though this might not have been true, these evening chats were justifiable, because they afforded the child an opportunity to unburden his mind of the little cares and worries of the day. In reality they seemed small only to adults, not to children.

PART VI

Feeling and Emotion in Relation to
Aesthetics and Religion

CHAPTER 30

THE RÔLE OF FEELING AND EMOTION IN AESTHETICS

HERBERT S. LANGFELD

Princeton University

The general subject of feeling and to a certain extent also that of the emotions form perhaps the most unsatisfactory chapters in the systematic psychology of the present day. It is therefore not surprising that in the literature on aesthetics there should be considerable vagueness and uncertainty regarding these experiences. Some writers use the words "feeling" and "emotion" interchangeably, while others separate the emotion from the affective experience to the extent of identifying the former with a confused manner of thinking. It is true that aestheticians are unanimous in the belief that the beautiful is pleasant and the ugly unpleasant, but this obvious fact is the only one upon which they are entirely agreed. When one seeks to discover the nature and function of this aesthetic pleasantness or unpleasantness, and the rôle, if any, which the emotions play, one encounters a variety of opinions.

It is far from my desire in this symposium to defend a theory of feeling or of the emotions, but it seems necessary at the outset to describe the theories which appear to me to be in best accord with my concept of the aesthetic activity, both productive and appreciative.

Pleasantness is a conscious state corresponding to successful adjustment of the organism—a state in which the organism is approaching and obtaining more of the stimulus. Unpleasantness is the conscious state where there is a motor conflict between two or more possible reactions, and a withdrawal from the stimulus. The states of pleasantness and unpleasantness do not accompany or follow these conflicts and adjustments; they are the conscious side of these particular states of organic response. When the motor inhibition or conflict is severe, there is a strong response of the muscles directly concerned with the conflict, and, through the spread of impulse, of muscle groups that are not directly essential to the particular adjustment in question. Under these conditions, the inhibitions are apt to be prolonged, and we speak of an unpleasantly toned emotion. The pleasantly toned emotions are more difficult to explain, but a possible solution of the problem is that there frequently occurs a correspondingly strong response of coordination and adjustment following a strong conflict, and a consequent emotion which is pleasantly toned as long as the motor responses are in harmony with the appropriate action. Frequently, however, conflicting and inappropriate responses follow the successful adjustment under the condition of strong stimulation, and the pleasant emotion goes over into an unpleasant one. For example, an author who is writing upon some scientific question comes to a point where conflicting theories occur to him and cause indecision. The situation becomes distinctly unpleasant and may go over into an emotion very like fear. After much thought, he sees the solution, and there is the accompanying emotion of joy, but, if he desires to continue his intellectual task, he may find that the emotion interferes with his further endeavors, and the emotional response then becomes distinctly unpleasant. Or one might take an example from direct action. An experienced golfer might indulge in the emotion of joy over a successful play, but he would be careful to inhibit such expression when taking his next shot. It is probably such experiences of emotional interference that make efficient workers consider all emotions, whether of joy or sorrow, love or hate, to be unpleasant *qua* emotions.

In the above description, I have said nothing of the response of smooth muscles because I believe they have only an indirect relation to consciousness, that is to say, only in so far as they affect the response of the striped muscles. It should also be indicated that, in such a theory of feeling, there is no place for a neutral affective tone. As long as we are conscious, we are making some sort of response, and are consequently either poorly or well adjusted to the situation. Does this hypothesis not fit the facts of experience? Are we not at all times in at least a slightly pleasant or unpleasant frame of mind, the so-called neutral state being a state of contentment which is pleasantly toned?

In a previous paper,[1] I have attempted to show the relation of motor inhibition to art production. The experience of artists seems to point to the fact that art production starts with some sort of conflict which cannot be resolved by direct action in the so-called world of reality. In the young child we see such conflict between random movements. There is a striving for coordination, and when it cannot be accomplished in the child's ordinary

[1] "Conflict and Adjustment in Art," in *Problems of Personality* (New York: Harcourt, Brace, 1925).

environment, play eventually ensues; and play, according to a majority of aestheticians, is the forerunner of art.

The conflict is a state of unpleasantness, which frequently goes over into an emotion, and this conflict (or unpleasantness, if one agrees that the terms are identical) is the urge towards continued action, whether "real" or in fancy, until an adjustment is made. Such an urge is present in artistic production.

It can, therefore, be said that emotions are at the root of aesthetic creation, but not as some mysterious driving force that guides the artist in his endeavors, or supplies the energy for his effort. Nor can it be said that a man is emotional because he is an artist, but rather he is an artist for the reason that he is emotional, or more explicitly, because his life is full of conflicts, which he is best able to overcome in artistic expression. All that is implied by this statement is that for artistic creation in the strict sense of the term, that is to say, production beyond mere hackwork, there must be disturbing problems in the life of the artist. I am reminded in this connection of the complaint of a short-story writer whose fiction was being rejected by a magazine which had formerly accepted everything she wrote. During her successful period she was greatly troubled by social problems, which were later resolved in a very favorable marriage. After a lapse of a few years, matrimonial perplexities began to appear, with the consequent return of her former creative ability.

There still remains to be explained why the activity does not always end in useless day-dreaming, in which all of us occasionally indulge. To answer this question satisfactorily would be to solve the centuries-old problem of the nature of creative genius. Although numerous attempts have been made, so far as I am aware no adequate psychological explanation has as yet been offered.

Freud, while not specifically referring to the problem of the emotions, has very clearly described the rôle of conflict in art. "The artist is originally a man who turns from reality because he cannot come to terms with the demand for the renunciation of instinctual satisfaction as it is first made, and who then in fantasy-life allows full play to his erotic and ambitious wishes. But he finds a way of return from this world of fantasy back to reality; with his special gifts he molds his fantasies into a new kind of reality, and men concede them a justification as valuable reflections of actual life."[2] Further on he makes the significant statement which is in accord with the theory of feeling which I have here accepted: ". . . happy people never make fantasies,

<hr />

[2] *Collected Papers* (London: Hogarth Press, 1925), IV, 19.

only unsatisfied ones."[3] We might add that there is probably no one who is perpetually happy, so there is no one entirely free from day-dreaming.

Although I agree in the broad with these statements of Freud, I do not wish to imply an acceptance of Freud's fundamental doctrine of the almost invariable functioning of childhood experiences. We can pass by this remark regarding erotic and ambitious wishes, since the term "ambitious wish" might easily be interpreted to cover any form of wish, even of the most trivial nature, but it seems to me that any relatively recent perplexity can be the incentive for a flight into the land of fantasy, and a spur for artistic effort.

The theory of relief from conflict in the production and appreciation of art has appeared to many writers to be similar to Aristotle's famous doctrine of *Katharsis:* "through pity and fear effecting the proper purgation of these emotions." Is it a matter of experience, however, that art frees us from our emotions in the sense that our emotional life becomes tempered through artistic creation and enjoyment? Can the theory mean any more than that the particular conflict and its corresponding particular emotion are resolved? The facts of experience, as well as the general laws of habit, seem to point to the opposite of a general catharsis of emotions. The artist, as long as he is creative, seems if anything to increase in emotional expression, and the devotee of the modern exciting drama or motion picture, as long as he is not worn out physically by his experiences, becomes rather more, than less, emotional. One only need point to the craving for excitement, for new experiences and emotional thrills, by the present generation, which night after night is held in dramatic suspense of almost unbearable length by the clever stage and screen craft of our modern producers. In short, although art offers us a means of adjustment toward fundamental problems of life and perplexing conditions of our environment, which we might not otherwise be able to obtain, it is very doubtful whether it often acts as a sedative.

It follows from what has been said concerning the artistic impulse toward creation that a certain degree of emotion is a necessary characteristic of that activity. This statement obviously refers to what can be considered an original contribution in the field of art. Much that goes by the name of art is mere imitation produced by so-called artists who are little more than thoroughly machine-like individuals. On the other hand, I do not mean to imply that the entire process of artistic creation is emotional or accompanied by emotional reactions. I have elsewhere[4] attempted

[3] *Ibid.*, p. 176.
[4] *The Aesthetic Attitude* (New York: Harcourt, Brace, 1920), pp. 6–13.

to describe the balance which probably exists between the intellectual and emotional life of most artists, and have suggested that the artist whose main attention is upon his own emotional responses, and who feels that he can only produce in the heat of what seems to him an inspirational state, is liable to become a mere sentimentalist and to produce a form of art which usually marks the extreme of a romantic movement. It is dangerous to generalize concerning the lives of artists, since there are as many different psychological states as there are forms of art, and what one would say of the poet would probably not be true of the musician; a description applicable to the classicist among the painters would probably be indignantly repudiated by the modernist. I should like to venture a guess, however, that while the inspiration to creative effort is an emotional experience, and while this emotional state may recur at intervals during the period of production, for the most part the creative work is carried on with great favor, and in a calm, controlled, and relatively unemotional state of mind. In short, an emotional reaction seems a necessary characteristic, but not a constantly present factor of artistic production.

Can the same thing be said concerning aesthetic appreciation? If we considered only music, which Ribot, among other authorities, believes to be the most emotional of the arts, we should be inclined to state that emotional response is as essential to appreciation as to the creative process. Wherever we have pronounced rhythm, we are likely to have an emotional arousal. In this connection, Ribot has pointed out the direct effect of music on animals, where the emotional response is frequently very much in evidence. The dance and the drama are also very strong emotional stimuli, and poetry might be placed on the same level, but painting, architecture, landscape-gardening, furniture and formal design, do not usually call forth ecstatic expressions of joy or sorrow, and when they do, one is apt to suspect a shallowness of experience. I am aware of the objection so frequently raised, that an unemotional, sophisticated attitude toward art is a purely intellectual affair, which resembles true aesthetic appreciation about as much as candlelight does the sunshine. It is a problem that cannot be answered to the satisfaction of all, since it is difficult, if not impossible, to convince those on the one side that their artistic response is that of the cold, calculating critic, and therefore not aesthetic. But both phylo- and ontogenetically, I believe we can trace in the development of aesthetic appreciation a gradual diminution of the emotional response. Primitive art was often primarily for the purpose of arousing fear and passion, and the child, when it has what seems like an aesthetic reaction, is generally highly emotional. The emotional response, when it becomes intense, is likely to take us out of a strictly aesthetic attitude, out of that peculiar state of detachment so essential to appreciation, and I suspect that it is the subconscious realization of this fact which induces many of us to practise a control over our responses.

Although the emotional response may be absent from the aesthetic appreciation, there is necessarily present a feeling-tone either of pleasantness or unpleasantness, wherever there is a true aesthetic experience, and not merely an intellectual one as to values. The problem is therefore presented as to whether there are any characteristics of pleasantness or unpleasantness which differentiate them from the affective tone of purely sensual experience. Introspection does not seem to reveal any differences in the degree of diffuseness or intensity in the two instances. Exact localization within the organism is equally difficult, and the scale of intensity seems to be equally extensive. On the expressive side, experiments have not, so far as I know, shown any changes in heart rate, breathing, blood-pressure, or psychogalvanic response, which might not have been obtained during a non-aesthetic experience; (the problem is complicated by the fact that it is difficult to determine, with any degree of certainty, whether or not the subject's response is to the beauty or to the merely sensual quality of the object). Attempts have been made to limit aesthetic feeling to those experiences which are obtained through the so-called higher senses, but it is easily demonstrable that although most of our perceptions of beauty come through the eye and ear, any sense may be the vehicle of such an experience. It is equally impossible to limit the experience to a particular category of objects. Bosanquet[5] has proposed three characteristics of aesthetic feeling—permanence, relevance, and community; our pleasure in beauty does not pass into satiety as do pleasures of eating and drinking, they are annexed to some quality of the object, and they are not diminished by being shared by others. Although these three characteristics seem in some degree to differentiate the aesthetic from the sensual, they are not exclusive characteristics of the former. Sensual pleasures may, under certain circumstances, be fairly permanent, they can be projected into the object as well as localized vaguely within the organism, and they can be shared by others. I surmise the problem is impossible of solution, as it has been stated. The aesthetic experience is a complex affair of feeling-tone and specific organic response or

[5] *Three Lectures on Aesthetics* (London: Macmillan, 1915), pp. 4 ff.

attitude. The experience is the total situation, and the aesthetic quality cannot be found in any of its parts.

I am fully aware that the views here formulated are based on scanty experimental evidence. Up to the present, the data in the field of aesthetics have had, for the most part, to be gathered from personal experience, from the lives of artists, and from their works. Further, an analysis of feeling and emotion has always been a difficult problem for the laboratory. The difficulty is increased when the problem concerns their rôle in the aesthetic experience. As an experimentalist, however, I hope that eventually our technique will allow us to present something more than suggestions for a possible solution.

DISCUSSION

DR. ENGLISH (*Antioch College*): I should like to ask Dr. Langfeld as to whether the negative attitude which he takes towards the Aristotelian catharsis would hold, at least for creative activity, if we interpret the catharsis as a purification of the emotions. I think we should all hesitate to suppose that there is any purification of the emotions in the matter of the movies which he mentions, but whether there is any type of purification, or, in Freudian terms, sublimation of the emotions in the case of the creative artist, is something more doubtful.

DR. LANGFELD: I think I did imply that in what I have said in my paper, and certainly Aristotle would have implied that, although we could not say how he would interpret it today, because it is a centuries-old problem for discussion as to just exactly what he did mean. He said only a few words, so we cannot tell.

DR. JASTROW: I find myself in the embarrassing position of agreeing so thoroughly with Dr. Langfeld's position that I merely want to emphasize a point that is implied, namely, that one of the few approaches to the study of aesthetics is through the ontogenetic series. We have taken emotion, as we have taken a great deal of our intellectual life, too high up. We have not started low enough, and we do not use the word aesthetic until the experience is fairly well matured. I should like to see someone devote half his lifetime to primitive aesthetics, and then the other half to enjoying the product of his work. I think that is what we need, the primitive idea of aesthetics, primitive aesthetics. There have been certain surveys and some remarkably interesting material, from the anthropological side, of the play of primitive children about which we know much. We of the present generation know more of primitive man than any other. The remarkable contributions are these amazing discoveries of what has been found in the caves of Northern Spain and Southern France. All of this remarkable material is now available for children, who are now for the first time seeing the aesthetic problems of the childhood of the race.

As for the next point that Dr. Langfeld so well emphasized, namely, that aesthetic experience runs through the whole series, we have a totally false view of aesthetics if we confine it to the ear and eye, and particularly the refinements of the ear and eye of which those of us who do not go to the movies still have an appreciation. The fact is that we must determine, first, what I should call the motor phase. I should say there is only one primitive art. That is dancing, the art in which you make the expression through the total human machinery. You do not have to have any instruments. You do it from within. That is necessarily a total motor response.

Let us take the idea of gratification. I think the most useful way is to regard the word "affect" as a conveniently large category, and by a category I do not mean a wastebasket. The point is we must have a term which does not imply a too specific connotation. Consequently, anything in this field has its affective side. Again, primitive affect would include those forms of gratification.

So again I have avoided the difficulties—it is one of the Freudian methods of escape, which is another word for ignorance—by calling it plus and minus. Anything that adds to our human content and adjustment, as Dr. Langfeld said, is plus. When we are in an adjusted state of content, we are likely to be on the plus side. Otherwise we would be a little pessimistic and there would be no difference of opinion. But if a person is in ordinarily good health, he has a little plus, he has a little balance in the bank. Consequently the plus and the minus feeling.

That, carried out, would give us a primitive aesthetics, not of the eye and ear, but of this great motor experience, for example, in the ordinary gratifications of food, taste, and smell.

My plea then is this, that in considering, as has been so helpfully done, the nature of the aesthetic experience, let us not focus too largely on the elaborate and the creative artist. The creative artist is fairly rare, and most of us, after we leave our childhood, have left all the glory we are ever going to have in life. We are interesting in the first four years. The number of geniuses in the first four years is remarkable, as family histories indicate. Consequently we have to emphasize this primitive aesthetics. I would not stop there. Let us say that the view of aesthetics is one with the view of a great deal of our affective study.

DR. REYMERT: I should like at this point from the Chair with your permission, to voice my perfect agreement with Dr. Jastrow and Dr. Langfeld as to the necessity of the ontogenetic approach to these aesthetic problems. And it may be interesting for you to hear that we have now some investigations going on here at the Wittenberg laboratory along ontogenetic lines, starting with young children, and it is amazing how much seems to come out of very simple studies like that. Our results so far seem to correlate very well with tentative results arrived at before from all of the studies we have on children's growing in Germany and in this country, and especially well with results from the Leipzig laboratory.

DR. DUNLAP: I wanted to ask Dr. Langfeld, first, about the use of his terms for feeling. I had a suspicion that he was using them in a way that I hope is not for qualitatively distinct entities, but rather as categories—wastebaskets if you please —into which for convenience we put many totally different things which have a connection in sometimes a very remote way. Is that what you mean?

DR. LANGFELD: Yes, that is why I expressed my skepticism in the first place.

DR. DUNLAP: If I may use another wastebasket term and leave it there, the term "desire," I wanted to ask you what you would say about the distinction between aesthetic and other emotional attitudes. I have been somewhat interested for years in this distinction, in which you might say that the one important characteristic of the aesthetic attitude is that it is free from desire, using desire in the rather commonplace way. One of the points that has occurred to me many times in that connection is the constant struggle over the presentation of the nude female figure in art and on the stage, and the statements of the moralists all seem to turn about that point—that if it produces desire, then it is not aesthetic; if it is aesthetic, it has not the considerations the moralists allege. And that has a bearing too, Dr. Jastrow, (I am not proposing this as anything more than a suggestion) not on the origins of art, nor of aesthetic feelings, but as to how far these primitive dances are merely sexual matters, which they are today among certain of the African villages. In this sense I should say there is nothing aesthetic about them, however important for human life they may be. So the question is of art in that sense and of the beginnings of aesthetics, if we may use those terms rather generally—whether they may not be found there. The dance may be art in one sense, but not in the aesthetic sense until later.

DR. LANGFELD: I am very glad that Dr. Dunlap brought up that matter of desire. I did not mention it in the paper because that would take you a little too far. I tried to make it plain in defining the aesthetic attitude, and I am not sure that I did not use almost the words that you use now in regard to the elimination of desire in the broad sense of the term. Of course, there is a desire of some sort, whether it is desire for art appreciation or whatever it is. In art I said we are rather led, as distinct from other forms of activity where we ourselves are active, that is, we desire and carry out our own wishes according to our own plan, rather than according to the plan of someone else. That seems to me to be the essential distinction, if one can express it in such broad terms. Now, I should like to get down to more specific terms if we possibly can do it in the future.

DR. PRINCE (*Harvard University*): I should like to ask Dr. Langfeld a question. I suppose he can hear me behind the board there. And that is, how much weight he would place upon the theory of subconscious activity in creative imagination, to use James's phrase in another connection, subconscious incubation of motives apart from the experiences of life? I ask that question because there is a good deal of evidence in specific cases of subconscious processes in creative imagination. In the literary art, a great many pieces, a great many productions, are introduced subconsciously. It is said that Stevenson, you know, dreamed his story of "Dr. Jekyll and Mr. Hyde." "Kubla Khan" is said to have been dreamed, and I am not certain about "The Ancient Mariner." But there have been many productions of that kind produced subconsciously. I have myself—I am only mentioning this to justify my question—I have myself quite a large collection of paintings and drawings done subconsciously through automatic activity. I have a large collection showing very marked constructive imagination. And also I have a very large collection of works of fiction produced in the same way. Now, how are we justified in generalizing from those incidents? That is another question. I remember the remark of a man who said, "All generalizations are untrue, including this one." I should like to hear from Dr. Langfeld as to how much weight he would lay on that.

DR. LANGFELD: I am glad you have mentioned "The Ancient Mariner" and "Kubla Khan," because I have just finished that most delightful of books by one of your colleagues, J. L. Lowes, *The Road to Xanadu*, in which he shows most conclusively where Coleridge got his visual imagery which he uses in "The Ancient Mariner" and to some extent in "Kubla Khan," because he had Coleridge's notebooks, and he did read everything that Coleridge had ever read during the period of his life before he had written "The Ancient Mariner." It is a most striking bit of research, the almost one-to-one correlation between the lines of "The Ancient Mariner" and the words and lines selected from the various readings that Coleridge had access to. Now, we know from psychology that at the time of creating "The Ancient Mariner" Coleridge was not conscious of all the books that he had read; that was not his method to have gone out into a card-index catalogue and picked out this image that he had got and say, "That is a good image for me to use." We know that it is not the process of creative art. And if he had done it that way, by a system of card catalogues and strictly conscious processes, we would not have had "The Ancient Mariner." We never would have had a work of art.

So I entirely agree with Dr. Prince that we have got to take into consideration the subconscious to a very great extent in creation, and that the period of so-called inspiration is very much a period where the facts of former experiences appear. I have used just that particular point to try to prove, or as part proof of, the necessity for the training of the intellectual side of art, the stirring of knowledge. And I have said it is only when we get the combination of the highly intellectual man and the man of feeling that we get great art. I think we can prove that by numerous examples throughout the whole history and development of art. It is not a one-sided man. It is not an emotional man. Nor is it an intellectual man. But it is that rarest of combinations. And that is why I think that genius is so rare. It is a thing we hardly ever meet among our friends—the man almost perfectly balanced between the two.

CHAPTER 31

PSYCHOLOGICAL AND PSYCHOPHYSICAL INVESTIGATIONS OF TYPES IN THEIR RELATION TO THE PSYCHOLOGY OF RELIGION

ERICH JAENSCH

University of Marburg

In German psychology the center of discussion is just now formed by the question whether there exists a unity in psychology, or whether our science is divided into two parts having to take separate ways, a "naturalistic" psychology and a "humanistic" psychology.

The unity of an extensive field can best be made clear by singling out some points as widely apart as possible from each other, and then showing them to belong to the same sphere in spite of their wide separation. Psychological investigation of types generally makes use of experimental means and does not disdain to investigate, in psychophysics and psychophysiology, processes of an elementary mental kind and even their bodily foundations. Therefore, at first sight, the doctrine of values seems very widely separated from it. Also, in the philosophy of values it has often been represented as a sphere entirely inaccessible to elementary psychology, and it was a special stronghold of the attempts to put the strictly empirical psychology into sharp contrast with entirely different methods of procedure.

Inside the range of values, the religious values again appear to be the most central and the highest ones. If it can be shown that it is necessary to comprehend all these different spheres in one glance, as it were, and that precisely in consequence of such a uniform contemplation of things apparently widely different the problems become clearer, an example of this sort can certainly help to demonstrate the unity of psychology.

In another place my co-workers and I have treated the integrated human type (*integrierte Menschentypen*) at length.[1] This

---

[1] A brief explanation is to be found in my pamphlet, "Die Eidetik und die typologische Forschungsmethode." These human types have been studied and represented more in detail in a book to be published soon by Otto Elsner (Berlin), *Grundformen menschlichen Seins und ihre Beziehung zu den Werten*. But the question discussed here, dealing with religious experience, has not yet been explicitly examined, and will be treated later on in a special series of monographs.

can be characterized briefly by saying that the partitions which usually separate the functions from one another have been, so to say, pulled down. The psychic processes influence and penetrate each other, and, in more strongly pronounced cases, psychic events also exercise a special influence upon physical events. Bodily events are here the expression of the mental.

One external characteristic of this type, therefore, is soulful, brilliant eyes, which in their constant mobility are a faithful mirror of the soul. This psychic and psychophysical interpenetration has been proved, in my Institute, in extensive psychological and psychophysical investigations. The spatial perceptions, the after-images (Nachbilder), and the processes of adaptation function in a different way from what physiology, always starting from the normal average adult, has described up to now.

In these elementary psychological processes of the senses it invariably appears as though concepts have here a stronger influence upon the processes. Here we can only superficially touch upon these phenomena without trying to explain them. Following them up would lead us into the deepest questions raised by psychology.[2] It is by no means true that conceptions or the contents of inner experience mix with the elementary feeling processes. What causes the impression that such an influence exists, is that the elementary processes of perception in this type have been shifted in the direction of the processes of conception. Briefly stated, they stand in a way between the processes of perception of the normal average adult, described by physiology, and the conceptions. The barriers which in the average adult usually separate perceptions and conceptions and generally the elementary mental processes from the inner life exist here to a far lesser degree. Eidetic phenomena may serve as an example. Pronounced eidetic phenomena are certainly frequently, but not invariably, a symptom of the integrated type of man. But wherever pronounced eidetic phenomena of this type exist conceptions can become visible in the literal sense of the word. This is one symptom amongst others, but it need not necessarily always occur. Yet it is an example in which the "integration" or "interpenetration of functions" appears with particular clearness and by means of which it can be very well demonstrated.

In a way conception and perception here penetrate each other. The partitions elsewhere separating them exist here to a much lesser degree. I repeat, with the integrated human type the

[2] On the basis of extensive experimental material, I have tried to investigate these questions in my book, Ueber den Aufbau der Wahrnehmungswelt und die Grundlagen der menschlichen Erkenntnis (2nd ed., Leipzig: Barth, 1927), Part I.

eidetic phenomena are often but not always present.[3] But invariably the principal characteristic of the integrated type consists in that functions, elsewhere separated, merely penetrate each other. Examined by more delicate tests, the integrated type proves to be widely spread. Certainly its frequency varies very much with different German tribes, and even more so, as we have been able to establish already, with different races and nations. But the integrated type becomes of general importance by the fact that children at certain ages have more or less of the characteristics of the integrated type, and because this psychic and psychophysical integration of juveniles is of great importance for the construction of the world of perception and of all mental life. As tests we made use of the different processes of perception and feeling. In what way the processes of spatial perception can be used for this purpose has been demonstrated in our larger publications.[4]

The elementary feeling processes, too, show here the characteristics of integration and are, therefore, employed as tests. The physiological after-images in integrated adults, and to a large extent also in children, behave quite differently from what physiology until now has always described, e. g., those of the normal adult.[5]

[3] Occasionally I have been represented as having tried to build up the whole of psychology upon "eidetics." Whoever has read the works of my Institute will know that this representation certainly does not correspond with the facts. Eidetics form only a small section of the work here.

[4] In *Ueber den Aufbau der Wahrnehmungswelt, usw.*, and especially in the monograph about to be published, *Grundformen menschlichen Seins, usw.*

[5] Compare with our older works (especially in the *Zeitschrift für Psychologie*) the work being published by W. Schmulling in the same review, "Aufdeckung latenter eidetischer Phänomene und des integrierten Menschentypus mit der Intermittenzmethode," a continuation of the intermittance method of the Englishman, Mills, and its application to the investigation of types. The publications recently made by Koffka and his pupils on after-images do not refute my theories, but rather throughout confirm the results and views published by myself and my pupils. Koffka affirms that the doctrines of physiology concerning the after-image are wrong, and he points out deviations, as we ourselves have been doing all along. But the teachings of physiology about the after-image are to a great extent correct; at least they are true for the average adult. On the contrary, they are not true for the integrated type and, therefore, to a large extent not for children. The deviations indicate a special type; and they can therefore be studied more profoundly in connection with typology, as I and my cooperators have already been doing.

Compare the article by W. Walker from my Institute, "Ueber die Adaptationsvorgänge der Jugendlichen und ihre Beziehung zu den Transformations-Erscheinungen," *Zeitschrift für die Psychologie*, CIII.

Compare in our publication, *Grundformen menschlichen Seins, usw.*, the passage written by Carl Köhler: "Das Verhalten des Pupillenreflexes und die psychophysische Integration der Jugendlichen und des integrierten Menschentypus."

With integrated people and children the elementary processes in dark adaptation also are of a special kind. They are more numerous and under certain conditions they can be influenced and altered from the sphere of conceptions. But the integration or interpenetration of functions does not only exist in the psychical but also in the psychophysical sphere, i. e., psychical processes influence not only one another, but also, to a high degree, bodily processes. Thus motor functions and also the eyes are here to a high degree organs of expression of mental life. This psychophysical integration of the integrate and of children has been proved with great exactitude, e. g., by studying the reaction of the pupils of the eye by means of Helmholtz's ophthalmometer.[6] It was shown that the reaction of the pupils here was influenced by central and psychical factors to a fairly high degree.

In this example of the integrated type it becomes evident that typology is important also for medicine. It is the integrated type on which psychoanalysts found their assertions. For the integrated type it is in fact true that the elementary psychic and even somatic occurrences are to a large extent dependent upon the contents of the higher mental life and upon conceptions,[7] of which the occurrences are the expression. But these observations, holding good for the integrated type, may not be generalized at once. The psychophysical study of constitution is, nevertheless, of far greater importance for medicine. Not only in psychiatry but also in internal medicine, the problem of constitution has stepped more and more into the foreground. Morbid processes are to a considerable degree anchored and performed in the constitution.

It has become evident that the psychophysical tests form a very delicate reagent for the discovery of important constitutional forms.[8] How the study of types is related to the questions of inner medicine can here, where we have to deal with entirely different matters, be only briefly hinted at. Psychophysical typology has to do with normal types. But the one-sided accentuation and exaggeration of these types lie on the way to certain forms of disease. Typology teaches us to discover their rudimentary forms, indicates those who are endangered, and thus

[6] See the third paragraph of footnote 5.

[7] E. R. Jaensch, "Ueber psychische Selektion: eine experimentelle Untersuchung über Beziehungen der wertenden zur vorstellenden Seite des Bewusstseins, mit Bemerkungen zu der durch die Psychoanalyse hervorgerufenen Erörterung," Zeitschrift für Psychologie, XCVIII (1925). Compare also the report of W. Jaensch, "Psychotherapie," Bericht über den allgemeinen ärztlichen Kongress für Psychologie, Baden-Baden, 1926.

[8] My brother has treated the psychophysical types of constitution from this clinical point of view. Cf. W. Jaensch, Grundzüge einer Physiologie und Klinik der psycho-physischen Persönlichkeit (Berlin: Springer, 1926).

opens up prophylactic possibilities; e. g., there are also internal diseases where the nervous system plays a decisive part. G. von Bergmann has shown this to be probable with certain forms of gastric ulcer. W. Jaensch and Kalk have made it extremely probable that our integrated type is very strongly represented amongst this kind of ulcer patient. The individuals of different fundamental psychophysical types also show, in their pronounced cases, different bodily characteristics. But the difference here is not anatomical—in the build of the body—but is functional. If, with the integrated type, the bodily characteristics are also strongly pronounced, we speak of the B-type. Usually we have then to do with strongly marked cases of the integrated type.

That this is the case of not only the psychic interpenetration but also the psychophysical interpenetration, is strongly pronounced, and, accordingly, so is the complex of bodily characteristics. We then find a functional preponderance, and increased irritability of the entire vegetative nervous system, which, according to Gildemeister's observations, is also highly integrated, i. e., works uniformly. To psychical and psychophysical integration of this type, there thus corresponds also a somatic integration. To the fundamental mental structure, therefore, the bodily constitution corresponds. But here we have to do with the purely psychological characteristics of types. Also here the fundamental characteristic of the integrated type again consists in this, that the psychic functions—in this case those of the higher mental life—penetrate each other. This explains the close relation between the integrated type and art. Artists express more or less the integrated type; inversely, the more gifted amongst the integrated adults are more or less aesthetically disposed. The reason is that aesthetic and artistic mentality stand in an essential relation to the integrated type, for art has always to do with the interpenetration of various mental functions. Certainly the work of art represents facts, but these at the same time always serve the needs of feeling (interpenetration of conception and feeling). Every great work of art interprets thoughts, not in a didactic form but in the form of sensuous perception (interpenetration of thought and perception). To the elements of all aesthetic and artistic experiences belongs *Einfühlung* (interpenetration of perception and feeling).

In the pedagogical movement in Germany it has long been asserted that there exists an intimate relation between the mind of the child and that of the artist, and that in view of this at a certain age teaching ought to assume a sort of artistic character. Typology justifies and explains these experiences of our practical pedagogues.[9] It shows that the integrated psychic structure is the elementary foundation of art, and at the same time is also, at certain ages, characteristic of the child's mind.

Only now do we come to the principal object of this brief treatise; but in order to make ourselves clearly understood, we had to begin with some observations about the more general results of psychological and psychophysical typology. Only in this way can it be achieved that the unity of psychology will appear in the particular subject which we are treating here.

For this purpose we had to point out, however briefly, how the types express themselves in the elementary psychic and even in the psychophysical sphere. So far we have treated elementary, indeed the most elementary, things. Now, however, we turn to the very highest spheres of psychic life. For there is no other sphere in which the innermost life of man manifests itself as strongly as in his religious life. The unity of psychology shows itself in this, that the same structural forms run through the most elementary as well as the highest psychic modes of being, determining both in the same way. We especially wished to emphasize this unity of psychology, for nowadays in Germany it is a bone of contention.[10]

To this basic psychic structure, too, corresponds the manner in which the individual experiences values and in which he approaches the highest, the religious values. Also, the realm of ideals and that which is actually given are for the integrate unseparated, that is, integrated. The ideal world and reality are a unity. These people stand in intimate coherence (*Kohärenz*) with their animate and inanimate surroundings, are open to everything, and, as it were, lovingly given to everything. As the lover the object of his love, so the integrate sees all things, as it were, transfigured. Values and ideals, as in the theory of ideas and manner of experience of Plato, seem to shine through the objects of sense. But that which is given can never be experienced alone, only in connection with everything else, as it corresponds to the process of integration.

The whole is always seen behind the individual. Hence, the

[9] Experimental and descriptive psychological investigations concerning this topic, as well as practical pedagogical experiments, will be found in our monograph, which is soon to be published: *Ueber die psychologischen Grundlagen des Künstlerischen Schaffens*. Very likely it will appear at Dr. Benno Fibert's, Augsburg. Compare also my report: "Psychologie und Aesthetik," Second Congress for Aesthetics and General Theory of Art, Berlin, 1924 (Stuttgart: F. Enke, 1925.)

[10] Compare also my lecture, "Die typologische Forschungsmethode," *Proceedings and Papers of the VIIIth International Congress of Psychology held at Groningen, 1926* (Groningen, 1927).

separate data have at the same time something cosmic. In the experience of the "cosmic" lies the connection between the experience of the infinite and the experience of value. In our records there are continual references such as this, that things are experienced in a finite and an infinite way at the same time, that, like the monads of Leibnitz, they mirror infinity, have a corona of infinity about them, or seem like an external facade of infinity. One subject drew it thus:

THE INFINITE

The Finite

The integrated type has different shades, and, according to them, the experience of finite-infinite takes on somewhat different forms. It can either form a constant undertone of being, or it can appear only at particular points in every state of feeling, or only in moments of special inner joy or exaltation. Of importance for this experience in every case, however, is the fact that the integrate stands in the closest coherence with his surroundings. He, therefore, experiences no separating barrier between himself and the cosmic, but appears, while experiencing objectivity as infinite, to be lifted up into this sphere of the cosmic. For example, all this is found with different intensity, very clearly, in the following record, which was given by a student of the history of art:

"At certain moments I believe I live in the cosmic. When that is the case, things are officially changed, they attain a size, a width, they are large in an optical sense. People are literally large and herewith is connected the feeling of a growth of the individual persons, corresponding to the tide of feeling which rules the moment and may appear in the aforementioned optical appearances. Everything that is inappropriate disappears from the figures. . . . ." He then feels himself just as large as, or larger than they. In a room, on this occasion, he may get a feeling as if he towers far above the ceiling, so that he, as it were, is above it and can span not only the room but the earth below it as well. He then has the feeling of being anchored in the cosmic and that a cosmic motion flows through him.

Changes in perception, as in this case, naturally do not necessarily need to be present. We have here a very pronounced integrate, with somatic characteristics as well—a B-type, therefore, in whom the world of perception usually is particularly fluid. For in the typological method we always start from strongly differentiated cases, and can then find the corresponding characteristics in the weaker cases, even though these are not as clearly defined. That which has been dealt with here refers throughout to a particular case of the integrated type, which we call the "type with general and externally directed integration" (*allgemein— und nach aussen hin integrierter typus*), or, in short, "i-type."

"Integration" is a very general characteristic and occurs in various special forms. The "general and externally integrated type" (i-type) is one of the most important cases within the wider group of the integrated type (I-type). We differentiate the i-type as the basis of experimental criteria and characteristics, which cannot be discussed in the brief space at our disposal.[11]

Some of its characteristics have been partially touched upon above, for at the beginning of this essay it was by means of this i-type that we explained the basis properties of integration, taking it as an example by means of which the properties of the whole species (I-type, integrated type) could be demonstrated with particular clarity. Of the i-type, it was only the fundamental characteristic which was of consequence in this connection; namely, that it stands in thoroughgoing coherence (in closest connection) with the external data.

Before discussing types in which the inner world dominates still more exclusively religious experience, we turn to a group in which the outer world, with its manifold inclines and color, dominates religious experience more strongly than is the case with the I-type, so that this religious experience by its primitiveness reminds one of the native races.

Between the I-type and the *synaesthetik* or S-type, to which we come now, there are certain connecting links. Thus, in childhood the "I" and "S" characters are widely coupled together.[12]

To understand the most characteristic, therefore, we must first of all turn to the most extreme synaesthetic types. The interaction of the senses here witnesses to a type of integration, which is always a destruction of barriers.

In pronounced synaesthesis the experiences combine, as it were, piecemeal; no unit or whole enters into the amalgam, as is always the case with the i-type. To the i-type, a favorite expression of the circle round George[13] is applicable: He is always "round," always "spherical." He puts into every detail the harmonic and closed unity of this "I" (ego) and at the same time the

[11] Some of them will be touched upon briefly later. The whole matter is thoroughly discussed in our monograph, *Grundformen menschlichen Seins, usw.*, which will appear shortly.

[12] My co-worker, H. Freilung, will prove this in a monograph, *Ueber die psychologischen Grundlagen der Arbeitsschule*, which is to appear shortly.

[13] Stefan George, famous poet and life-reformer.

closed unity of his "cosmic" conception of the universe. The characteristic synaesthetic has no such unity, no uniform "I," but also no uniform, closed world—therefore, no cosmos. Nevertheless he, too, is integrated, and so the fragment of his inner world and the fragments of his outer world form a firm amalgam. As a result, religious experience in the characteristic cases of the S-type, which are far removed from the i-type, is primitively archaic, fetishistic, demonic, at most similar to polytheism. Other things, too, have an influence in the same direction.

The stronger and more pronounced the synaesthetic type is, the more completely he lives in archaic strata of consciousness. Everything appears living and ensouled; for many individuals of this type dead things simply do not exist. While the I-type feels himself into his animate and inanimate surroundings, the synaesthetic projects his feelings, or rather feeling-fragments into them. For the characteristic I-type *Einfühlung* predominates, for the S-type *Zufühlung*. For the latter, therefore, facts have above all a symbolic value. The world of sense perception is often extraordinarily fluid; its contents are of importance above all according to the symbolic value of the very often primitive affects, and in their sense are extensively remodelled. According as *Zufühlung* predominates over *Einfühlung* and the S-type recedes from the I-type, all mundane experience, as well as religious experience, becomes more autistical, more unintelligible to others.

We men have the "schizoform synaesthetic type." We next give a portion of the record of a synaesthetic woman who is still close to the I-type and whose demonic, almost polytheistic conceptions are at any rate still quite intelligible.

"The sea is strongly felt as female; she is the infinitely great woman, with very deep blue eyes. When I suddenly talk of storm, she laughs aloud and tosses her hair. Similarly with the wind, who is felt more as male, a man with the gigantic, gray storm-mantle. As I went along the road, the storm whistled past, threw his gray mantle around me, the trees bent before him, he did not heed them and passed over them.

"In the roots of trees I continually see faces; when I lie in the forest and gaze into the distance, everything around me is full of the ghostly doings of gnomes and animals. They come towards me, have long hair, are threatening and hideous. When someone scolds me, the whole room is filled with darkness, the scolding person seems to touch me—to attack me, so that I hold out my arms to defend myself and retreat to the wall, just as when a child I used to hide myself. The question as to the reality or unreality of these contents of experience is not put at all—it is left completely in the air. . . . . ."

The description of his religious experience by a characteristic synaesthetic, who is far removed from the i-type, is far more artistic. He is a student and passionately fond of boxing. In other aspects of his life he is also somewhat primitive, but at the same time is very talented.

"The luminous twilight of Gothic churches forces me to holy devotion, which at the same time is coupled with the feeling of inner exaltation and fervor. It becomes clear to me what the love of God means—one wants to thank someone that one is able to achieve this intense realization of one's humanity. I had this feeling most strongly in the Egyptian temple in the old museum in Berlin; when the two Rameses colossi glimmered in the dim light, I wanted to fall on my knees; the feeling of holy awe is intensified by the smell of stone so prevalent in Gothic churches. I am inspired by a heroic thought in archaic form. I am happy that as a human being one can take part in it.

"Even though the idea of battle cannot be realized in that form today, one can still achieve admiration and love (as a wounded hero on the battlefield). There is a rapture in the thought of this dream-world turned to stone, which, for example, in its highest power embodies within itself all expression of a warrior's strength. Involuntarily an erotic thought vibrates in unison, that the most beautiful woman belongs to the hero. . . . A ceremonial liturgy, when the priests of Isis strike the gong and the temple-girls perform a ritual dance, could force me to my knees by its monumental monotony.

"Religious aspirations are awakened in churches only by monotonous chants and liturgies. I can designate this musing in my world of dreams as something different from the aesthetic and artistic, namely as 'religiosity.' The sight of the Pyramids could make me weep because in them my dream-world towers into the real. Eternal happiness for me would be to live my life as a lost and wandering Odysseus, an Egyptian Pharaoh, in heroic-antique-archaic wise. This dream-world was already mine when I still believed in eternal life, at the age of fifteen; afterward I thought God would furnish me with a stone, heroic-antique-archaic wise, on which I would live and taste all modes of existence, Odysseus, Pharaoh, Centaur, till the end of time."

The origin of the demonic in fear is quite plain in the case of our characteristic synaesthetics, and this fear again arises from the torn and disunited character of this type. I once more quote a part of the record of the boxer, who in many respects is not at all timid:

"When I have to pass through many doors, I rush because I believe a ghost is following me to plunge a dagger between my head and cervical vertebra. I duck, jump aside, and, quick as lightning, slam the door behind me so that the ghost cannot follow. · The world is peopled with demons. During an evening's walk, I lose my psychic balance; it seems to me I have gone down in a ship and, separated from all living things, am walking along the sea bottom. The evening sky appears like the surface of the sea, which is sky-high above me. Shuddering terror overcomes me that a shark may grab me from behind. I dare not go through parks, because a shark might be hidden in the jungle of seaweeds. In between times is a quiet battle of reason. The question of whether reality is attributable to these ideas or not remains unsettled, although they determine the action. . . . This fear of ghosts is intensified in states of depression. One may not leave a leg hanging out of bed, because outside the bed it would come within the reach of bad demons. . . . ."

Basing his stories on such experiences, he writes grotesque, phantastically gruesome tales after the manner of Edgar Allen

Poe. His bizarre fancy reminds one of the synaesthetic Victor Hugo and of the pronounced archaism of the synaesthetic Richard Wagner.

We now return to the i-type, the type with general and outwardly directed integration. We throw a brief glance upon the types resulting when the integration outwards recedes more and more, together with the external world, and when at the same time the integration is inwards and together with it the inner world steps more and more into the foreground. In purely experimental researches on integration, it first became necessary to differentiate between a T-1 and a T-2 type.[14] Experiments which with T-1 at once gave positive results did so with a second group, which we called T-2, only under certain conditions, namely, only by means of vivid imagining.

A third group which did not react at all (they are those who are not at all outwardly integrated) need not be considered here. We find, for example, with the T-1 types that if, during the contemplation of a line drawn upon a piece of paper, one pulls their arms, there very often suddenly takes place an optical change in the length of the line. With T-2 this does not manifest itself at once but only as soon as the subjects vividly imagine that such pulling forces as they have just experienced act on the line also. In the inner psychic life corresponding phenomena take place as in these elementary strata. These people too stand in coherence (*Kohärenz*), in connection with the world, but, exactly as in the above-mentioned experiment, always through the medium of an inner world of conceptions and ideas, which here has a firm existence of its own. They do not surrender themselves to everything, like the naïve and ever plastic, ever regenerative type T-1, but only to that which corresponds to their determinate, rigid world of ideas and of ideals. Unmistakably even here we always have to do with an outward integration, because we see that even these ideal worlds do not entirely lack perceptual elements, but somehow bear the features of the external world. But the ideal and the divine here do not shine forth as immediately from out the real as with type T-1. Type T-2 loves veils and distances. For him the ideal world is not so near that he can touch it; it is not immanent to facts but it lies beyond the hills or in temporal distance, though it still bears the features of the transfigured real. They also can still be poets and artists. Lucke, experimentally and by means of structural philosophy, compares the T-1 types investigated by him to the Goethe type, the T-2 to the Schiller type.

---

[14] Further details appear in the dissertations of V. Lucke and H. Weil, which are about to be published.

On the other hand, those who are purely inwardly integrated
can in general not become poets or artists. Here there exists
no surrendering to the outer world and to things, no binding to
the world given by perceptual experience. The purely inward
integration or interconnection consists here in there being a firm
line of life, faithfulness to one's self, genuineness. Here it is mental
complexes, belonging purely to the life of mind and will or to a
sense of duty, which bring about integration, the unity of personality. It is only when these complexes are touched, as when
man gets immersed in himself and retires from the outer world,
that the outward sign of integration also shows itself. Only then
the otherwise dim eye becomes brilliant, whereas with type T-1
we might say that it always carries the soul outside. Sensuous
conceptions, especially of a visual kind, are here mostly absent,
to a degree which would be surprising in other types. There does
not exist any inner connection with things, quite the reverse;
things can serve only as material for actions, for practical work,
or for the fulfilment of duty in the sense of Fichte.

Only immersion into the dark depths of the self and into the
origins of the inner line of life can be experienced as religious.
Only here the connection with the divine is sought.

In all these cases the most pronounced form of religious experience is not yet to be found. It is only in converts that it manifests itself. The converts who have been treated on the basis of
vast material by E. Schlink, one of my co-workers, have the
aspects of a change of axis. The axis round which existence
revolves moves out of the world and the axon "ego" merges into
God, into whose hands the convert feels himself to be completely
surrendered. And yet, in spite of this conformity, how enormously
different, according to the type, the experiences in conversions are!
I limit myself here to the quotation of some passages from our
records. The first is taken from an integrate: the second from
a non-integrate. In the first case, God is experienced entirely
emotionally, nearly sensuously and bodily; in the second case,
emotion is entirely absent. The experience is quite unsensuous
and abstract.

The first case shows the characteristics of the integrated T-1
type. Before being converted, as a young girl, she always had

"so much fancy, such an impulse towards something exalted. Especially in
autumn I could hardly bring myself to stay in the house. Away! Out of doors!
Into the forest! I was as if drunk, as if I must die if I did not get outdoors. It
was a passionate clinging to nature. But I am now freed from it by the Lord. I
am entirely in the Lord. It still gives me pleasure, but it no longer seems to draw
me away.   .   .   .

"To be in God, to be near God, I feel as something sublime. One cannot describe it. . . . There are services and hours when God can be felt in us." ("Can you paraphrase the feeling more in detail?") "If I may say so it is a divine feeling of awe! As of being entranced. . . . When I rose from prayer, I felt reborn. . . . I have experienced God almost bodily. It is a youthful force arising out of the inner life and taking hold of my body."

Again and again the characterization, "quite different." Divine joy is a joy "quite different" from any ordinary joy.

Not only here but also elsewhere we are reminded of the characterizations of the "luminous" in Rudolf Otto's classical work *Das Heilige* (*The Divine*). But none of the persons we examined were influenced by it. They are simple people and have never taken any interest in theology and philosophy.

Another example is that of a man with a hard nature, a pronounced soldier type, in his profession as a teacher feared on account of hardness and severity, in war a reckless leader of attacking detachments (*Sturmtruppe*). Conversion took place when his child met with a fatal accident.

"My conversion was a purely rational decision. With me principally the merely rational facts have been at play, nothing else. I had a life without God behind me; then my attention was drawn to this and God revealed himself to me by the love of his judgment. And then, as a cool, reflective man, having stood under the discipline of mental training, one is naturally ready at once to sum up the results. 'Now go and submit yourself unto this God.' My conversion was a purely rational decision. Feelings were quite spared to me in it. Also at my child's death I was entirely spared pain. Everything was more rational. It had become dear to me that my child had to die, in order that my God might prove his love for me.

"I always kept myself quite free from feelings. I was quite clear about it, that this (i. e., the communion with God) is a deadly serious affair. I was quite clear that the dangerous side in the communion with God is that one's emotions can go astray. I always was repelled by people who spoke emotionally of the divine. I then knew: 'Either this man is in danger of going astray, or he has gone astray already.' The Lord also has kept people away from emotions. Let the dead bury their dead!"

Occasionally the doubt has been raised that the investigation of types might make truth relative, by taking everything equally seriously, i. e., by taking nothing seriously. I am going to contradict this entirely mistaken view in other articles in a more detailed way. Investigations of types do not lead to relativism, but to a standpoint of relativity, to a neo-Leibnitzian perspective. In the doctrine of knowledge, which as a basis makes use of the typology of thinking and knowing, it can be demonstrated very precisely that the mental structures of the different types comprehend different sides, so to say, different perspective views of the real.[15] In this article there is only space to prove my view

[15] This is proved in a *Kategorienlehre* on which the author is now working.

that in religious life the same rules hold good as in the sphere
of values.

We are convinced that the importance of such typological researches goes beyond the range of psychology and into that of
the philosophy of values. A philosophy of values, having as
basis the knowledge of the different forms of the experience of
values, will see clearer in many questions. Such a doctrine of
values will possess a theoretical but especially a great practical
importance. It will lead to a deeper tolerance. Many discussions
in the sphere of the philosophy of values suffer from the author's
knowing only his way of experiencing values, and from his quite
ignoring the other ways. For everybody is, so to speak, fettered
to the barriers of his own type. Scheler, for example, in his
important writings on the philosophy of religion proves himself
to belong entirely to the T-1 type. Herein lies the weakness of
his excellent works. His polemics against modern times and
against the Protestant world, and his exclusive glorification of
the Roman Catholic Middle Ages, especially of Augustinism,
are brought about chiefly by his not knowing the T-2 type and those
who have only inward integration. He, therefore, does not know
people who are religious in quite a different way, whether they
are Roman Catholics or Protestants.

In studying mental structures one recognizes how values and
non-values are coupled together, and in consequence of this
knowledge one will learn better how to avoid non-values. We
have mentioned already that the records of our first case of
conversion, where we had to do with a simple person who had
not the slightest knowledge of theology, reminds one of Otto's
description of the "luminous." In the second case, on the contrary, we have to do with an experience of God quite free from
feeling and purely rational, which seems originally to underlie
another theological line of thought nowadays very widespread
in Germany. But just because religious experience here bears
a purely rational character, there is great danger of gliding into
dialectic construction and thereby stepping out of religious
experience altogether. In fact this line of thought has often met
with the reproach that it is too much inclined to dialectic construction and that it abandons the ground of religious experience.
It is manifest that there is a form of religious experience which
essentially contains this danger; thus the investigations of types
will be able to indicate in many cases the non-values coupled with
values and even dangers.

Thereby we have hinted already that such a study of types not
only serves the psychological description of the experience of

values but also the discovery of the values themselves, and thus also general philosophy and culture. In this connection it is an important circumstance that the study of types brings about a widening of the horizon and an eye for values. It breaks up the narrow bounds in which we are confirmed by our own type for experiencing values, and it teaches us to know kinds and interconnections of values which otherwise would remain a closed book for us. And progress in this sphere inevitably depends upon our having as wide an outlook as possible upon the sphere of values, for progress here is chiefly brought about by a synthesis of different values. It is accomplished by various, even contradictory values being united in a higher synthesis and thereby coming to agreement amongst one another.[16] The strongest obstacle acting against a synthesis of this sort consists in the barriers of individuality and type, in which we are all locked up. Typology, opening for us an insight into the world of other people, is an efficient means of eliminating or at least weakening this obstacle.

Thus the work of psychology and philosophic anthropology takes its place in the wider field of philosophy, that philosophy which does not disdain its foundation on empirically assured facts.

From Descartes up to Kant and his successors, modern philosophy has been struggling with the question concerning the meaning of consciousness. Idealism, which gave a definite answer to this question and which dominated the last phase of philosophizing, had overemphasized the importance of consciousness. At the present time, idealism is believed to have failed, and nowadays, in the so-called ontological lines of thought, the opposite mistake is being committed of ascribing hardly any importance whatever to consciousness. But it is certain that consciousness is a system of coordinates, a basis of reference in which the real is given, whatever the essence may be, and different structures of consciousness are different coordinate systems. Idealism was bound to fail on account of its lack of a well-derived and insured doctrine of consciousness and because it fought against the recognition of the real. Our psychological and anthropological work aims at such a doctrine of consciousness, and, by being founded upon facts, will avoid all the exaggerations of idealism, helping at the same time to detach from it that timeless

---

[16] It seems as if Aristotle, the real founder of scientific ethics, had already known this, or at least had had a presentiment of it. At any rate Nicolai Hartmann (Berlin & Leipzig: E. Urik, 1926) interprets the Aristotelian concept in this sense. According to him, Aristotle did not really mean an average of values but a synthesis of values. This historical interpretation has not been left unchallenged, however.

nucleus which can be taken over into the realistic epoch of thinking of the future.

Every correct and tenable insight holds good also in practice. The treatment of philosophic questions on the basis of psychology and philosophic anthropology will not only open up important theoretical insights but will also assume practical importance. That can best be explained by the example of typology discussed here. We have hinted already that such a typological treatment of fundamental mental questions must lead to a wider tolerance. This is of importance with regard to the re-ordering of human relationships which is being aimed at everywhere in the world today and which is to be based upon men's no longer fighting and destroying one another, but striving to come to a mutual understanding. Here we, once more, refer to the examples discussed in this short article.

According to our experiences, the general and outwardly integrated type is much commoner and much more pronounced in the west of Germany than in the north. Our most pronounced cases of the T-1 type came from western Germany. On the other hand, the purely inwardly integrated type seems to prevail in northern Germany and at the coast. Most of the subjects of this kind examined by us came from there. The west of Germany is predominantly Roman Catholic—the north, Protestant. It now seems to me certain that the stronger inclination of the west towards Catholicism and that of the north towards Protestantism are connected with the different diffusion of human types and their different ways of experiencing the world. For it is clear that the T-1 type, generally and outwardly integrated, stands in an inner relationship to Catholicism, and that the not at all outwardly but purely inwardly integrated type stands in an essential relation to Protestantism, because Protestantism leads man to depend exclusively upon his inner being and thus corresponds to the nature of the inwardly integrated type. Catholicism seeks to bring the inner and the outer world into harmony, corresponding to the way the generally and outwardly integrated type experiences the world. Also the innermost being of man, his religious experience, is here connected with the outer. It is represented by symbols which appeal to the senses, and man appears within his innermost nature not solely dependent upon himself, but belonging to an outward community, the Church. Both kinds of experience have their deeper meaning. If through the doctrine of types we learn to know their peculiarity and their significance, we shall also do justice to people who are constituted differently from ourselves. The representatives of the various faiths will then no longer fight each other but will rather strive towards mutual understanding.

And with nations it is the same as with faiths. Nations also stand in relation to the psychophysical fundamental types: in one people one fundamental type prevails, in another people another type. We have experimental results for this contention too. Here, too, typological contemplation will lead to a more deeply rooted tolerance. It will bring about peace, or, let us rather say, it will prepare the way for peace. For that is a great and heavy task. Its solution will require patient work for a long time to come. But science must help according to its powers. The study of the fundamental psychophysical types also promotes the study of nations and puts the merits of each single nation into the best light. It explodes all barriers of individuality, which prevent us from seeing strange values. Typological contemplation leads us to a conception which considers the separate types, as well as the various nations, as being instruments of a great orchestra. It will be everybody's first duty to take care that his own voice gives a pure tone but he will honor the others too, conscious that all are necessary and must complement each other in harmonic cooperation.

CHAPTER 32

FEELINGS AND EMOTIONS IN THE PSYCHOLOGY OF RELIGION

D. Werner Gruehn

University of Berlin

Every science has its Achilles' heel. It has problems which seem difficult or even impossible to solve. It has results which lack the certainty and precision of exact science. We know of such problems also in modern empirical psychology. This will not surprise us if we know the history of psychology and its unparalleled development in the twentieth century. It has, in point of fact, been authoritatively stated that in a hundred years the history of scientific psychology will begin with the year 1900. Consequently, we need not give up the hope that some problems which are unsolved today will yet be solved satisfactorily as investigation advances.

In present-day psychology the status of the doctrine of feeling is particularly confused. And yet it is precisely in this field that practical life demands peremptorily a clear answer. This is true of all feelings, especially of the aesthetic, moral, and religious feelings. In the school we try to educate our children to reverence, piety, and trust. But what do we mean when we speak of reverence, piety, and trust? It is obvious that they are mental states and that only a science of mental life can make out what they are. In the church we cultivate various feelings: solemnity, devoutness, meditation, abandonment, active love. What sort of feelings are these? It is obvious that psychology must know the answer. Ever since Schleiermacher, which means for the last one hundred and twenty-eight years, all religious processes have been quite generally referred to the affective side of mental life. If, then, the investigation of feeling cannot answer these questions, the cultivation of the spiritual life must of necessity remain purely external—as external as the raising of hothouse plants when their cultivator knows nothing about all his various plants except that they belong to the large group of "flowers."

Such deficiency will be felt in particular when very rare and delicate plants are intrusted to the gardener. It is then certain that in the hands of a gardener so uninformed the very best and finest plants will be ruined. And do not the aesthetic, moral, and religious feelings belong to the noblest and most delicate experiences which a man can have? Are not the finely shaded, deeper feelings, which take place in the mind of a highly civilized man (*Kulturmensch*), an irreplaceable condition for any profound and genuine civilization (*Kultur*)? However one may regard religion, one must admit that these very delicate feelings of evaluation require tender care if they are not to perish utterly in a harsh, material world. But before we can cultivate feelings we must know them.

I. The Situation in Modern Psychology

Let us look for a moment at present-day psychology, as far as the time placed at our disposal permits. What can it tell us concerning the study of feeling, particularly religious feeling?

Six years ago there appeared a searching investigation of the mental structure of religious experience by my late teacher, Karl Girgensohn. That work, which was originally intended as a contribution to the theory of religious feeling and as an exact test of Schleiermacher's theory of religion, attracted so much attention that, despite its scope and the poverty of the years after the World War, it was fully sold out in only five years. In a first section the book gives a brief exposition of the various contemporary theories of feeling. Practically all psychologists who have worked at feeling are quoted: W. Wundt, O. Külpe, H. Ebbinghaus, K. Bühler, E. Dürr, S. Witasek, A. Messer, C. Stumpf, and also R. Lagerborg, W. James, C. Lange, T. Ribot, H. Münsterberg, G. Störring, F. Jodl, T. Lipps, H. Maier, O. v.d. Pfordten, R. Müller-Freienfels, R. Hönigswald, K. Oesterreich, J. Orth, and others.

And what are the established results? The answer is a crushing one for scientific psychology. It can be put in a few words: Psychology is very far from agreement on what feelings are, what mental states belong under them, and what their principal classes are. When every investigator today sets up his own theory of feeling, it simply means that psychology as science must answer honestly: ignoramus. And of religious feeling we know least. It is but slight consolation to know that the expression "feeling" (*das Gefühl*) occurs for the first time in the year 1691 (J. Orth), and that it was introduced into scientific psychology only a hundred years later by Tetens and especially by Kant, while thought (ideation) and will have been elaborated for centuries. In view of the situation described, we may well surmise the presence of important methodic errors which hinder the steady advance of the modern investigation of feeling.

No change in this situation is indicated by the present attempt to carry on again with a purely rational psychology—to elucidate the nature of feeling in a purely conceptual manner (the Austrians: A. v. Meinong, W. Schmied-Kowarzik, and others; in part also the phenomenologists: E. Husserl, M. Scheler, and others). Such work is, of course, meritorious. It must, however, be joined to empirical observation of actual mental life; it must follow, not precede. If not, it becomes speculative; it brings certain theories arbitrarily into the actual state of affairs, and so confuses, instead of amplifying, the psychological picture; it generalizes before it has apprehended the fullness of reality, and so makes for triteness. From this error, J. Leuba, S. Freud, and E. Jones are not altogether free. The apparent unanimity which distinguishes this group of rational theories of feeling favorably from all other theories is, consequently, merely artificial; it is obtained through the relinquishment of exact observation.

If science has not yet been able to set up a consistent theory of feeling, it seems reasonable to turn back to the language of everyday life. This method is also followed, as we know, by the experimental psychology of the higher mental life; its most refined analyses always start out from the subjects' everyday vocabulary. So we inquire: What do we mean in ordinary life when we speak of feeling? What mental processes are in that case reckoned among feelings?

The answer goes as follows: In everyday life we are acquainted with an infinite number of feelings. Every dim or obscure stirring of mental life is designated by that name. Indeed, the concept, feeling, has become a veritable lumber-room into which we promptly throw any internal process that we cannot or will not designate clearly. A large number of such feelings have been already recognized by the so-called pure psychologists, who, since the beginning of the last century, have opposed the psychology of associationism, who stress exact description, and make no resort to experiment: F. Brentano, Volkelt, W. Dilthey, E. Spranger, T. Elsenhans, F. Jodl, v. Aster, Pfänder, and others; my Munich teacher, T. Lipps, also takes a leading position among them. In the field of the psychology of religion we can mention R. Otto, F. Heiler, I. W. Hauer, and, in part, W. James and M. Scheler. They have the merit of having directed attention to the large variety of religious feelings: fear, fright, awe, regret, calm, exaltation, devoutness, and so on.

E. B. Titchener, in his *Text-Book of Psychology*,[1] mentions casually 54 different feelings. A. Messer, in an experimental investigation (1906), also makes casual mention of 70 feelings. I have in my possession a list, which I happened to find four years ago and which has not yet been published; in it are discriminated 525 feelings of common parlance. The number has since further increased by about 50 feelings, and can easily be still more amplified. Wundt, consequently, was right in his surmise that the number of feelings is larger than the number of sensations, as of these it is already possible to differentiate 1300 separate kinds (Orth).

But what can we do with so many feelings? Obviously, nothing more than with the two feelings, pleasantness and unpleasantness. Application requires an ordering, a grouping of this multiplicity; else nothing can be done with it. We have just seen, however, that scientific psychology has so far been unable to give us such an arrangement. Neither the logicians, who wrongly call themselves *Analytiker*, nor the pure psychologists, now known also as phenomenologists, go very much further than ordinary observation does. It is obvious that science must take altogether new roads in order to get ahead in this difficult field. Let us now turn to these new roads, and first of all to the important question of method.

II. METHODS

In the history of psychology the year 1900 means very much, because at about that time Oswald Külpe had already found altogether new methods for the exact determination of the higher mental life. He was a pupil of Wilhelm Wundt, and had been trained by this great man of science in precise experimental observation. The significance and the limits of the Wundtian experimental procedure and his doctrine of feeling are so generally known that we can pass over them. Külpe was not content with measuring, as Wundt had done, only the external reactions of feeling. He went much farther. He was primarily concerned with obtaining as complete a description as possible of the internal processes.

The details of our inner life we know only through self-observation. If our self-observation were, in fact, reportable with full precision and exactness, we should now be already excellently informed concerning our inner life. Everything, therefore, depends upon improving self-observation as much as possible. How is this improvement to be obtained? There are three places in an

[1] German edition by O. Klemm, *Lehrbuch der Psychologie* (Leipzig: Barth, 1910), I, 225.

experiment where it comes in: in the experience, in the observation, and in the report. More precisely, it means that the desired experience of the subject can be produced in accordance with a regular plan; that the subject's self-observation can be made very much more exact by the aid of special measures; and that the subject's report of the results of his observation can be rendered as precise as possible (by recording it immediately, by the use of shorthand, by increased practice, and so on). In the simple formula, experience-observation-report, is in fact summed up the whole of the ingenious technical advance which Külpe achieved. How great this advance is we realize also when we consider that, methodically, even the remarkable psychological descriptions of the poets have a similar origin. What gives their portrayals its exclusive value is the depth and the individuality of their experience, the accuracy of their observation, and the consummate art of their narration.

The practical success of the Külpean procedure has been demonstrated by his pupils, the so-called Würzburg School: K. Marbe, H. J. Watt, A. Messer, K. Bühler, A. Grünbaum, G. Störring, B. Schanof, O. Selz, L. Rangette, J. Lindworsky, A. Westphal, N. Ach, J. Orth, K. Koffka, A. Mager, Segal, Legowsky, Michotte, Prüm, (in the psychology of religion especially) T. L. Häring, K. Girgensohn, W. Stählin, A. Canesi, W. Gruehn, and others. As I showed in my 1924 review, this school has subjected to exact investigation the most varied provinces of mind: ideational activity, thought, the processes of volition and the affective life (Orth and Störring), the processes of aesthetics, choice, and evaluation, and the religious experience.

The progress thus achieved is not slight. To be sure, in comparison with the great advances which, with the help of improved methods, can certainly be made in the next decades, it is infinitesimally small. It is not small when compared with our psychological knowledge to date. For it is quite astonishing how every one of the investigations already made has brought to light from the depths of mental life utterly new material. Connections, acts, even the course of individual acts, which formerly were closed to observation, are becoming clearly discernible. Most important of all, almost every investigation confirms the results of preceding investigations, so that in this way we are finally getting again in psychology concordant, hence certain, scientific judgments. The sole disadvantage, the laboriousness, and the length of these investigations, does not counterbalance seriously the great advantages. We may then expect that this experimental mode of research will soon receive another impetus, after having suffered in Europe from Külpe's death and from the post-war mania of uncritical speculation.

Just a few words more about the methods of investigation of religious feeling. I disregard A. F. Shand's thoroughgoing investigation, since it analyzes primarily the instinctive life and, furthermore, pursues different methods.

Already in 1903, J. Orth published results in accordance with the Külpean method. His stimuli were tuning-fork tones, odors, colored figures, noises, lines, and points. The concrete results were rather slight. Yet the discovery of a particular class of experiences, *Bewusstseinslagen*, as he called them on Marbe's suggestion, was a very valuable outcome. Though before unknown, they play a big rôle in the mental states which are designated as feeling. They enter into connection with the feelings of doubt, certainty, uncertainty, contrast, acquiescence, immediate cognition, and so on.

In 1914, W. Stählin went farther. He presented to his subjects selected religious passages. These passages evoked certain impressions and feelings, of which a detailed report was required. He, too, came across peculiar, as yet unknown factors of feeling, which became understood as a result of later studies.

Then came K. Girgensohn. In his work, which we have already mentioned, he followed up the religious feelings in a most comprehensive manner. He presented to his subjects carefully selected religious compositions, which he had them read a number of times during the experimental period. After every reading, the subject had to report in detail upon his experiences during the reading. There were twenty-eight compositions and fourteen subjects. There were also supplementary association experiments, carefully planned conversations on religious questions, and the like. It will interest Americans to know that this study was preceded by experiments, in 1909–10, which were carried out with a combination of Starbuck's questionnaire. The results of this most important work will be treated in the following section. The method is still imperfect, as Girgensohn himself admitted. It gives us insight more into the statics than into the dynamics of religious life. Yet Girgensohn, like James, knows how to handle masterfully an imperfect method.

In 1913, and independently of Girgensohn, T. L. Häring, another pupil of Külpe, published a study of the processes of evaluation. Provided with a large stock of stimulus-words and carefully chosen instructions, he follows up the processes, which have not yet received experimental treatment, of logical, economic, aesthetic, and moral evaluation. But his results, as I have shown and as Häring admitted, still do not go very deep and are important chiefly to logical evaluation. The lack of preliminary work in this difficult field and a pronounced speculative disposition rendered the getting of new facts difficult.

I began my studies of the experience of evaluation in 1913 by building upon the methods of my predecessors. Instructions and stimulus-words were brought into closer relation to each other, reaction-times were reduced, and the stimulus-words were shortened. In this way I succeeded not only in scrutinizing minute processes but also in uncovering previously unknown mental structures. Girgensohn, in particular, repeatedly pointed out the advance here achieved.

Afterward, H. Lorenzsohn, one of my pupils, made a detailed study, by a similar method, of the most central religious feelings. It is to be hoped that he will soon be able to publish the results, which are novel in part and very interesting. Other pupils of Girgensohn's, C. Schneider and E. Nobiling, have studied the individual and genetic aspects of religious experience.

A. Canesi, a pupil of Gemelli and Külpe, went so far as to investigate experimentally the life of prayer. He follows Girgensohn's investigations and mine, but he believes that he can do without a more refined experimental technique because his subjects are all selected and very pious. This is a very instructive error. To be sure, in this way Canesi obtained results of a very high religious status; but the reports are not precise. Thus his results, like those of Stählin, who came at the beginning of this series, in spite of a wealth of material derived from many subjects, are quite hazy and not perspicuous. The attempts show convincingly that no other advantages can replace refinement of psychological technique.

Looking back, we see in the methodic development of the study of religious feeling an unretarded progress in depth. The method has already become indispensable. From fruitless speculations, from theories of the seat of feeling, from discord-producing conceptual analyses, and so on, our methods turn more and more to the individual concrete phenomena of mental life which are not too distant from ordinary life, and, by intensified self-observation, try to penetrate deep into the structure of mind. Thus they come closer and closer to real life, which the results in the last section will confirm.

Truly, the more precise these observations become in detail, the more do they require supplementary methods. Microscopic observation must be supplemented with macroscopic observation. The larger connections of mental life must not be forgotten on account of the details. At this point the methods of pure psychology

(J. Volkelt and T. Lipps) and of phenomenology (E. Husserl and M. Scheler), which we criticized earlier, become extraordinarily important. The same is true of the modern psychology of Gestalt, whose need was early recognized by D. F. Schleiermacher, H. Cornelius, C. v. Ehrenfels, and others, and which is now successfully represented by M. Wertheimer, W. Köhler, K. Koffka, F. Krueger, K. Bühler, F. Sander, and others. It has grown out of the realization that a one-sided analysis of mental life, a mere resolution into elements, is dangerous to scientific psychology and breaks up mind in an unreal manner. At the same time it tries to find clear concepts for the unresolvable totality-character of mental life and of its individual structures and phenomena. Yet it seems to me that this tendency which is gaining ground in Germany is to be invoked not in opposition to but as supplementing experimental analysis. This was the standpoint of Girgensohn in his description of the religious states of pleasantness and unpleasantness (*supra*, p. 383 ff.). In my *Religionspsychologie*, I, too, devoted a separate section to synthetic normal psychology (p. 106 ff.). Decisive advances in getting new facts are to be expected, as I believe I have shown, chiefly from analytical experimentation.

III. RESULTS

Girgensohn's impressive analyses will long remain a model for the study of religious feeling. He shows that subjects mean very different things when they talk of feelings, but, in the main, two classes of experiences. In the first class, the observer's self plays a decisive role, either as self-perception or as self-function. Girgensohn mentions in this connection agreement and rejection (cf. *supra*, J. Orth, activity and passivity). Thus it is certain acts, activities of the self, that are termed feelings. In the second class, feeling has definite contents. Either organic sensations appear (cf. James-Lange's theory, Leuba, Freud), or the well-known feelings of pleasantness and unpleasantness, intuitive thoughts, or reproductive bases, memories, and impalpable cognition (cf. *supra*, J. Orth). Here very refined mental operations are regarded as feelings. We can only mention the fact that Girgensohn has also very significant evidence for the nature of intuitive thinking, for the importance of organic sensations, for the topography of the field of consciousness, and the like.

The following result is particularly important. If we take together all the mentioned factors of the religious affective life, we come close to the experience which Schleiermacher understood by the terms, religion or feeling. In the genuine religious experience, ideas, discursive thinking, and processes of volition are secondary. The experimental psychology of religion has brought us farther. It shows us that religion, or what is ordinarily understood as religious feeling, is a specific compound, synthesis, or Gestalt, in which the two groups just mentioned appear in intimate fusion with each other. It is at the same time self-function and mental operation.

Of special interest are the self-functions, a class of elementary mental processes for whose emphasis Girgensohn deserves credit. In these functions or mental acts, the total self, the personality, enters into intimate personal relation with the idea of God. It is already clear how important these results are to pedagogy. Rationalism, voluntarism, the Herbartian one-sided stress upon sense-presentation in education, impersonal "objective" religious instruction are absolutely mistaken. The sources of the religious affective life lie elsewhere.

In my studies of the experience of evaluation, I tried to supplement and carry on the investigations of Girgensohn. His definition of self-function is still very ambiguous. We have seen that he subsumes under it activity, and he does the same with attention and the like. I succeeded—a point which Girgensohn himself had stressed—in throwing more light upon these self-functions.

The central group I have called acts of appropriation. They are specific mental acts which bear the character of experiences of inner contact. Whatever thus comes into touch or most intimate contact with the self becomes a personal possession of the self, becomes a part of it. These processes bear the character of experiences in the highest degree; they are "events" in mental life; they bear the character of microscopic conversions (*Bekehrungen*), as E. D. Starbuck has described them. The impressions thus received form the depths of mental life. They seem to have an outstanding share in the building-up of the individual self. A peculiar hierarchical arrangement, a "monarchical principle" (O. Külpe), brings the individual ideas and thoughts into a systematic connection of superordination and subordination. In my *Religionspsychologie*, I described the course and the stages of these acts. In my *Psychologie des Jugendlichen*, I pointed out pedagogical consequences of this discovery. It appears that the important religious acts or "feelings" of faith and love follow exactly the same laws as the self-functions. Indeed, that was to be expected.

I must content myself with the results I have given as examples of the modern investigation of religious feeling, although there are other most noteworthy things to report upon in the above-mentioned works. It is generally admitted that the published protocols deserve special attention. For they offer the possibility of studying with great refinement the true life of mind.

It is especially important that these results may already be regarded as secure. For we can clearly observe—in the studies of Orth, Stählin, Girgensohn, Gruehn, Canesi, and also Häring, A. Bolley, and in those not yet published—how the same central processes, though variously and independently executed and guided by different motives, appear again and again, are apprehended from quite different points of view, but, as the method progresses, can be diagnosticated more and more univocally.

At the same time, we find confirmation of certain casual (all the more refined non-experimental results are in a measure accidental), very interesting, but frequently contested results of non-experimental psychologists; in a larger context they become comprehensible. So, it seems to me, the doctrine of self-functions throws light upon some peculiar observations of medical psychology and of pure psychology: the concept of transfer (Freud), identification (A. Maeder), empathy (Lipps, Volkelt), love and hate (Brentano, Scheler), and the concept of a depth dimension in mental life (J. S. Mill, Volkelt, Lipps, Scheler, Schmied-Kowarzik, Orth, Krueger, and others).

If we take the results here described and those only indicated, Girgensohn is quite right in saying that the first task of the psychology of religious feeling can now, thanks to experiment, be regarded as solved, namely, the analysis of the fundamental elements and structures of religious life. We are now faced with the second task, equally important and no easier, of the unitary arrangement of the most important religious feelings and the deeper understanding of all the immense variety of forms of religious life from the newly obtained unitary points of view. The execution of this task also opens up very wide perspectives.

For the progress of the doctrine of religious feeling here sketched is of no small importance for the whole of mental life. Let us, at the conclusion as we have done at the beginning, look into these distances. One hundred years ago German classical idealism (Kant, Fichte, Schelling, Hegel) made the gigantic attempt of creating a unitary and comprehensive world-view of the whole of modern science and civilization (*Kultur*). After Plato and Aristotle, it was the second attempt of the sort in the history of man. The attempt failed, and led, as we now clearly see, to the terrible debacle of present European civilization. But now we see even more clearly the mistakes which frustrated the attempt.

First, the last peaks of mental life were sought in mysticism (Fichte), and in religious rationalism (Hegel)—not in that still higher sphere in which, as I have shown, the inwardness of mysticism and the spirituality of intuitive thought combine into the mysterious experience of true piety. As a result of this error, the nineteenth century clung to a false religiosity, and neglected those genuine sources out of which the peoples and civilizations of earlier centuries drew, again and again, rejuvenating power.

The second error was seen, but could not then be eliminated. Kant wanted to establish exact mental sciences—this was one of the starting-points of his famous *Kritiken*—which were to be as securely founded as the natural sciences. To do this he had to have very comprehensive and precise work chiefly in the field of mental life, the common basis of all the mental sciences. Since this work was not available, there resulted the familiar one-sided structure of science and civilization, the underestimation of the mental and the spiritual, the perverse overestimation of the material world, and the spiritual debility of Europe. These two errors stand in perspicuous connection with the doctrine of religious feeling.

Humanity is today working again with profound earnestness at a re-establishment of the whole of its material and spiritual possession. Again, as a hundred years ago, the unsolved problems come up. Will we succeed in the exact treatment of the profound problems and in the attainment of the goal which Kant saw? That it is not unattainable is shown in small part by the progress of experimental research in the field of religious feeling.

SELECTED BIBLIOGRAPHY

I. Logische Psychologie

1. Husserl, E. Logische Untersuchungen. Halle: Niemeyer, 1912.

2. Meinong, A. v. Psychologisch-ethische Untersuchungen zur Werttheorie. 1894.

3. Müller, A. Psychologie. Berlin: Dümmler, 1927.

4. ————. Gotteserlebnis und Welterkenntnis. Festschrift für J. Volkelt. Munich, 1918.

5. Scheler, M. Zur Phänomenologie und Theorie der Sympathiegefühle. Halle: Niemeyer, 1913, 1923.

6. Schmied-Kowarzik, W. Umriss einer analytischen Psychologie. Leipzig: Barth, 1912.

II. Reine Psychologie

1. James, W. The principles of psychology. New York: Holt, 1890.

2. ————. The varieties of religious experience. New York: Longmans, Green, 1902.

3. LIPPS, TH. Vom Fühlen, Denken, und Wollen. Leipzig: Barth, 1902, 1907.

4. MAIER, H. Psychologie des emotionalen Denkens. Tübingen: Mohr, 1908.

5. RIBOT, TH. La psychologie des sentiments. Paris: Alcan, 1896.

6. SCHLEIERMACHER, D. FR. Reden über Religion. 1799.

III. EXPERIMENTELLE PSYCHOLOGIE

A. *Allgemein*

1. KRUEGER, F. Die Tiefendimension und die Gegensätzlichkeit des Gefühlslebens. Festschrift für J. Volkelt. Munich, 1918.

2. ————. Komplexqualitäten, Gestalten und Gefühle. Munich: Beck, 1926.

3. LEUBA, J. Psychologie der religiösen Mystik. Munich: Bergmann, 1927.

4. McDOUGALL, W. An introduction to social psychology. London: Methuen, 1908, 1922.

5. SHAND, A. F. The foundations of character. London: Macmillan, 1920.

6. STARBUCK, E. D. The psychology of religion. London: Scott, 1899, 1901.

7. TITCHENER, E. B. Lectures on the elementary psychology of feeling and attention. New York: Macmillan, 1908.

B. *Würzburger Schule*

1. BOLLEY, A. Die Betrachtung als psychologisches Problem. *Bonner Zeitschrift für Theologie*, 1924.

2. CANESI, A. Ricerche preliminari sulla psicologia della preghiera. *Contributi del laboratorio di psicologia della Università Cattolica del Sacro Cuore, Milano*, Series I, Vol. I (1925), No. 4, pp. 247–315.

3. GIRGENSOHN, K. Der seelische Aufbau des religiösen Erlebens: eine religionspsychologische Untersuchung auf experimenteller Grundlage. 1921.

4. ————. Die Erscheinungsweisen religiöser Gedanken. *Bericht über den VIII. Kongress für experimentelle Psychologie*, 1924.

5. ————. Religionspsychologie, Religionswissenschaft und Theologie. Leipzig, Erlangen: A. Deichert, 1923, 1925.

6. GRUEHN, W. K. Girgensohns religionspsychologische Entwicklung. *Archiv für die gesamte Psychologie*, LV (1926), 219–250.

7. ————. Das Werterlebnis: eine religionspsychologische Studie auf experimenteller Grundlage. Leipzig: Hirzel, 1924.

8. ————. Religionspsychologie. Breslau: Hirt, 1926.

9. ————. Psychologie des Jugendlichen mit besonderer Berücksichtigung der religiösen Erscheinungen. Handbuch für d. ev. Jungmännerarb. Deutschlands, ed. by E. Stange, I (1927).

10. HÄRING, TH. L. Untersuchungen zur Psychologie der Wertung. *Archiv für die gesamte Psychologie*, 1913.

11. KÜLPE, O. Grundriss der Psychologie. Leipzig: Engelmann, 1893.

12. ————. Vorlesungen über Psychologie. Ed. by K. Bühler. Leipzig: Hirzel, 1920, 1922.

13. MESSER, A. Psychologie. Stuttgart: Deutsche Verlag, 1914.

14. ORTH, J. Gefühl und Bewusstseinslage: eine kritisch-experimentelle Studie. Berlin: Reuther & Reichert, 1903.

15. RAITZ VON FRENTZ, E. Bedeutung, Ursprung und Sein der Gefühle. *Scholastik*, II (1927), No. 3.

16. Stählin, W. Experimentelle Untersuchungen zur . . . Religions-psychologie. *Archiv für Religionspsychologie,* I (1914).

17. Störring, G. Psychologie des menschlichen Gefühlslebens. Bonn: Cohen, 1916.

IV. Medizinische Psychologie

1. Adler, A. Ueber den nervösen Charakter. 1922.

2. Freud, S. Studien über Hysterie. 1895.

3. Schultz, I. H. Seelische Krankenbehandlung. Jena: Fischer, 1918, 1922.

DISCUSSION

Dr. Reymert: Dr. Gruehn's paper is now open for discussion. May I call upon Dr. Bühler to please voice his opinion?

Dr. Bühler *(University of Vienna)*: I do not want to speak first in this discussion. I should prefer to be the last speaker. Dr. Schneider can answer as well as I. Do you agree to that?

Dr. Reymert: Surely. Any questions or comments from anyone? I believe from my own impressions at several national conventions of psychology in America, at which I have been present, that the experimental attack on the psychology of religion, as we should know it through the Külpe-Girgensohn method, and from the work of Bühler, Schneider, and others, is somewhat unknown among American workers as yet. I think that we should use this opportunity, having both Dr. Bühler and Dr. Schneider here, to ask any questions our hearts desire. Let us start in.

Dr. Weiss *(Ohio State University)*: I should like to ask for a more complete analysis of the self-function. In religious feelings two kinds were mentioned, the self-function and the object-function.

Dr. Schneider *(Wittenberg College)*: This is not easy to explain in the short time at our disposal. It means that finally all religious experience can be analyzed into two functions: we may say, in the more popular terminology, into an emotional function and an intellectual function, that is, the self-related function or ego-function, which has qualitative tones of emotional character. At the same time every religious experience goes inherently together with an objective relation, a more or less intuitive thought process. This thought process is an experience of a transcendent object. These two functions may be found in the psychology of Augustine. He makes a difference between *amare* and *intellegere* in the religious experience. We also have it in the psychological observations of the mysticists.

Dr. Weiss: I understand, then, that this ego-function, so far as religious feelings are concerned, is dominant.

Dr. Schneider: Yes, yes.

Dr. Bühler: Yes.

Professor Crowl *(University of Michigan)*: As I understand it, the chief characteristic of the technique under discussion was that of having persons explain, at some sort of request, their feelings which are supposed to be of a religious nature. Without meaning to criticize, I should like to ask the speaker what his opinion is of a supplementary method, that of employing the spontaneous religious writings of adolescents as apparent from diaries and religious poetry?

Dr. Schneider: We do not put questions to our observers. I think Dr. Gruehn has been misunderstood. The process is that we give religious stimuli, religious poems, or better, short striking religious sentences; we have tried it also with pictures, and I tried it here with religious tunes and melodies. We give the stimulus and then the observer has, with his definite *Einstellung,* to read, hear, or see this stimulus and then give us an introspective report. All other methods would be useful as supplementary methods, and when you read Girgensohn's books you will find he also has often used such supplementary methods.

DR. ERICSON (*Upsala College*): Has it been observed in these experiments that the subject really changes his report, i. e., that his reaction is reported differently at different times? What came to my mind was the suggestion given somewhere of the possibility that the physiological condition of the subject has something to do with his reaction to the religious stimuli.

DR. SCHNEIDER: Certainly it has. A complete description has to include all these things: physiological condition, *Einstellung*, i. e., "general mood." Dr. Ericson's question refers to a genetic process. Some religious experiences continuously change, but we can also observe some structural lines which run through all protocols, under all possible conditions. To bring this out in detail I should have to cite too many instances.

DR. BÜHLER: I think Dr. Schneider has answered all questions so well and so definitely that I have nothing more to add.

PART VII

History of the Psychology of
Feelings and Emotions

CHAPTER 33

HISTORICAL DEVELOPMENT OF THE THEORY OF EMOTIONS

G. S. Brett

University of Toronto

It seems proper that in a symposium on feelings and emotions some account should be given of the long history of the subject. The development of all the sciences has been so rapid in the past century that no one can expect to find in the records of antiquity, or even of comparatively recent times, any significant addition to knowledge. But the function of the historian is quite distinct from that of the experimenter or the theorist. In the common language of today, history is a cultural subject. It serves to open the mind to the long periods of time during which men have pursued truth. It also provides a perspective in which it is possible to see the variety of interests which dominate research, often influencing the whole trend of thought for long periods of time and inclining men to accept theories which afterwards appear misguided and limited. The historian, for better or for worse, is committed to the labor of going back along the highway of progress and discovering the ideas and suggestions which, though no longer remembered in their original form, are none the less landmarks in the general advance.

In the limited time which this subject can claim on the program it would be futile to attempt any detailed history of what has been said about emotions. Omissions will be numerous and can easily be pardoned. While some subjects in the field of psychology have been more or less adequately traced by historians, there seems to be no adequate survey of the theories of emotion, and it is to be hoped that the task will be undertaken some day by someone with sufficient leisure and ability. A probable reason for this state of affairs is the fact that no subject in the whole field of psychology is more complex or indeterminate than the emotions. The conditions under which they can be observed are not such as would naturally produce exact results; but those conditions are so common and so frequent that descriptions and classifications have been recorded from the earliest times and exist in bewildering confusion.

All scientific work emerges from a background of uncritical observation. Though the earliest efforts may have little permanent value, they often contain elements of truth which help to direct thought into the right channels. In so large and difficult a field as that of human behavior it would not be surprising if some shrewd observer, unhampered by the accumulation of theories, were to make a contribution as valuable as it was simple. Though the Greeks were by no means primitive, they came very near the beginning of Western civilization, and they may be said to have created the first systematic account of the human organism and its functions. In so doing they started from a pure and unprejudiced naturalism, which stands out in the history of thought as distinctively as Greek sculpture. For the Greek thinker, man was an animal, distinguished from other animals by two characteristics—the power of calculative reason and the capacity for social organization. The science of human conduct was a part of natural science, and the two great exponents of this theory, Plato and Aristotle, constructed their interpretation of human life on the basis of the contemporary science of medicine. Though the nervous system was at that time undiscovered, the apparatus at their disposal was not wholly inadequate. The "humors" were a good basis for clinical descriptions. The idea of a physiological balance was expressly formulated; disease, mental and physical, could be usefully catalogued in terms of the excess and defect in the quality and quantity of the humors. The Hippocratic School was responsible for the authoritative statement which put all diseases on the same natural level and banished the supernatural from the sphere of medicine.

The mental and the physical are only known in correlation; he would be a bold man who would assert more than that. It is therefore not contrary to the logic of scientific thought that sometimes one and sometimes the other should exhibit an independent advance. Psychology as a science of behavior can go a long way in the analysis of conduct without committing itself to physiological dogmas. The fact that Greek physiology was not within sight of the real truth most of the time is not a reason for refusing to acknowledge the contributions made to psychology. As a historical fact it is clear that the psychological descriptions succeeded in spite of the defective physiology. In the subjects with which we are now concerned the fundamental concept employed was that of activity or vital motion. With a large and generous outlook Plato calls this *eros*, popularly translated love but more correctly interpreted by the word libido. Greek naturalism, consciously opposed to the Oriental sentiments, took its stand on the three fundamental ideas of food and drink and sex. Accordingly the emotional life is mainly dependent on the various manifestations of these three primary drives. But the virtue of the Greek method is found in the skill with which these elementary forces are kept in relation with the progressive civilization of the human animal. As the level of development rises, the nature of the satisfaction changes; aesthetic and intellectual satisfaction are as real as food and mating. What Plato called *eros* Aristotle described as *orexis*, the conation of the later Latin writers. This is simply the biological will-to-live, the life-energy itself. In Aristotle the details are more systematically elaborated and we have a remarkably complete sketch of the evolution of conduct. The primary elements are the purely somatic energies—the ferocity of the animal in defending its life and the hunger that seeks food. But with the expansion of life these develop into acquisitiveness, desire for fame, sensitiveness to insult, and all the other modifications which accompany the evolution of the social group. This sense for the different forms of the original affective state is a very interesting point. Fear, for example, covers a variety of states ranging from timidity and dread of pain to that kind of fear which is only possible to a creature that hopes and plans. Many things cause fear, but they are all reducible to one class: the typical fear is fear of death, and all other causes are forms of this original type. Similarly Aristotle makes a significant point when he distinguishes between the feeling which belongs to natural hunger and the craving which results from acquired habit and self-indulgence.

These suggestions must suffice at the present time to support the claim that the Greeks hold an important place in the history of this subject. By taking a simple basis of "motion to" and "motion from," the seeking and the avoiding reactions of modern writers, they were able to construct a plan of behavior which still repays consideration. The affective states were recognized as a distinct class; in them the subject undergoes a change in some way distinct from the changes which constitute perception. They are more deeply organic than intellectual processes; they move to action, for intellect cannot produce motion. They are the various forms in which the original dynamic energy of life is expressed; for desire is the primary factor in life and the emotions are the deeper stirrings of nature. That Aristotle thought feeling is controlled chiefly by success or failure in the realization of purpose, conscious or unconscious, seems clearly indicated by his definition of pleasure as "the accompaniment of unimpeded activity."

In popular thought the Stoics and Epicureans are considered to have been excessively preoccupied with the problems of feeling and emotion. There is truth in this view, but the popular tradition omits the subtlety of their actual theories. Both parties accepted the view that emotions are actually forms of motion, of being "moved," as we say; emotions were reduced to the formula of positive and negative directions of motion. In the normal state the emotion in the proper sense was not found; all emotions were forms of disease, or, as we should say, abnormal states of excitement. The normal state was a point of equilibrium called tranquillity, a point on the scale of feeling to which the person returns after divergence either toward elation or toward depression. Amid the lengthy moralizing of a school more interested in controlling than analyzing emotions, there are many acute descriptions which seem to express in cruder language the ideas of tension, relaxation, sthenic or asthenic states, and similar classifications revived in the last century. Moreover this doctrine was not merely theoretical, for the variations of the pulse were elaborately studied by the Alexandrian schools of medicine. There is an old story of the Arab physician who discovered by variations of the pulse which lady of the harem was disturbing the tranquillity of the royal patient. The fact that this story appears in several forms is good evidence of the extent to which the volume-pulse method was practically applied when emotional disturbances were suspected.

The Oriental writers invariably describe emotions in terms of somatic conditions, and such picturesque phrases as "the bowels of mercy" perpetuate their memory. The Greeks, too, employed a language which showed that they assigned emotional states a place in the middle parts of the body. In spite of this there seems to be a widespread notion that all the older theories were intellectualistic and took no account of anything but a vague entity called a soul. It is true that as the science of behavior became more complex it was felt necessary to give the psychic factors a place in the description of emotions; but even so the important writers continued a form of bookkeeping by double entry: anger, for example, might originate in the idea of the wrong inflicted but it was also a "boiling of the blood about the heart." Psychologists, along with other people, will have to revise their ideas of mediaeval doctrines and cease to refer to that period as though it were exclusively an age of theological abstractions. The chief defect of that age was a love of formal classifications and it is more than probable that we have not yet recovered from the influence it exerted on the earlier modern writers It is to be recorded as a virtue of the classical Greek writers that they made no attempt to devise a complete list of emotions. Fear, pity, love, hate, and some others are quoted as examples, but there is no systematic order and no finality is attempted.

The Revival of Learning merely brought into vogue the original Aristotelian and Stoic views. Aristotle had expressly likened animals to machines operated by the inner forces just as a puppet is worked by wires. Descartes, anxious to exploit his physiology, revived this method of treatment. It was an easy way of shaking off many difficult problems and offered a prospect of reducing emotions to the laws of mechanics; the dynamics of expansion and contraction were adequate to explain the affective or passive states. The fashion spread rapidly, because all theory was temporarily in bondage to the clearness and distinctness of the ideas which Galileo formulated. It was a fallacious simplicity, but of a kind which has often made an equally successful appeal. Also it could easily be combined with the formulae that survived in the Aristotelian tradition. Hobbes, inspired by Galileo, proceeded to reduce all mental phenomena to modes of motion and reproduced verbatim his own translation of Aristotle's *Rhetoric*. Malebranche, intoxicated by the Cartesian wine, emphasized contractions and dilatations so effectively that he has been proclaimed the forerunner of James and Lange, a discovery which is less remarkable when we remember that Lange refers to Malebranche as virtually anticipating his theory. The "machinamentum corporis" was a regulative idea in the eighteenth century and slowly penetrated the last strongholds of rationalism. But it remained a barren theory, a testimony to the futility of all attempts to reduce experience to the artificial language of mechanics.

The subject of emotions was saved from complete extinction by the influence of two new movements—the novel and biology. The sudden emergence of the novel in the middle of the eighteenth century is a curious event. There can be no reasonable doubt that it was a by-product of the individualistic philosophy which had conquered England and France. The sentimental superseded the rational; the sentimental journey and the sentimental novel were now fashionable, and the rigidity of logical systems was ignored. The Romantic School was interested in the variety of human emotions and popularized the idea that emotions were really important. As students of life the Romantics joined hands with the biologists, notably in the case of Goethe who was an epitome of the whole movement. There are still no greater descriptions of the emotional life of individuals than those produced during this period. Psychologists have made too little use of this literature, though Shand set a good example and Miss Edgell has recently drawn attention to it. On the more scientific side we find at this period a revived interest in the physical expression of the emotions. Sir Charles Bell's *Anatomy and Philosophy of Expression* may be called the first attempt to make a science of expression. The way for this had really been prepared by the great artists—to artists and actors the psychologists owe a considerable debt.

From this point progress during the nineteenth century has been considerable and varied. The names of Wundt, Darwin, and Bain naturally rise in the mind, and at the present time in this, as in all branches of psychology, we may say of the workers that their name is legion. The object of this rapid survey is twofold. First, in the interests of the historical approach I have aimed to suggest how much there is to correct in current opinions about our predecessors and how much might be gained by adorning psychology with the greatness of its own tradition. Secondly, I have tried to trace the variety of interests which converge on this subject of emotions. At the present time they seem to run parallel. There are first, the description and classification of normal emotions; second, the experimental analysis; third, the contributions from the field of abnormal psychology, psychoanalysis, and the like. In all this there is great confusion and variety of opinion. A list of emotions implies that there are emotions to be listed. If the list is correlated with a list of instincts, there is a double implication; namely, that there are both instincts and emotions and that they are related in some definite way. This structure would collapse if either instincts or emotions were found to be illusory entities. There is no doubt about the utility of such schemes but at the same time there is no guarantee of their finality or adequacy. We must accept the lesson of history, that a new truth is generally discovered later to have been a half-truth. The experimental approach has a hard task in the case of emotions. It plays its part in determining the endosomatic responses and they are perhaps the most definite factors today in the whole range of literature on the emotions. But whether we talk of secretions or galvanometric measurements it is very obvious that we are only selecting one aspect of a total response; there is no successful generalization of the facts and no satisfactory explanation of the causation or the correlation implied.

When we turn from the experimental to the clinical approach, we seem to be in another world. For those who reject the unconscious altogether, there can be little interest in the study of this material and the opponents are apparently irreconcilable. I cannot pretend to pass any judgment on the merits of the case, but a study of the recent works in this field suggests the need for some distinction between the emotions as usually described and the kind of experience which the clinical psychologist describes. The influence of animal psychology and of the physiological schools that flourished in Germany has been allowed to obscure the possibility of an evolution of the emotions. There is no a priori reason why the emotions should not evolve; the assumption that they do not seems to be little more than an oversight. If they did, the most natural and obvious mistake would be to confuse the different levels. This has been the worst effect of the interpretation usually put on such theories as the James-Lange; because they are indisputably right up to a certain point they are stretched over the rest of the area. It is noticeable that some writers are addicted to the use of the word biological; we are assured that the instincts and their visceral accompaniments are what they are because of their biological importance. But, properly speaking, this importance is known only to the theorist; an animal certainly does not exhibit fear or rage because self-preservation is the first law of life. The word biological, if it is given an exact meaning, implies a relation between the act and the consequences of the act for either the individual or the race. This relation is no part of any behavior unless we assume that the behavior is influenced by memory or purpose. Behavior is only biological for the scientific observer; for the agent it is psychological. If the psychologist is confident that emotions are gut-reactions, he need not complicate matters by calling them biological. We may, presumably, accept as an established fact that instincts are equivalent to muscular reactions and emotions equivalent to visceral reactions. On this basis it would seem advisable to attempt a comparative study of emotions. It may be that all the theories are right, but that they require to be sorted out on some evolutionary principle. At one end of the scale the types of reaction would approximate a type of compound reflex response. The instinct and the emotion would then be so far undifferentiated that the terms need not be discussed; the general diffusion of excitement would adequately account for all forms of behavior at this level. The emotion as a differentiated factor would then emerge at that point on the scale of development at which we are prepared to say that a situation has meaning, using that word to denote any form of connection between the given situation and other situations either remembered or anticipated. This higher level, defined in terms of organic development and ultimately of brain-development, would carry with it more or less modified forms of the primitive type of reaction; it would be emotional both on account of the bodily reverberation and the psychic tension. In defense of this suggestion I would appeal to the very significant results reported by Helga Eng in the book called *Experimental Investigations into the Emotional Life of the Child Compared with that of the Adult*. The results reported in this work are derived from exact experiments in which the measurement of physiological expression is the method of investigation. The definition of the emotion is therefore derived from the bodily changes and the investigation is in line with the modern methods in this respect. But the conclusions show important modifications and are particularly significant in demonstrating the difference between children and adults. It is reported that in the case of stimuli employed objectively by the experimenter, there was no difference between children and adults. This is natural, because the stimuli were sensory and there would be no ground for supposing that a direct response to such stimuli would differ in adults and children. But it is reported that "in the spontaneous curves where the changes are caused by free personal psychic activity the matter is otherwise." Here a real differentia seems to be introduced by the more complex mentality of the adult; the relation between ideas comes into play and the character of the emotions changes.

The author of the work says: "If a few of those investigators who have carried out plethysmograph investigations, such as Mosso and Canestrini, find that the results point to the dependence of mind on matter, this must rest on an acquired materialistic view of life." That expression indicates the important point that a theory may be influenced by the fashion of the time at which it appeared. In the reaction from a peculiar form of vagueness which belonged to Germany in the early nineteenth century, there was an almost hysterical demand for what was tangible and demonstrable to the senses. This was the time when it seemed plausible to say man is what he eats. But that epoch is definitely ended; nothing remains of it but the limited doctrine that physiological data are a part of all human behavior. For the other part we are compelled to accept a type of causation which is psychic and consists of antecedent events which qualify the subsequent acts either as memories or as subconscious factors. This point of view makes it possible to unify the general theory of emotions with the theory of abnormal phenomena. All emotions begin from a stimulus which disturbs the balance of the organism. The response varies with the nature of the organism and is more or less complex according to the level of development. Fear, for example, may induce flight and thereby cease to exist as an emotion, or it may induce a complex state of antagonistic impulses producing inhibitions which augment the emotion; or it may persist as a conflict between a conscious purpose and an unconscious or co-conscious factor, which is equivalent to a reduction of energy with a sense of defective power. This condition is a state of fear such as occurs when there is no apparent cause of fear but nevertheless the situation is made the object of genuine fear.

The historical development which has been sketched seems to end in confusion and a demand for a reconstruction of the theory of emotions. The most recent efforts to satisfy all the requirements have not been described in detail because that process would be too fatiguing. But their significance seems to lie in the direction indicated by all evolutionary methods. The human animal has reached its present state of development through slow processes of growth and integration which are admitted to be the explanation of special cognitive functions. There is no ground for divorcing these functions from general bodily states, but there is also no reason for ignoring the possibility of great differences arising from the degree of cerebral development and integration. This seems to be the element of truth in the distinction which James retained between the "coarser" and the "subtler" emotions. But that distinction smacks of a theory of values which is not wholly relevant to psychology. The amendment which it requires must be looked for in another direction. Instead of opposing one class of emotions to another we must recognize that any emotion may have distinct forms, as distinct as animal rage from righteous indignation. As the one form has evolved from the other, in conformity with the general evolution of man, it may easily retain associations with its more primitive type or with allied types. In any case the relation between the emotion and the expression will become less fixed as the organism develops away from instinctive and stereotyped forms of reaction. The more complex emotions (i.e., the subtler), having had no specific associated reaction (such as is typical of animal behavior), will be capable of varied expression, and the expression will have no intimate connection with the cognitive element—a point which might considerably assist the theorists who try to decide why we weep as successfully for joy as for sorrow.

DISCUSSION

Dr. Reymert: May I be permitted a few remarks from the Chair about the small investigation of Helga Eng, to which Dr. Brett seemed to attach altogether too much significance, and to which he referred at length. This study was undertaken at the University of Oslo, from which I hail. It meant a following-up of the well-known works of Lehmann in Copenhagen—using his expressive method. The arrangement of the plethysmographic apparatus was minutely done by the director of the Physiological Institute, Dr. Torup.   As far as I remember, Dr. Eng had just a few children and very few adult observers, most of them not psychologically trained.   We all know the tremendously many sources of error in plethysmographic work in general—and from this knowledge it should a priori be almost impossible to undertake such work with children.   From the small number of observers and from the application of the method to children, it seems to me that all the many conclusions which the author draws from these experiments have at best only a hypothetical value.   The high-sounding title of such a limited study seems pretentious, and when Dr. Eng even goes so far as to offer a solution of the general body-mental problem—on the basis of such experimentation—then we are way outside the simplest scientific logic.   I have permitted myself these remarks because it often happens that philosophers are apt to use quotations and conclusions of this kind, without—as may be reasonable—being able to weigh or scrutinize the limitations and the possible sources of error inherent in the experimental method employed.

PART VIII

Emotion in Relation to
Education

CHAPTER 34

TRAINING THE EMOTIONS

JOHN S. TERRY
New York City

Those of you who have listened to the learned and scientific papers on the feelings and emotions delivered here since last Wednesday, doubtless feel like the twelve-year-old boy who not long ago was presumably taking part in an arithmetic class. The private school which he attended was a very modern one, using all up-to-date methods. His teacher in this particular class noticed that he was not paying attention, and finally, when she asked him a question, he blandly ignored her.

"Why don't you answer the question, John?" asked the teacher.

"Oh, I'm relaxing," replied John.

One of his other teachers had told the children that when they felt a nervous strain they should relax. Arithmetic made John nervous. Perhaps psychology has done the same for you.

I recently read an account of a visit by two parents to another very modern school. The children were *learning by doing*. As the parents went through one classroom they noticed that two boys were beating another over the head with a club.

"But," asked the mother, "aren't they hurting the child?"

"Oh, yes," replied the teacher. "These children are studying the Whiskey Rebellion."

"Why, they're drunk," said the mother.

"Certainly," said the teacher. "They're drunk and they'll soon be sick. We use real equipment when possible. But today even the schools can't get decent whiskey for their work."

The parents would not visit the class in literature studying "The Murders in the Rue Morgue."

At the very outset I want it clearly understood that my knowledge of psychology is not enough to permit me to understand what its battles are about. And as to scientific knowledge of the emotions, I remember that William James, after reading the classics on the subject, said that he would as lief read verbal descriptions of the shapes of rocks in a New England field.

In spite of these facts, I hope to give you in the next few minutes

[1] Portions of the discussion of Mr. Terry's paper have been published in *School* during December, 1927, and January, 1928, and in subsequent issues.

some thoughts on the need for more wholesome emotion in the life of America, for more attention to the emotional lives of the children in our schools, and to suggest a few methods that have been or might be used in this work.

A new emphasis is needed in our education, I feel sure. We have gone ahead too much with the idea that training the minds of children is enough. We give them intelligence tests, measure their mental possibilities *after a fashion*, classify them, and then put them through their intellectual paces, just as if their minds were the controlling factors in their lives. As a matter of fact, I think it is generally believed that the intellect plays not fifty per cent in determining what people are going to do with their lives. Environment and circumstances play their parts, but emotionalized attitudes play a much more important part. In life, the heart plays a much bigger rôle than the head.

James Harvey Robinson, in his notable plea for science and the scientific method, recognized this when he said that only through a change in man's attitude can intelligence play its part in civilization.

In December, 1925, I came to the conclusion that the schools were neglecting to fulfil their duties in guiding the emotional development of children. I visited a New York City junior high school for girls. The principal told me of a serious problem case.

A girl had gone to a dance with a high-school boy. He escorted her home and told her good-night. The girl did not enter her home, but decided to see more of night life. She wandered along the streets, bent on flirtation. It happened that the man she finally spoke to was sensible enough to take her to a policeman. She then pretended to be suffering from that tabloid disease known as amnesia.

I asked about the girl's school record. It was excellent. Her grades were high; her conduct, good. But her teachers investigated and found that outside the school this girl went to all the dances she possibly could. She was a constant viewer of lurid moving pictures, in which virtue usually triumphs in order to please the censor, but always rather late. Her home was crowded. She had no privacy. In other words, her whole life was being moulded not so much by her mental training in her school, as by outside forces playing on her emotions. She frankly admitted that while she enjoyed school, it had little influence in determining her conduct after she left it in the afternoon.

I realized that here was a girl whose emotional life was an un-weeded garden. She was evidently fearless, too much so; she was adventurous, even in the realm of lying. And her school was making no particular effort to guide her and show her how to develop her life emotionally.

I began to look around me, and saw that while we have an excess of emotional stimulants in American life, too many of them are of the wrong sort. I agree with the editors of *Civilization in the United States* that "the most moving and pathetic fact in the social life of America is emotional and aesthetic starvation."

I find Americans attempting to feed their emotions. They are avid for thrilling moving pictures and for jazzy radio programs; they buy tabloid magazines and confession magazines by the millions.

Sinclair Lewis criticizes the Babbitts for the poor intellects they display. The Rotarians are not after intellect. In their business they use their brains. In their get-togethers and social activities they try to feed their emotions. Booth Tarkington has given a better picture of Babbitt in his novel *The Plutocrat*. Tarkington shows the zest a Babbitt gets from his good fellowship and showing-off. No heartburnings here; rather a childlike zest in living.

I believe the fact that ours is called the jazz age is significant. "Let me write a nation's songs, and I'll let who will write its laws," said some wise man. Americans have been wrought upon by jazz music until the greater part of our social life, from "speak-easy" to ball-room, is negroid. This jazz music is easily reacted to, and it sets a whole nation dancing to primitive rhythms. I wonder what is the effect on a sedate North Dakota family of radio jazz music and cutting-up broadcast from the Silver Slipper night club on footloose Broadway. I read recently of a psychologist who had a jazz band perform for the sake of an elephant. The elephant soon routed the players with well-directed spouts of water. Perhaps he had more than human intelligence.

Americans enjoyed the World War immensely. It gave them a chance to blow off the lid of the emotional reservoir. The lid has blown off only once since the war—when Charles A. Lindbergh stirred the nation to transports such as were never before aroused by one man's heroic deed.

After the war there developed a mood of futility that exists yet. If you want to see how cynical and hopeless young America is, read *The American Caravan*, a collection of short stories, plays, and poems, that the magazines wouldn't print.

Even the best of our creative artists seem terribly depressed. Sinclair Lewis has studied religion and I hear that he is actually so wrought up that his favorite sport is getting a crowd of boon companions together to sing hymns. I believe that the man may become a revivalist at any minute. There's no doubt in my mind that Lewis is emotionally starved. The hymns do him good.

I think that the intelligentsia in America are in the same plight that Darwin found himself in, in his later years. In his youth he got the greatest pleasure from music. In his old age he expressed profound regret that his intellect had so dominated his life that his emotional and aesthetic nature was atrophied.

I believe these generalizations are worth thinking about. All psychologists agree that the emotions are extremely important. I expect that every scientist envies the fervor of the religious man and knows that his own life is colorless in comparison.

The crime situation, with preachers, judges, and newspapers seeking panaceas, has brought about a great outcry for character training in the schools. They would train character, but they don't know what it is. They know it only when they see it manifested.

Various groups are trying to find out what character is. One scheme for finding out is most interesting. The researchers plan to investigate how men and women of acknowledged success and character react in certain social and moral situations. They plan to ask the men and women to tell them. It is devastating to think what a lot of lies, conscious and unconscious, will be told by those who are asked to give their reactions. As one man put it, every autobiography is a lie. People refuse to undress their minds and souls for the public gaze.

Another method has been followed by President Daniel L. Marsh of Boston University. Last year he asked several hundred business men and his thousand seniors and graduate students what qualities or ideals a good man should possess. The composite answers named the following qualities: honesty, love, reverence, loyalty, industry, intelligence, a moral sense, courage, justice, self-control, and patience. Four ways of attaining these were given: example and environment; education, that is, definite instruction; experience; and precept.

Such inquiries seem to me of little practical worth. My reasons are obvious. We all agree, for example, that loyalty is a desirable quality. But loyalty to what? John Galsworthy in his play *Loyalties* has given us some idea of the complexity of the question. Shall we be loyal to self, to family, to friends, to race, to city, to state, to nation; to the ideal or to the practical? If a man begins consciously to try to be loyal, he's apt to land in a mad house. So it is with love.

Just one reference to a related field of inquiry. Drs. Hugh Hartshorne and Mark A. May have been using provocations tests. They are making an investigation in cooperation with the Institute of Social and Religious Research, New York, in Teachers

College, Columbia University. They have been asking children all sorts of questions, from why they like their friends to what they would do in certain situations.

In one of the provocations tests they asked this question: "Henry saw a big bully strike a little boy, so Henry walked up and gave the bully a real hard blow and knocked him down." "Was Henry's action right, excusable, or wrong?" Eighty-five per cent of the sixth-grade children questioned said that Henry's action was right, six per cent said it was excusable, and nine per cent said it was wrong. Forty-five per cent of a class of graduate students thought Henry did right in knocking the bully down, forty-two per cent thought Henry's deed excusable, and thirteen per cent thought he did wrong. Messrs. Hartshorne and May had three points of value for the decisions. They voted two points that Henry did wrong, and one that he was to be excused. I expect the majority of us would agree with the judgment of the sixth-grade children.

I believe that such questions and answers are also of little practical value, for we cannot possibly tell how we would act, and therefore cannot safely pass judgment on others. The only way to find out what we would do in Henry's situation would be to see a bully strike a child.

I suppose that it is practically impossible to determine just how important a part the intellect plays in determining what people will say and do under any stated conditions. There is certainly no way at present to tell. However, there is much good authority which favors emotional attitudes as the strongest determinant of conduct. There is strong distrust of the intellect as arbiter and guide. Associate Superintendent Joseph M. Sheehan of New York City recently quoted George Eliot as saying that to train a child to reason about everything is to make him a monster. This statement is in agreement with my belief that the feelings and emotions play a large part in determining a man's action and worth.

Dr. Cyril Burt, the English psychologist, defines character as "the sum total of those personal qualities of mind which do not constitute, or are not pervaded by intelligence. They are marked by feeling rather than skill." Roback declares that character is "an enduring psychophysical disposition to inhibit instinctive impulses in accordance with a regulative principle." Herbert Martin in his study *Formative Foundations of Character* states: "Intelligence has long been regarded not only as of doubtful worth in the realm of morals, but as an altogether perilous possession. Knowledge and moral peril vary directly." Adam and Eve found this to be true.

I agree with Dr. Ira S. Wile, who has quoted these authorities,[2] that the motor part of emotion determines action and character; that the intelligent child is often harder to train in desirable habits just because his intelligence shows him how better to feed his desires through habits of his own formation.

I believe, therefore, that psychologists and educators should try to shape the emotional attitudes of pupils, despite the fact that there is no scientific working basis for procedure in the work.

Perhaps you will say that it is impossible directly to train the emotions. Of course a teacher cannot tell his pupils to register love, tenderness, hate, fear, as would a movie director. But we have found methods by which to train the mind. These methods are indirect too. The educator can only teach. The child must do the learning—so with the emotions.

I wish you'd all think back over your school years. Did anyone ever tell you the importance of the feelings and emotions in your lives? I'm afraid not.

Of course I'm rather late in urging training of the emotions. Christ did it about two thousand years ago. I feel that He would have had more success with His doctrines if St. Paul and some of His other followers had not intellectualized them. Saul's conversion left him still a man of intellect, and he wrote too many letters.

Christ said to his disciples, "Love one another." He also commanded them to love God with all their hearts. St. Paul preached this too, but rather unconvincingly. As Dr. William Dygnum Moss has often said to me, "Christ knew that a good man is a person of fine feeling. The man with the right feeling will do the right thing in practically every situation." Christ was moral without trying to be. But St. Paul was intellectual; he had a thorn in his flesh.

The influence of all religious leaders has been due to the emotions. Their whole success has depended on whether or not they could develop desired emotional attitudes in their followers. Mohammed fired his followers with a flame that swept over Asia and Africa, and seared part of Europe.

I think the weakness of many religious organizations today lies in the fact that they have forgotten the fundamental need of emotional appeal. The fundamentalists still use this appeal, but the modernists have lost ground through appealing chiefly to the intellect. It seems to me that the Catholic and the Christian Science Churches have been the most successful trainers of the emotions. Please understand that I adhere to neither faith. The

[2] *Intelligent Parenthood* (Chicago: The University of Chicago Press, 1926), p. 241.

Roman Catholics have this work down to a science. The Christian Science Church is certainly one of the most successful of all modern cults. Study of the work of these two institutions should be a challenge to psychologists. The Catholic ritual, confessional, and discipline have helped make success along this line possible. The Christian Scientists train themselves by a kind of mental hygiene to forget the evil in life. They sometimes succeed. "God is love," they say, until they actually believe it. Their work offers a wealth of material to show how the mind can control health, now the primary aim in education.

The schools themselves have, of course, attempted to develop attitudes, but more or less haphazardly. The good teacher has always created interest by his enthusiasm and his ability to stir the curiosity of his pupils. William Heard Kilpatrick has for years been pounding home the need for purposeful activity and performance followed by satisfaction. The junior high schools are using pupil clubs to bring about a sense of social cooperation. Dr. Harold Rugg, who was, I believe, formerly an engineer, and is now a psychologist in the Lincoln School, Teachers College, is an advocate of education in which art has at least three-fourths of the curriculum. But the schools have not as yet any practical scientific knowledge as to how they should proceed in the cultivating of right emotional attitudes.

This province of the emotions educators have too long left to the artists. It seems to me that teachers have the greater opportunity. I shall now give some of the methods which I think they might use to direct the emotional lives of children.

First of all, parents should understand to as great an extent as possible the emotions and how to build up good ones and destroy or replace evil ones. Second, teachers should be required to master all the available scientific knowledge as to methods of guiding the child's emotional life and of stimulating good reactions and replacing or killing bad ones. There is very little knowledge available as yet. Third, parents and teachers should cultivate the best emotional attitudes in themselves.

After these three, which are fundamental, come the ones directly affecting the child so as to develop good emotionalized attitudes. The six which follow were listed by Professor Thomas H. Briggs: (4) precept, (5) formal instruction, (6) incidental instruction, (7) personal example, (8) experience followed by satisfaction, (9) ritual.

The next, number 10, Associate Superintendent Gustave Straubenmüller of New York City, thinks most important of all. It is to guide children properly to influence each other.

Number 11 is the use of personal conferences between pupil
and teacher, a kind of modified confessional.

While number 12 may be closely related to many others, it is
worth a place of its own. It is this: The child's curiosity should
be aroused so as to stir his interest.

Number 13: Teaching and learning should be cooperative enter-
prises, with the teacher a co-worker with the pupil.

Number 14: Children should be made conscious that their
emotions affect their lives and should, with the greatest care and
skill, be made to analyze their past emotional reactions, with the
consequent effects.

Number 15: All teaching should be bent toward educating the
child for freedom, setting free his latent abilities, and developing
his powers.

Number 16: The child should be given opportunity to learn to
appreciate art in all its branches, and to develop any talent that
he may show in art.

There are many possible ways, but these seem to me most important. A brief discussion of these suggested methods may serve
to give an idea as to how I think they might be used.

It is axiomatic that the knowledge, attitudes, and work of
parents and teachers are paramount. Here we can hope for progress because of the ever growing movements for parent-teacher
cooperation and for adult education.

As to the use of *precept*, I'm rather doubtful. It seems wrong to
flood children with a lot of idealistic language which they may or
may not understand or heed. Most of us preach too much. Pre-
cepts seem to have been used from the beginning of the world,
but even children are apt to see that many of them are half-truths
or worse.

Their reactions may be surprising. A father had two sons who
drove recklessly. He put up a sign on the wall of the boys' room:
"Safety First." The boys turned the sign to the wall and wrote
on the other side, "Aw, take a chance!"

Formal instruction, such as courses in ethics, religion, etc., have
been largely used, but the most valuable, it seems to me, is that
which trains children through the use of situations that arise in
their schools and in their neighborhoods.

Incidental instruction is perhaps the most easily available method. Superintendent of Schools William J. O'Shea of New York
City has stressed the necessity for teachers' using all subjects to
develop the emotional and aesthetic aspects of the child's nature.
On October 11 he issued a pamphlet explaining how study should
be directed and with what aims. The first aim, he said, should be

insights, appreciations, attitudes. The second, moral traits and habits. The third, the teacher should make himself useless by directing the student to take control of his own education.

Dr. O'Shea has constantly encouraged the teaching that stresses the higher and finer elements of personality, and has decried the emphasis placed on methods of teaching, the imparting of facts, and testing, at the expense of the more important aim. He has declared that it is not so important that the pupils know all the facts of the American Revolution as that they be stirred by the spirit of sacrifice, patriotism, and democracy that made possible the birth of a new nation on this continent. He has urged that geography be taught so as to develop appreciation for the majesty of nature and its contributions to man's life. Associate Superintendent Gustave Straubenmüller, as teacher and as official, has made geography one of the most vital, interesting, and inspiring of all the elementary school subjects in New York City.

The schools, from the elementary grades through the university, have made the mistake in many subjects of neglecting this great emotional appeal. Strangely enough, they have made their greatest mistake in teaching literature. The child is not taught so much to appreciate the life that is in a poem or story as he is the language that is used to express it. He is all too often driven to hate reading and books. Our colleges and universities do even worse. The students must learn all the known facts of the author's life, the sources of his plots and ideas; they must study texts and language, and pay the scantest attention to the beauties before them. Poems, novels, plays, and short stories are primarily emotional, but one would never think so from seeing how they are taught.

I once heard John Erskine say that he would like to make an experiment with two students. One would spend four hours a day for ten years with Milton; the other, with Whitman. At the end of the ten years Erskine said he would analyze the minds and hearts of the students and find what the effects had been.

Without a doubt, incidental instruction, not only through the particular subjects studied but also through the use of current events, can be a most powerful lever in influencing the emotions of pupils.

The use of *personal example* is of great importance. Here hero-worship can play its part. Rudolf Steiner said that if a school has a good, strong, wholesome principal everything else can be taken for granted.

But in this field other problems arise. Children are usually taught to reverence men high in public life. Here the emotional appeal is easily used, for the majority of political leaders who make a success do so through their appeal to the emotions. I imagine, however, that the teachers of Indiana and Indianapolis would be opposed to this method now. As one man remarked recently, only dead heroes are safe to be used in teaching youth. The live ones are apt to get into trouble. Charles A. Lindbergh seems to be one live hero who is all right for teaching purposes.

In the matter of example, the teacher himself is most important; his influence may be incalculable.

Experience followed by satisfaction is so obvious a necessity in all human activity that it is accepted without question, though this, too, should be subjected to some careful analysis. We must realize that there are many kinds of satisfaction, some of them not particularly desirable. A burglar doubtless enjoys experience followed by satisfaction when he gets away with a lot of swag.

Ritual we have great need of in our lives. It seems necessary, and the schools are trying schemes which make use of it. The Knighthood of Youth, with all the romance, trappings, and ceremonies of chivalry, is perhaps the most outstanding one. The saluting of the flag is another great ritualistic scheme.

Guiding children rightly to influence each other is of utmost importance. Drs. Hartshorne and May, after prolonged research, have reported that their findings show the home to be the greatest influence in determining the child's knowledge of right and wrong, that the club leaders may possibly have a slight influence, but that there is no evidence that day-school or Sunday-school teachers are contributors to the moral knowledge of children either directly or indirectly. But there is much evidence that friends come second in importance after the home, and really do much to determine the child's attitudes and actions. Here, of course, lies the use of pupil clubs, boy scout troops, and self-governing organizations. If the pupils are allowed to work out problems of their own freely in the school through social cooperation and learning to work with one another, and incidentally to respect the rights of others, they are apt to carry over the attitudes formed into their outside activities.

The use of *conferences between pupil and teacher* would be a great boon. Some believe that the teacher cannot be the father confessor, but I doubt that. I believe that the confessional, now being used in so many ways by psychologists and others, is one of the chief sources of strength of the Catholic Church. Of course, the Church requires that suffering or penance follow sin, and at least the intent that the sin be not committed again.

In their conferences the teachers would find most difficult

problems to solve, but with study and experience would come wisdom. The visiting teachers are doing immensely valuable work in this field. They, like the priest, persuade the sinner to give up his sin.

Curiosity is the greatest spur to interest, for it creates the desire to know and to experience. Here is a subject related to incidental instruction, but, as I have already said, important enough for a separate classification. As Bertrand Russell states, the pupil's interest and not the teacher's authority should be the motivating power in education. Education would not have to be easy, even if this were the sole motivating power. The teacher should know how to arouse the curiosity of his pupils to such a pitch that they would work to find the truth just as the athlete bores himself with arduous training in order to win a football game, and incidentally builds a strong body.

My next point closely follows that of interest. *Teacher and pupil should be cooperative workers* searching for interesting truth. There should be no sense of superiority in the teacher. He should grow as he teaches even little children—for the small ones are just as interesting, emotionally and mentally, as adults. The teacher should not be so much the instructor, pouring knowledge in, as the educator who shows the pupil how to draw out of himself his abilities and powers. Children do not need teaching; they need understanding and freedom. The teacher has no right to impose adult conceptions on children. He should be a guide and a liberator.

Any real discipline in the home or in the school grows out of leadership. This ideal of leadership is widespread now, and there is every sign that it will grow in strength and influence.

While the next suggestion may be dangerous, nevertheless I believe that it should be attempted. It seems to me that *children should be made to analyze their own emotions* (of course, after the emotions have been experienced) *and to consider the consequent effects.* They should be made aware of the power of feelings and emotions in their lives, either for enriching or destroying. There is danger that the child might become morbidly introspective, and a moral prig; therefore I was glad to learn that this practice did not work harm when it was tried by Bronson Alcott in his school in Boston. He was extremely successful in it.

In this work there is enough to keep the teacher busy always. Perhaps one of the simplest ways to begin would be to have children define some common words with worlds of meaning. I'll guarantee that few people ever stop to ask themselves the difference between happiness and pleasure. Many think they are the same thing. Children should know the difference between these two states of being, as well as other important distinctions between related words—words such as knowledge and wisdom, license and liberty. They would not have to be philosophers to know the differences between these words—I mean the deep underlying differences, which, understood, might influence attitudes and actions. By knowing the differences, children might avoid confusion.

They should also know that all things called by the same name do not mean the same thing. Dr. Johnson's famous definition of patriotism as the last refuge of a scoundrel seems all too true, if we may consider for a moment the patriotic conflict Mayor Thompson of Chicago is now waging with Superintendent William McAndrew. Intelligent diagnoses of such words as patriotism might bring children to realize that they have responsibilities as citizens, and that citizenship means more than a glow of enthusiasm when they salute the flag.

In the problem of direct teaching of children how to safeguard their emotional lives, methods used by religious organizations again offer help. Many of them specifically warn their adherents to avoid all places, persons, and things that might cause them to commit sin. Children might learn to foresee and avoid places, persons, and things that would be harmful to them emotionally.[3] Of course, I realize that the decision to do the avoiding must be the child's, for the warning by adults is more than apt to arouse curiosity and interest that would lead the child to seek the forbidden.

Some would teach the child not to fear, but to do this would be absurd. Intelligent fear may be one of our most useful emotions, causing us to avoid that which would harm us. Fear should be changed to positive action.[4] It really seems quite difficult to build up intelligent fear in human beings, or so many of them would not get killed by automobiles.

In this phase of training many educators are now interested in changing what seems to be one of the strongest motives in human nature. · They would have the schools teach pupils that competition is damnable. Wells has told how Sanderson of Oundle did fine work along this line.

Suggestibility! The power of suggestion is another great force for use in training the emotions. Professor Herbert Martin has said that "our ideas and beliefs, our ethics and our religion, our arts, science, and politics *are* through suggestibility." Certainly our feelings and emotions, and our emotionalized attitudes are

[3] *Curriculum Problems* (New York: Macmillan, 1926), p. 57.
[4] *The Problem Child* (New York: McBride, 1927), p. 157.

built up around our families, cities, states, and nations. These institutions were moulded by the feelings and emotions of our ancestors. Surely the best way to bring about any desired changes is through using the emotions of their descendants.

Our principal effort in Americanization is to create a love for our institutions in the hearts of new citizens. For example, recently a ritual for awarding citizenship papers was instituted in New York City. All of us are more apt to resent an insult to the flag, which represents an emotionalized attitude, than we are an intellectual jibe at our institutions. If Mencken had insulted the flag physically as he has our governmental philosophies and institutions intellectually, he would have been lynched long ago.

Freedom must be the goal of all educational training. As I have said in another connection, I believe that in all the work of the schools there should be no attempt to force children to adopt the preconceived attitudes of teachers. In this work there would be the inevitable temptation for the teacher to make the child accept the teacher's attitudes as correct. The child's own attitudes may be the better for him and for his progress than would be the teacher's. I think that if training in emotionalized attitudes would result in forcing children to adopt the preconceived attitudes of others, such training had better be neglected.

As A. S. Neill said in pleading this same cause,[5] educators with schemes of life and philosophy are humbugs. To impose adult conceptions and values on children is not what I desire. I merely ask that children be shown how to develop through their own initiative and power the qualities that will help make them stronger and happier.

To paraphrase D. H. Lawrence, it seems that the whole of humanity has certain ideas in common: truth, duty, honor, love. But each idea may represent a different kind of feeling in each individual. Few of us would agree that anyone has the right to tell us what to feel and do. We do not know what another man ought to feel. Certainly every man has his right to his own special reactions. Educators ought not to want children to feel alike. All of them have different natures and so they should feel differently about practically everything. We don't want to produce standardized feelings.

Love cannot be created; it can only be set free. Demand it and you don't get it; you only produce hypocrisy. Children are usually naturally friendly and draw friendship from others.[6] In other words, the whole problem in this work is how to help

[5] *The Problem Child* (New York: McBride, 1927), pp. 115–116.
[6] *Education and the Good Life* (New York: Boni & Liveright, 1927), p. 207

children freely to develop themselves as emotionally balanced individuals.

Before leaving this phase of the subject I wish to point out a few aspects of the emotions that do not come under any of the heads that I have suggested. No one would try to create despair in a child. Yet, strangely enough, despair has often been one of the greatest incentives to accomplishment. Schubert, a most unhappy man, unable to sell his songs, kept on composing until he gave us six hundred of them. Beethoven was driven to despair by his tyrannical father, who made his son's life a burden by requiring him to practice too much on the piano. The son would have given up music, but later, under an inspiring teacher, he received the inspiration that was necessary to revive his interest in music, and to express his creative faculties. Despair, instead of helping him, had almost wrecked his powers. But despair has also been found to whet the desires. John Keats was told to go back to his pill-boxes. Schumann-Heink was told to go back to her wash-tubs. Paderewski was told that his fingers were too thick and blunt. Beethoven always did better work after suffering great disappointment. He composed his *Eroica* when he thought that Bonaparte would lead France to freedom. When Napoleon crowned himself emperor, Beethoven removed all references to his former hero and immediately composed some greater music.

Other peculiarities in human nature must be taken into consideration. Ideals are often more forceful in getting action when they are expressed in the negative.[7] A teacher in a tough neighborhood realized that talking about sanitation in the usual way would do no good. At first she planned to use the negative statement, "Boys, don't spit on the floor." Instead she said, "If you spit on the floor at home, spit on the floor here!" Whereupon one boy spat, and explained that he had done the same thing at home and his father knocked him down, but that the teacher couldn't beat him. The teacher's negation might have worked better. While working for good ends with some resourcefulness, she had not impressed her reasons nor created attitudes in her pupils with regard to sanitation.

We are all more or less interested in shaping people according to our ideas of what they should be like. Practically every educator has some philosophy which he uses as a guide. His philosophy grew out of his own attitudes. Deep down in his heart he admits that he does not know what education really is. He rarely knows what the child's life is going to be. But in spite of this lack of knowledge, educators try to express their ideals and lose

[7] *Curriculum Problems* (New York: Macmillan, 1926), p. 138.

themselves in vague terms.   For instance, Bertrand Russell
wants four qualities developed by education: vitality, courage,
sensitiveness, and intelligence.   Think of how these qualities
might be misused.   In his school he proposes to have no obstacles
to knowledge, but to "seek virtue by the right training of passions
and instincts."

He is most fearful of the power placed in the hands of educators.
He says that "the power of moulding young minds which science
has placed in our possession is a very terrible power, capable of
deadly misuse; if it falls into the wrong hands, it may produce a
world even more ruthless and cruel than the haphazard world of
nature."

The knowledge that I have asked for—that to be used in training the emotions—is even more dangerous, for in the past the
feelings and emotions have kept human nature fairly wholesome.

To see the danger of wrongly used emotion we need only glance
casually at history.   Whole nations have been led to feel that
they were crusaders for a holy cause, when really the leaders were
merely working selfishly for their own power.   A play recently
produced on Broadway, Spread Eagle, showed how possibly a
powerful and influential group, close to the government, might
in a few hours by propaganda broadcast through radio and
press, stir up a war fever that could not be denied.   Of course,
in every war, emotion plays the biggest part.   The sinking of the
"Lusitania" and emotional phrases like "Make the World Safe
for Democracy" did more to throw America's power in with
the Allies than did reason.

Perhaps if people's minds were brought consciously to bear
on their emotions, they would try to practice more intelligent
control of them during great crises   The schools have long
been about the work of developing emotionalized attitudes and
establishing habits, but without any definite scientific knowledge,
and without placing enough emphasis on the problem.   Some
schools of psychology may claim that they have set forth methods
of procedure that could be used in this work, but I know that their
methods are not being used to any great extent.

In my hasty summary of methods that have been or might be
used in this work, I have doubtless overlooked many important
things.   And right here I wish to say that I know that many of
the methods suggested are being used splendidly by our educators.

On December 10, 1925, I urged editorially in School that
psychologists and educators pay more attention to the uncharted
jungles of men's emotions and attempt to discover scientific
methods by which children could be so taught that they would
develop life-enriching emotional attitudes.   I then asked Associate

Superintendent Gustave Straubenmüller, chairman of New York City's Committee on the Study and Revision of the Curriculum, to make a special study of the subject. He did so, and found that psychologists had paid very little attention to the subject, and that many textbooks in education omitted it entirely. He recorded his findings and conclusions in an article called "Importance of the Emotions in Education and How to Use Them," which was published in *School*, June 3, 1926. As chairman of the important committee charged with the remodeling of the course of study, he has constantly emphasized the need for giving the greatest thought and attention to this phase of education.

On February 25, 1926, Superintendent of Schools William J. O'Shea in an address before the executive session of the Department of Superintendence of the National Education Association in Washington, on the subject, "Changes in the Course of Study for the City of New York," declared that "the fundamental aim in education is the development of moral character." In his speech he mentioned, among others, two aims which he declared were of paramount importance. "One of these," he said, "is the development of the emotional and aesthetic aspects of the child's nature; the other is the development of moral character."

"The schools," he continued, "must perform their full duty of developing in school children good taste and good manners, high and noble ideals, consideration for others, 'charity toward all,' those indefinable attributes of personality, outlook, temperament, and conduct for which we use the term *character.*"

He declared that today teachers seem to underestimate the importance of this aim in education, that "methods of teaching, the imparting of facts, and testing are being emphasized to the neglect of the higher and finer elements of personality." He stated that the courses of study and syllabuses should be the instruments for the realization of this aim in education.

The problem of training so as to develop emotionalized attitudes was stated in a book, *Curriculum Problems*, by Professor Thomas H. Briggs of Teachers College, Columbia University, which was published in July, 1926. Dr. Briggs also stated that the greatest problem now facing educators is how to cultivate emotionalized attitudes. He declared that he could not answer the question, but that he was merely bringing it to the attention of educators. This was, I believe, the first book to ask recognition for the same need that was pointed out by me in *School* on December 10, 1925, by Superintendent O'Shea on February 25, 1926, and in elaborated form by Associate Superintendent Straubenmüller on June 3, 1926.

New York City is already proceeding to work out its curriculum so as to develop the proper emotionalized attitudes. This city, with its million school children, drawn from practically every race, has a problem astounding in its complexity, but its officials are working manfully to solve it.

During the past month Chairman Straubenmüller and his Committee on Character Education have had their proposed course printed, but its contents have not yet been made public. The whole scheme is planned to develop emotionalized attitudes in children. The basic aim will be health, then self-reliance, self-control, kindness, honesty, and other desirable qualities, including sportsmanship. Definite methods of procedure will be given all teachers for every grade, but chiefly as suggestions. Every teacher may put his own ideas into operation, using the course as a guide. I believe that Dr. Straubenmüller and his committee have done a magnificent piece of work, one that the great majority of adults might well study and apply to their own lives.

Explanations of why this important phase of education has been so long neglected are not hard to find. In the first place, religious organizations have long been trying to handle this part of training. But now the school is more and more taking over the duties of the home and the church. The public is demanding it.

But there is a second and a more important reason. We cannot measure the intangible things called personality and the soul. The teacher desiring promotion knows, however, that the pupil's mental progress can be measured. Therefore he crams the child's head with knowledge, often of the poorest kind, fact-knowledge, and gives what time is left to the heart. The teacher himself, perhaps, has only vague notions of the child's emotional and spiritual progress.

This neglect will be no longer possible in New York City. Associate Superintendent Straubenmüller has placed emphasis here in his work in revising the curriculum. His character-education program will, I believe, bear immortal fruits.

No one knows what the results of attempting to develop emotionalized attitudes will be. Teachers may still find the most useful materials to be those given us by the artist. However, they can bring their own minds and those of their pupils consciously to bear on the emotions, and try to cultivate by the help of the reason and will-power the good feelings and emotions and to avoid the bad ones.

One thing I know. Teachers must be artists. Art is the expression of fine emotion, crystallized in some form. Teachers have the privilege of working with living materials. Surely they should so work that their pupils become living embodiments of all that is nourishing in the emotions as well as in the intellect.

Of failures there will be a plenty. You remember how recently one well-known psychologist, a child specialist, suffered the loss of his own adolescent son by suicide. And how, some years ago, a woman who went about the country lecturing on how to bring up children properly, was shocked when her own son, a medical student, killed the schoolgirl whom he had ruined. But from failure may come value. The adolescent son of one of America's best-known poets recently committed suicide. The poet has dedicated his life to helping solve the problems of youth.

In the beginning, perhaps, it is necessary to urge that emotional training be not carried to extremes and therefore become absurd. The children themselves would be the first to rebel against any such overdoing. They are usually able to take care of themselves and will continue to do so.

Whatever we may be able to accomplish in this field, the truth remains that everything we do and are, our outlooks on life, our interpretations of the universe, our religions, are basically determined by our emotional attitudes.

We have sought relief in science and not found it. Science has contributed to man's material and intellectual progress as has no other power. But it can answer only four of the great questions: *What*, *Where*, *When*, *How*. It cannot answer the question that demands knowledge of first principles: *Why*. Men have tried to answer this question through their emotions, their religions. Psychologists have done prodigious labor in studying man's mind, and have given immeasurable aid to education. But so far they have neglected the feelings and emotions.

I believe, therefore, that this symposium is among the most significant ever held. It will focus attention on the most important and most unexplored phase of education. It may be the first move toward a really cooperative, practical, and scientific study of the feelings and emotions, and may mark an evolutionary as well as a revolutionary step in education.

If from this beginning grows a science by which teachers may be guided in developing good emotional attitudes, education may become a spiritual and emotional adventure. To bring this about, I can imagine no greater opportunity than this symposium has offered.

"What is truth?" said jesting Pilate, and would not stay for an answer. Perhaps, since Francis Bacon, we have too long sought for truth in the intellect. Mayhap by searching in the emotions, we may come nearer to the answer.

I read not long ago how "when Zola's remains were being removed to the Pantheon, an anti-Semite fired a shot at Dreyfus. In the trial, the defendant made the plea that he bore no hatred toward Dreyfus, that he had not even aimed at him. 'My action was symbolic, and I fired a shot at an idea.'"

APPENDIX

APPENDIX A

ADDRESS OF WELCOME*

REES EDGAR TULLOSS
President of Wittenberg College

It is with profound satisfaction that I welcome to the Wittenberg Campus this distinguished assembly of participants in the Wittenberg Symposium on Feelings and Emotions.

Preparations for this conference have been made in the confident expectation that the results will constitute a real contribution to scientific thought in an important field of psychological investigation.

This seems assured by the character of the contributors to this Symposium. Some thirty-five of the world's most distinguished workers in our field find place upon the program. Professor Dallenbach is probably correct when he writes that they constitute "the most illustrious group of psychologists who ever participated in any symposium."

Another consideration seems to justify the expectation of results highly important to scientific advancement. I refer to the particular field to the consideration of which these days are to be devoted. Of all phases of human behavior, the feelings and emotions have most persistently resisted the attacks of the experimentalists. We may almost say that no general attack upon the problems has yet been made. We have, as it were, made minor skirmishes and done some effective scouting. But the field of feelings and emotions remains for the most part an unconquered and unexplored territory.

This is, of course, entirely understandable and expectable. The great substrata of human experience are built up of our emotional reactions. Such more superficial phases of behavior as our sensational experiences, our habit formations, and our thought processes, have naturally received first attention. They have to some degree yielded up their secrets. But who will venture to say that we have gone far into the understanding of the more ancient, fundamental, and deeply hidden elements of our experience and behavior which are involved in the feelings and emotions?

The program has been prepared upon the basis of the belief that the time is now ripe for a gathering of the forces of psychology for an attack upon this important field; and that the form of attack most likely to achieve results of consequence is that of experimental procedure. If this conference can help to show that a study of the feelings and emotions is scientifically desirable and practically very deeply needed, and if it can further emphasize the experimental method as the procedure toward which we may now most hopefully turn, it will amply justify the labors of those who have undertaken the task of its arrangement.

Dr. Reymert has been kind enough to refer to the cooperation and encouragement which, in the development of this project, he has received from the Wittenberg administration. That has been only a small contribution, made with genuine personal pleasure. Let me bestow credit for the bringing about of this important gathering where credit belongs, placing it upon the vision and energy of my friend and co-worker, Dr. Reymert. His wide acquaintance with the psychologists of all lands, acquired through his study in America, his teaching experience in Europe, his editorship of the *Scandinavian Scientific Review*, and his intense interest in the field here to be dealt with, have fitted him uniquely for the task of convening this conference. Its results will stand as a memorial to his organizing ability.

---

* October 19, 1927.

Permit me in a closing word to express my heartfelt thanks and appreciation to all who have answered Dr. Reymert's call to contribute to the Symposium as stated speakers or writers of papers. May you have the reward of the satisfaction of having cooperated in a worthy project.

Permit me to remind you also that the value of the Symposium will depend in no small measure upon the degree to which those of you who listen to the papers and addresses participate also in the discussion.

The Honorary Chairman of the Conference, Dr. J. McKeen Cattell, will be introduced later during the day. At this time it is my pleasure to present to you the Chairman of the Symposium, Professor M. L. Reymert, head of the Department of Psychology at Wittenberg College.

APPENDIX B

WHY FEELINGS AND EMOTIONS?*

MARTIN L. REYMERT
Wittenberg College

Mr. President, Ladies and Gentlemen:

Our science evolved out of philosophy. It received its great impetus in the middle of the nineteenth century from the natural sciences—physiology, physics, biology, and anthropology. Its history clearly shows that the field of feelings and emotions has been puzzling to savants of many departments of organized knowledge from the very beginning of scientific pursuit. Scholars have always been aware of this intangible and intricate "something" which we may call feeling, as a very essential and perhaps the most dominating aspect of mental life. We find numerous endeavors toward a hypothesis of explanation and a search for rational methods of attack. Looking out over human history in a philosophical light we find a clear division line already drawn in ancient Indian philosophy, in its differentiation of *love* and *thought*. Greek classical philosophy shifts its differentiation to *mood* and *intellect*. The scholasticism and mysticism of the Middle Ages are charged, the first, with *intellect* and, the second, with *emotion*. In our own times we are isolating what we call the *emotional* and the *intellectual*.

Many scholars have emphasized the rivalry between heart and head. It is apparent from their writing that this struggle accompanies the development of psychological thought from the most primitive forms of philosophy and religion up to the psychological problems of our day. As is well known, various periods of European history have been christened by scholars in accordance with the way in which the *intellectual* or the *emotional* factors have been dominating; as for instance, romanticism, scholasticism, and mysticism.

The fact that science has been so conspicuously slow in trying to dissipate the fog of the emotional states, may have its general explanation primarily in the fact that man has always been reluctant to undertake the study of his own real self. Again, and perhaps more clearly, it may have its origin in the seemingly inherent tendency of man toward mysticism; certain desires acting as prohibitive agencies against such destruction of the emotional complexes in him, as would bring him out of his beloved, elated, or depressed self. A third reason may be found in obstacles due to the unstable and fleeting characteristics of emotional experiences, and the difficulty of finding expressions for the highly complicated factors of emotional patterns. With the birth of experimental psychology, whether along strictly psychological or biological lines, the intellect of man for the first time arrives at a systematic study of the entire range of mental phenomena, getting its sails filled from the spirit of the natural sciences. As a result we very soon witness the application of exact methods to this important study. From the enthusiasm of the earliest workers, such as Fechner, Weber, Helmholtz, and Wundt,[1] it is apparent that these scholars had the aspirations and hope that this scientific method would in time solve all problems and enigmas of mental life. The primary desire within the sphere of natural science being to find basic elements, we observe a wealth of research

---

* Opening address, October 19, 1927.

[1] Wundt, like G. Stanley Hall, William James, and Edward L. Thorndike, in this country, can be mentioned only with restrictions. Wundt's interest in social psychology shows that he knew the limitations of the laboratory method.

with noteworthy results on the senses and the sensations, on imagery and intellectual elements. It is, however, almost with reluctance that an experimental psychologist has to admit that this tendency of the most extreme analysis has lasted up to the present time, thereby blinding and misleading the investigators into a piece-meal psychology.[2] There are exceptions of course. T. H. Lipps regarded feelings as a manifold of total and unanalyzable functions. C. von Ehrenfels and H. Cornelius discovered and propounded, long before the Berlin Gestalt School, the emotional importance of qualities of shape as experienced qualities resisting a complete dissection into elements.[3] Thus it is rather strange to know that while the element which we may call "simple feeling" was truly recognized from the very start, we now and then find rather strange methods of experimental attack, and various and often extremely insufficient theories proclaimed in explanation of the more complicated feeling and emotional patterns. We observe this fact in the earliest psychology of feeling in Wundt, Münsterberg, Titchener, Külpe, and others.

I am happy to say that recently a new trend is making itself apparent in psychology, emphasis shifting as regards both viewpoint and method, a trend which not only promises to revive scholarly interest in the field of feelings, but also foreshadows fruitful results. A number of the papers at our Symposium will doubtless bear witness to this. The fact is also clearly revealed in the psychological literature of today. Such a new orientation has rapidly been coming to the fore. It does not disregard analysis, but restricts analysis in such a way that it shall not be used to the extent that it will destroy or alter the more complex mental phenomena as entities in and by themselves, to be described and investigated in and by their own natural attributes.

We observe this in the psychology of *Ganzheit* (Leipzig), claiming that a psychological entity or "whole" is always more than the sum of its elements and that this "more" is of the greatest importance; and in the psychology of Gestalt (Berlin) with similar claims, but going still further in its condemnation of analysis (almost disclaiming it altogether). We further find this tendency in the psychology of understanding (*Verstehende Psychologie*) of Eduard Spranger, and in the systems of the psychoanalytic schools. In this connection we should also mention the more recent English psychology of "relations" (Spearman and Aveling) the beginnings of which might already be detected in Lord Shaftsbury's psychology, and which also has in Italy an able exponent (Rignano) who interprets Spearman's "relations" as feelings. In this country, Madison Bentley with his psychosomatic structures, and H. L. Hollingworth in his original use of the "redintegrative sequences" are pointing out new methods toward systematic unity. It is also significant that the more recent studies emanating from the Cornell laboratory and from close adherents to the Titchener school definitely show similar trends. From William McDougall's dualistic purposivism arose the first systematic view of society as a psychological unit. Even recent behaviorism points more and more to observation of genetic as well as of social totalities; as may be evinced from the biosocial

---

[2] The writer has no patience, however, with certain modern scholars who disregard the importance of the historically necessary and highly valuable analytical trend in our science. While, as stated above, this trend might be said to have delayed the investigation of more complicated processes in their true form, it, nevertheless, has to be looked upon as an inevitable background for the beneficial reaction to this method which is now to be witnessed in several psychological movements. Even scholars of today who ostensibly sponsor "description" in place of analysis, do not seem fully to realize that any "description" presupposes in all cases a certain amount of analysis.

[3] The preludes of these pioneers just mentioned sounded upon deaf ears while being played, and it seems that some of the present performers of similar melodies are very little aware of the original composers.

systems of Max Meyer and A. P. Weiss. We may observe this tendency also within several other departments of contemporary science. Thus we find it in the biology of Driesch and Erich Becher; in the physiology of W. B. Cannon; and in the sociology of Dilthey, Litt, Durkheim, Lévy-Bruhl, Bartlett, and others, who in all their attempts at explanations of social phenomena, put the main emphasis upon society as a unit. We have reflections of this also in recent philosophy—compare movements and systems as Stern's personalism, J. Dewey's social philosophy, Krueger's neo-idealism, N. Hartmann's phenomenology, etc. For psychology then these recent changes in attitude have brought about a new interest in emotions, a domain in our science on which, to my knowledge, we have had no monograph and no systematic bibliography since Ribot.

While all these new efforts indeed seem to promise much of real value for the future, we nevertheless must admit reluctantly that at this particular moment we are as yet not far removed from the state of mere hypothesis, theories, and opinions in the field of feelings and emotions. Let us just mention a few vital problems still open: Why is an emotion? What is an emotion, i. e., the rise, the life, and the decay of a particular emotion in the individual as well as within social units? What are the laws governing the interplay of the different feelings and emotions, again individually and socially? How far are we justified in dealing with "elementary" feeling as against "higher" feelings, or in accepting any one of the now existing systems of classification? Have we been blinded by sensualistic psychologies to the paramount importance of research and systematic study of such more complex but highly important phenomena as *moods* and *sentiments*? Shall we ever arrive at such entities as national and racial moods? May certain national groups be more marked by the contemplative moods, so highly essential for cultural and scientific pursuit?

Our Symposium, it seems to me, has two valid *raisons d'être*. First of all, we shall be taking stock internationally of our present status; secondly, from the platform thus afforded, we should arrive at a clearer and more fruitful perspective which in turn may show problems as well as ways and means which should occupy our attention in the immediate future. In this connection I am glad to announce to you that our present meeting is not meant only as a passing show in the history of psychology, but that, with the hearty endorsement of the administrative authorities of this institution, and, as we hope, with the continuous interest of all psychologists, it is our hope to repeat such an International Symposium on Feelings and Emotions every fifth year.

It should not be inferred from the above that we are interested in the general psychology of feelings and emotions only, since our endeavor is to cover the field in the broadest way and in all possible phases. Thus we shall not overlook the importance of our subject for individual psychology, a field which has already been entered, thanks to the original points of view and the methods instigated by such pioneers as Cattell and Stern. We are also fully aware of the crying need for further and more minute and extensive work from the point of view of both individual and general psychology in such spheres of interest as religion, aesthetics, education, law, psychotherapy, business, and industry. If in this way we could be of some aid in the work toward a real factual knowledge of feelings and emotions, this should lead also to a new epistomological and general philosophical era. In this latter conjecture we find ourselves in full accord with views expressed by Bergson, F. Krueger, Müller-Freinfels, Rignano, Jaspers, Spengler, and others.

You will find in the selection of contributions to this Symposium, as will also be the case for those in the future, a strong emphasis placed upon the genetic approach It seems to me that we now witness an altogether too artificial division line drawn between the investigations of momentary consciousness and behavior in laboratory adult psychology on the one hand, and a study of the growing mental-bodily structure of the child on the other. This might have been natural hitherto; but that it has not been easy is readily apparent, e. g., from the excursions into the genetic field which Titchener finds necessary in so many of his writings. May it be possible then that a systematic work of comparison and correlation of these two so intimately interrelated aspects may receive its impetus from this Symposium?

Considered from all angles we cherish the hope that the Wittenberg Symposium on Feelings and Emotions of 1927 will prove to be of real value to the history of our science.

EARLY PSYCHOLOGICAL LABORATORIES*

J. McKeen Cattell

*Formerly Professor of Psychology in the University of Pennsylvania
and in Columbia University*

Laboratories for research and teaching in the sciences are of comparatively recent origin. They may be regarded as part of the industrial revolution, for there is a close parallel in causes and effects between the development of the factory system and of scientific laboratories. The industrial revolution began with the exploitation by machinery of coal and iron in England; it may perhaps be dated from the use of the steam engine of Watts's in the coal mines of Cornwell about a hundred and fifty years ago.

The laboratory had its origin fifty years later in Germany as part of the scientific renaissance following the Napoleonic wars. The University of Berlin was founded by Wilhelm von Humboldt and Frederick William III in 1810. The first laboratory of chemistry was opened by Justus von Liebig at Giessen in 1824. This was followed by similar laboratories at Göttingen under Wöhler in 1836, at Marburg under Bunsen in 1840, and at Leipzig under Erdmann in 1843. The first English laboratory was the College of Chemistry, now part of the Imperial College of Science and Technology of the University of London, which was opened in 1845 by von Hofmann, brought from Germany by Prince Albert. Benjamin Silliman founded at Yale University the first American laboratory for the teaching of chemistry. Laboratories in France and in other countries were of later origin. Prior to the industrial revolution the artisan worked at home, sometimes with apprentices, who were often his children. The factories, the mines, and the systems of transportation, with their machinery, their skilled overseers, and division of labor, their owners and entrepreneurs, their exchange of commodities and ideas, created a remarkable economy in production, so that now each individual may perhaps work half as long and consume twice as much wealth as formerly. But there are serious drawbacks in the lack of freedom and initiative of the workman, in the loss of joy in creative work. The situation in the laboratory is similar. A professor may have many associates, assistants, and students; expensive apparatus and extensive libraries may be installed; division of labor in each laboratory and among laboratories can be planned; there may be exchange of ideas and of information on the progress of research; students are taught in large groups. Production is greatly increased, perhaps quadrupled, as in the industrial system. But the scientific man is subject to administrative controls; he is no longer free; he must compromise with others and teach all sorts of students. The system is useful for the production of a large mass of routine work; it may not be favorable to creative genius.

Anatomy has been called the mother of the sciences; dissecting rooms go back to the medieval universities of Italy. Observatories, museums, botanical gardens, academies of science, and university schools, where research was undertaken and in which students and assistants were taught and trained, preceded organized laboratories. Chemistry is the gold transmuted through alchemy; we have all seen on the stage the laboratory of Faust. Tertullian and other Christian fathers say that when "the sons of God saw the daughters of men, that they were fair and

---

* Address on the occasion of the inauguration of the Psychological Laboratory of Wittenberg College, October 21, 1927.

they took them wives" as told in the sixth chapter of Genesis, these fallen angels taught the fair daughters of men the arts of astrology and alchemy. Scientific men who do not care for special creations may assume that there has been a gradual development from the time of the first experiment by an anthropoid ape, or it may be by a paramecium or an electron. If, however, we want an official beginning for the first scientific laboratory, it will be the laboratory of chemistry at Giessen, the hundredth anniversary of whose foundation was celebrated three years ago.

Chemical laboratories were followed by laboratories of physics and biology. I worked in the first American biological laboratory in its early days. It was established at The Johns Hopkins University by Newell Martin, a student of Huxley who at the Royal College of Science had founded the first laboratory of biology. From the laboratories of Martin and Brooks at The Johns Hopkins have proceeded many of our most eminent biological workers. The Johns Hopkins also led in the establishment (under Welch, Mall, Abel, and Howell) of laboratories in the medical sciences. But there is obviously no sharp line of demarcation between the modern laboratory and earlier groups of workers such as the great school of zoölogy conducted by Agassiz at Harvard.

The first laboratory of psychology was established by Wilhelm Wundt. In an article on the Leipzig laboratory, published in *Mind* in 1888 and submitted to Professor Wundt, I give the date as 1879. The fiftieth anniversary of the founding of the laboratory was, however, celebrated at Leipzig in 1925. Wundt published his *Grundzüge der physiologischen Psychologie* in 1874 and was called from Zurich to a chair of philosophy at Leipzig in 1875. The Psychologische Institut there was a gradual development. Wundt writes in his autobiography *Erlebtes und Erkanntes,* published in 1920, that Kraepelin, Lehmann, and I were his three earliest *Arbeitsgenossen* who remained faithful to psychology and that we worked with him at a time when the institute was his private undertaking and lacked official recognition on the part of the university. The first research published from the Leipzig laboratory was apparently a doctor's dissertation by Dr. Max Friedrich carried out during the winter semester of 1879–80.

Wundt writes in the preface to the *Physiologische Psychologie* that it undertakes "*ein neues Gebiet der Wissenschaft abzugrenzen,*" but he was partly anticipated by Hermann Lotze whose *Medizinische Psychologie* was published in 1852. Both Lotze and Wundt had a medical education and were professors of philosophy. Their books are landmarks in the history of our science. It was my privilege to hear the last course of lectures on psychology by Lotze given at Göttingen in the winter semester of 1880–81. In accordance with the custom of that university Lotze dictated summaries which could be written down verbatim even by one who had little psychology and less German. The *Dictata* of that year were published and have been translated into English. In the spring of 1881 Lotze, then seventy-four years of age, migrated to Berlin and died, according to Göttingen opinion, of homesickness.

Herbart, whom Lotze succeeded at Göttingen, had tried to give a mathematical formulation to psychology as Spinoza had to philosophy. He published the first edition of his *Einleitung in die Philosophie* in 1813. There followed Drobitsch, Lindner, Benecke, Volkmar, and other German psychologists. In England we have the notable development of association and analytic psychology from Locke through Berkeley, Hume, the Mills, and Bain to Ward. The first edition of Carpenter's *Mental Physiology*, today a useful and readable book, was published in 1874, the same year as Wundt's *Grundzüge*. In England and in France there were numerous workers in the fields of physiological and pathological psychology.

The most important developments for laboratory psychology were through the great German physiologists and physicists, most of all Helmholtz, who passed from physiology to physics. His *Physiologische Optik*, recently translated under the editorship of Professor Southard and published as an act of piety by the Optical

Society, and his *Tonempfindungen* of which there is an earlier translation, are classics in the history of science. E. H. Weber became professor of anatomy at Leipzig in 1818 at the age of twenty-three, being later transferred to physiology. The law that bears his name was stated in his *Annotationes*, published from 1834 to 1851. Fechner was appointed professor of physics at the same university in 1834; his *Zendavesta* was published in 1851, his *Elemente der Psychophysik* in 1860. When I was a student at Leipzig he was over eighty-five years old and blind from experiments on vision, a charming man, intensely interested in his psychophysical experiments, though chiefly in philosophical interpretations.

The middle fifty years of the last century were the golden age of the German University and of science, its *Wunderkind*. It is marvelous what was accomplished then and there. Thus in the little corner of the field of science concerned with the psychology of the sense of vision there worked, in addition to Helmholtz and Fechner, a notable company, including Aubert, Brücke, du Bois-Reymond, Donders (in Holland), Exner, Fraunhofer, Fick, von Graefe (who examined my eyes when I was a child of eight), Hering, Hermann, von Kries, Listing, Johann Müller, Nagel, Purkinje, Vierordt, the Webers, and many more. In England there were Brewster, Maxwell, and others. There is no such group in the world today working on vision or in any other part of experimental psychology. At that time the investigation of the other senses, of movement, of the time of reaction, and much else was pursued probably to greater effect than in all the innumerable laboratories of today.

The fields so fertile in the nineteenth century were, of course, cleared at an earlier time. Experiments on vision go back to Kepler, Huygens, and Newton. Weber's law was anticipated by Bouguer and Lambert; Fechner's law by Bernouilli and Laplace; the personal equation by the astronomers. Observations on after-images were made not only by Goethe, the elder Darwin, Buffon, and Newton among others, but also by Augustine and Aristotle. Very curiously the problems of psychological measurement were clearly stated by the poet Shelley who more than a hundred years ago wrote: "A scale might be formed, graduated according to the degrees of a combined scale of intensity, duration, connection, periods of recurrence, and utility, which would be the standard, according to which all ideas might be measured."

When I came across this passage in Shelley it seemed almost incredible that he of all men should have written it, as indeed it is that the most unearthly of poets should have been the son of a country squire. But England has always given birth to great men in families, and as sports. It has been said that Graham Bell (he too was British) could not have invented the telephone if he had been a physicist, for he would have known that it was impossible; so it may be said that Francis Galton could not have accomplished his great work toward founding modern psychology if he had been a psychologist, for he would have known that it was not psychology. Galton, like Darwin his cousin, had no university position and no laboratory. He published his *Hereditary Genius* in 1869, his *Inquiries into Human Faculty* in 1883.

With intermissions I was a student at Leipzig under Wundt from 1881 to 1896, serving during the last year as laboratory assistant in psychology, the first to be appointed there or anywhere. Wundt had a higher opinion, doubtless with good reason, of American enterprise than of American scholarship. In his reminiscences he writes that with "*bekannter Amerikanischer Entscholssenheit*" I approached him and declared: "Herr Professor, you need an assistant and I shall be your assistant." He was the most kindly of men and was much worried lest I should not pass my doctorate examination in physics under Hankel and in zoölogy under Leuckhart, but these distinguished professors also fortunately made due allowance for a child of the wilderness. Wundt's combined courtesy and remoteness from the modern world may be illustrated by an incident. At that time women were seldom admitted to university lectures, but at my request he gave permission to an American woman of fine intelligence to attend his course on psychology. This was frequented by some two hundred students, among them the most stupid in the university, for all theological students were required to attend. One day he said: "I am sorry that I let Miss X attend my lectures; it embarrasses me; I feel that I ought to speak in a way that a woman can understand."

When I showed Wundt an outline of the work that I proposed for a doctor's thesis on reaction-time, including complicated responses and a study of individual differences, his comment was: "*ganz Amerikanisch.*" As a matter of fact I did the work in my own rooms and with my own apparatus. At that time students were expected to work in the laboratory on a subject assigned by the professor during certain definite hours in the afternoon and with the apparatus supplied, which had to be put away neatly in the cases after a two-hour period. We used two batteries of Daniel cells and when these were set up and got into running order it was nearly time to take them apart, wash the zincs and coppers, and put the fluids into bottles. As in this process we were likely to splash sulphuric acid on our clothes we kept handy a bottle of ammonia which was very promptly applied to the stains. At that time I anticipated Dr. Watson in an observation on the unconditioned reflex, for when the German student who worked with me drew a mouthful of dilute sulphuric acid through the syphon that we used, he immediately reached for the ammonia bottle and took a mouthful of that.

In the early eighties Wundt's laboratory was housed on the top floor of the Convict building, where indigent students had their meals. He used to walk through the laboratory after his lecture, always courteous and ready to answer questions, but, as I remember it, usually limiting his visit to five or ten minutes. He was interested in the laboratory as a system and as a method of introspection, but he was not himself a laboratory worker. His interests were very broad, a less friendly word would be voluminous. His *Logik*, first published from 1880 to 1883, contains in the second edition 1995 pages; his *Ethik*, also published while I was at Leipzig contains in its third edition 933 pages. The *System der Philosophie*, published in 1889, contains in its third edition 738 pages. The last edition of the *Physiologische Psychologie* contains 2317 pages; the *Völkerpsychologie*, 3161 pages.

These books and others Wundt composed on a typewriter that I gave him, one of the first in Germany. Avenarius once remarked that I had by this gift done a serious disservice to philosophy, for it had enabled Wundt to write twice as many books as would otherwise have been possible. At that time the relations of German professors were curious from an American point of view. Wundt was not in friendly relations with Helmholtz, Stumpf, Müller, and others. Stumpf, next to Wundt the most distinguished of German psychologists, was professor at Halle, only three quarters of an hour by train from Leipzig, and Wundt was asked for an introduction. He said that he was sorry that he could not give it as he did not know Professor Stumpf personally; it was better so, for they could then write more freely when there was a difference of opinion—and they did so a couple of years later.

At the beginning of the semester, students who wanted to undertake experimental work stood before Wundt in a row and from a slip of paper that he held in his hand he assigned topics in order. The year that I appeared there were six or seven of us, representing nearly as many nationalities. I was assigned the problem of reacting to colored lights; first, when the light was seen; and second, when the color was distinguished, and by subtracting one time from the other of obtaining what Wundt called the "*Apperceptionszeit.*" This I could not do, but the problem was most useful to me, for it led me to realize the limitations of introspection and to base my work on objective measurements of behavior. Wundt's refusal to admit any subject to the laboratory except a psychologist who could use the results introspectively was also useful, for it led me to transfer the work to my rooms and make there the first psychological measurements of individual differences and to attempt to develop the useful applications of psychology with both of which efforts Wundt had no sympathy.

Wundt rejected as a doctorate dissertation Münsterberg's very able monograph on *Die Willenshandlungen* because it did not coincide with his own theories. He calls Stanley Hall's excellent sketch of his life and work an *"erdichtete Biographie die von Anfang bis zu Ende erfunden ist."* But such things were only the righteous indignation of the Hebrew prophet denouncing the enemies of the Lord. The academic life in Germany in those days was truly exalted. The nation, the university, the professor, were sacrosanct. It was a fine experience to be admitted to the outer court of the temple before the money changers had entered. Wundt himself was the ideal German professor, with boundless learning shading toward the pedantic, fully conscious of his plenary inspiration, yet withal, most modest, shy, and kindly; a seer before his students, a child at home, a truly great man.

Wundt's laboratory of psychology was international in its reputation and influence, attracting students from all parts of the world, Americans and Russians predominating. In 1892 it received larger quarters and in 1897 was removed to one of the buildings vacated by the Medical School where fourteen rooms were remodeled for its purposes. In the late eighties there were beginnings of laboratories under Ebbinghaus at Berlin, under Müller at Göttingen, and under students of Wundt who were my contemporaries and friends: Münsterberg at Freiburg, Martius at Bonn, and Lehmann at Copenhagen.

The second laboratory of psychology was organized by G. Stanley Hall at The Johns Hopkins University early in the year 1883. I was there before Hall, holding a fellowship in philosophy, this award for a thesis on Lotze having been made by the professor of Latin who knew even less about philosophy than I did, or the fellowship would have been given John Dewey. He was there as a student, as were also Joseph Jastrow and H. H. Donaldson. We helped Hall set up a modest laboratory in a private house adjacent to the center of ugly little brick buildings and great men that formed the university. The small group of professors working there included Remsen, Rowland, Sylvester, Gildersleeve, Haupt, Adams, Brooks, and Martin.

It is a curious fact that neither of the founders of our first two psychological laboratories was a laboratory worker. Hall's chair, like Wundt's, was not limited to psychology; he lectured on philosophy and he also conducted courses in pedagogy. The range of his interests was large, but it was the human aspects of life that he cared for rather than abstract quantitative measurements. Like James he was a man of literary genius swayed by the emotions, which are such a large part of life and yet such a small part of our science. Minot, the distinguished Harvard embryologist, once said that he envied my occupation with a science concerned with human interests. My reply was that my experiments had as little to do with such things as his had with love and children. Hall wrote about children, adolescence and senescence, religion and sex, the drama of life. He and James were giants in the land, over-towering their descendants of a work-a-day world.

As Wundt established the *Philosophische Studien* to publish the work from his own laboratory and his own articles on psychology and philosophy, so Hall established the *American Journal of Psychology*. The early volumes give a survey of the work done in Baltimore, which was largely physiological and psychiatrical. Hall was much interested in insanity and other pathological aspects of psychology and we used to go regularly to the Enoch Pratt Hospital for the insane. These interests were maintained and in the last conversation that I had with him in his lonely house at Worcester he wanted especially to know why orthodox American psychologists cared so little for Freud and psychoanalysis. He showed me a mass of publications and notes that he had collected on the subject.

Hall was called upon to organize Clark University in 1888 and gathered there a group of outstanding scientific men including Michelson, Webster, Bolza, Nef,

Whitman, Mall, Donaldson, Lombard, McMurrich, and Boas. The financial support of the university by Mr. Clark was less liberal than had been anticipated and Dr. Harper took over in a body a large part of these men for the faculty of the new University of Chicago. Hall remarks in his *Life and Confessions:* "I felt his act comparable to that of a housekeeper who would steal in at the back door to engage servants at a higher price." Sanford went with Hall from The Johns Hopkins to Clark and became director of the laboratory of psychology which was opened in 1889. The Johns Hopkins laboratory was closed and the apparatus dispersed until it was re-established by Professor Baldwin and Professor Stratton in 1904. Hall and Clark University long maintained a dominant position in psychology and the psychological side of education. In his death there ends the romantic and heroic era of our science.

The laboratory of psychology at the University of Pennsylvania was founded in 1887, though it was only in January, 1889, that a special laboratory with adequate equipment of apparatus was opened. The laboratories at Leipzig and The Johns Hopkins were for research students, and psychology was only part of the field covered by the professor. At the University of Pennsylvania a professorship of psychology was established and laboratory courses for students were given. It might consequently be argued by a partial advocate that this was the first laboratory of psychology in the sense that Liebig's chemical laboratory at Giessen was the first scientific laboratory. More significant is the circumstance that in this laboratory the research work and the courses for students were based on objective measurements of responses to the environment with special reference to individual and group differences and to the useful applications of psychology, thus leading to the development of modern educational, clinical, and industrial psychology.

In 1888 I was also lecturer at Bryn Mawr College and at the University of Cambridge, conducting in both institutions laboratory courses for students. At Cambridge the work was in conjunction with the lectures of Professor James Ward and in the Cavendish laboratory of which the present Sir Joseph Thomson was the director, having just before at the age of twenty-six succeeded Maxwell and Rayleigh in the professorship of physics. In the Cavendish laboratory apparatus for research work was also set up, and this was the beginning of the first British laboratory of psychology. At that time I had the privilege of assisting Galton in setting up the Anthropometric Laboratory in the South Kensington Museum and we began in cooperation the preparation of a book of instructions for a laboratory course in psychology.

The five-year period from 1887 to 1892 is distinguished for the development of laboratories of psychology in the United States. For earlier work tribute should in passing be paid to James McCosh, Presbyterian clergyman from Scotland and president of a Presbyterian college, who at Princeton promoted the study of organic evolution and physiological psychology. George Trumbull Ladd, also a clergyman, was called to Yale in 1881 and developed there courses in physiological psychology, leading to the publication in 1887 of his *Outlines of Physiological Psychology.* With James and Hall he shares the honor of leading in the development of psychology in America. The laboratory at Yale was organized by Professor Ladd in 1892 with Dr. E. W. Scripture as instructor.

Work in experimental psychology leading to the establishment of a laboratory was begun by Professor Joseph Jastrow at Wisconsin in 1888. His service as professor of psychology is the longest in the history of our science. A year or two later laboratories were established at Indiana University by President W. L. Bryan, at the University of Nebraska by Professor H. K. Wolfe, at Brown University by Professor E. B. Delabarre, and at Stanford University by Professor Frank Angell. Professor J. Mark Baldwin was called to Toronto in 1890 and established there a psychological laboratory as he did at Princeton when he returned to that university in 1893. In 1895 we together founded *The Psychological Review* which, with its children, *The Psychological Monographs, The Psychological Index, The Psychological Bulletin, The Journal of Experimental Psychology,* and the newly established *Psychological Abstracts,* have now, through the generous cooperation of Professor Warren, been acquired and are being conducted by the American Psychological Association.

The professorship of psychology and the laboratory of psychology at Columbia University date from 1891. The following year is notable for the establishment of the psychological laboratories at Harvard and Cornell and the calling to America of Hugo Münsterberg and E. B. Titchener. At Cornell the traditions of the Leipzig laboratory have been best maintained. Titchener brought to us the high standards and some of the idiosyncrasies of the Oxford don and the German professor. Now he has followed James, Hall, and Münsterberg, leaving the world more drab and empty.

Where James, Royce, and Münsterberg were, was the center of psychology. James was appointed professor of psychology at Harvard in 1889, having been from 1872 to 1880 instructor and assistant professor of comparative anatomy and physiology, after 1880 assistant professor of philosophy, becoming again professor of philosophy in 1897. His great work *The Principles of Psychology* was published in 1890. In a letter addressed to me as editor of *Science* in 1895 James tells of the development of work in experimental psychology at Harvard: "I, myself, 'founded' the instruction in experimental psychology at Harvard in 1874–75, or 1876, I forget which. For a long series of years the laboratory was in two rooms of the Scientific School building, which at last became choked with apparatus, so that a change was necessary. I then, in 1890, resolved on an altogether new departure, raised several thousand dollars, fitted up Dane Hall, and introduced laboratory exercises as a regular part of the undergraduate psychology course. Dr. Herbert Nichols, then at Clark, was appointed in 1891 assistant in this part of the work; and Professor Münsterberg was made director of the laboratory in 1892."

With the publication of James's *Principles of Psychology* in 1890, the opening of the laboratories at Harvard, Yale, and Cornell in 1892, and the establishment of the American Psychological Association in the same year, the earlier period of psychology in America may be closed. The few survivors may look back upon it as the golden age of our science, but that is doubtless due only to the presbyopia that obscures the vision of objects near at hand. In the thirty-five years that have since elapsed the number of our workers in psychology has increased to an extent perhaps without parallel in any other science or in any other country. We welcome the opening at Wittenberg College of a new laboratory, which under the direction of Professor Reymert will become a new center for psychological research, auspiciously inaugurated by this conference to advance our knowledge of the problems of feeling and the emotions.

Chemistry is the earliest, and psychology is the latest, of the laboratory sciences. It is of interest that we meet today to dedicate a building built for laboratories in these two sciences which I understand will be given equal opportunities at Wittenberg College. Psychology as the youngest child of the family has in our universities usually been given the outgrown clothes of the older sibs. Here, for almost the first time, it is treated on terms of equality. It is also significant that in an institution that is designated as a college rather than a university, there should be provided men and equipment for advanced teaching and research in psychology. It will be a fine development worthy of a truly democratic nation, if each of the better colleges of the class of Wittenberg, if each of all the thousand colleges of the country, will take up some one or two subjects in which high standards of research and scholarship are maintained. They will be leaven for the college, beacon lights for the state.

LO, THE PSYCHOLOGIST!*

Joseph Jastrow
University of Wisconsin

There are interludes when attention may be diverted from the play to the players. The psychologist, responsive to encouragement, steps before the curtain and addresses, in his own behalf, as if over the radio, a small present and a larger invisible audience. There is current a gentle libel that a psychologist is one who tells what everyone knows in language that nobody understands. The aggressively up-to-date psychologist has changed all that: he tells what, as yet, nobody knows in language that everybody understands, and cultivates the art of persuading enterprising editors to reward him handsomely for his reckless ingenuity.

At a ceremony similar to the present I was introduced as one of the small company who had taken the sigh out of psychology, and did not resent the unearned compliment; thus proving my sympathy with the popularization of all sound knowledge. Particularly have we psychologists gained and not lost by becoming intelligible. But the lure of the footlights and the glare of the headlights tend to obscure the steady, modest lamp of learning. The psychologist should not be dazzled by the ready and undiscriminating demand for his services; his responsibility remains. He cannot, though at times he pretends to, be all things to all men and even more to some women. Yet it is not my unpopular purpose to impose a personality-inventory upon the psychologist, nor yet to subject him publicly to a psychoanalysis that might even in private prove embarrassing.

I prefer to acknowledge gratefully his good fortune in being accorded the public ear, and to suggest the obligations of this privilege. We are not likely to overlook the circumstance that the typical psychologist is a professor, however little the typical professor is a psychologist. But the implications as well as the prerequisites of what some call a career and others a misfortune have altered notably in our scholastic generation. The days when the university had any of the configuration or Gestalt, or presented even remotely the behavior-patterns of a cloister, are so far in the past that no one of us remembers them. It is only in such archaic traditions as those that survive on the stage and in the press that the professor is still portrayed as an absent-minded beggar, whose reputed mentality is spent upon unprofitable mysteries of his own beclouded making, though a half-truth remains in the beggarliness of his salary. His alert presence of mind is his indispensable asset to hold his job. In his distracting versatility he often longs for a bit of a retreat where the students cease from troubling, and the tax- or fee-paying parents are at rest. Far from suffering, as did his predecessor, from the view of his *Fach* as something to learn in order to teach others to learn to teach it to still others in a squirrel-cage rotary continuum called the curriculum or educational running-track, he is under diverse pressure from the world without to make his wares marketable. He is training a select group of practical-minded scholars, and talks to many so intensely practical that they do not take him seriously.

The ambition, at one time attributed to college presidents with more energy than erudition, to make culture hum, now affects the psychologist with the determination to make psychology pay. The psychology of advertising has so subtly taken posses-

---

* Address given at the dedication of the Chemistry-Psychology Building at Wittenberg College, October 21, 1927.

sion of the academic premises as to emerge as the advertising of psychology. The tail of applied psychology impudently wags the dog, and I am doubtless betraying my senility in bemoaning the anatomical innovation. Pure psychology needs no plea, and I am not disposed to make a plea for a pure psychologist or even a pure professor. Every complete professor is something more than he professes. A pliable versatility offsets the danger of too specialized interests. Since the only person who glories in being addressed as "professor" is the dancing-master, most of us prefer to travel incognito, and are delighted to be mistaken for men of the world. Through the popular practicality of psychology, it has come about that in some quai rs a psychologist is expected to read your character or, if you lack that superfluous appendage, your palm or your bumps, to inoculate you with success germs, and reveal either your past or your future, according to whichever is the more presentable or promising. If of a certain kidney, he undertakes to double your future income by removing some of your present cash. Nor can one dismiss the peripatetic reapers of shekels as psychologists of the slums, since some of them have dwelt in college halls while others in prison walls.

There is the like temptation in the quite legitimate fields occupied by the legitimate profession. I am not ready to greet as a philanthropist the confident adviser of manufacturers, showing them how to avoid unnecessary movements in making still more unnecessary articles, or developing a technique of reducing recalcitrant buyers (still retaining a moronic delusion that they know what they want) to helpless victims of the salesman's craft. The enterprising psychologist bent upon practicality is prepared to measure intelligence even when it is conspicuously absent, and to reduce to a score anything from a fingerprint to a belief in immortality. For more complicated mortals there is the devastating penetration of X-raying psychoanalysis; while the more simple-minded can have their behavior recorded and their careers shaped to any desired pattern by a conditioned response applied early and often. You can have your mind lifted or acquire a permanent wave of your psychic head-gear if you pursue the proper cult with faith and fees. To make people efficient though incompetent is no longer the exclusive prerogative of the colleges.

Supporting the ambitious superstructure of many such claims, pursued even by able and reputable psychologists not wisely but too irresponsibly, is a solid body of sound information and an important approach attained by well-tested methods of well-organized research, together with much more of similar intention but carried through with halting comprehension. Psychology has in fact advanced man's knowledge of the human make-up, has furthered the better direction and control of human energy in fields as various as the spread of human interests. Lo, the psychologist has come to his own! In a sense never before so appropriate, we live in a psychological age; but equally the improper as well as the proper study of mankind is man. So long confused by the products of his traditionally and economically hampered activities, he has awakened to the realization with a newer insight that it is imperative to take stock of human motives and conditions and thereby test the value of his strivings.

We have at command, as has had no previous generation, a modernized and humanized and scientized outlook, all as potent to influence human welfare as the transformations wrought in the human scene by autos and airplanes and radios and X-rays and floating palaces and soaring skyscrapers and the more than nine-times-nine wonders of the modern world. How we think and what we believe, how we influence and minister to minds in the making, how we attempt to control the conflicts of men's interests and the clashes of their jealousies and ambitions, is more significant than how we move and live and maintain our physical being. To select but two high points of the psychologist's insight, there is the revelation of the nature and unsuspected significance of early childhood, and the equally significant story of man's liabilities in mental disorder and defect. Both are imbedded in the human heritage. The child as early man, as well as primitive man himself, still active in the cave-man that survives, though the modern cliff-dweller ascends to his eeried office by express elevator, sets the problem of human direction, whatever the occupations that engage the same hands, the same brain, that made possible his ascent. It is in this complicated world that the psychologist operates; and it is important that he should not be confused by its din and machinery, that he should join the small remnant of creative and progressive thinkers who can see even this bewildering world soundly and see it whole. Such is part of the psychologist's responsibility. Hence the necessity to him of an adequate background, of a comprehensive outlook. However engaging and legitimate the study of trees, the psychologist is a forester in human nature and must attain that position whether through the laboratory, or through analysis of the behavior of human minds in the records of history and literature and science, or by direct contact with the streams of activity, mingling with men and their many affairs.

It is, I believe, in his response to the practical pressure of our times that the psychologist will show his worth. He must continue to maintain that the problems of greatest moment are those that arise within the science itself. In this the lessons of the story of all science are clear. The great advances have come from those who found their problems by the light of their own concentration. Galileos and Newtons and Darwins are too rare to afford a working model for the rest of us gleaners. But so far we can all accept the guiding principle of their endeavors: to find the supporting motives for our intellectual life in the interpretation of that aspect of nature that we chose by dominant interest and studious possession.

Lo, the expert psychologist! There was a certain dignity in the older name of physics as natural philosophy, and the term naturalist deserves a more liberal currency. We are all naturalists: the chemist studies the inner nature of the make-up of things; the psychologist, the inner nature of the make-up of mind. We should never need the cry, "Back to Nature," which was Rousseau's slogan for a too sophisticated social world, a world since his day jazzed to a feverish pace out of all resemblance to that which aroused his revolt; because we should never move away from nature, as nature never moves away from us, however much we try to escape her conditioning hand. Because nature conditions art, psychologists must keep the direction of advance in their own control. However ready to serve, they cannot be subservient to a practical perspective imposed from without.

The sterility of many movements in psychology even within the early laboratory period resulted mainly from the too academic pursuit and framing of problems; the lesson that all function has a natural setting was not yet learned. This correction has been made; the psychologist has a biological grasp. The present danger is just the opposite—that psychology will take its problems too largely from the stress of application, which is just as artificial in another sense, and irrelevant and disturbing as well.

The psychology of advertising may in itself be a matter of slight moment, just a section of the far larger and more consequential psychology of persuasion; and it cannot be glorified into importance because vast sums of money are spent or misspent in this amazing exhibition of the lack of self-direction of human sheep. Science must set the standards of importance. The psychology of the nervous or the gifted child, the psychology of the variant specimens of humanity whether delinquent or defective, are a hundred times more significant and more difficult to pursue than the psychology of advertising which a properly directed human society would reduce to a minimum.

As I look about to find some common factors of the misdirection or abuse of psychological interests, I seem to discover first the lure of simplicity. Sound psychology simplified in statement by all means, but not by sacrifice of perspective and truth, nor yet in a flippant disregard of the difficult paths by which the stages of insight have been reached. The actual behavior of human beings and their psychological problems that arise out of them are not simple. Simplification not well steadied distorts, misleads, and obstructs. As so many leave home-work for factory-work and home-making for making things for the market, because the factory side of life is so much simpler than the home side, so may the lure of the practical be but a phase of the lure of simplicity as well as the hope of quick returns. Both lead to a superficial psychology; and we need more than ever a deep psychology. I find it necessary to place in this same misleading tendency a movement for which, within its domain, I have the highest respect—that too limitedly called behaviorism. With few exceptions, all psychologists are behaviorists, and with just as few exceptions psychologists refuse to follow the ambitious negations and conclusions of extreme behaviorism. The attraction of the radical behavioristic doctrines is their simplicity, yet also the next lure, that of novelty. The confusion of the new and the true is a widespread fallacy. Since everything that ever led to human progress was at one time an innovation, the novel, always attractive in its own engaging charm, gets a hearing; and a following uncritically heralds it as an advance and a correction and an emancipation. But this is too momentous a matter for brief consideration. One may simplify anything by ignoring its complications; and in the negations of radical behaviorism, as well as in its cavalierly dismissal of the essential problems, there is a pitfall for the unwary.

The psychoanalyst is a deep psychologist in all truth. His is the opposite danger of making mountains out of molehills. He may well profit by the rigid exactions of the behaviorist's technique. The behaviorist's facts will stand though we challenge the practical consequences which he deduces from them; the over-zealous psychoanalyst insists that the facts must be as his conclusions demand, and he has a technique that favors finding what you look for. Both are on the search for mechanisms, but are angling at different depths. The psychoanalyst is persuaded that the behaviorist is catching nothing but minnows and ignores the complications of deep-sea life; the behaviorist is persuaded that the psychoanalyst's monsters of the deep are hatched in an imaginary aquarium. Clearly, the psychologist is in no immediate danger of finding his occupation gone through a dreary unanimity of opinion. Man is still an enigma, and the nature of the human mind not a dead issue but a live controversy. Lo, the psychologist has his hands full, and the public awaits his deliveries!

As the largest asset of the advertiser is the habit of reading advertising, so the most valued asset of the psychologist is the public faith or hope that he has a message for the man of the street and the office and the home and the school and the church and the courts and the political and social life generally. If as the result of a campaign of enlightenment, one could broadcast the conviction that practically all advertising is bunk, and every he-man would show his masculinity and every she-woman her native insight by resisting every advertising appeal and establishing a boycott for all advertised goods, that hugest industry of the modern world would crumble to the dust, and the glare of Broadway be sobered down to a pleasing and decorative illumination. By quite the same argument (and doubtless the issue is just as probable) if all men could be made to resist the temptation to take what is not nailed down, all locks and bolts and steel vaults and armored cars and the rest of the world of steel against steal would be so much junk. In the one instance people would be so inhumanly intelligent that they would know what they want, and in the other case so inhumanly honest that they wouldn't take it when they saw it. And lo, the psychologist as well as the advertiser and the preacher and the lawyer and the judge would have their occupations reduced to a pleasant employment of their superfluous energy, while now they all work overtime and with questionable profit to their several flocks and charges!

But even in post-prandial mood I am not optimistic enough to indulge in Utopias. I use the idea only to place the responsibility of the psychologist in the present instance, of every other profession in turn as their devotees assemble, plainly before them. We must retain the popular ear and confidence, for we are convinced that what we have to offer has an important share to guide aright the course of many lives, to contribute to the pool of knowledge that we call modern science, humanized science particularly. We live in a journalistic age. The sources of distribution exert the most powerful control over what people will accept, whether in things or ideas, for such is the texture of human suggestibility. One editor in an influential position, I will not say with a perverted but with a less than worthy policy of adapting what people will accept to what is good for them, can do more to offset the work of all the rest of the educational forces directed toward stabilizing the present generation (I use the word because "uplifting" has acquired a suspicious repute) than any agency as yet developed. The yellow peril by which we are threatened is not a racial one in the far East, but is blazoned forth in all colors on every newsstand. One of the outstanding jobs for the Hercules among psychologists is to develop a journalistic hygienic technique to clean out the garages of high-powered presses.

We must popularize as we advance and advance as we popularize; and because of the special temptation to the psychologist to yield to the clamor for the simple, the predigested and misinterpreted, the novel and upsetting and surprising, the sensational when it is sufficiently off-color, is it permitted, even while he steps before the curtain to receive the applause which he so artfully arranged that it seems to be spontaneous, for a fellow psychologist to speak to his guild in words of congratulation not unmixed with warning.

The current reply to all this is: "Highbrow stuff not wanted!" Apparently, we are still willing to be called, "the heirs of all the ages," but have no aversion to herding with narrow foreheads vacant of our glorious gains. Addressing, as I have the futile habit of doing, audiences of all sorts and conditions of men, I am quite intimately aware of the difficulty of steering between that which demands the slightest mental effort on the part of the hearer and that which demands no effort at all on the part of the speaker. Perhaps some are expert in thus striking the proper cranial altitude between the high-brows and the low-brows. With me it is hit or miss; and, unlike the shooting gallery, one gets the report when one fails to score; nor have I any great interest in keeping score. So I fall back on the conviction that, however poor my sermon, I have a good text. I am convinced that psychology has a message that can be "put over" (to use "journalese") not by the arts of the advertiser and the exploiter, but by the same loyalty to a sense of truth and value that advances the search for knowledge and its sober and critical application. I even entertain the hope that there may come the day when some mind as great in insight as that of Newton for the physical world, of Darwin for the biological world, will appear as a great psychologist combining in one composite all the several congenial insights that make up the present heritage of such a body as is here assembled to dedicate another center of dissemination of learning. May he be greeted: "Lo, the great psychologist!"

APPENDIX E

CHEMISTRY AND PSYCHOLOGY*

EDWIN E. SLOSSON

Science Service, Washington, D. C.

In speaking at the dedication of a chemistry-psychology building I have attained a lifelong ambition. I am filled with that feeling of satisfaction, that peace of mind, which arises from the synthesis of two diverging desires, the appeasement of a conflict that tore my soul in twain at the critical period of adolescence.

The day I left the University of Kansas in 1891 I had two jobs offered me. One was the offer from G. Stanley Hall of a fellowship in experimental psychology at the newly established Clark University. The other was to become the assistant in chemistry in the newly established University of Wyoming. I was drawn in opposite directions, east and west, after the ancient mode of torture. I felt like the Italian lover in Daly's ballad:

> "I gotta love for Angela,
> I love Carlotta, too!
> I no can marry both of dem,
> So what I gonna do?"

Since in those days I could not combine the rivals—no such building as this having been erected—I chose chemistry and rejected psychology. Since it is nowadays permissible to admit that our decisions are not determined purely by intellectual arguments, but are sometimes swayed by the emotions, I may now admit that my choice was influenced by the fact that the eastern fellowship was celibate whereas the western position allowed me to take a wife. Owing to this, that my decision was dictated by my optic thalamus more than my cerebrum, I am in the chemical section of this symposium instead of the emotional section.

A few years later a student entering graduate work came to me to get me to suggest a novel and promising field for research for his Ph.D. *Arbeit* (as we used to call it before the war). No easy task to be asked to give offhand a subject on which a young man might spend profitably three years and $3,000! But I was young and more ready to give advice to other people; less willing to admit that I did not know everything.

So I resorted to generalities, as we all do when we are at a loss for particulars. I discoursed to him on the fundamental principles of the scientific method.

"All Nature is one," I said. "So at least we believe, and it is the object of science, as it is of religion, to prove its faith in practice. Science consists in showing the relationships between things. As Poincaré says of mathematics, 'It is the art of giving the same name to different things.' Everything in the universe is related to everything else, but the relationship is often not apparent but has to be disclosed. The more remote the relationship, the greater the triumph of its discoverer.

"Now put yourself in the place of a matrimonial matchmaker. Look around the circle of the sciences, pick out two of them that no one has ever thought of bringing together, and marry them. Never mind if it may be considered by the world a *mésalliance*. In the history of science, unlike biology, the hybrid sciences prove most fertile of offspring."

---

* Address given at the dedication of the Chemistry-Psychology Building at Wittenberg College, October 21, 1927.

"But how can I think of two sciences that no one has ever thought of joining?"
"Resort to chance, my boy. Chance has a wider imagination than any human intellect. Write out on separate slips of paper the names of all the sciences and subsciences. Put them in your hat, shake them up, shut your eyes, and draw out two of them. Then write your dissertation on the connection between the two. If fortune favors you she may call upon you to marry such dissimilar sciences as 'astronomy and conchology' or 'herpetology and metallurgy' or 'psychology and chemistry.'"

But at that the young man went away sorrowful, for he thought I was joking at his serious dilemma. No one is more serious than a student in search of a thesis subject.

I must admit that my advice seemed absurd, especially the idea of there being any connection between psychology and chemistry. For in my time—I use the phrase in its customary sense, meaning when I was in my twenties, the age we all are in our dreams—chemistry and psychology were not on speaking terms. They moved in different social circles. Teaching psychology was a white-collar job. There was no taint of stinks and stains. The Chancellor of the University taught it to seniors out of Porter or McCosh in the classroom opposite his office at the front entrance, while chemistry was put in the basement or attic where it would be most out of the way.

But times have changed. I have been recently in psychological laboratories where rats and monkeys were being educated and the smell was worse than in my old chemical laboratory in the basement. I suspect that the presence of psychologists in this building will be quite as obnoxious to the chemists as the chemists will be to the psychologists. But I hope there are no impermeable partitions. I trust that ideas will be allowed to seep through by mental osmosis.

Such partitions are doing a great damage to science nowadays. Some of the sciences are hardly on speaking terms with one another. According to the familiar definition: "A specialist is a man who is learning more and more about less and less." The same principle seems to apply in research as in boring for petroleum; the deeper the well the narrower becomes the bore.

Specialization, matchless method of research, has been carried so far as to remind one of the study of the elephant by the six blind men. The one who touched the side reported that the elephant was "very like a wall." The one who embraced the leg concluded that the elephant was "very like a post." The one who was entangled in the trunk said that the elephant was "very like a snake," and so forth. These investigators were all quite correct, yet it would have been better if they all could have got a glimpse of the beast as a whole before beginning their specialized researches.

So, too, it seems to me advisable to give our pupils a glimpse of nature in its wholeness before we begin to partition it among the several sciences. It is the custom at hotel dinners to bring in the roast turkey or the planked steak and exhibit it in its entirety to the guests before it is carved up into portions for the particular plates where it is to be still further reduced by each to masticable morsels.

The slicing up of a subject into separate sciences is as necessary a preliminary to its complete assimilation as is the carving of a turkey. But both processes are irreversible reactions. It is difficult to get from the consideration of hash an integral idea of what creature supplied the meat.

Not long ago I was in the study of the head of the biological department of one of our colleges when he said to me: "You are going about the country a good deal, can't you help me to get a professor of zöology?" I replied that that ought to be easy.

"No," he said, "I have been trying to find one for the last three years. You see I want a zöologist of very unusual qualifications."

"What sort of a man do you want?" I asked.

"I want a professor of zoölogy who knows something about animals. But the universities don't seem to be turning out such nowadays. I can get a man who knows all about the hydrogen ion concentration of the blood or who can count the chromosomes or who is familiar with museum specimens, but they do not seem to be acquainted with animals that are alive and whole."

It seems to me that what we need in our educational institutions is a combination of specialized research and synthetic education. Yesterday evening at the dinner given in honor of Professor Linn, I had the pleasure of sitting beside Dean Shatzer and found that he feels as strongly as I do about the importance of closer cooperation between diverse departments of education. "At present," he told me in substance, "our studies are taught as though they were islands rather than parts of a continuous continent of universal knowledge." It is to prevent the students from living the lives of intellectual Robinson Crusoes that progressive colleges are attempting to introduce some sort of synthetic or orientation courses.

I am glad to see that in spite of the partitions of our curriculum, diverse training, and trade-union spirit, the several and separated sciences are spreading into each other's provinces. A growing science is like an overpopulated state. It cannot be kept to the bounds of the map.

Chemistry since my time—using the words in the same sense as before—has invaded the field of biology and even the field beyond, that of psychology.

This week thirty-five of the leading psychologists of the world have, at Wittenberg, been studying the feelings and emotions of man—and, I suppose, of woman. But in this province chemistry is the dominant science. For feelings and emotions of every sort can be instantaneously suspended by a whiff of ether. And a few more whiffs of ether will abolish them permanently. The chemist would then leave the psychologist nothing to study.

So you have done wisely, I think, in planning this program so that the psychologists and chemists meet at the same time, though I am sorry you did not force them to sit together in the same room and listen to each other in discussing the emotional side of human conduct.

"Until this paragon of spheres
By philosophic thought coheres
The vast machine will be controlled
By love and hunger, as of old."

Now love and hunger are based upon definite chemical reactions. They can be excited or allayed by certain compounds, some of which are already known. By chemical means affection can be stimulated or transformed into indifference or into aversion.

One of the most powerful of the emotional factors among the higher animals is maternal affection. Yet lack of an infinitesimal amount of a chemical compound may annihilate or even reverse maternal affection. I allude to vitamin X or E. It has been found that feeding rat mothers on a diet containing this vitamin they nurse their young, cover them from the cold, make straw beds for them, wash them with their tongues, even protect them at the risk of their lives.

But change the diet to one without vitamin E, although equally nutritious, digestible, and tasty, and the attitude of the mother rat changes. She refuses to suckle her offspring or care for them, shoves them out of the nest into the cold, thrusts them out of the cage to fall on the floor and perish. She may even eat them up.

Here is a chemical transformation from maternal affection to maternal cannibalism. Some day we may assume the maternal vitamin or hormone will be isolated, even synthesized in the laboratory. We may also assume that what has been found true about rats may be applied to humans. At least psychologists and physiologists commonly assume this. If so, we may expect that it may be possible to instill the maternal instinct by administering the missing ingredient to the females of our species who are nowadays too often destitute of it.

In proof of the power of the chemist to control the other ruling passion of the world, hunger, the experiment just performed in this room is most convincing. We all, however diverse in temperament, were drawn here simultaneously by a common motive, the feeling for food. It is a sort of chemico-psychic impulse, which psychologists who experiment with bugs and worms call chemotaxis. But within the hour by the aid of that branch of applied chemistry known commonly as "cookery" the passion of hunger has been amputated from the bodies of all of us by a painless, indeed pleasurable, operation.

Scents, savors, and colors are silent and subtle in their sway over emotions, and emotions move the world. When the mother advises her daughter that "The way to a man's heart is through his stomach"; when the florist advertises, "Say it with flowers"; when the confectioner suggests, "Take a box of candy with you when you call on her," they are recommending chemical courtship—the oldest way in the world, the method that prevails all through the animal kingdom from the insects up to mankind. When the poet wishes to play most powerfully upon our emotions, he resorts to chemical allusions. Let me read you what seems to me the most tasty stanza in all poetry, the courtship scene from Keats's *Eve of St. Agnes*.

> "And still she slept in azure-lidded sleep,
> In blanched linen, smooth and lavendered:
> While he from forth the closet brought a heap
> Of candied apple, quince, and plum, and gourd:
> With jellies soother than the creamy curd,
> And lucent sirups, tinct with cinnamon;
> Manna and dates, in argosy transferred
> From Fez; and spiced dainties, every one,
> From silken Samarcand to cedared Lebanon."

You will see that he said it with polysaccharides and coal-tar compounds, and you know how well it worked. They eloped that very night. Keats was a chemist before becoming a poet. We will not properly understand the world's great literature until the teaching of English is transferred to the department of chemistry, or at least until the professors of English study chemistry.

The same is true of history. The history of the world will remain a riddle, an inexplicable succession of chance happenings, until we recognize the chemical factors in the course of events. It is like looking at a tapestry from the wrong side; but when we turn it over the design becomes plain.

What was it that drew Columbus across the Atlantic? What was it that enticed Vasco da Gama to India around the Cape of Good Hope? What was it that sent Magellan around the world? It was "the spicy breezes that blow soft o'er Ceylon's Isle." The great explorers followed that spoor as the bee scents out the flower or the vulture his game. Chemotaxis gives the clue to many an historical mystery.

In the past the chemist has controlled the course of civilization through such gross means as the introduction of a new food or fuel, or in entions like glass or paper. But he is now beginning to get his hands upon minuter means of control which are more direct and vastly more powerful in their influence upon the human race. Chemical changes of almost inconceivable minuteness are found to affect the balance of the body. The growth of young rats is perceptibly promoted by the addition to their daily diet of much less than a hundredth of a milligram of vitamin A from codliver oil. An infinitesimal amount of pollen protein may not only start a new plant to growing but may start a big man to sneezing. This is Nature's sternutatory gas, the chemical warfare service of the ragweed.

Adrenalin produces a perceptible effect upon the tissues in a dilution of one part in 330,000,000. The hormone that Professor Abel has extracted from the pituitary body has still higher potency, for it can be detected in a dilution of more than 18,000,000,000. "A deviation in the acid-alkaline balance of the blood no greater than that between tap water and distilled water is fatal" to human beings.

The conventional classification of animals and plants from the time of Aristotle and Linnaeus has been chiefly based on morphology, just as mineralogy was in its early days mostly a matter of crystalline form. But nowadays we know that minerals can better be classified according to chemical composition than by their shape, color, hardness, and other visible characteristics. A similar change must take place in the field of biology, for it is already apparent that the forms of all creatures from the microbe to man are determined by certain chemical compounds in extremely minute amount. This may put it in the power of the chemist to control the size and shape of plants or animals, to fix the number and location of their branches and leaves, or legs and eyes, to modify color or complexion, and to determine or alter sex. The factors of heredity and the origin of species, when you get down to bedrock, are chemical problems.

But this is not all. The chemist will soon have power, not only to control the course of life in the future, but he will be able to reinterpret the past.

We already hear endocrine explanations of the character and career of Napoleon and Roosevelt, and may look forward to a new school of historical writers, the chemical interpretation of history, based upon the composition of the blood of the leaders of thought and action in the past. But chemical analysis may extend much further than man into the past. We already know something of the chemical causes of the development of organs and excrescences in animals, and we may in time be able to tell the true story of "How the Camel Got His Hump" and "How the Dinosaur Got His Horns." The chemist of the future may be able to measure the pH concentration of the blood of prehistoric monsters of millions of years ago as he can now follow the gyrations of the electrons in stars billions of miles afar. Neither time nor space can curtail the scope of chemistry.

Hitherto the chemist has confined himself to the humble task of providing the conveniences of life. In the future he may gain control of life itself. He may mold stature and character as the sculptor molds his clay. The world knows too well the evil influences on the race of certain chemicals such as alcohol, opium, and cocain, but some day the chemist will turn his attention to the preparation of compounds that will contribute to human welfare instead of woe and will stimulate virtues instead of vices.

The way is open. We know now that what we value as individuality—the familiar features; the fascinating temperament; the charms of vivacity, wit, and sympathy; all the peculiar qualities that attract or repel us in a personality are due to definite hormones, some of which are already known as chemical compounds. The new theory of hormones reminds one of the old theory of humors which were supposed to regulate health and determine temperament. The hyperthyroid type corresponds closely to the choleric and the hypothyroid to the melancholic temperament.

Diabetic patients taking insulin tell me the first effect of an overdose is a feeling of formless·fear, a vague apprehension, a sense of futility and failure, a shiver of anxiety. Their courage can be at once restored by sucking a lollipop. A variation of a few hundredths of one per cent in the glucose of the blood may make the difference between cowardice and courage, may determine whether a man shall be shot as a slacker or medaled as a hero. Courage is not a matter of "sand," but of sugar. In the excitement of combat the secretion of adrenalin is stimulated and this causes more sugar to be released to the blood and so strengthens a man's valor and endows him with greater strength.

Sugar fed to plant lice will so sweeten their dispositions that they will grow wings, while the administration of alcohol has, as we should expect, the opposite effect, and prevents any approach to the angelic state.

The chemist can so sensitize a man with an injection of hematoporphyrin that he will be light-struck and die if he ventures out of doors, even on a cloudy day, and yet would feel well so long as he remained in the house.

According to Goldschmidt, sex in birds and mammals depends upon a balance of opposing hormones both present in both sexes. "In the female the production of female hormones is more rapid than that of male hormones, the opposite is the case in the male."

It seems, then, that we must regard sex, with all it means throughout the range of animate nature, with all its influence on the development of art, literature, morals, and social life, as essentially a chemical affair, regulated, repressed, stimulated, or reversed by minute amounts of certain definite compounds in the blood or food. Experimentation is already active in this field and no one can foretell how far it will lead. The experiments of Evans and Bishop in the University of California, of Sure in the University of Arkansas, and of Stone in Stanford University indicate that a specific vitamin in food is necessary for reproduction, in addition to those essential for growth and health. This, too, may involve a reinterpretation of history, for it may be that what has been called "race suicide" in a class or nation may be sometimes due to a change in diet to a new one, which, though quite as nutritious and more tasty, is deficient in vitamin X or E.

That sex itself can be reversed at adult age by chemical means, at least as high up in the scale of life as birds, is proved by Dr. Crew of Edinburgh, who observed the transformation of a hen into a cock, and by Dr. Oscar Riddle, of the Carnegie Station for Experimental Evolution, who reports the change of a female pigeon to a male.

It is apparent that we have it in our power to modify the characteristics of plants and animals in two ways, biologically by eugenics, and chemically by such agencies as vitamins and hormones.

It is evident that we are entering upon a new epoch in medicine, for when the physician injects into the blood a hormone, such as insulin, thyroxin, or adrenalin, he is not introducing a foreign compound, such as strychnine, quinine, or arsenic, but merely restoring a natural compound unnaturally deficient. It is more like a food than a medicine.

Several of the hormones and vitamins have now been isolated; some even have been synthesized. We may reasonably expect that in the course of time many, if not all, of them will be made in the laboratory, But the chemist does not stop with the imitation of nature. He produces metals, building materials, dyes, scents, and foods not found in nature, and having, for human purposes, certain superiorities over natural products. Why should not the chemist be able to create hormones and vitamins not found in nature but capable of producing greater or different effects? And why should not these effects be desirable as well as undesirable? Why should it not be possible by chemical means to improve the stature, looks, longevity, or capabilities of human beings?

Dietetic physiology has been investigated for some years. Dietetic psychology has only recently been recognized as a field of research, while dietetic sociology is far in the future.

But it is already obvious that all these fields of chemical research are likely to elicit lessons of great value to humanity. The consumption of a few hundred calories of common food may completely alter a man's attitude toward the universe, including his wife and children.

By changing the diet a colony of rats may be, at will, converted into militants or pacifists. Chemists do not seem to have yet accomplished the production of anything corresponding to that human hybrid, the militant pacifist.

There is a certain drug known to organic chemists which is so potent that a single dose of it may within a few minutes incite a well-disposed and peaceable man to attack his best friend and beat his wife, or, on the other hand, cause him to weep on the shoulder of his worst enemy. On account of its powerful and incalculable effect on the emotions, the manufacture and sale of ethyl hydroxide has been prohibited in this country.

The effect of ethyl hydroxide on the cerebral functions, causing temporary anaesthesia and ataxia, was discovered by Noah in the year 2349 B.C., shortly after the world had gone wet. Like a true scientist he experimented upon himself and the results were conspicuously successful and decisive. Nevertheless, many of his descendants have thought it desirable to repeat the Noachian reaction even to this day.

History unconsciously records many cases where a change in the character of a race coincides with a change in diet. When a tribe of nomads, living almost exclusively on meat and milk, settles down to agriculture and vegetarianism, when a frugal band of mountaineers from the cold and arid uplands invades tropical territory where they live in luxury, the alteration in diet must be a formative factor of their future as well as the change in climate and mode of life.

I hope I shall avoid the mistake so often made by theorists of attempting to unlock all doors with the same key. In particular I do not mean to add another to the already too long list of the causes of the fall of Rome. But I cannot forebear calling your attention to the fact that when the Romans rose to power they were living on their own land, that is, on fresh fruits, vegetables, meats, and milk, and that in the days of their decline they were dependent upon oversea supplies, mostly grains which are deficient in the vitamins essential to the maintenance of health and fertility. The cry of the Roman populace was for *panem et circenses* (bread and circuses), neither of which was good for them.

This is a delicate question at the present day so I merely venture to suggest in passing that the student body in our colleges may likewise be suffering from an overdose of starch and stadium.

Whenever the psychologist enters a new field of investigation the chemist follows close at his heels and claims possession of it. Recently psychologists have been actively pushing forward into a new territory, that of dreamland, not properly to be called "new territory," since it was in this field that the psychologists of antiquity first gained fame and fortune. But this field was overexploited in ancient times so psychologists have left it fallow for some centuries until in the 20th they are again engaging in the interpretation of visions.

But here also the chemist can file a claim to be considered. A psychoanalyst may interpret your dreams as he likes best, but a chemist can give you any kind of dream you like by a dose of hasheesh, strychnine, or opium; or you may get dreams of a kind you don't like from an untimely mince pie or an unruly Welsh rarebit.

America has contributed the means of approach to a new artificial paradise like those described by Baudelaire and Havelock Ellis, the peyote or mescal buttons. A church has been chartered in Oklahoma where chewing the peyote is used to evoke visions of saints and angels of Heaven and its antithesis. It is called "The American Church" for the membership claims to be of native American stock although the aboriginal blood may have been diluted by admixture with the invading pale faces. The Oklahoma legislature at its last session tried to suppress the church by law but the chiefs of the Indian tribes appeared in a body and protested that the partaking of peyote was their form of communion and so could not be prohibited by the Food and Drug Act.

I tried an involuntary experiment recently on the effect of chemicals on vision. I am extremely defective in visual imagery. If I try to recall a picture of an old friend, a familiar building, or this morning's breakfast table (as James advised), I get only faint and fugitive pictures, very elusive, indefinite, and only in black and white. But once taking a prescription containing a little laudanum I was entranced when I closed my eyes by a succession very vivid, minute, and brilliantly colored pictures, from memory or imagination, like the little landscapes the Japanese paint on rice paper, or those seen through an inverted opera glass. I saw then what I had missed. I was convinced of what others had said of their visual ability. We may anticipate that drug-stores will sell such visions and dreams as they do post-cards, one cent plain, five cents colored.

The influence of chemistry upon art opens up another unexplored field. I do not mean painting or printing or motion pictures but on the models which set the artistic ideals of a generation. The dwarf and giant gods of antiquity and other monstrosities are easily explainable by endocrinology, Bes of the Egyptians, the Titans, Gog and Magog, triple-headed Cerberus, many-armed Briareus, multi-mammiferous Diana of the Ephesians.

We can see where Michelangelo got his masculine sybils of the Sistine Chapel and Fra Angelico the anaemic angels of the monastery.

Botticelli set an example for the consumptive as an ideal of art. His famous Venus arising from the sea—you know the one I mean, it might be called "Venus on the Halfshell"—was modeled from La Bella Simonetta, mistress of de Medici, who died at the age of 23 from tuberculosis.

The Pre-Raphaelites' school made the goiter popular. The model in this case was an ill-nourished seamstress whom Dante Gabriel Rossetti made his wife. The "Blessed Damozel" as she leans out over the bar of Heaven is in a posture to show her enlarged thyroid admirably. In "Rosa Triplex," Rossetti has portrayed three goitrous girls in a row. The Pre-Raphaelite movement might have been prevented by the administration of iodine.

The endocrine theory of art would also throw light on dark periods in history. It has been recently pointed out that the infant Jesus as portrayed by northern painters following the thirty years' war is deformed by rickets. The Babe in the manger shows the squared head, shrunken chest, and bow-legs due to lack of vitamin D. The artists would not, of course, intentionally depict the infant Jesus as inferior. Quite the contrary, so it is evident that rickets was so common among the best babies in those distressful days that they regarded the pitiful types they portrayed as normal children.

I have given here a few casual illustrations of the human side of chemistry and especially its influence on psychology. The topic would be equally fruitful if approached from the opposite point, to show the influence of psychology on chemistry. I have here time for only one instance. I can stand six feet in front of a man weighing not over fifty kilograms and raise the percentage of dextrose in his blood without touching him. I should do it by making faces at him or calling him a liar. I stipulate that the body weight of the subject stripped shall be less than fifty kilograms because otherwise the reaction might be reversed.

Chemists and psychologists can learn much from each other. I hope that at the next conference at Wittenberg they will meet together and not be segregated.

I now yield the floor to Professor Jastrow to whom I owe my initiation in the methods of experimental psychology when in 1893 he allowed me to aid him in preparing the mental tests used at the Columbian World's Fair, which was, I believe, the first time such tests were applied in mass to thousands of individuals.

INDEX

INDEX

[References to papers of the symposium, as indexed under the author's name, are printed in bold-face type; references to illustrations are in italics.]

CLASSICS IN PSYCHOLOGY

AN ARNO PRESS COLLECTION

Angell, James Rowland. **Psychology: On Introductory Study of the Structure and Function of Human Consciousness.** 4th edition. 1908

Bain, Alexander. **Mental Science.** 1868

Baldwin, James Mark. **Social and Ethical Interpretations in Mental Development.** 2nd edition. 1899

Bechterev, Vladimir Michailovitch. **General Principles of Human Reflexology.** [1932]

Binet, Alfred and Th[éodore] Simon. **The Development of Intelligence in Children.** 1916

Bogardus, Emory S. **Fundamentals of Social Psychology.** 1924

Buytendijk, F. J. J. **The Mind of the Dog.** 1936

Ebbinghaus, Hermann. **Psychology: An Elementary Text-Book.** 1908

Goddard, Henry Herbert. **The Kallikak Family.** 1931

Hobhouse, L[eonard] T. **Mind in Evolution.** 1915

Holt, Edwin B. **The Concept of Consciousness.** 1914

Külpe, Oswald. **Outlines of Psychology.** 1895

Ladd-Franklin, Christine. **Colour and Colour Theories.** 1929

Lectures Delivered at the 20th Anniversary Celebration of Clark University. (Reprinted from *The American Journal of Psychology*, Vol. 21, Nos. 2 and 3). 1910

Lipps, Theodor. **Psychological Studies.** 2nd edition. 1926

Loeb, Jacques. **Comparative Physiology of the Brain and Comparative Psychology.** 1900

Lotze, Hermann. **Outlines of Psychology.** [1885]

McDougall, William. **The Group Mind.** 2nd edition. 1920

Meier, Norman C., editor. **Studies in the Psychology of Art: Volume III.** 1939

Morgan, C. Lloyd. **Habit and Instinct.** 1896

Münsterberg, Hugo. **Psychology and Industrial Efficiency.** 1913

Murchison, Carl, editor. **Psychologies of 1930.** 1930

Piéron, Henri. **Thought and the Brain.** 1927

Pillsbury, W[alter] B[owers]. **Attention.** 1908

[Poffenberger, A. T., editor]. **James McKeen Cattell: Man of Science.** 1947

Preyer, W[illiam] **The Mind of the Child: Parts I and II.** 1890/1889

The Psychology of Skill: Three Studies. 1973

Reymert, Martin L., editor. **Feelings and Emotions: The Wittenberg Symposium.** 1928

Ribot, Th[éodule Armand]. **Essay on the Creative Imagination.** 1906

Roback, A[braham] A[aron]. **The Psychology of Character.** 1927

I. M. Sechenov: Biographical Sketch and Essays. (Reprinted from *Selected Works* by I. Sechenov). 1935

Sherrington, Charles. **The Integrative Action of the Nervous System.** 2nd edition. 1947

Spearman, C[harles]. **The Nature of 'Intelligence' and the Principles of Cognition.** 1923

Thorndike, Edward L. **Education: A First Book.** 1912

Thorndike, Edward L., E. O. Bregman, M. V. Cobb, et al. **The Measurement of Intelligence.** [1927]

Titchener, Edward Bradford. **Lectures on the Elementary Psychology of Feeling and Attention.** 1908

Titchener, Edward Bradford. **Lectures on the Experimental Psychology of the Thought-Processes.** 1909

Washburn, Margaret Floy. **Movement and Mental Imagery.** 1916

Whipple, Guy Montrose. **Manual of Mental and Physical Tests: Parts I and II.** 2nd edition. 1914/1915

Woodworth, Robert Sessions. **Dynamic Psychology.** 1918

Wundt, Wilhelm. **An Introduction to Psychology.** 1912

Yerkes, Robert M. **The Dancing Mouse** and **The Mind of a Gorilla.** 1907/1926